Philadelphia & the Amish Country

11th Edition

by Jay Golan

HUNGRY MINDS, INC.

New York, NY • Cleveland, OH • Indianapolis, IN
Chicago, IL • Foster City, CA • San Francisco, CA

ABOUT THE AUTHOR

Jay Golan has been writing about travel in Europe, Asia, and the United States since college. Educated at Harvard, Oxford, and Columbia Universities, he has worked for major cultural institutions in Boston and New York for 20 years, most recently at Carnegie Hall. He and his young family live in New York City and frequently visit relatives and friends in Philadelphia. This edition is dedicated to his two most reliable critics, Emma and Sophie, and to Barat.

Published by:

HUNGRY MINDS, INC.

909 Third Ave.
New York, NY 10022
www.frommers.com

ISBN 0-7645-6212-6
ISSN 0899-3211

Editor: Alice Fellows
Production Editor: Heather Gregory
Photo Editor: Richard Fox
Design by Michele Laseau
Cartographer: Roberta Stockwell
Production by Hungry Minds Indianapolis Production Services
Front cover photo: Society Hill

SPECIAL SALES

For general information on Hungry Minds' products and services, please contact our Customer Care department; within the U.S. at 800-762-2974, outside the U.S. at 317-572-3993 or fax 317-572-4002. For sales inquiries and reseller information, including discounts, bulk sales, customized editions, and premium sales, please contact our Customer Care department at 800-434-3422.

Manufactured in the United States of America.

5   4   3   2   1

Contents

List of Maps   viii

1   Introducing Philadelphia   1

1 Frommer's Favorite Philadelphia
   Experiences   2
2 Best Hotel Bets   4
3 Best Restaurant Bets   6

2   Planning a Trip to Philadelphia   10

1 Visitor Information
   & Money   10
2 When to Go   11
   *Philadelphia Calendar of
   Events*   11
3 Insurance   15
4 Tips for Travelers with Special
   Needs   16
   A Little Book Learnin'   18
5 Getting There   19
   Cyber Deals for Net Surfers   20

3   For Foreign Visitors   23

1 Preparing for Your Trip   23
2 Getting to & Around the United
   States   25
   *Fast Facts: For the Foreign
   Traveler*   27

4   Getting to Know Philadelphia   30

1 Orientation   30
   The Neighborhoods in Brief   32
2 Getting Around   33
   Fast Facts: Philadelphia   38

5   Where to Stay   42

1 Historic Area   43
2 Center City   48
   Family-Friendly Hotels   57
3 University City (West
   Philadelphia)   58
4 Near the Airport   60
5 City Line & Northeast   61
6 Hostels   62

6   Where to Dine   63

1 Restaurants by Cuisine   64
2 Historic Area   65
3 Center City   74
   *A Taste of Ethnic Philly: Reading
   Terminal Market*   83
   Family-Friendly Restaurants   84
4 South Philadelphia   84
5 University City (West
   Philadelphia)   86
6 Chinatown   89
7 Manayunk   90
8 Local Favorites: Cheesesteaks,
   Hoagies & More   91

7   Exploring Philadelphia   95

Suggested Itineraries   98

1 Independence National Historical Park: America's Most Historic Square Mile   98

2 The Top Museums   103

3 More Attractions   106

Philadelphia's Oddball Museums   115

Did You Know?   121

4 Parks & Penn's Landing   122

5 Especially for Kids   126

6 Organized Tours   127

7 Outdoor Activities   128

8 Spectator Sports   131

8   City Strolls   134

Walking Tour 1: Historic Highlights & Society Hill   134

Architectural ABCs   139

Walking Tour 2: Old City   143

Walking Tour 3: Midtown & the Parkway   147

9   Shopping   153

1 The Shopping Scene   153

2 Shopping A to Z   155

Manayunk Shopping   160

10   Philadelphia After Dark   168

1 The Performing Arts   169

2 The Club & Music Scene   174

Sleepless in Philadelphia   175

That's Amore: Italian Crooning in South Philly   180

3 The Bar Scene   181

4 The Gay & Lesbian Scene   183

5 More Entertainment   184

6 Late-Night Bites   185

11   Side Trips from Philadelphia   187

1 Bucks County & Nearby New Jersey   187

Where Washington Crossed the Delaware   188

2 Valley Forge   195

3 Exploring the Brandywine Valley   198

Did You Know?   198

12   Lancaster County: The Amish Country   204

1 Introducing the Pennsylvania Dutch Country   204

2 Essentials   208

3 Exploring Amish Country   210

The Bridges of Lancaster County   211

Did You Know?   213

4 Especially for Kids   213

5 Shopping   214

6 Where to Stay   217

7 Where to Dine   220

Appendix: Philadelphia in Depth   223

1 History 101: The Philadelphia
   Story   224
   Dateline   224
   *A Portrait of the
   Philadelphians*   230

2 Recommended Books
   & Films   230

Index   234

General Index   234
Accommodations Index   241

Restaurant Index   241

List of Maps

The Eastern Seaboard   3

Philadelphia Neighborhoods   34

Philadelphia Accommodations   44

Philadelphia Dining   66

Philadelphia Attractions   96

Fairmount Park   123

Walking Tour: Historic Highlights & Society Hill   135

Walking Tour: Old City   145

Walking Tour: Midtown & the Parkway   149

Bucks County   189

Valley Forge   197

The Brandywine Valley   199

Lancaster & the Pennsylvania Dutch Country   205

AN INVITATION TO THE READER

In researching this book, we discovered many wonderful places—hotels, restaurants, shops, and more. We're sure you'll find others. Please tell us about them, so we can share the information with your fellow travelers in upcoming editions. If you were disappointed with a recommendation, we'd love to know that, too. Please write to:

Frommer's Philadelphia & the Amish Country, 11th Edition
Hungry Minds, Inc.
909 Third Avenue
New York, NY 10022

AN ADDITIONAL NOTE

Please be advised that travel information is subject to change at any time—and this is especially true of prices. We therefore suggest that you write or call ahead for confirmation when making your travel plans. The authors, editors, and publisher cannot be held responsible for the experiences of readers while traveling. Your safety is important to us, however, so we encourage you to stay alert and be aware of your surroundings. Keep a close eye on cameras, purses, and wallets, all favorite targets of thieves and pickpockets.

WHAT THE SYMBOLS MEAN

✪ **Frommer's Favorites**

Our favorite places and experiences—outstanding for quality, value, or both.

The following abbreviations are used for credit cards:

AE	American Express	DISC	Discover
CB	Carte Blanche	MC	MasterCard
DC	Diners Club	V	Visa

FIND FROMMER'S ONLINE

www.frommers.com offers up-to-the-minute listings on almost 200 cities around the globe—including the latest bargains and candid, personal articles updated daily by Arthur Frommer himself. No other Web site offers such comprehensive and timely coverage of the world of travel.

Introducing Philadelphia

Philadelphia today is an inseparable mix of old and new. Scratch the surface of William Penn's "Green countrie town" and you'll find both a wealth of history and plenty of modern distractions.

Philadelphia has the largest original and surviving district of colonial homes and shops in the country, with dozens of treasures in and around Independence National Historical Park. It boasts the most historic square mile in America, the place where the United States was conceived, declared, and ratified—and you can see the Liberty Bell to prove it. It offers some of the best dining values and several of the finest restaurants in America. Philadelphia is a stroller's paradise of restored Georgian and Federal structures integrated with smart shops and contemporary row-house courts to create a working urban environment. It's a center of professional and amateur sports, with more than 9,800 acres of parkland within the city limits. It's a city filled with art, crafts, and music for every taste, with boulevards made for street fairs and parades all year long. From row-house boutiques to the Second Continental Congress's favorite tavern, from an Ivy League campus to street artists and musicians, from gleaming skyscrapers to Italian marketplaces, Philadelphia is a city of the unexpected.

The earlier colonial view of Philadelphians as reflective, sophisticated, and tolerant has long been succeeded by the brash, good-hearted "Rocky" stereotype. Philadelphia is "The place that loves you back," as the current marketing campaign puts it. Of course, both characterizations have some grain of truth to them. There's a tremendous diversity among the 1.4 million residents of this city, spread over 129 square miles—and it's a long way from the boxes at the Academy of Music and the dining room of Zanzibar Blue to the bleachers of Veterans Stadium.

Geographically, Philadelphia sits pretty. Some 60 miles inland, it's the country's busiest freshwater port, controlling the Delaware Valley. Philadelphia occupies a tongue of land at the confluence of the Delaware—one of the largest U.S. rivers feeding into the Atlantic—and the Schuylkill (*school*-kill) rivers. The original settlement, and the heart of Center City today, is the band of solid ground about 5 miles north of the junction's marshland. Since then, of course, the city has drained and used the entire tongue to the south and has exploded into the northeast and northwest. The city is a natural stopping place between New York and Washington, D.C., with easy access to both by rail and road. And the casinos and beaches of Atlantic City, the Revolutionary War sites of Valley Forge and Brandywine, the great Du Pont family mansions, and Pennsylvania Dutch country all lie within 90 minutes of the city.

1 Frommer's Favorite Philadelphia Experiences

- **Taking Afternoon Tea at the Swann Lounge:** The quintessential luxury tea is found at the Four Seasons, overlooking one of the city's finest squares with fountains on both sides.
- **Visiting the Barnes Foundation:** The Barnes Foundation Gallery in Merion houses the most important private collection of Impressionist and early French modern paintings in the world, displaying more Cézannes than all the museums of France put together. Try to schedule a visit around its open hours from Friday to Sunday (or Wed to Fri in summertime).
- **Wandering Through Fairmount Park:** It would take dozens of outings to fully explore the 100 miles of trails in this 8,900-acre giant of an urban park—some of them are virtually unchanged since Revolutionary times. We'll settle for the hundreds of flame azaleas that bloom behind the Art Museum in spring and the dozen Georgian country mansions kept in immaculate condition.
- **Shopping on First Friday:** On the first Friday of every month, the galleries, stores, and studios of Old City—just above Independence National Historical Park—remain open with refreshments until 9pm. Wander along the cobblestone streets, stopping into one of the many coffee bars or bistros.
- **Stepping Back in Time in Historic Philadelphia:** Everyone knows about the miraculous reclamation of this country's colonial capital, from the Liberty Bell to hundreds of row houses with their distinctive bricks and 18th-century formal gardens (and welcoming benches). But the new tours (especially the nighttime "Lights of Liberty" show), the costumed town criers with free maps, and the Revolutionary War–era street theater bring the experience even closer. Just wander; they'll find you.
- **Snacking on Pretzels, Hoagies, and Philly's Famous Cheesesteaks:** Philadelphia has a rich tradition of cuisine from haute (as in the shad roe from fish caught in the Delaware River each April) to hot (the warm, soft, salty pretzels served slathered with mustard at stands all over town or at the Pretzel Museum in Old City). The hoagie is something else—cold cuts, lettuce, and onions layered with oil and vinegar—along with its cousin the cheesesteak, also served on an enormous elongated bun.
- **Strolling Around Independence Square at Night:** The combination of history, elegance, and proportion among the three main buildings that contained America's first government always induces a sense of wonder at this country's good fortune in its founding citizens. You might even feel the urge to jump aboard one of the horse-drawn carriages lined up in front of the square.
- **Enjoying the Lights at Night:** As of January 2000, the William Penn statue atop City Hall and seven Schuylkill River bridges are permanently lighted, joining the pinlights that outline the boathouses along the Schuylkill River. Sheer magic.

A Central City

Thirty-eight percent of the nation's population lives within a 4½-hour drive from Philadelphia.

- **Listening to Hot Jazz and Blues:** There are at least half a dozen clubs with world-class, down-home, accessible, and affordable American music any night you're in town, very possibly with local sons like Grover Washington Jr. and Christian McBride.
- **Touring an Open House:** If you're in the city at the right time, don't miss the tours of restored mansions in Society Hill, Rittenhouse Square, or Fairmount Park for a delightful lesson in interior design and Americana. They're scattered throughout the year, but I especially love the pre-Christmas season.
- **Checking Out Penn's Landing and the Delaware Waterfront:** With the newly opened Independence Seaport Museum, historic ships, throbbing pier lounges and discos, and spanking-new sidewalks and street life, Philadelphia has definitively reclaimed its waterfront for tourism. The massive project now under construction will add a hotel, an FAO Schwarz toy store, a children's museum, and multimedia family fun to the mix by 2003.
- **Breathing Deeply at the Philadelphia Flower Show:** In early March, the scent-sational Flower Show—the largest and most prestigious indoor exhibition of its kind in the world—descends on the Pennsylvania Convention Center.
- **Rubbing Elbows at the Philadelphia Museum of Art:** It has a stupendous collection of masterpieces, period rooms, and crafts, and is becoming one of the hottest museums in the country for special exhibitions. Look for more

blockbusters like the recent van Gogh and Cézanne exhibitions. The late Wednesdays have become one of the city's trendiest social scenes.

- **Cheering the Regattas Along the Schuylkill:** On any spring weekend, stand along Boathouse Row just north of the Philadelphia Museum of Art. Crews race each other every 5 minutes or so, with cheering friends along the riverbanks.
- **Stocking Up at the Reading Terminal Market:** From Bassett's ice cream to Bain's turkey sandwiches to the food of the 12th Street Cantina, this is the century-old mother lode of unpackaged, fresh, honest-to-goodness provisions. Amish farmers come every Thursday to Saturday to sell their custards and scrapple (a kind of herbed pork casserole held together with cornmeal and fried before serving, either hot or cold). And what could be more convenient than its being right underneath the Convention Center?
- **Exploring South Philly:** Exuberant attitude punctuates every interchange you'll have, whether on a stroll with samples through the Italian Market or wandering farther south to seek out the area's great pizzas, cannoli, or famed cheesesteaks.
- **Dining on Walnut and Sydenham Streets:** This particular corner near Rittenhouse Square has more world-class restaurants within mere feet of each other— Le Bec-Fin, Circa, Striped Bass, Brasserie Perrier, Susanna Foo, and Il Portico—than any other spot anywhere in the world. Whatever your taste or price range, you should try one of them.

2 Best Hotel Bets

For all the details on the hotels below, see chapter 5.

- **Best Historic Hotel:** Well, it's only the "lite" version of what it used to be, when Thomas Edison designed the fixtures and the top-floor ballroom virtually defined swank. But the top floor of the **Park Hyatt at the Bellevue,** Broad and Walnut streets, or 1415 Chancellor Court, between Walnut and Locust streets (☎ 800/223-1234), with its occasionally oddly proportioned rooms, carries traces of a century's worth of history on South Broad Street.
- **Best for Business Travelers:** Even though it's the largest hotel in the state, you can still figure out the layout and amenities of the **Philadelphia Marriott,** 12th and Market streets (☎ 800/228-9290), pretty easily. The rooms have great work spaces with a second modem jack instead of a breakfast table, and the business center on the fifth floor is quite efficient. The service staff is truly excellent.
- **Best for a Romantic Getaway:** Some people like a slick, cosmopolitan suite in the clouds for romance. But I'll take the **Penn's View Hotel,** Front and Market streets (☎ 800/331-7634), any day. Even at the noisy corner of Front and Market streets, the upper floors feel like an exquisite club, with views over the Delaware River. And how could you vote against the largest wine bar in the world downstairs?
- **Best Hotel Lobby for Pretending You're Rich:** There's no place like the cool, plush **Four Seasons Hotel,** 1 Logan Sq. (☎ 800/332-3442), for rubbing elbows with the monied elite. The Swann Lounge overlooking Logan Circle is a constant stream of chic outfits, custom suits, and the frequent black tie.
- **Best for Families:** The new **Inn at Penn,** in West Philadelphia at 3600 Sansom St. (☎ 800/809-7001), is a crosstown ride from the historical sites, but offers the whole family space to roam among spacious corridors, ever-present fruit to munch on or tea to sip in a comfortable library lounge, plus TV for children to

watch while parents exercise. Also, the campus of U. Penn. across the street is perfect for throwing a Frisbee or climbing statues. Slightly tattered but more moderately priced is the **Embassy Suites Center City,** 1776 Benjamin Franklin Pkwy. at Logan Square (☎ **800/362-2779**), with cute little open-air balconies (yes, the railings are sturdy), and an opulent buffet breakfast at the TGI Friday's at street level. It's 5 minutes to the premier children's museums and Logan Circle. And, of course, all the rooms are suites, so parents still can have their privacy.

- **Best Moderately Priced Hotel:** The spanking new **Hawthorn Suites,** adjacent to the Convention Center at 1100 Vine St. (☎ **800/527-1133**), is the best choice in its price range. A suite with two double beds and a sofa bed in the living room goes for $149 but can often be had for as little as $119. Full breakfast and afternoon hors d'oeuvres are included, along with in-room microwaves, refrigerators, and coffeemakers.
- **Best B&B:** Many, many more B&Bs are listed through A Bed & Breakfast Connection/Bed & Breakfast of Philadelphia (see "B&B Agencies," in chapter 5) than those that list themselves independently. My favorite among the latter is **Shippen Way Inn,** 418 Bainbridge St. (☎ **800/245-4873** or 215/627-7266), a tiny row house in Queen Village built around 1750 and lovingly maintained. You might also try **Ten Eleven Clinton** (☎ **215/923-8144**), an elegant 1836 Federal townhouse on a quiet tree-lined street.
- **Best Service:** The training process set up by the Ritz Carlton group's C.O., Horst Schulze, for every employee of every **Ritz-Carlton** hotel is legendary, and the new hotel at 10 Avenue of the Arts (☎ **215/735-7700**) is no exception. Guests pay top prices (actually, weekend packages are quite affordable) to be pampered before they have to face the tough world outside. It's a fantasyland of amenities; service attendants earn points for thinking of extras like both foam and down pillows in the closets and bookmarks in the *TV Guides.*
- **Best Location:** Assuming we're visitors who have come to see Independence Park, why not wake up looking at it through the floral chintz curtains at the **Omni Hotel at Independence Park,** 4th and Chestnut streets (☎ **800/ 843-6664**)? All 155 guest rooms have views of the Greek Revival Second Bank of the U.S. and a half-dozen of America's Georgian jewels. And the clip-clopping of horses and carriages below maintains the sense of history.
- **Best Health Club: The Wyndham,** 17th and Race streets (☎ **800/996-3426**), with 758 rooms—second only to the Convention Center Marriott—has the best facilities for hotel guests, including a 45-foot indoor pool, a track, three racquetball courts, three squash courts, outdoor handball, and two tennis courts—all on the third-floor lobby roof. Weights and Nautilus machines round out the picture inside.
- **Best Hotel Pool:** I'm actually cheating a tiny bit here, but part of the garage complex of the **Park Hyatt at the Bellevue** (see "Best Historic Hotel," above) is the Sporting Club, with its four-lane, junior Olympic pool. Only hotel guests and local members can use the pool.
- **Best Views:** Many of the hotel listings in chapter 5 specify one side or another as preferable. In Center City, rooms at **The Rittenhouse,** 210 W. Rittenhouse Sq. (☎ **800/635-1042**), are on floors five to nine, and all have wonderful views, from the colorful park below on the east to the western view of the Schuylkill and the Parkway.
- **Best Hotel Restaurant:** The Zagat 2000 guide to local restaurants lists the **Fountain Restaurant** in the **Four Seasons** (see "Best Hotel Lobby for Pretending

You're Rich," above) as one of the country's top 50 dining spots—and many other publications have concurred. Natural light streams over fresh flowers, tapestries, and wide armchairs. It's virtually flawless, with prices to match.

3 Best Restaurant Bets

For full details on the restaurants below, see chapter 6.

- **Best Spot for a Romantic Dinner:** Antique tables and a flowery back garden with bright yellow umbrellas make **The Garden,** 1617 Spruce St., near Rittenhouse Square (☎ **215/546-4455**), the perfect spot for lingering over a long meal. The predominance of chocolate, exemplified in the sampler plate dessert, is guaranteed to leave you on a high.
- **Best Spot for a Business Lunch:** The **Fountain** of the Four Seasons Hotel, 1 Logan Sq. (☎ **215/963-1500**), fulfills every requirement: It's quiet, the tables are well spaced, the decor and service are impressive, and the cuisine—top-of-the-line steak, chops, and fish—is elegantly presented. The Georgian and mahogany paneling is lightened by magnificent windows on the water-sprayed gardens of Logan Circle.
- **Best Spot for a Celebration:** If you have a special occasion to celebrate—even if it's just being in Philadelphia—**Le Bec-Fin,** 1523 Walnut St. (☎ **215/567-1000**), is the clear choice. The cuisine under chef Georges Perrier has an international reputation, and the opulence of the fixed-price meal is staggering. And those dessert carts—unforgettable! Advance reservations are a must.
- **Best Decor:** This is necessarily a personal evaluation, but I figure if you're in Philadelphia, you're interested in a sense of history and old-style elegance. If so, head for the **Paris Bar & Grille,** in the stunning rotunda of the recently renovated bank now housing the Ritz Carlton Hotel at 10 Avenue of the Arts (☎ **215/735-7700**), in the center of town. Surrounded by the soaring dome and windows, the American organic cuisine has a tall bill to fill but seems to be up to the task.
- **Best View:** Crowds make the **Chart House,** 555 S. Columbus Blvd. (formerly Delaware Ave.) at Penn's Landing (☎ **215/625-8383**), the Convention Center of Philadelphia restaurants, but the food is amazingly good for the size of the place, and the views of the Delaware River from its own pier are spectacular. All this, plus reasonable prices for steak and lobster.
- **Best Wine List:** I can't resist mentioning two, since they're only a block apart and owned by the same people. **La Famiglia,** 8 S. Front St. (☎ **215/922-2803**), offers one of the finest wine cellars in the world, according to *Wine Spectator* magazine. One block north, the **Ristorante Panorama,** in the Penn's View Inn at Front and Market streets (☎ **215/922-7800**), is a charming Italian trattoria that reportedly has the largest single wine-dispensing machine in the world, with 120 different bottles available by the glass ($2.75–$30 per 5-ounce glass). What's really fun, though, is to order a "flight"—five glasses grouped around a theme, in the $12 to $16 range.
- **Best Value:** For its unbeatable central location and elegant surroundings (in a retro-fitted bank), I'm always happy to dine at **Circa,** 1518 Walnut St. (☎ **215/545-6800**). Most dinner entrees are less than $20, and lunch is even cheaper. Stick around for the great dance club action after 10pm on weekends.
- **Best Value, Fixed-Price Meal:** The $13.95 Tuesday night dinner at **Painted Parrot Café,** 211 Chestnut St. (☎ **215/922-5971**), in the heart of the historic

district, offers superb soup or salad, a choice of pasta entrees, great bread, and one of the city's best desserts (served with La Colombe brand coffee). Get there before they come to their senses; but the other à la carte nights won't break your bank, either.

- **Best for Kids:** If your kids are like mine, they like the broad selection and energy that a mall-type food court gives them. The **Food Court at Liberty Place,** between Chestnut and Market streets and 16th and 17th streets, has old city stalwarts like Bain's Deli and Bassett's Original Turkey, along with out-of-towners like Sbarro and Mentesini Pizza. It's spotless, large, and steps away from the city's best urban mall.

- **Best Date Restaurant:** I'd pick two relative newcomers here. For a classy bistro with contemporary combinations in Old City, I would go for **Fork,** 306 Market St. (☎ **215/625-9425**). In the heart of Center City, you'll find the warm and exotic fusion of South American flavors under candlelit sconces at **Pasion!,** 211 S. 15th St. (☎ **215/875-9895**).

- **Best American Cuisine:** Jack McDavid is the *enfant terrible* of Philadelphia chefs. His warm, homey **Jack's Firehouse,** 2130 Fairmount Ave. (☎ **215/232-9000**), features the most dramatic juxtapositions of American ingredients and flavors in town, with special emphasis on rare and ethnic fare. It isn't every day you'll have the occasion to try bear or beaver tail, or such a selection of organic ingredients.

- **Best Chinese Cuisine:** A reserved former librarian, born in inner Mongolia and raised in northern China and Taiwan, has quietly built up a national reputation with **Susanna Foo,** 1512 Walnut St. (☎ **215/545-2666**). Her innovative mix of East and West relies on reductions rather than dashes of soy sauce and ginger, and skillets and saucepans rather than a wok. The dim sum—appetizer-sized portions—are a city favorite.

- **Best Continental Cuisine:** The **Fountain** at the Four Seasons Hotel, 1 Logan Sq., between 18th Street and Franklin Parkway (☎ **215/963-1500**), is consistently rated best in town for understated, complex versions of classic continental dishes. Since the food is so uniformly excellent, my advice is to go with the chef's choice on the fixed-price menu.

- **Best French Cuisine:** Most Frenchmen have never tasted a meal remotely as good as what Georges Perrier prepares at **Le Bec-Fin** (see "Best Spot for a Celebration," above). A meal here can be the food event of a lifetime.

- **Best Italian Cuisine:** Philadelphia must have 1,000 Italian restaurants, but I especially like **The Saloon,** 750 S. 7th St. (☎ **215/627-1811**), the type of dignified, elegant place that draws everyone in town sooner or later. For up-to-date style and modern interpretations of classic dishes, try **Aglio,** 937 E. Passyunk Ave. (☎ **215/336-8008**).

- **Best Seafood:** As you would expect, Philadelphia has a superb reputation for fish houses, but the best in town is **Striped Bass,** 1500 Walnut St. (☎ **215/732-4444**), in the most chic dining block in the city. New chef Terence Feury has continued to create a menu breathtaking in its unusual treatment of fish and seafood.

- **Best Steakhouse:** Philadelphia has always been more of a seafood and pasta town than a steak town. The top choices are both imports: **Ruth's Chris Steak House,** 260 S. Broad St. (☎ **215/790-1515**), a butter-laden sizzling chain from New Orleans, and **Morton's of Chicago,** 1411 Walnut St. (☎ **215/557-0724**), a quiet refuge with a 24-ounce porterhouse.

- **Best Burgers and Beer:** In this case, bigger is better. The new **Dock Street Brew Pub at Reading Terminal,** at 1150 Filbert St., right under Reading Terminal Headhouse (☎ **215/922-4292**), has hundreds of seats, all happily occupied with diners chowing down beer-batter fried and sundaes to boot. An on-site brewery produces six different ales, porters, and lagers fresh each day. No reservations for parties under six.
- **Best Pizza: Marra's,** 1734 E. Passyunk Ave., between Morris and Moore streets (☎ **215/463-9249**), in South Philadelphia, has thin crusts and delicious, spicy traditional toppings, baked in brick ovens; enjoy them in those old wooden booths.
- **Best Desserts:** Apart from the dessert cart at **Le Bec-Fin** (see "Best Spot for a Celebration," above), the best sweet show in town is to be found at **Painted Parrot Café** (see "Best Value, Fixed-Price Meal," above); choices range from harlequin mousse tart and other chocolate delights to fruit. Wednesday is "all-you-can-savor dessert buffet" (a dangerous concept!) starting at 5pm.
- **Best Bread:** It's "only" bread—but they do make it better than anyone else at **Metropolitan Bakery,** 262 S. 19th St. (☎ **215/545-6655**), and 1114 Pine St. (☎ **215/627-3433**). They use organic fruit starters rather than commercial yeast, French willow baskets for the final rise, and bake in a steam-process brick oven. Try San Francisco Sourdough, Chocolate Cherry, or Olive Thyme.
- **Best Breakfast:** The **Down Home Diner** at Reading Terminal Market (☎ **215/627-1955;** see "A Taste of Ethnic Philly: Reading Terminal Market," in chapter 6), open from 7am, has wonderful blueberry pancakes, fresh eggs with garlic grits, and a breakfast "pizza" with sausage biscuits, smoked cheddar, and tomato. All ingredients are fanatically organic, from small-scale producers wherever possible. Lunch has its charms too, with meatloaf, black-eyed pea and ham-hock soup, and pecan pie. The vintage jukebox plays great old American tunes.
- **Best Brunch:** Nearly every restaurant offers Sunday brunch, ranging from standard bagels with spreads to a full brunch menu. The **White Dog Cafe,** 3420 Sansom St. (☎ **215/386-9224**), in West Philadelphia, can swing either way, in a completely comfortable, unpretentious environment.
- **Best People Watching:** No place is hotter than Manayunk, halfway between Center City and Bryn Mawr. The window seats at **Sonoma,** 4411 Main St. (☎ **215/483-9400**), are great for watching thousands of people stroll by, hour after hour, between noon and midnight. The vodka bar is legendary. For spotting a celebrity, head for one of the Stephen Starr-owned operations such as **Buddakan,** 325 Chestnut St. (☎ **215/574-9440**).
- **Best Afternoon Tea:** The advent of true luxury hotels in Philadelphia has brought exquisite afternoon teas all over town. I love the Cassatt Lounge at the **Rittenhouse Hotel,** 210 W. Rittenhouse Sq. (☎ **215/546-9000**), for its cheery decor, tucked-in garden, and Mary Cassatt's drawings commemorating her brother's house that once stood on the site. For a more solid, English burgher version, try the **Dickens Inn,** 421 S. 2nd St. (☎ **215/928-9307**), in Head House Square.
- **Best for Pretheater Dinner:** It's had some ups and downs recently, but I am partial to **Toto's,** 1407 Locust St. (☎ **215/546-2000**), just steps from the Academy of Music and the Merriam. It has always looked spectacular, and now serves a simpler, less over-the-top Italian menu.
- **Best Outdoor Dining:** In the historic district, the back garden of **City Tavern,** 138 S. 2nd St., near Walnut Street (☎ **215/413-1443**), belongs to Independence

National Historical Park, and diners are surrounded by century-old trees and Federal-style landmarks while they imbibe their strong ale or punch, or dine on a historically faithful 18th-century potpie. In Center City, you'll be heading for 18th Street along Rittenhouse Square, between Walnut and Locust streets: Anywhere you park among **Devon Seafood Grill, Rouge,** or **Bleu** (the last has the best cuisine) on that block is fine.

- **Best Late-Night Dining:** When it's after midnight, I head for Chinatown. **Shiao Lan Kung,** 930 Race St. (☎ **215/928-0282**), while not much on decor, has wonderful hot pot dishes, and you can order fresh sea bass from the tank.
- **Best Ice Cream: Bassett's Ice Cream** (☎ **215/925-4315**), an original 1892 tenant of Reading Terminal Market (see "A Taste of Ethnic Philly: Reading Terminal Market," in chapter 6), has long claimed supremacy for its rich and smooth flavors, and they make a terrific milkshake. A second location, at the Food Court at Liberty Place, carries the quality but lacks that turn-of-the-century soda fountain ambience.

2

Planning a Trip to Philadelphia

This chapter is devoted to the where, when, and how of your trip—the advance-planning issues required to get it together and take it on the road.

1 Visitor Information & Money

VISITOR INFORMATION

TOURIST OFFICE   The **Philadelphia Convention and Visitors Bureau,** 16th Street and John F. Kennedy Boulevard, Philadelphia, PA 19102 (☎ **800/537-7676** or 215/636-1666), should be your first resource. It offers a wealth of publications, from seasonal calendars of events to maps; knowledgeable volunteers staff the phones. Definitely ask for the "Official Visitors Guide," a seasonal compendium. It also offers an increasing number of package tours combining special museum exhibitions, concerts, or sporting events with discount hotel prices, free city transit passes, and Amtrak discounts. Once you're in town, note that many bus tours, historic trolley rides, and walking tours start from here, including tours of City Hall.

WEB SITES   For the growing number of visitors who have access to the Internet, there are a growing number of Web sites that you'll find helpful. Chief among them is the Convention and Visitors Bureau site **www.libertynet.org/phila-visitor**. Other sites include: **www.netscape.digitalcity.com/philadelphia**, which contains a great deal of user feedback and opinions along with excellent and pithy summaries of events, sites, and restaurants; **www.gophia.com** and **www.phillyvisitor.com**, which are driven by paid advertisers and hotlinks; and **www.cityspin.com/philadelphia**, which basically consists of a listing of options.

MONEY

Except for truly deluxe experiences, you will find moderate prices in Philadelphia, less than those in New York and on a par with, or slightly above, those in Washington, D.C.

Minimal cash is required, since credit cards are accepted universally and automatic-teller machines linked to national networks are strewn around tourist destinations and increasingly within hotels. To find ATMs on the **Cirrus** network, call ☎ **800/424-7787;** for the **PLUS** system, call ☎ **800/843-7587.**

Lost or Stolen Credit Cards

Credit cards usually have a toll-free number on the back. But that doesn't help you much if the card was stolen, does it? **Citibank Visa**'s U.S. emergency number is ☎ **800/645-6556**. **American Express** cardholders and traveler's check holders should call ☎ **800/221-7282** for all money emergencies. **MasterCard** holders should call ☎ **800/307-7309**. For any other toll-free number, call 800 information at ☎ **800/555-1212**.

The three major traveler's check agencies are **American Express** (☎ **800/ 221-7282**); **BankAmerica** (☎ **800/227-3460**); and **VISA** (☎ **800/227-6811**). See chapter 3.

2 When to Go

Philadelphia is great to visit any time, although given the city's popularity, the constant flow of conventions, and the current hotel shortage, you'll find better deals in the fall and winter. Concert and museum seasons run from early October to early June.

The city has four distinct seasons with temperatures ranging from the 90s (°F) in summer to the 30s in winter. (Below-zero temperatures normally hit only one out of every four winters.) Summers, the height of tourist season, can get swelteringly humid. In the fall, the weather becomes drier. Spring temperatures are variable; count on comfortable breezes.

Average Temperatures & Precipitation in Philadelphia

	Jan	Feb	Mar	Apr	May	June	July	Aug	Sept	Oct	Nov	Dec
High °F	40	41	50	62	73	81	85	83	77	66	54	43
Low °F	26	26	33	43	53	63	68	66	60	49	39	29
Precip. in days	11	9	11	11	11	10	9	9	8	8	10	10

Philadelphia Calendar of Events

For more details and up-to-the-minute information, contact the **Convention and Visitors Bureau,** 1515 John F. Kennedy Blvd. (at 16th St.), Philadelphia, PA 19102 (☎ **215/636-1666**); www.libertynet.org/phila-visitor.

January

✪ **Mummer's Parade.** Starting at 8am and lasting most of the day, 30,000 spangled strutters march with feathers and banjos in a celebration that must have been pagan in origin. (The word "mummer" comes from the French *momer*, meaning "to go masked.") The parade starts at 5th and Market streets, proceeds west to City Hall, and finally goes counterclockwise around City Hall, passing the judging stand at Juniper and Filbert streets. If you have visited the Mummer's Museum beforehand, the gaudiness and elaborateness of the costumes won't amaze you quite so much, but the music (everyone ends up humming "Oh, Dem Golden Slippers") and festivity will have you entranced. You can get reserved seats, available for $2 from early December at the Convention and Visitors Bureau. Call ☎ **215/336-3050** for details. January 1 (or the following Sat in case of bad weather).

- **Benjamin Franklin's Birthday.** The Franklin Institute Science Museum (see chapter 7) celebrates its namesake's birthday with scientific demonstrations and a big birthday cake. Call ☎ 215/448-1200 for details. Second or third Sunday of the month.

February

- **Black History Month.** The Afro-American Museum, 7th and Arch streets, offers a full complement of exhibitions, lectures, and music. Call ☎ 215/574-0380 for details. All month long.
- **Chinese New Year.** You can enjoy dragons and fireworks at 11th and Arch streets, traditional 10-course banquets, or a visit to the Chinese Cultural Center at 125 N. 10th St. Call ☎ 215/923-6767 for details on the festivities. Mid- to late February.
- **George Washington's Birthday.** Valley Forge National Historical Park holds a Cherries Jubilee weekend. Call ☎ 610/783-7700 for details. Third Sunday and Monday of the month.
- **Comcast U.S. Indoor Tennis Championships.** This event, held at the Spectrum, features some of the world's best players. Call ☎ 215/947-2530 for particulars. Third weekend of the month.

March

- ✪ **Philadelphia Flower Show.** Now held in the Convention Center, it's the largest flower show in the country, with acres of gardens and rustic settings. With the citywide institution of Flower Show Week, it's even bigger and better than before. You can usually get tickets at the door, but the Pennsylvania Horticultural Society at 325 Walnut St. sells them in advance. Call ☎ 800/611-5960 for information or for tour packages. Late February to early March.
- ✪ **The Book and the Cook Festival.** For the past decade, Philadelphia has combined its love for reading and eating into this festival. For five days, eminent food critics, cookbook authors, and restaurateurs are invited to plan dream meals with participating city restaurants. If you're a foodie, you know that the chance to stroll through Reading Terminal Market with Alice Waters, or to dine on what she cooks up, is not to be declined. The festival has recently expanded into food samplings and wine and beer tastings all over town. The list of participating restaurants is published in January, and many get booked quickly. Call ☎ 215/686-3662 for a schedule and to make a reservation. Usually the third week of the month.
- **St. Patrick's Day Parade.** The parade starts at noon on 20th Street and the Parkway, turns on 17th Street to Chestnut Street, then goes down Chestnut Street to Independence Mall. The Parkway is the most spacious vantage point, and the Irish Pub at 2007 Walnut St. will be packed. Call the Convention and Visitors Bureau for details (☎ 215/636-1666). Sunday closest to March 17.

April

- **Philadelphia Antiques Show.** Started in 1961, this antiques show is probably the finest in the nation, with 50-odd major English and American exhibitors. It's held at the 103rd Engineers Armory, 33rd and Market streets. Call ☎ 215/387-3500 for information. First weekend of the month.
- **American Music Theater Festival.** In its 18th year in 2001, this festival offers premieres of musical theater works by major American artists, ranging from traditional Broadway-bound musicals to avant-garde works. Call ☎ 215/893-1570 for information. Runs through June.

- **Easter Sunday.** This day brings fashion shows and music to Rittenhouse Square. The Easter Bunny usually makes an appearance at Lord & Taylor's and the Gallery. Call ☎ **215/686-2876** for details.
- **Spring Tour of Fairmount Park.** The dogwood and cherry trees along both sides of the Schuylkill are in blossom. Trolley buses make a special run along Wissahickon Creek, a lovely woodland minutes away from Center City. Call ☎ **215/636-1666** for details. Last Sunday of the month (or first Sun in May).

May

- **Philadelphia Open House.** These tours give you a rare chance to see Germantown, Society Hill, and University City mansions. Call ☎ **215/928-1188** for information. Late April to early May.
- **Mozart on the Square.** Also around Rittenhouse Square, this festival brings about 20 chamber performances of younger talent to town. Performances cost $5 to $15; for information, contact P.O. Box 237, Merion Station, PA 19006 (☎ **215/668-1799**). All month long.
- **Dad Vail Regatta.** This is one of the largest collegiate rowing events in the country. You can picnic on East River Drive near Strawberry Mansion. Call ☎ **215/542-7844** for details. Second week of the month.
- **Israel Independence Day.** This holiday brings a Center City parade and day-long Israeli bazaar to the Parkway. Call ☎ **215/922-7222** for details. Second or third Sunday of the month.
- **Rittenhouse Square Flower Market.** This market has been an annual event since 1914. Plants, flowers, baked goods, and lemon sticks are some of the irresistibles for sale. The more than 2,000 azaleas and rhododendrons in bloom behind the Museum of Art literally stop traffic with their brilliance. Call ☎ **215/525-7182** for details. Third Thursday of the month.
- **International Theater Festival for Children.** This festival takes place on or near the University of Pennsylvania campus, based at 3680 Walnut St. Call ☎ **215/898-6791** for programs and prices. Last week of the month.
- **Jam on the River.** This was cooked up as Philadelphia's homage to New Orleans and has expanded to include blues as well as jazz. It's based at the Great Plaza at Penn's Landing. In recent years, Dr. John and the Preservation Hall Jazz Band have been in attendance. Call ☎ **215/636-1666** for particulars. Late May.
- **Devon Horse Show,** Route 30, Devon. This event outside Philadelphia includes jumping competitions, carriage races and a great country fair with plenty of food stalls—burgers as well as watercress sandwiches—under cheerful awnings. Call ☎ **610/964-0550** for details. End of the month.

June

- **Head House Square.** Local craftspeople, food vendors, and street artists set up shop on Saturday noon to midnight and Sunday noon to 6pm. Throughout the summer.
- **Elfreth's Alley Days.** Row-house dwellers, many in colonial costumes, open up their homes for inspection and admiration. There are reenactments of colonial crafts. Call ☎ **215/574-0560** for details. First weekend of the month.
- **First Union Pro Cycling Championships.** The 156-mile course of this country's premier one-day cycling event starts and finishes on the Parkway, following the incredible climb up the cliffs at Manayunk. First weekend of the month.
- **Rittenhouse Square Fine Arts Annual.** Philadelphia moves outdoors with this event, in which hundreds of professional and student works of art go on sale. Call ☎ **215/634-5060** for details. First 2 weeks of June.

- **Betsy Ross House.** Flag Day festivities are held here at 12:30pm, usually with a national guard band and a speech. Call ☎ **215/627-5343** for details. June 14.
- **Bloomsday.** The Rosenbach Museum and the Irish Pub at 2007 Walnut St. both celebrate the 24-hour time span of James Joyce's novel *Ulysses.* June 16.
- **Mellon Jazz Festival.** A top-drawer collection of artists is featured at the Mann Music Center and the Academy of Music. Second or third week of the month.

July

✪ **Sunoco Welcome America!** The whole town turns out for this weeklong festival to celebrate America's birthday with fountains, theater, free entertainment, and assorted pageantry. The Fourth of July brings special ceremonies to Independence Square including: a reading of the Declaration of Independence, a presentation of the prestigious Freedom Medal, and an evening parade up the Parkway. There's also a Schuylkill regatta on the Fourth. Principal locations are the terrace by the Philadelphia Museum of Art, City Hall (where the world's largest hoagie is assembled), and Independence Mall. Call ☎ **215/636-1666** or log onto www.americasbirthday.com for information. The week before July 4, with fireworks on the Delaware River July 3.

- **Philadelphia Orchestra Summer Concerts.** Mann Music Center in Fairmount Park. The concerts are free on Monday, Wednesday, and Thursday through August. There are also pop concerts at low prices at Robin Hood Dell East and dancing at Art Museum Terrace. See chapter 10 for more information about the concerts, or call ☎ **215/567-0707** for a schedule.

August

- **Pennsylvania Dutch Festival.** Reading Terminal Market is the venue all week for quilts, music, food, crafts, and such. Call ☎ **215/922-2317** for more information. First week of August.
- **Philadelphia Folk Festival.** Suburban Poole Farm, Schwenksville. This festival offers bluegrass, Irish, Cajun, Klezmer, and cowboy music, as well as dancing, juggling, puppetry, and crafts. It has a national reputation and draws major crowds. Call ☎ **215/247-1300** for details. Usually late in the month.

September

- **Philadelphia Fringe Festival.** Inaugurated in 1997, this festival brings up to 500 cutting-edge performances, experimental films, and art installations to nooks and crannies of Old City throughout the first half of the month.
- **Fairmount Park Festival.** This festival, which runs through November, includes the Harvest Show at Memorial Hall and parades of varying themes down the Parkway. Call ☎ **215/685-0052** for details. Most weekends.
- **Philadelphia Distance Run.** One of the nation's premier tests, it's a half marathon through Center City and Fairmount Park. In town, it's bigger than the November marathon and gets plenty of national running figures. Call ☎ **215/665-8500** if you wish to join the field of 7,500. Usually the third Sunday of the month.

October

- **Columbus Day Parade.** There's a parade along the Parkway; also look for South Philadelphia fairs. Second Monday of the month.
- ✪ **Super Sunday.** Think of a party for an entire city—that's Super Sunday, held on the Benjamin Franklin Parkway from Logan Circle to the Museum of Art. There are clowns, jugglers, mimes, rides, craft vendors, and a flea market. The museums and academies along the Parkway have sponsored this event since 1970, rain

or shine, and most have reduced admissions and special programs. This is one day when parking on the grass won't get you a ticket. Call ☎ **215/665-1050** for information. Third Sunday of the month.

November

- **Philadelphia Marathon.** The marathon starts and finishes at the Art Museum, passing through Fairmount Park, Center City, and Independence Hall. Call ☎ **215/683-2070** for more information. Usually a Sunday in the middle of the month.
- **Virginia Slims Women's Tennis Championships.** The matches are played at the Spectrum in South Philadelphia. Call ☎ **215/568-4444** for details. Second week of the month.
- **Philadelphia Museum of Art Craft Show.** This preeminent exhibition and retail sale of the finest American contemporary craft involves clay, glass, fiber, jewelry, metal, wearables, and wool. Tickets are $10 (2 days for $15). At the Convention Center. Call ☎ **215/684-7930.** Usually the second weekend of the month.
- **Thanksgiving Day Parade.** This parade features cartoon characters, bands, floats, and Santa Claus. Thanksgiving Day.

December

- **Holiday Activities Around Town.** Christmas occasions many activities in Center City, beginning with the tree lighting in City Hall courtyard. The Gallery at Market East, "A Christmas Carol" at Strawbridge and Clothier, a Colonial Christmas Village at Market Place East, and Hecht's all host elaborate extravaganzas, with organs and choruses. The Society Hill and Germantown Christmas walking tours are lovely, with the same leafy decorations as Fairmount Park. Throughout the month.
- *Nutcracker* **Ballet.** The Pennsylvania Ballet performs Tchaikovsky's classic at the Academy of Music, Broad and Locust streets. Call ☎ **215/551-7014** for details. Throughout the month.
- **Private Lights.** For an unusual Christmas experience, visit the 2700 block of South Colorado Street, south of Oregon Avenue, between 17th and 18th streets. The sight of some 40 houses bathed in interconnected strands of holiday lights is spectacular. The lights usually go up right after Thanksgiving.
- **Lucia Fest.** American Swedish Historical Museum, 1900 Pattison Ave. in South Philadelphia. It sounds Italian, but the Lucia Fest is a Swedish pageant held by candlelight. Call ☎ **215/389-1776** for information. First weekend of the month.
- **Christmas Tours of Fairmount Park and Germantown.** Colonial mansions sparkle with wreaths, holly, and fruit arrangements donated by local garden clubs. Call ☎ **215/787-5449** or 215/848-1777 for details. Tours begin mid-month.
- **New Year's Eve.** Fireworks are held at the Great Plaza of Penn's Landing on December 31.

3 Insurance

There are three kinds of travel insurance: trip cancellation, medical, and lost luggage. Trip cancellation insurance is a good idea if you have paid a large portion of your vacation expenses up front, but the other two types of insurance don't make sense for most travelers.

Your existing health insurance should cover you if you get sick while on vacation. If you belong to an HMO or have a managed plan, you should check to see whether you are fully covered when away from home. Your homeowner's insurance should cover stolen luggage if you have off-premises theft. Check your existing policies before you buy any additional coverage. The airlines are responsible for $1,250 on domestic flights if they lose your luggage; if you plan to carry anything more valuable than that, keep it in your carry-on bag.

Some credit cards (American Express and certain gold and platinum Visas and MasterCards, for example) offer automatic flight insurance against death or dismemberment in case of an airplane crash. If you still feel you need more insurance, try one of the companies listed below. But don't pay for more insurance than you need. For example, if you only need trip cancellation insurance, don't purchase coverage for lost or stolen property. Trip cancellation insurance costs approximately 6% to 8% of the total value of your vacation. Among the reputable issuers of travel insurance are:

Access America, 6600 W. Broad St., Richmond, VA 23230 (☎ **800/ 284-8300**).

Mutual of Omaha, Mutual of Omaha Plaza, Omaha, NE 68175 (☎ **800/ 228-9792**).

Travel Guard International, 1145 Clark St., Stevens Point, WI 54481 (☎ **800/826-1300**).

Travel Insured International, P.O. Box 280568, East Hartford, CT 06128 (☎ **800/243-3174**).

4 Tips for Travelers with Special Needs

FOR TRAVELERS WITH DISABILITIES

An excellent resource for travelers with any type of disability is **Mobility International USA,** P.O. Box 10767, Eugene, OR 97440 (☎ **541/343-1284,** voice and TDD; www.miusa.org), a nonprofit organization involved in promoting travel awareness for people who have difficulty in getting around. The organization publishes *A World of Options,* a 658-page book of resources for disabled travelers, covering everything from biking trips to scuba outfitters ($45).

If you're plugged in, **Access-Able Travel Source** (**www.access-able.com**) is an all-purpose on-line resource. You can get information here on travel agents that have tours or can plan trips for special needs; links to other disability and travel Web sites; lists of disability organizations, magazines, and newsletters, and more.

Travelers with disabilities will find the tourist areas of Philadelphia accessible. Even though some streets in Society Hill and those bordering Independence National Historical Park have uneven brick sidewalks, and Dock Street itself is paved with rough cobblestones, all curbs are well cut at intersections.

Parking is tough, however, as ISA-designated spots are rare. The same is true for Chestnut Street, the Parkway, and the University of Pennsylvania campus. Independence National Historic Park's Visitor Center has a level entrance and publishes "Accessibilities," a brochure detailing all park sites.

Virtually all theaters and stadiums accommodate wheelchairs. Call ahead to plan routes. To aid people with hearing impairments, the Academy of Music provides free infrared headsets for concerts; the Annenberg Center rents them for $2.

A national resource, the **Travel Information Service** at Moss Rehabilitation Hospital will provide telephone information at ☎ **215/456-9603.**

For basic information, contact the **Mayor's Commission on People with Disabilities,** Room 143, City Hall, Philadelphia, PA 19107 (☎ 215/686-2798). SEPTA publishes a special "Transit Guide for the Disabled"; you can request it from **SEPTA Special Services,** 1234 Market St., 4th Floor, Philadelphia, PA 19107 (☎ 215/580-7145). All SEPTA bus routes are lift-equipped. Market East and University City subway stations are wheelchair accessible, but most other stops are not. The airport has a variety of services including 15 TDD telephones, elevators and escalators, Braille ATMs, and curb cuts.

The Free Library of Philadelphia runs a **Library for the Blind and Physically Handicapped,** very conveniently located at 919 Walnut St. (☎ 215/683-3213); it's open Monday to Friday 9am to 5pm. It adjoins the **Associated Services for the Blind,** which offers transcriptions into Braille for a fee.

If you travel with Amtrak or Greyhound/Trailways, be aware that on the former you can receive a 25% discount and a special seat with advance notification (☎ 800/523-6590), and on the latter a free seat for a companion (☎ 800/345-3109).

Many of the major car-rental companies now offer hand-controlled cars for disabled drivers. Avis can provide such a vehicle at any of its locations in the United States with 48-hour advance notice; Hertz requires between 24 and 72 hours advance reservation at most of its locations. **Wheelchair Getaways** (☎ 800/873-4973; www.blvd.com/wg.htm) and **Wheelers East** (☎ 800/862-7475) rent specialized vans with wheelchair lifts and other features for the disabled in more than 100 cities across the United States.

FOR GAYS & LESBIANS

Center City is used to, and tolerant of, gays and lesbians, and the rectangle bordered by 9th and Juniper streets and Walnut and South streets is filled with gay social services, restaurants, bookstores, and clubs. See chapter 10 for specific clubs and bars. You might also check the weekly *Philadelphia Gay News* (www.epgn.com), which is widely available. The lesbian-oriented *Labyrinth* is available free at Giovanni's Room (see below), which is 'ground zero' for media at 12th and Pine streets. Outside the city, New Hope (see chapter 11) is a popular destination for gay and lesbian travelers.

For meetings, classes, gallery exhibitions, and social events, consult **William Way Community Center,** 1315 Spruce St. (☎ 215/732-2220), or drop by **Millennium Coffee,** 212 S. 12th St. (☎ 215/731-9798), a sleek scene open until midnight. The **Blackwell Center for Women,** 1124 Walnut St. (☎ 215/923-7577), can direct you to health clinics. The **Women's Switchboard** is at ☎ 215/829-1976.

The bookstore **Giovanni's Room,** 345 S. 12th St., Philadelphia, PA 19107 (☎ 215/923-2960), is a 25-year-old national resource for publications produced by and for gays and lesbians as well as for feminist and progressive literature.

A national **Gay/Lesbian Crisisline** (☎ 800/767-4297) can provide instant medical or legal counseling and local support listings as well. The **Gay Switchboard** (open daily 7–10pm) is at ☎ 215/546-7100; the **Lesbian Hotline** is at ☎ 215/222-5110.

To report antigay violence or discrimination, call the **Philadelphia Lesbian and Gay Task Force Hotline** at ☎ 215/563-4581. **ACT UP/Philadelphia** meets on Monday; call ☎ 215/731-1844.

FOR SENIORS

Many city attractions grant special discounts to seniors, especially during weekdays. Some hotels, too, will shift their rates, particularly on weekends. The Convention and Visitors Bureau publishes "Seniors on the Go," which lists dozens of specific benefits around town—from flat taxi fares to museum admissions; write ahead or pick it up at the Convention and Visitors Bureau. Senior citizens should bring some form of photo ID.

If you haven't already done so, think about joining the **American Association of Retired Persons (AARP)**, 1909 K St. NW, Washington, DC 20049 (☎ **202/ 872-4700**). Its Purchase Privilege Program unlocks an incredible trove of discounts on car rentals, hotels, restaurant meals, and museums, as well as discounts from participating retail stores.

Many seniors prefer places with convenient local transportation between sites, and Philadelphia is wonderful in this regard. Seniors might consider the two unlimited day public transport options: the SEPTA DayPass ($5), available at the Convention and Visitors Bureau at 16th Street and John F. Kennedy Boulevard, and the purple PHLASH vans ($4), which loop around all day to Center City's most popular destinations.

You can pick up a **Golden Age Passport** at Independence National Historical Park if you are 62 or over. Since this park is free, it won't matter there, but the passport provides free admission to all parks, monuments, and recreation areas operated by the National Park Service.

Some educational programs run by **Elderhostel** are in the Philadelphia area. You must be over 60 (and your spouse or companion over 50) to participate. For information, contact them at 75 Federal St., 3rd Floor, Boston, MA 02110 (☎ **617/ 426-7788**).

FOR FAMILIES

Planning is essential for success in Philadelphia—I know from personal experience! Airlines and Amtrak both let children under 2 years old travel free and offer discounts for children and/or families. Once you arrive, children under 12 (in some cases, 18) can stay free in the same room as their parents in virtually all Philadelphia hotels. Be sure to reserve cribs and playpens if needed in advance. Restaurants

---

A Little Book Learnin'

If your kids are old enough, encourage them to read something about Philadelphia ahead of time. Robert Lawson's classic *Ben and Me* tells of Ben Franklin's career from a mouse's point of view. Katherine Milhous's *Through These Arches: The Story of Independence Hall* is an engaging illustrated book. For younger readers, there's Elvajeen Hall's *Today in Old Philadelphia*, which combines historic buildings and sights with a description of daily life in the past. John Loeper's *The House on Spruce Street* uses the restoration of a grand old Society Hill house to discuss Philadelphia history. Elizabeth Gray Vining's *The Taken Girl* is a lovely story about an orphan girl who becomes involved in the antislavery movement after being taken on as a helper in the 1840s Quaker household of John Greenleaf Whittier. In Susan Lee's *The Fall of the Quaker City,* a Quaker family must decide whether to support the American Revolution.

all over the country are increasingly aware of the need to provide the basics, and the "Family-Friendly Restaurants" featured in chapter 6 will point out some favorites.

The best current resource for family travel in Philadelphia is *Metrokids,* a bimonthly newspaper available at the Convention and Visitors Bureau at 16th Street and John F. Kennedy Boulevard. It lists all cultural attractions geared toward families, along with special issues on factory tours, the Camden aquarium, and the like. Call ☎ **215/735-7035** with specific questions.

FOR STUDENTS

It's not well known, but there are more colleges and universities in and around Philadelphia than any other city in the country—so students will find a warm reception from area vendors and sites. A valid student ID will get you special discounts on cultural sites, accommodations, car rentals, and more. The **Council on International Educational Exchange,** or **CIEE** (www.ciee.org), will set you up with an ID card. While in Philadelphia, students might head for the **University of Pennsylvania,** 34th and Walnut streets (☎ **215/898-5000**); **Temple University,** Broad Street and Montgomery Avenue (☎ **215/787-8561**); or **International House,** 3701 Chestnut St. (☎ **215/387-5125**). All publish free papers listing lectures, performances, films, and social events.

5 Getting There

BY PLANE

THE MAJOR AIRLINES   By air, Philadelphia is 2½ hours from Miami or Chicago, and 6 hours from the West Coast. To Philadelphia, 24 carriers fly from more than 100 cities in the U.S. and 16 destinations abroad. You can check flight schedules and make reservations on the following domestic airlines:

American Airlines and **American Eagle** (☎ 800/433-7300 or 215/365-4000; www.americanair.com); **America West** (☎ 800/235-9292; www.americawest. com); **Continental Airlines** (☎ 800/525-0280; www.flycontinental.com); **Delta Air Lines** (☎ 800/221-1212 or 215/667-7720; www.delta.com); **Midway Airlines** (☎ 800/446-4392; www.midwayair.com); **Midwest Express** (☎ 800/452-2022; www.midwestexpress.com); **Northwest Airlines** (☎ 800/225-2525 domestic, or 800/447-4747 international; www.nwa.com); **TWA** (☎ 800/221-2000, 215/923-2000 domestic, or 800/892-4141 international; www.twa. com); **United Airlines** (☎ 800/241-6522 or 215/568-2800; www.ual.com); and **USAirways** (☎ 800/428-4322; www.usairways.com). **Midway Airlines** and **USAirways** use Philadelphia International Airport as a hub.

For international carriers with direct flights, see chapter 3.

FIGHTING THE AIRFARE WARS   Airfares are capitalism at its purest. Passengers within the same cabin on an airplane rarely pay the same fare. Rather, they pay what the market will bear.

Business travelers who need the flexibility to purchase their tickets at the last minute, who change their itinerary at a moment's notice, or who want to get home before the weekend pay the premium rate, known as the full fare. Passengers who can book their tickets long in advance, who don't mind staying over Saturday night, or who are willing to travel on a Tuesday, Wednesday, or Thursday pay the least, usually a fraction of the full fare.

The airlines also periodically hold sales, in which they lower the prices on their most popular routes. These fares have advance purchase requirements and date of

Cyber Deals for Net Surfers

It's possible to get some great deals on airfare, hotels, and car rentals via the Internet. So go grab your mouse and start surfing before you take off—you could save a bundle on your trip. The Web sites highlighted below are worth checking out, especially since all services are free.

Travelocity (**www.travelocity.com; www.previewtravel.com; www. frommerstravelocity. com**)   Travelocity is Frommer's online travel-planning/ booking partner. In addition to its "Personal Fare Watcher," which notifies you via e-mail of the lowest airfares for up to five different destinations, Travelocity will track the three lowest fares for any routes on any dates in minutes. You can book a flight right then and there, and if you need a rental car or hotel, Travelocity will find you the best deal via the SABRE computer reservations system (another huge travel agent database).

Flifo Global (**http://travel.yahoo.com/travel/**)   This Yahoo site has a feature called "Fare Beater," which will check flights on different airlines or at different times or dates in hopes of finding the cheapest fare.

Microsoft Expedia (**www.expedia.com**)   The best part of this multi-purpose travel site is the "Fare Tracker": You fill out a form on the screen indicating that you're interested in cheap flights from your nearest gateway, and, once a week, they'll e-mail you the best airfare deals. The site's "Travel Agent" will steer you to bargains on hotels and car rentals, and you can book everything, including flights, right on-line. This site is even useful once you're booked: Before you go, log on to Expedia for oodles of up-to-date travel information, including weather reports and foreign exchange rates.

Trip.Com (**www.thetrip.com**)   This site is really geared toward the business traveler, but vacationers-to-be can also use Trip.Com's valuable fare-finding engine, which will e-mail you every week with the best city-to-city airfare deals on your selected route or routes.

E-Savers Programs   Several major airlines, many of which service Hong Kong, offer a free e-mail service known as **E-Savers,** via which they'll send you their best bargain airfares on a regular basis. Here's how it works: Once a week (usually Wed), or whenever a sale fare comes up, subscribers receive a list of discounted flights to and from various destinations, both international and domestic. Here's the catch: These fares are usually only available if you leave the very next Saturday (or sometimes Fri night) and return on the following Monday or Tuesday. It's really a service for the spontaneously inclined and travelers looking for a quick getaway. But the fares are cheap, so it's worth taking a look. If you have a preference for certain airlines (in other words, the ones you fly most frequently), sign up with them first.

travel restrictions, but you can't beat the price: usually no more than $450 for a cross-country flight. Keep your eyes open for these sales as you are planning your vacation, then pounce on them. The sales tend to take place in seasons of low travel volume. You'll almost never see a sale around the peak summer vacation months of July and August, or around Thanksgiving or Christmas when people have to fly, regardless of the fare.

Consolidators, also known as bucket shops, are a good place to check for the lowest fares. Their prices are much better than the fares you could get yourself and are often even lower than what your travel agent can get you. You see their ads in the small boxes at the bottom of the page in your Sunday travel section. Some of the most reliable consolidators include **1-800-FLY-4-LESS** or **1-800-FLY-CHEAP.** Another good choice, **Council Travel** (☎ **800/226-8624**), caters especially to young travelers, but their bargain basement prices are available to people of all ages.

Another way to find the cheapest fare is by using the Internet to do your searching for you (see below), or by going to the individual airlines' Web sites.

BY CAR

It's no wonder that 67% of all visitors arrive by car—Philadelphia is some 300 miles (6 or so hrs.) from Boston, 100 miles (2 hrs.) from New York City, 135 miles (3 hrs.) from Washington, D.C., and 450 miles (9 hrs.) from Montreal. Tolls between Philadelphia and either New York City or Washington come to about $12.

Philadelphia is better served than ever before by a series of interstate highways that circle or pass through the city. Think of Center City as a rectangle. I-95 whizzes by its bottom and right sides. The Pennsylvania Turnpike (I-276) is the top edge, just widened to six lanes with the same E-ZPass electronic toll system that the New Jersey Turnpike and New York City use. I-76 splits off and snakes along the Schuylkill River along the left side into town. I-676 traverses Center City under Vine Street, connecting I-76 to adjacent Camden, New Jersey via the Ben Franklin Bridge over the Delaware. The "Blue Route" of I-476 forms a left edge for the suburbs, about 15 miles west of town, connecting I-276 and I-76 at its northern end with I-95 to the south.

Here are routes to City Hall, in the very center of town, from various directions.

NEW JERSEY TURNPIKE SOUTHBOUND EXIT 6   Take the Pennsylvania Turnpike westbound to the first exit, exit 29, and change to U.S. 13 southbound. Follow the signs a short distance to I-95 southbound and enter at exit 22, heading south. Exit for Center City at I-676 (Vine St. Expressway) westbound to 15th Street, then turn left and travel southbound 2 blocks.

NEW JERSEY TURNPIKE EXIT 4   Take N.J. 73 northbound to N.J. 38 westbound, then change to U.S. 30 westbound (the signage is abominable) and follow it over the Ben Franklin Bridge ($3 this way, but free eastbound) to I-676. Go south on 6th Street to Walnut Street (historic district will be on the left), turn right, and travel westbound to 15th Street.

FROM I-95 NORTHBOUND   Just past Philadelphia International Airport, take Pa. 291 toward Center City, Philadelphia. Cross the George C. Platt Memorial Bridge and turn left onto 26th Street, then follow 26th Street directly onto I-76 (Schuylkill Expressway) westbound to exit 39 (30th St. Station). Go 1 block to Market Street and turn right. Go east on Market Street to City Hall, which will be in front of you.

FROM THE PENNSYLVANIA TURNPIKE (I-76)   Take exit 24 to I-76 (Schuylkill Expressway) eastbound to I-676 (Vine St. Expressway). Take I-676 eastbound to 15th Street, turn right, and proceed southbound 2 blocks.

BY TRAIN

Philadelphia is a major Amtrak stop (☎ **800/USA-RAIL;** www.amtrak.com). It's on the Boston–Washington, D.C., northeast corridor, which has extensions south to Florida, west to Pittsburgh and Chicago, and east to Atlantic City. The Amtrak terminal is Penn Station (30th St.), about 15 blocks from City Hall. Regular service, called Northeast Direct, from New York City takes 85 minutes; Metroliner service is 70 minutes for the same trip, or 5 hours from Boston and 100 minutes from Washington. The new Acela, once implemented in 2001, should trim the Boston trip to 4 hours.

SEPTA commuter trains (☎ **215/580-7800;** www.septa.com) also connect 30th Street Station and several Center City stations to Trenton, New Jersey, to the northeast; to Harrisburg to the west; and directly to airport terminals to the south.

Sample round-trip fares on Amtrak as of press time were: New York City to Philadelphia, $88 peak, $80 excursion; Washington to Philadelphia, $82 peak, $70 excursion; one train daily to or from Chicago, around $200. Peak hours are Friday and Sunday, or days surrounding major holidays, from 11am to 11pm. These rates are subject to change, of course, but they'll give you an idea.

Keep in mind that Philadelphia trips can be much cheaper if you take **New Jersey Transit** (☎ **800/582-5946,** 215/569-3752, or 973/762-5100) commuter trains out of Penn Station in New York City or Newark to Trenton, then switch across the platform to the R7 Philadelphia-bound SEPTA commuter train that makes several convenient Center City stops before heading out to Chestnut Hill. The New Jersey Transit train from New York to Trenton travels every 20 minutes from 6am to 1:45am, takes 80 minutes, and costs $9.45 one-way or $14 round-trip. The SEPTA portion costs another $5 each way, $9.50 round-trip and takes about 30 minutes. (Rates and times are, of course, subject to change.)

BY BUS

Peter Pan/Trailways, the chief U.S. intercity operator, operates a great new office and terminal on 11th Street between Filbert and Arch streets, right across from the Convention Center (☎ **800/343-9999** or 215/931-4000; www.peterpanbus.com). Depending on advance purchase and length of stay, a round-trip ticket to or from New York City is $39 for the 2-hour trip; one way is $20. **Greyhound Bus Lines** (☎ **800/229-9424;** www.greyhound.com) carries service to and from New York every half hour 7am to 11:30pm at identical prices, and also serves Washington, D.C. from the same terminal. **New Jersey Transit** (☎ **215/569-3752**) also operates buses out of Philadelphia, with terminals at Camden, Atlantic City, and other nearby destinations.

For Foreign Visitors   3

This chapter provides specific suggestions about getting to the United States as economically and effortlessly as possible, plus some helpful information about how things are done in Philadelphia—from receiving mail to making a local or long-distance telephone call.

The **International Visitors Center** at 1 Parkway, 1515 Arch St., 12th Floor, Philadelphia, PA 19102 (☎ **215/686-4471**), offers special services to overseas visitors to the city.

1 Preparing for Your Trip

ENTRY REQUIREMENTS

DOCUMENT REGULATIONS   Canadian citizens may enter the United States without visas; they need only proof of residence.

British subjects and citizens of Australia, New Zealand, Japan, and most western European countries traveling on valid national (or EU) passports may not need visas for fewer than 90 days of vacation or business travel in the United States, providing that they hold round-trip or return tickets and enter the United States on an airline or cruise line that participates in the visa waiver program. (Citizens of these visa-exempt countries who first enter the United States may then visit Mexico, Canada, Bermuda, and/or the Caribbean islands and then reenter the United States, by any mode of transportation, without needing a visa. Further information is available from any U.S. embassy or consulate.)

Citizens of countries other than those above must have two documents: (1) a valid passport, with an expiration date at least 6 months later than the scheduled end of the visit to the United States; and (2) a tourist visa, available without charge from the nearest U.S. consulate.

To obtain a visa, the traveler must submit a completed application form (either in person or by mail) with a 1½-inch square photo and demonstrate binding ties to a residence abroad. Usually you can obtain a visa immediately or within 24 hours, but it may take longer during the summer rush from June to August. If you cannot go in person, contact the nearest U.S. embassy or consulate for directions on applying by mail. Your travel agent or airline office may also be able to provide you with visa applications and instructions. The U.S. consulate that issues your visa will determine whether you will be issued a multiple- or single-entry visa and any restrictions regarding the length of your stay.

MEDICAL REQUIREMENTS   No inoculations are needed to enter the United States unless you are coming from, or have stopped over in, areas known to be suffering from epidemics, especially of cholera or yellow fever.

If you have a disease requiring treatment with medications that either contain narcotics or require a syringe, carry a valid, signed prescription from your physician.

CUSTOMS REQUIREMENTS   Every adult visitor may bring in free of duty: 1 liter of wine or hard liquor; 200 cigarettes or 100 cigars (but no cigars from Cuba) or 3 pounds of smoking tobacco; and $100 worth of gifts. These exemptions are offered to travelers who spend at least 72 hours in the United States and who have not claimed them within the preceding 6 months. It is altogether forbidden to bring into the country foodstuffs (particularly unpasteurized cheese, fresh fruit, or cooked meats) and plants (vegetables, seeds, tropical plants, and so on). Foreign tourists may bring in or take out up to $10,000 in U.S. or foreign currency with no formalities; larger sums must be declared to customs on entering or leaving.

INSURANCE

There's no national health-care system in the United States. Because the cost of medical care is extremely high, we strongly advise every traveler to secure health insurance coverage before setting out. You may want to take out a comprehensive travel policy that covers (for a relatively low premium) sickness or injury costs (medical, surgical, and hospital); loss or theft of your baggage; trip-cancellation costs; guarantee of bail in case of arrest; and costs associated with accident, repatriation, or death. Such packages (for example, "Europ Assistance" in Europe) are sold by automobile clubs at attractive rates, as well as by banks and travel agencies.

MONEY

CURRENCY & EXCHANGE   The U.S. monetary system has a decimal base: One American **dollar** ($1) = 100 **cents** (100¢). Dollar **bills** commonly come in $1 ("a buck"), $5, $10, $20, $50, and $100 denominations (the last two are not welcome when paying for small purchases and are usually not accepted in taxis or at subway ticket booths). There are also $2 bills (rarely encountered).

There are six coin denominations: 1¢ (one cent, or "penny"); 5¢ (five cents, or "nickel"); 10¢ (ten cents, or "dime"); 25¢ (twenty-five cents, or "quarter"); 50¢ (fifty cents, or "half dollar"); and $1 pieces (both the new golden dollar coin and the smaller Susan B. Anthony coin). The last two coins are not very common.

TRAVELER'S CHECKS   Traveler's checks denominated in U.S. dollars are accepted at most hotels, motels, restaurants, and large stores. Sometimes photo identification is required. The best place to change traveler's checks is at a bank. Do not bring traveler's checks denominated in a currency other than U.S.

CREDIT CARDS   The most widely used method of payment credit or charge cards: Visa (BarclayCard in Britain), MasterCard (Eurocard in continental Europe, Access in Britain, Diamond in Japan), American Express, Diners Club, enRoute, JCB, and Carte Blanche. You can save yourself trouble by using "plastic" rather than cash or traveler's checks in most hotels, motels, restaurants, and retail stores (most large food and liquor stores now accept credit cards). You must have a credit card to rent a car. It can also be used as proof of identity, or as a "cash card," enabling you to draw money from automated teller machines (ATMs) that accept it.

You can telegraph (wire) money, or have it telegraphed to you very quickly using the **Western Union** system (☎ **800/325-6000**).

SAFETY

U.S. cities tend to be less safe than those in Europe or Japan, but you shouldn't have any trouble in the major tourist areas. Visitors should always stay alert and be aware of their immediate surroundings. Wear a money belt—or, better yet, check valuables in a safety-deposit box at your hotel. Keep a close eye on your possessions and be sure to keep them in sight when you're seated in a restaurant, theater, or other public place. Be especially careful in neighborhoods around college campuses, in North and West Philadelphia, and if you are staying out late, avoid deserted streets at night.

Remember also that hotels are open to the public, and in a large hotel, security may not be able to screen everyone entering. Always lock your door—don't assume that once inside your hotel you are automatically safe and no longer need to be aware of your surroundings.

DRIVING   Safety while driving is particularly important. Question your rental agency about personal safety, or ask for a brochure of traveler safety tips when you pick up your car. Obtain written directions from the agency or a map with the route marked in red to show you how to get to your destination. If possible, arrive and depart during daylight hours. Don't leave valuables in your car—even in the trunk, and never leave any packages or valuables in sight. Always keep your car doors locked, whether attended or unattended. Be cautious at night when unlocking doors or leaving your car for any reason.

Recently more and more crime has involved cars and drivers. If you drive off a highway into a doubtful neighborhood, leave the area as quickly as possible. If you have an accident, even on the highway, stay in your car with the doors locked until you assess the situation or until the police arrive. If you are bumped from behind on the street or are involved in a minor accident with no injuries and the situation appears to be suspicious, motion for the other driver to follow you to a police station or safe, lighted area where there are other people. *Never* get out of your car in such situations.

If you see someone on the road who indicates a need for help, do not stop. Take note of the location, drive onto a well-lighted area, and telephone the police by dialing ☎ **911.** Always park in a well-lighted, well-traveled area if possible.

If someone attempts to rob you or steal your car, do not try to resist—report the incident to the police department immediately.

2 Getting to & Around the United States

GETTING TO THE UNITED STATES

Overseas travelers can take advantage of the **APEX (Advance Purchase Excursion)** fares offered by major U.S. and European carriers. International carriers that fly into Philadelphia International Airport (☎ **215/937-6800**) include **Air Canada** (☎ 800/268-7240 in Canada), **Air Jamaica** (☎ 800/523-5585); **British Airways** (☎ 0345/222-111 in London); and **Swissair** (☎ 01/258-3434 in Zurich, or 022/799-5999 in Geneva). From Ireland, **Aer Lingus** (☎ 01/844-4747 in Dublin, or 061/415-556 in Shannon) can fly you into New York and arrange an add-on flight to Philadelphia. From New Zealand and Australia, there are flights to Los Angeles on **Qantas** (☎ 008/177-767 in Australia) and on **Air**

New Zealand (☎ 0800/737-000 in Auckland, or 3/379-5200 in Christchurch); both airlines can book you through to Philadelphia.

The visitor arriving by air, no matter what port of entry, should cultivate patience before setting foot on U.S. soil. Getting through Immigration Control may take as long as 2 hours, especially on summer weekends. Add the time it takes to clear Customs and you should make a very generous allowance for delay in planning connections between international and domestic flights—figure on at least 2 or 3 hours.

In contrast, travelers arriving by car or by rail from Canada will find border-crossing formalities streamlined to the vanishing point. And air travelers from Canada, Bermuda, and some places in the Caribbean can sometimes go through Customs and Immigration at the point of departure, which is much quicker and less painful.

GETTING AROUND THE UNITED STATES

BY PLANE   Some large airlines (for example, TWA, American Airlines, Northwest, United, and Delta) offer transatlantic and transpacific travelers special discount tickets under the name **Visit USA,** allowing travel between U.S. destinations at minimum rates. They are not on sale in the United States—they must be purchased before you leave your foreign point of departure. This system is the best, easiest, and fastest way to see the United States at low cost. You should obtain information well in advance from your travel agent or the office of the relevant airline, since the conditions attached to these discount tickets can change at any time.

BY CAR   The automobile is the major means of local and national transportation everywhere in the United States. To rent a car, you'll need a major credit card. The minimum driver age is usually 21, and you'll need a valid driver's license. Foreign driver's licenses are recognized in most states, but you may want to get an international driver's license written in English. See chapter 4 for more information about car rentals and insurance.

BY TRAIN   Long-distance trains in the United States are operated by **Amtrak** (☎ 800/872-7245). International visitors can also buy a **USA Railpass,** good for 15 or 30 days of unlimited travel on Amtrak. The pass is available through many foreign-travel agents. Prices in winter 2001 for a 15-day pass are $260 for nationwide off-peak travel, $190 if you stay in the Northeast; a 30-day pass costs $345 for nationwide off-peak travel, $196 for the Northeast only. (With a foreign passport, you can also buy passes at some Amtrak offices in the United States, including locations in San Francisco, Los Angeles, Chicago, New York, Miami, Boston, and Washington, D.C.) Reservations are generally required and should be made for each part of your trip as early as possible.

Visitors should also be aware of the limitations of long-distance rail travel in the United States. With a few notable exceptions (for instance, the Northeast Corridor line between Boston and Washington, D.C.), service, schedules, and convenience are rarely up to European standards.

BY BUS   The cheapest way to travel in the United States is by bus. Greyhound (☎ 800/231-2222), the sole nationwide bus line, offers an **Ameripass** for unlimited travel. At press time, a 7-day pass was $209, a 15-day pass was $319, and a 30-day pass was $429. Bus travel in the United States can be scenic, but both slow and uncomfortable, so this option is not for everyone.

Fast Facts: For the Foreign Traveler

Automobile Organizations   Auto clubs can supply maps; recommended routes; guidebooks; accident and bail-bond insurance; and, most important, emergency road service. The major auto club in the United States is the **American Automobile Association** (**AAA**), with national headquarters at 1000 AAA Dr., Heathrow, FL 32745 (☎ **800/336-4357;** www.aaa.org). AAA can provide you with an international driving permit validating your foreign license. The local office is Keystone AAA, 2040 Market St., Philadelphia, PA 19103 (☎ **215/864-5000**). For local emergency road service, call ☎ **215/569-4411.**

Business Hours   Banks are generally open Monday to Friday 9am to 3pm, in some cases Friday until 6pm and Saturday morning. Post offices are open Monday to Friday 8am to 5:30 or 6pm, Saturday 8am to noon. Store hours are Monday to Saturday 9 or 10am to 5:30 or 6pm, though often on Wednesday until 9pm in Philadelphia. Most shopping centers, drugstores, and supermarkets are open Monday to Saturday 9am to 9pm, with some open 24 hours a day. Public and private offices are usually open Monday to Friday 9am to 5pm. Also, see "Business Hours" in "Fast Facts," in chapter 4.

Climate   See "When to Go," in chapter 2.

Currency   See "Preparing for Your Trip," earlier in this chapter.

Currency Exchange   You can exchange money at the following places in Center City: American Express Travel Service, 2 Penn Center Plaza (☎ **215/587-2342** or 215/587-2343); Thomas Cook Currency Services, 1800 John F. Kennedy Blvd. (☎ **800/287-7362**); CoreStates First Union, 16th and Market streets (☎ **215/973-6812**); Dickens Inn, Head House Square at 2nd Street (☎ **215/928-9307**); Meridian Bank, 1700 Arch St. (☎ **215/854-3549**); and PNC Bank, Broad and Chestnut streets (☎ **215/585-5178**).

Drinking Laws   You must be 21 or older to consume alcohol in public. In Philadelphia, establishments may serve alcoholic beverages from 9am to 2am (private clubs may serve until 4am). Purchasing liquor in Pennsylvania is quite restricted (see chapter 9).

Electricity   U.S. wall outlets give power at 110 to 120 volts AC (60 cycles), compared to 220 to 240 volts AC (50 cycles) in most of Europe. In addition to a 110-volt converter, small appliances of non-American manufacture, such as hair dryers and shavers, will require a plug adapter with two flat parallel pins.

Embassies and Consulates   All embassies are located in Washington, D.C.; some consulates are located in major cities, and most nations have a mission to the United Nations in New York City. You can get the telephone number of your embassy by calling information in Washington, D.C. (☎ **202/555-1212**).

   Most European countries have consulates in Philadelphia; call information at ☎ **215/555-1212** for the telephone number. The British Consulate is at 226 Walnut St. (☎ **215/925-0118**).

Emergencies   Dial ☎ **911** to report a fire, call the police, or get an ambulance. This is a toll-free call (no coins are required at a public telephone). You can also report an emergency by dialing **0** (zero, *not* the letter "O") and contacting the telephone-company operator.

   If you encounter such travelers' problems as sickness, accident, or lost or stolen baggage, call the local chapter of the **Travelers Aid Society** at

☎ **215/546-0571.** This organization specializes in helping distressed travelers, whether American or foreign.

For medical emergencies at Philadelphia International Airport, call ☎ **215/937-3111.**

Gasoline (Petrol)   One U.S. gallon equals 3.75 liters, while 1.2 U.S. gallons equals 1 imperial gallon. You'll notice there are several grades (and price levels) of gasoline at most gas stations. And you'll also notice that their names change from company to company. The unleaded grades with the highest octane are the most expensive, but most rental cars take the least expensive "regular" unleaded. Leaded gasoline is rarely used anymore. Gas stations are both self-serve and full-service.

Holidays   On the following national legal holidays, banks, government offices, post offices, and many stores, restaurants, and museums are closed: January 1 (New Year's Day); third Monday in January (Martin Luther King, Jr. Day); third Monday in February (Presidents' Day, marking Washington's and Lincoln's birthdays); last Monday in May (Memorial Day); July 4 (Independence Day); first Monday in September (Labor Day); second Monday in October (Columbus Day); November 11 (Veterans Day/Armistice Day); fourth Thursday in November (Thanksgiving Day); and December 25 (Christmas). The Tuesday following the first Monday in November is Election Day and is a legal holiday in presidential election years.

Legal Aid   If you are stopped for a minor infraction (say, speeding on the highway), never attempt to pay the fine directly to a police officer; you may wind up arrested on the much more serious charge of attempted bribery. Pay fines by mail or directly to the clerk of a court. If you're accused of a more serious offense, say and do nothing before consulting a lawyer. Under U.S. law, an arrested person is allowed one telephone call to a party of his or her choice. Call your embassy or consulate.

Mail   If your mail is addressed to a U.S. destination, don't forget to add the five-figure postal code or ZIP code after the two-letter abbreviation of the state to which the mail is addressed (CA for California, MA for Massachusetts, NY for New York, PA for Pennsylvania, and so on).

Rates in 2001 for international mail are: post cards, 70¢ to everywhere except Mexico and Canada (50¢); basic letters cost 80¢ to everywhere except Mexico and Canada (60¢). Aerogrammes are 70¢. U.S. postage is 20¢ for postcards, 34¢ for letters.

Philadelphia's main post offices are located at 9th and Market streets and across from Penn Station at 30th Street.

Safety   See "Safety," above.

Taxes   In the United States there is no VAT (value-added tax) at the national level. Every state and each city, can levy its own local tax on purchases, including hotel and restaurant checks, airline tickets, and the like. It is automatically added to the price of certain services, such as public transportation, cab fares, phone calls, and gasoline. Philadelphia's sales tax is 7%, except for clothing, which makes visits to outlet malls such as Franklin Mills so popular with international tourists.

In addition, each locality can levy its own separate tax on hotel occupancy. In Philadelphia, in addition to your hotel rate, you pay 7% sales tax plus a 5% surcharge.

Telephone and Fax   The telephone system in the United States is run by private corporations, so rates, especially for long-distance service and operator-assisted calls, can vary widely—even on calls made from public telephones. Local calls usually cost 35¢.

Generally, hotel surcharges on long-distance and local calls are astronomical. These are best avoided by using a public phone, calling collect, or using a telephone charge card or prepaid card.

Most long-distance or international calls can be dialed directly from any phone. For international calls, dial 011, followed by the country code, then the city code and the number of the person you wish to call. For calls to Canada and other parts of the United States, dial 1 followed by the area code and seven-digit number.

For reversed-charge or collect calls, and for person-to-person calls, dial 0 (zero, *not* the letter "O") followed by the area code and number you want; an operator will then come on the line, and you should specify what you want. If your operator-assisted call is international, ask for the overseas operator.

For directory assistance ("information"), dial **411;** for long-distance information, dial 1, then the appropriate area code and **555-1212.**

Most hotels have fax machines available for their customers, and there is usually a charge to send or receive a fax. You will also see signs for public faxes in the windows of small shops.

Time   The United States is divided into six time zones. From east to west, these are Eastern Standard Time (EST), Central Standard Time (CST), Mountain Standard Time (MST), Pacific Standard Time (PST), Alaska Standard Time (AST), and Hawaii Standard Time (HST). Always keep changing time zones in your mind if you are traveling (or even telephoning) long distances in the United States. For example, noon in Philadelphia (EST) is 11am in Chicago (CST), 10am in Denver (MST), 9am in Los Angeles (PST), 8am in Anchorage (AST), and 7am in Honolulu (HST). Daylight saving time (DST) is in effect from the first Sunday in April to the last Saturday in October, except in Arizona, Hawaii, part of Indiana, and Puerto Rico. Daylight saving time moves the clock 1 hour ahead of standard time.

Tipping   This is part of the American way of life, on the principle that you must pay for any service received. A service charge is never included in restaurant checks or hotel bills. Bartenders should receive 10% to 15%; bellhops, 50¢ per bag; cab drivers, 15% of the fare; hotel service personnel, $1 a day; waiters, 15% to 20% of the check.

Toilets   As elsewhere in the United States, there are no public kiosks in Philadelphia; your best choice is to use rest rooms in museums, historic sites, or malls. Independence National Historical Park sites have very clean, free rest rooms. Within Center City, most hotel lobbies have public rest rooms, and many restaurants will allow you to use theirs during off-peak hours. Also, see "Rest Rooms" in "Fast Facts," in chapter 4.

4

Getting to Know Philadelphia

This chapter sets out to answer all your travel questions, furnishing you with the practical information that you'll need to handle any and every experience during your stay in Philadelphia—from the city layout and transportation to emergencies and business hours.

1 Orientation

ARRIVING

BY PLANE All flights into and from Philadelphia use **Philadelphia International Airport** (☎ 215/937-6800; www.phl.org), at the southwest corner of the city. For up-to-the-minute information on airline arrival and departure times and gate assignments, call ☎ 800/PHL-GATE. With 24 million passengers in 2000, it's one of the country's fastest growing airports. There are flights to more than 100 cities in the United States and more than 1,000 arrivals and departures daily.

The airport is laid out with a central corridor connecting the five basic depots. Terminal B is the place to catch taxis, buses, and hotel limousines. The areas with the most amenities are between Terminals B and C and Terminals D and E.

Drivers have three parking options: short term, garage, and economy (long term). Economy parking is available for $6.50 per day at more distant lots, while garage parking is $14 per day. Short-term parking is $2.50 for the first 30 minutes, $12 for up to 3 hours, $16 for 3 to 4 hours, and $30 for 4 to 24 hours.

For medical emergencies at the airport, call ☎ 215/937-3111.

Getting Into Town From the Airport A high-speed rail link with direct service between the airport and Center City runs daily every 30 minutes 5:30am to 11:25pm. Trains leave the airport at 10 and 40 minutes past the hour; they follow the loop of a raised pedestrian bridge, stop in front of every terminal and are easy to find. Trains to the airport depart from Market East (and a Convention Center connection), Suburban Station at 16th Street, and 30th Street Station. The 30-minute trip costs $5 for adults; children's fares are $1.50 weekdays and $1 weekends; and the family fare is $15.

A taxi from the airport to Center City takes about 25 minutes and costs a flat rate of $20 plus tip.

If you're interested in airport limousines or shuttles to garages, hotels, or area destinations, fares range from $8 to $16. Try **Airport-Limelight** (☎ **800/342-7121** or 215/342-5557), **Deluxe Limo** (☎ **215/463-8787**), 6am to 11pm, **Lady Liberty** (☎ **215/724-8888**), 5am to midnight, or **Philadelphia Airport Shuttle** (☎ **215/333-1441**), 5am to 10pm. **BostonCoach** (☎ **800/342-7121**) quotes sedan rates of $46 from the airport to a Center City address; $96 to Valley Forge; and $135 to Atlantic City; the others listed above are $30 to $50 cheaper.

All major car-rental operations have desks at the airport and Zone 2 pick-up. These include **Alamo** (☎ 800/327-9633); **Avis** (☎ 800/331-1212); **Budget** (☎ 800/527-0700); **Dollar** (☎ 800/800-4000); **Hertz** (☎ 215/654-3131); and **National** (☎ 800/227-7368).

BY TRAIN   Trains arrive at Penn (30th St.) Station in West Philadelphia, just on the other side of the Schuylkill River from Center City, and about 15 blocks from City Hall. Take a taxi or SEPTA (see below) from the station to your hotel.

VISITOR INFORMATION

The **Philadelphia Convention and Visitors Bureau,** 1515 John F. Kennedy Blvd., Philadelphia, PA 19102 (☎ **800/537-7676** or 215/636-1666; www.libertynet. org/phila-visitor), is one of the very best in America. It looks like a shiny layer cake between Suburban Station and City Hall, and its reception desk is staffed by enthusiastic and knowledgeable volunteers. You can pick up coupons for reduced admission to many museums and attractions here, as well as free aids for persons who are blind or have disabilities.

The visitors bureau parcels out free tickets to the New Year's Day Mummer's Parade and to the Mann Music Center for summer concerts in the park. They also sell such tickets as the SEPTA DayPass ($5) and "A Gift of Gardens" for 14 regional sites. Many bus tours, trolley rides, and walking tours conveniently begin here. Some floor space has been devoted to a city gift shop.

The bureau is open daily 9am to 5pm (except Christmas Day), and until 6pm on summer weekdays. If you're planning in advance, call ☎ **800/537-7676** to get material on all the special seasonal promotions. If you show up at noon in summer, there's usually outdoor entertainment on the adjoining plaza, which anchors one end of the Benjamin Franklin Parkway (known simply as "the Parkway").

CITY LAYOUT

MAIN ARTERIES & STREETS   Unlike Boston, Philadelphia has no colonial cow paths that were turned into streets. If you can count and remember the names of trees, you'll know exactly where you are in the Center City grid. For the overview, go to (or pretend you're at) the top of **City Hall,** that over-iced wedding cake in the very center of things, at the intersection of Broad and Market streets. **Broad Street** runs 4 miles south, where the Delaware and Schuylkill flow together, and 8 miles north—all perfectly straight. The other major north-south streets are numbered. Except for a few two-way exceptions, traffic on even-numbered streets heads south and on odd-numbered streets, north. **Front Street** (should be 1st St.), once at the Delaware's edge off to the right, and neighboring **2nd Street** were the major thoroughfares in colonial times. In-between streets are named. The major east-west streets in Philadelphia's Center City run from Spring Garden Street to the north to South Street. You'll spend much of your time between Arch and Pine streets, especially south of Chestnut Street, both for the historical attractions and for the current restaurant and nightlife vibrancy.

The colonial city, now **Independence National Historical Park,** with its reconstructed row houses grew up along the Delaware north and south of **Market Street,** extending west to 6th Street by 1776. The 19th century saw the development of the western quadrants (including most museums and cultural centers) and suburbs in every direction. The city blocks planned by William Penn included five parks spaced between the two rivers. Four parks have been named for local notables (including George Washington, who headed the federal government here in the 1790s). The fifth supports City Hall. A broad northwest boulevard, dividing the grid like a slice of Paris, ends in the majestic arms of the Philadelphia Museum of Art. The entire quadrant west and north of City Hall has been the site of intensive development and redevelopment of hotels, office buildings, and apartment houses.

Just beyond, the Schuylkill separates Philadelphia from West Philadelphia from 24th Street to about 30th Street—if you're looking for an address in this area, ask which side it's on. **Fairmount Park** lines both sides of the Schuylkill for miles above the museum.

FINDING AN ADDRESS   Addresses on these streets add 100 for every block away from the axis of Market Street (north-south) or Front Street (east-west): 1534 Chestnut St. is between 15th and 16th streets, and 610 S. 5th St. is between 6 and 7 blocks south of Market.

STREET MAPS   The **Philadelphia Convention and Visitors Bureau,** 1515 John F. Kennedy Blvd. (☎ **800/537-7676** or 215/636-1666), has a very good street map in its "Official Visitors Guide." You can pick it up at the Visitors Bureau and at all hotels.

The Neighborhoods in Brief

Philadelphia is more of a collection of neighborhoods than a unified metropolis. Here are short descriptions of those likely to come your way.

Chestnut Hill   This enclave of suburban gentility with a "Main Street" flavor, centered around upper Germantown Avenue, is the highest point within city limits. It's filled with galleries and boutiques, tearooms, and comfortable restaurants.

Chinatown   Nowadays it's largely commercial rather than residential, but there are lots of good restaurants, a growing number of hotels, and cheaper parking only 5 minutes from the Convention Center. And it stays awake forever.

Germantown   One of Philadelphia's most ancient settlements, this area was founded by German émigrés, attracted by Penn's religious tolerance. Outside of its wonderful historic mansions, however, it is not especially attractive now.

Manayunk   This neighborhood, 4 miles up the Schuylkill River from Center City, has rocketed to gentility in the last decade, with many of the city's hottest boutiques, galleries, and cafe/restaurants on Main Street, overlooking a 19th-century canal adjoining the river. It's a picturesque and vital place for an afternoon stroll, and there's a great farmer's market. Visit it virtually at www.manayunk.com.

Old City   In the shadow of the Benjamin Franklin Bridge just north of Independence National Historical Park lies an eclectic blend of row houses dating from William Penn's time, 19th-century commercial warehouses, and 20th-century rehabs à la SoHo in New York City. It even has its own Web site: www.oldcity.org. If you're interested in either the very old or the very new, this is the place to spend a few hours. The odd alleyways between the city grid streets here provide nooks for quaint and quiet cafes and shops. The first Friday night of every month is like a giant block party, with all the galleries and stores open until 8pm.

Queen Village   On a pleasant day you'll want to walk south from Society Hill along the Delaware or 2nd Street (known as "Two Street" among old Philadelphians). The Swedish originally settled this area, along with the river islands below the confluence with the Schuylkill, and some of their buildings remain. There are lots of small, reasonably priced cafes and bistros here, and pedestrian bridges constructed over I-95 have recently reconnected it to the waterfront.

Rittenhouse Square   This urban park connotes the elegance, wealth, and culture of pre-skyscraper Philadelphia. The world is much bigger and more diverse now, but many traces linger on. From the Rittenhouse Hotel on a sunny day, walk through the square to Walnut Street, which can rival any district in Paris or London for charm and sophistication.

Society Hill   This heart of reclaimed 18th-century Philadelphia is loosely defined by Walnut and Lombard streets and Front and 7th streets. Today, it's a fashionable section of the old city, just south of Independence National Historical Park, where you can stroll among restored Federal, colonial, and Georgian homes—even the contemporary "infill" is interesting and immaculately maintained.

South Philadelphia   It's Rocky Balboa and more. Three hundred years of immigration have made South Philadelphia the city's most colorful and ethnically diverse neighborhood, although the feel is distinctly Italian (circa 1910s Calabria). I love strolling the Italian Market at 9th and Christian and heading south, snacking all along the way until dinner.

South Street   Located below Society Hill and above Queen Village, South Street was the city limit in William Penn's day. The 1960s saw bohemian artists reclaim this street in the name of peace and love; newer spirits, just as young and somewhat cockier, have replaced the previous hipsters, but it's undeniably hopping day or night. Look for good restaurants and bars, bookstores, hoagie shops, contemporary handcrafted furniture stores, natural-food stores, European-style cafes, and art galleries. The neighborhood has an appropriately retro Web site at www.southstreet.com.

University City   West Philadelphia was farmland until the University of Pennsylvania moved here from 9th and Chestnut streets in the 1870s. Wander through the main campus for the architecture and the cultural amenities. The original college quadrangle built in 1895 was modeled on Oxford and Cambridge, with the added touch of Dutch gables. Penn is pumping in development and enticing major cinemas and bookstores to gentrify the area, following a long slump.

2 Getting Around

BY PUBLIC TRANSPORTATION

SEPTA (Southeastern Pennsylvania Transportation Authority) operates a complicated and extensive network of trolleys, buses, commuter trains, and subways. In the past 10 years the capital budget for new equipment has increased from $20 million to $120 million; new cars gleam on the Broad Street line.

Fares for any SEPTA route are $1.60, with 40¢ more for a transfer, and *exact change or tokens are required.* You can purchase a 5-pack for $5.75 or a 10-pack for $11.50. Seniors pay nothing and passengers with disabilities pay half-fare during off-peak hours. Certain buses and trolleys run 24 hours a day.

Philadelphia Neighborhoods

Kelly Dr.
↖ To Manayunk
25th St.
24th St.
Fairmount Ave.
Azalea Gardens
Wallace St.
Mt. Vernon St.
Fairmount Waterworks
23rd St.
22nd St.
Green St.
Schuylkill Expressway
West River Dr.
Philadelphia Museum of Art
Fairmount Park
Spring Garden St.
Eakins Oval
Hamilton St.
19th St.
18th St.
17th St.
16th St.
15th St.
32nd St.
76
Rodin Museum
The Benjamin Franklin Parkway
Callowhill St.
Free Library of Philadelphia
Powelton Ave.
676
Winter St.
Logan Square
Race St.
†
76
Cherry St.
33rd St.
Amtrak 30th St. Station
Arch St.
PARKWAY/MUSEUMS DISTRICT
JFK Blvd.
Philadelphia Stock Exchange
Market St.
Market St.
Market-Frankford Subway
Subway-Surface
UNIVERSITY CITY
Drexel Main Building
Ludlow
Chestnut St.
Chestnut St.
RITTENHOUSE SQUARE DISTRICT
Mandell Theater
Sansom St.
Airport Train
Walnut St.
Walnut St.
†
Palestra
Locust St.
Rittenhouse Square
Franklin Field
Spruce St.
Schuylkill River
Schuylkill River Park
Fitler Square
Delancey Pl.
☆
Philadelphia Civic Center
South St. Bridge
26th St.
25th St.
24th St.
23rd St.
22nd St.
Pine St.
20th St.
19th St.
18th St.
17th St.
16th St.
15th St.
Lombard St.
South St.

Manayunk

↑ To Germantown & Chestnut Hill
Fairmount Park
Pensdale St.
Wissahickon Dr.
Levington Ave.
Green Lane
Lyceum St.
Levering St.
Carson St.
Manayunk Ave.
Ridge Avenue
Tower St.
Terrace
St.
Umbria St.
Cresson St.
Main Street
Manayunk
Canal
Flat Rock Rd.
Belmont Ave.
Venice Island
Schuylkill River
Approx. 7 miles to Center City →
76
Schuylkill Expressway

Edgar Allan Poe
Nat'l Hist. Site

German Society
of Philadelphia

Spring Garden St.

13th St.
12th St.
Broad Street Subway
11th St.
10th St.
9th St.
8th St.
7th St.

Hamilton St.
Noble St.
Broad St.

Callowhill St.

Legend

✝ Church
✉ Post Office
✡ Synagogue
▬ Subway stop

95

Pier 24

Vine St.

Vine St.

✝ Vine St.

Painted Bride
Art Center

To
New Jersey →

CONVENTION CENTER DISTRICT

Franklin
Square

676

Benjamin Franklin
Bridge

Pennsylvania
Convention
Center

CHINATOWN

Cherry
St.

Chinese Cultural
Center

Race St.

U.S.
Mint

Cherry St.

Elfreth's
Alley

Betsy Ross
House

Pier 5

Franklin St.

Pier 3

Reading
Terminal
Market

Chinese
Friendship
Gate

Arch St.

U.S.
Federal
Building

✡

OLD CITY
CULTURAL
DISTRICT

Arden
Theater

Delaware River

(Delaware Ave.)

Christopher Columbus Blvd.

City
Hall

Market St.
St. Stephen's
Alley Theater

The Liberty
Bell

The Bourse

Chestnut St.

Penn's
Landing

Juniper St.
13th St.
12th St.
11th St.
10th St.
2nd St.
Front St.

✉

Sansom St.

Thomas Jefferson
University

Independence National Park

Walnut St.

Forrest
Theater

WASHINGTON
SQUARE
DISTRICT

Washington
Square

Tomb of the
Unknown Soldier

✝

3rd St.

Dock
St.

95

SOCIETY HILL

Locust St.

Merriam
Theater

nmel Performing
s Center
University
of the Arts

Spruce St.

Pennsylvania
Hospital

✝

✡

Delancey St.

"Antique Row"

9th St.
8th St.
7th St.
6th St.
5th St.
4th St.

Pine St.

Lombard St.

Head
House
Square

Broad Street Subway

SOUTH STREET

South St.

Walkway

Bainbridge St.

Pier 34

Fleischer Art
Memorial

Fitzwater St.

Catharine St.

"Fabric
Row"

Queen St.

SOUTH
PHILADELPHIA

Passyunik Ave.

Christian St.

QUEEN
VILLAGE

Swanson St.

Italian
Market

Carpenter St.

Washington Ave.

To Airport ↓

If you have questions about how to reach a specific destination, call SEPTA at ☎ **215/580-7800** between 6am and midnight—but expect to wait.

BY SUBWAY-SURFACE LINE   This "local" connects City Hall and 30th Street Station, stopping at 19th and 22nd streets along the way. West of the Amtrak station it branches out, moving aboveground beyond U. Penn to the north and south.

BY RAPID TRANSIT   In Center City, these fast cars speed under Broad Street and Market Street, intersecting under City Hall. The Broad Street line now connects directly to Pattison Avenue and Philadelphia sporting events to the south. The Market Street line stops at 2nd, 5th, 8th, 11th, 13th (Convention Center), 15th, and 30th Street stations and stretches to the west and northeast. Both lines run all night, but exercise caution during late-hour use.

BY PATCO   This commuter rail line (☎ **215/922-4600**) begins at Walnut and Locust streets around Broad Street, connects with rapid transit at 8th and Market, and crosses the Ben Franklin Bridge to Camden. To get to the aquarium, transfer at Broadway in Camden to the New Jersey Transit's Aqualink Shuttle. Transfers connect to the Jersey shore from Lindenwold.

BY BUS   Those purple vans with the turquoise wings go pretty much everywhere tourists want to go. Every 10 minutes between 10am and 12:30am in summer (until 6:30pm mid-Sept to mid-May) the **PHLASH Bus** service (☎ **215/ 474-5274**) links Independence Park sites, the Delaware waterfront, the Convention Center, Rittenhouse Square shopping, and the cultural institution at Logan Circle. The total loop takes 50 minutes and makes 30 stops. A one-time pass is $2, but get the all-day unlimited ride-pass for $4 per person or $10 per family. Passes are not transferable to SEPTA. Children under 6 ride free.

Route 76, the **Ben FrankLine,** is also a subsidized tourism deal at 50¢. It connects Society Hill at 3rd and Chestnut streets to the Parkway all the way to the Museum of Art and the zoo. It operates every 10 minutes weekdays, every 20 minutes weekends. The first trip from 3rd Street is at 9am, and the last pickup at the Museum of Art is at 6:11pm.

For a straight crosstown route, you'll often find yourself on Chestnut Street, and bus no. 42 swoops along Chestnut from West Philadelphia to 2nd at all hours. Several bus routes serve Market Street; the **Mid-City loop** ($1.50, with a 40¢ transfer to another bus) goes up Market and down Chestnut between 5th and 17th streets. Route 32 goes up Broad Street and the Parkway and through Fairmount Park to Andorra; the full trip is 15 miles.

BY TROLLEY   There are no more "true" city trolleys such as you would find in Boston or San Francisco. A privately operated **Penn's Landing Trolley** chugs along Christopher Columbus Boulevard (formerly Delaware Ave.) between the Benjamin Franklin Bridge and Fitzwater Street; you can board at Dock Street or Spruce Street. The fare is $1.50 for adults, 75¢ for children, and the trolley runs Thursday to Sunday, 11am to dusk in the summer.

Buses that are replicas of 1930s open-air trolleys are operated by **American Trolley Bus** (☎ **215/333-0320**) and **Old Town Trolley** (☎ **215/928-8687**). Guides point out all the high spots. Tour prices range from $7.50 to $16, depending on tour length and family size. Pickup spots include Liberty Bell Pavilion, Independence Park Visitors Center, and the Franklin Institute.

BY TRAIN   The Philadelphia area is served by one of the best commuter-rail networks in America. Chestnut Hill, a wealthy enclave of fine shops and restaurants,

Ride Cheap

A $5 DayPass is good for all buses, subways, and one ride on the Airport loop. A weekly TransPass, good from Monday to the next Sunday, is $16.

can be reached from both Penn Center (Suburban) Station at 16th Street and John F. Kennedy Boulevard and Reading Terminal at 12th and Market streets; the two are now connected by the new rail link. What in the suburbs would interest you? Merion is home to the great Barnes Foundation art collection and the Buten Museum of Wedgwood. Bryn Mawr, Haverford, Swarthmore, and Villanova are sites of noted colleges. Devon hosts a great horse and country fair. One-way fares for all destinations are less than $6, and you can buy tickets at station counters or vending machines.

BY CAR

Philadelphia's streets were once considered so wide that there was room for market stalls in the divides. Unfortunately, that was 200 years ago—today, there's little room on Center City streets for parked or moving cars. You might try the streets below Chestnut: Locust, Spruce, and Pine are often the best. Be forewarned that *all streets are one way*—except for lower Market Street, the Parkway, Vine Street, and Broad Street. The Convention and Visitors Bureau at the foot of the Parkway offers a Center City traffic map. Traffic around City Hall runs counterclockwise, but traffic lights seem to follow a logic of their own.

Since Philadelphia is so walkable, it's easier to leave your car while you explore. Many hotels offer free or reduced-rate parking to registered guests.

If you need emergency car repair, try **Center City Auto Care,** 901 N. Broad St. (☎ 215/763-8328), or **Mina Motors,** Broad and Fitzwater streets (☎ 215/735-2749), for same-day service. **Keystone AAA** is at 2040 Market St. (☎ 215/864-5000).

RENTALS   Philadelphia has no shortage of rental cars and very good rates as a consequence. For example, you can pick up a weekend sedan from **Avis** (☎ 800/331-1212) for $49 per day, with unlimited mileage, at one of their lots: 2000 Arch St. (☎ 215/563-8976), 30th Street Station (☎ 215/386-6426), or near Independence Hall at 37 S. 2nd St. (☎ 215/928-1082). Avis and all other major renters maintain offices at the airport. These include **Alamo** (☎ 800/327-9633); **Budget** (☎ 800/527-0700, 215/492-9447 at the airport, or 215/492-9400 at 21st and Market); **Dollar** (☎ 800/800-4000, or 215/365-2700 at the airport); and **Hertz** (☎ 800/654-3131 for all locations). Also check smaller local companies and car dealers like **Sheehy Ford** (☎ 215/698-7000).

On top of the standard rental prices, other optional charges apply to most car rentals, including liability insurance (if you harm others in an accident), personal accident insurance (if you harm yourself or your passengers), and personal effects insurance (if your luggage is stolen from your car). If your own insurance doesn't cover you for rentals, you should consider the additional coverages. But weigh the likelihood of getting into an accident or losing your luggage against the cost of these coverages (as much as $20 per day combined), which can significantly add to the price of your rental.

What's in a Name?

Philadelphia's opulent "Main Line" suburbs take their name from the old Pennsylvania Railroad line, built after the Civil War, which once ran through them from Suburban (now Penn Center) Station to Harrisburg.

PARKING   Call the Philadelphia Parking Authority (☎ **215/683-9600**) for current information.

Garage rates are fairly similar: Outside of hotels, no place exceeds $25 per day, with typical charges of $5 per hour and $12 for an evening out.

Parking can be found for **Independence Park** at 125 S. 2nd St. (Sansom St. is the cross street); Spruce Street between 5th and 6th streets (private lot); and Head House Square, 2nd and Lombard streets (city meters). **Convention Center Area** parking includes Kinney Chinatown at 11th and Race streets (private garage); Kinney underneath the Gallery II mall at 11th and Arch streets; the Autopark beside the Gallery mall at 10th and Filbert streets; or the garage underneath the adjoining Marriott at Arch and 13th streets. **City Hall Area** parking is underneath Lord & Taylor (formerly Wanamaker's), between Market and Chestnut streets at 13th Street; a private garage adjoining the Doubletree Hotel at Broad and Spruce streets; and Kennedy Plaza, 15th Street and John F. Kennedy Boulevard (underground city garage; enter on Arch, 1 block north of the plaza).

BY TAXI

Philadelphia's notorious shortage of taxis is improving, with about 1,400 currently licensed. Under 1991 legislation, gypsy cabs have been outlawed in return for increasing the number of taxi medallions. Cabbies must maintain clean vehicles and pass stringent tests on their knowledge of the city. Fares are currently $1.80 for the first one-seventh mile and 30¢ for each additional one-seventh mile or minute of the motor running. Tips are expected, usually 15% of the fare.

If you need to call for a cab while in the city, the three largest outfits are **Olde City Taxi** (☎ **215/338-0838**), **United Cab** (☎ **215/291-0203**), and **Quaker City** (☎ **215/728-8000**).

Fast Facts: Philadelphia

American Express   There are AmEx offices at 16th Street and John F. Kennedy Boulevard (☎ **215/587-2342**) and at the airport (☎ **215/492-4200**).

Area Code   Philadelphia's telephone area code is **215.** Bucks County and half of Montgomery County also use **215,** but the Brandywine Valley area of Delaware, Chester, and half of Montgomery have switched to **610.** Lancaster County and the Pennsylvania Dutch region use area code **717.**

Baby-sitters   Check with your hotel, or contact Rocking Horse Child Care Center at the Curtis Center, Walnut and 6th streets (☎ **215/592-8257**); rates are $8 per hour for children under 2, $7 per hour for ages 3 to 6. Call-A-Granni, 1133 E. Barringer St. (☎ **215/924-8723**), is comparable.

Business Hours   Banks are generally open Monday to Thursday 10am to 3pm, Friday until 6pm, with some also open on Saturday 9am to noon. Most bars and restaurants serve food until 10 or 10:30pm (some Chinatown places stay open until 3am), and social bars are open Friday and Saturday until 1 or 2am. Offices are open Monday to Friday 9am to 5pm. Stores are open daily 9am to 5pm, and most Center City locations keep the doors open later on Wednesday evening. Old City, South Street, the Delaware waterfront, and Head House Square are the most active late-night districts. Some SEPTA routes run all night, but the frequency of buses and trolleys drops dramatically after 6pm.

Business Services   Most hotels have onsite business facilities, but for quick professional production of materials, try Printers Place near the Convention Center at 1310 Walnut St. (☎ **215/546-6562**), or the various 24-hour Kinko's, whose downtown locations include 2001 Market St. (☎ **215/561-5170**). For shipping, the local UPS is at ☎ **215/895-8984.**

Car Rentals   See "Getting Around," earlier in this chapter.

Dentist   Call ☎ **215/925-6050** in a dental emergency.

Doctor   Call the Philadelphia County Medical Society (☎ **215/563-5343**). You can always dial **911** in an emergency. Every hospital in town has an emergency room.

Drugstores   See "Pharmacies," below.

Embassies and Consulates   See chapter 3.

Emergencies   In an extreme emergency, dial ☎ **911.** In case of accidental poisoning, call ☎ **215/386-2100.** For police, call ☎ **215/231-3131;** for fire and rescue, call ☎ **215/922-6000.** Ambulance and emergency transportation can be summoned through Care & Emergency (☎ **215/877-6300**), or SEPTA Paratransit (☎ **215/574-2780**). For 24-hour pet emergencies, call (☎ **215/ 898-4685**).

Hospitals   Medical care in Philadelphia is excellent. Major hospitals include Children's Hospital, 34th Street and Civic Center Boulevard (☎ **215/590-1000**); Allegheny Graduate Hospital, 1800 Lombard St. (☎ **215/893-2000**); Allegheny Hahnemann, Broad and Vine streets (☎ **215/762-7000**); University of Pennsylvania Hospital, 3400 Spruce St. (☎ **215/662-4000**); Pennsylvania Hospital, 8th and Spruce streets (☎ **215/829-3000**); and Thomas Jefferson, 11th and Walnut streets (☎ **215/955-6000**).

Information   See "Visitor Information," earlier in this chapter.

Liquor Laws   The legal drinking age is 21, and closing time for bars (as opposed to private clubs) is 2am, 7 days a week. You can buy wine and spirits only in state stores, which are usually open Monday to Wednesday 9am to 5pm and Thursday to Saturday 9am to 9pm. Beer, champagne, and wine coolers are available at most supermarkets and delis. See chapter 9 for the best state store locations.

Lost Property   If you lose something on a SEPTA train or subway, try the stationmaster's office in Suburban Station (☎ **215/580-7800**).

Newspapers and Magazines   Philadelphia has two main print journals, both now owned by the same firm. You'll want to check out the Friday "Weekend" supplement of the *Inquirer* for listings and prices of entertainment as well as special events and tours. The *Daily News* has more local news. Free tabloid weeklies with surprisingly good articles and listings include *City Paper* and *Philadelphia Weekly;* you'll find them at record and bookstores and in street-corner boxes. For the most complete selection of journals and newspapers, try Avril 50, 3406 Sansom St. (☎ **215/222-6108**), in University City. The Society Hill equivalent is Popi, 526 S. 4th St. (☎ **215/922-4119**), and 116 S. 20th St. (☎ **215/557-8282**), near Rittenhouse Square.

Pharmacies   There's a 24-hour CVS at 1826 Chestnut St., corner of 19th Street (☎ **215/972-0909**), and at 10th and Reed streets (☎ **215/465-2130**) in South Philadelphia. For northeast locations, try the 24-hour Pathmark at City Line and Monument avenues (☎ **215/879-1322**). The Medical Tower Pharmacy, 255 S. 17th St. (☎ **215/545-3525**), is open until 9pm on Monday to Friday and until 6pm on Saturday. During regular hours near Independence Hall, try Green Drugs, 5th and South streets (☎ **215/922-7441**).

Police   The emergency telephone number is ☎ **911.**

Post Office   The main post office at 2970 Market St. (☎ **215/596-5577**), just across the Schuylkill and next to 30th Street station, is always open; you can reach its 24-hour window at ☎ **215/895-8989.** The post office on the subway concourse at 2 Penn Center, 15th Street and John F. Kennedy Boulevard, is open Monday to Friday 7am to 6pm, Saturday 9am to noon. You can also go to the post office Ben Franklin used, at 316 Market St.

Radio   There's intense competition among more than 60 stations, so the following programming emphasis is subject to change: all news, WKYW (1060 AM); album-oriented rock, WMMR (93.3 FM); classic rock, WYSP (94.1 FM); oldies, WOGL (98.1 FM); soft rock, WIOQ (102.1 FM); country, WCZN (1590 AM) and WXTU (92.5 FM), ethnic urban orientation; WUSL (98.9 FM); WDAS (1480 AM); WHAT (1340 AM); and National Public Radio, WHYY (91.0 FM) and WXPN (88.5 FM).

Rest Rooms   Public rest rooms can be found at 30th Street Station; the Independence National Historical Park Visitors Center; and at major shopping complexes such as Liberty Place, the Bourse, the Gallery, and Downstairs at the Bellevue. You can usually use hotel lobby and restaurant facilities.

Safety   Philadelphia has many of the preconditions of crime: It's large and populous and suffers from overall job losses in the last decade and a widening gap between haves and have-nots. You won't see too much of this underside if you concentrate on major tourist destinations but stay alert and be aware of your immediate surroundings. Keep a close eye on your possessions. If you are planning to explore in unusual neighborhoods, around college campuses in West Philadelphia, at unusual hours, or in a style that makes you conspicuous, be especially careful. Center City has recently responded to visible signs of urban distress, including tourist crime, with a combination of police staffing and specially identified "Community Ambassadors," so incidents are rare under normal circumstances.

Taxes   Hotel-room charges incur a 7% state tax and a 5% city surcharge. There is a 7% tax on restaurant meals and on general sales. Clothing is tax-free.

Taxis   See "Getting Around," earlier in this chapter.

Television   Network affiliates include Channel 3 (CBS), KYW; Channel 6 (ABC), WPVI; Channel 10 (NBC), WCAU; Channel 12 (PBS), WHYY; and

Channel 29 (FOX), WTXF. Most hotels have cable with offerings like HBO, CNN, ESPN, and Disney.

Time Zone   Philadelphia is in the Eastern Time zone—Eastern Standard Time (EST) or eastern daylight time, depending on the time of year, making it the same as New York and 3 hours ahead of the West Coast.

Transit Information   To find out how to reach a specific destination, call SEPTA headquarters at ☎ **215/574-7800**—but expect to wait.

Weather   Call ☎ **215/936-1212.**

5 Where to Stay

A century ago, Philadelphia was full of inns, hostelries, and European-style hotels for all pocketbooks and tastes. Today, after decades of frankly disappointing choices, Philadelphia has begun paying serious attention to the comfort of its guests again, and it shows.

Philadelphia hotels are currently booming, thanks in part to the dozens of conventions being booked by the new Pennsylvania Convention Center. Not even the adjoining Philadelphia Convention Center Marriott, the largest hotel in the state, with 1,200 rooms, can soak up all this demand. Exactly 5,711 hotel beds were added to the city between January 1999 and May 2000, and 3,000 of these are within 2 blocks of the Convention Center. Hampton Inn, Hilton, Hyatt, Loews, Marriott/Courtyard by Marriott, Ritz Carlton, Sofitel, and Sheraton are all in the game, either in new or rehabbed buildings. A sign of the times: Four of these buildings were originally constructed for banks.

Prices hit new levels with the 2000 Republican National Convention. There's no indication that prices won't continue to rise, so you'll have to look a little harder for discounts and promotions—especially at luxury and near luxury hotels. Concentrate on the great weekend packages around town, particularly near the airport, where $100 to $110 specials abound. Find several hotels that look appealing and call their toll-free numbers or check out their Web sites to find out about package deals. Many hotels also advertise in the travel sections of major newspapers. Ask about senior citizen discounts, or holiday, family, or all-inclusive packages with meals or sightseeing tours. No matter where you decide to stay, *always ask for the lowest-priced package available.* Remember that reservation agents won't necessarily volunteer the cheapest rates—you might have to insist. And check out the increased bed-and-breakfast and smaller inn listings, many spurred by the Convention Center, for a cheaper, fresh alternative. Ask about the hotel plus special admissions to sites packages offered through the Convention and Visitors Bureau.

Geographically, look to hotels in the Rittenhouse Square area for larger, more individualized prewar spaces. Other large hotels in town serve corporate headquarters in the northwest quadrant between City Hall and the Philadelphia Museum of Art. Medium-size hotels are surging in historic Society Hill, Chinatown, and residential blocks. Business amenities such as Internet access ports, voice mail, and functional desks have become standard.

There are an additional 9,000 hotel beds within a 20-mile circumference outside of town. This includes a full complement of airport hotels 20 minutes away, many of them recently opened in response to the growth of the airport itself. Two fine hotels sit atop a bluff near I-76 that overlooks the downtown skyline. Roosevelt Boulevard hides some smaller properties, about 20 minutes out of town.

Outside the city you can find plenty of lovely old inns like Evermay-on-the-Delaware in Bucks County—see chapter 11 for listings. The **Visitors Center,** 16th Street and John F. Kennedy Boulevard, Philadelphia, PA 19102 (☎ **215/ 636-1666**), can help with any questions.

RATES   Unless otherwise specified, all prices quoted are for double occupancy and all rooms have private bathrooms. You can count on a state tax of 7%, plus a city surcharge of 6%. Remember that the prices listed here are "rack rates"—the room rate charged without any discount—and you can usually do better. Be sure to ask about parking and/or arrangements for children.

B&B AGENCIES   The region has more than 250 bed-and-breakfasts, each as charming and/or eccentric as its owner. One good agency to contact is **A Bed & Breakfast Connection/Bed & Breakfast of Philadelphia,** Box 21, Devon, PA 19333 (☎ **800/448-3619** or 610/687-3565; fax 610/995-9524; www. bnbphiladelphia.com; e-mail: bnb@bnbphiladelphia.com). This reservation service represents more than 100 personally inspected accommodations in Philadelphia, Valley Forge, the Brandywine Valley and in Lancaster, Montgomery, and Bucks counties. The agency has assembled a group of interesting, warm hosts, including linguists, gourmet cooks, and therapists. Philadelphia accommodations include a contemporary loft with a spectacular view of the Delaware River, a mid–18th-century inn, a Victorian home with a magnificent 3-story open staircase, and a town house tucked in an alley seconds from Rittenhouse Square. In greener pastures, you could pick from the second oldest house in Pennsylvania, a former stagecoach stop, or a converted carriage house complete with pool.

Prices range $50 to $225 for a couple. Many at lower prices have shared bathrooms, and children are a point to discuss. The agency will select a compatible lodging for you or send you its free brochure. American Express, VISA, and MasterCard are accepted; phone reservations can be made Monday to Friday 9am to 6pm, and Saturday 9am to 1pm.

Janice Archbold at **Guesthouses,** Box 2137, West Chester, PA 19380 (☎ **610/ 692-4575;** fax 610/692-4451), has more than 200 host situations lined up, not only in Philadelphia but also throughout the mid-Atlantic region. Most buildings are architecturally or historically significant, and rates average $80 and up. Monthly rentals are also available.

The **Association of Bed and Breakfasts in Philadelphia, Valley Forge, and Brandywine,** P.O. Box 562, Valley Forge, PA 19481 (☎ **800/344-0123,** or 215/783-7838 for reservations 9am–9pm daily; fax 610/783-7783), is a no-fee reservation service with 600 rooms in more than 130 town-and-country choices, from Main Line to Bucks County, Lancaster County, and West Chester. Singles start at $35 per night, and doubles at $45.

1 Historic Area

VERY EXPENSIVE

○ **Omni Hotel at Independence Park.** 4th and Chestnut sts., Philadelphia, PA 19106. ☎ **800/843-6664** or 215/925-0000. Fax 215/931-1263. www.omnihotels.com. 150 units.

Philadelphia Accommodations

Alexander Inn **20**

Bank Street Hostel **25**

Best Western Independence Park Inn **24**

Clarion Suites **6**

Comfort Inn
Downtown/Historic Area **28**

Courtyard by Marriott **7**

Crowne Plaza Philadelphia Center City **12**

Doubletree Hotel Philadelphia **18**

Embassy Suites Center City **5**

Four Seasons Hotel **4**

Hawthorn Suites **2**

Holiday Inn–
Independence Mall **27**

KormanSuites Hotel and
Conference Center **1**

The Latham **14**
Loews Philadelphia Hotel **9**
Omni Hotel at Independence Park **23**
Penn's View Hotel **26**
Philadelphia Marriott **8**
Philadelphia Park Hyatt
  at the Bellevue **17**
Rittenhouse Hotel **15**

Ritz Carlton Philadelphia **10**
Rodeway Inn **19**
Sheraton Rittenhouse Square **16**
Sheraton Society Hill **21**
Sofitel Hotel **13**
Thomas Bond House **22**
Westin Philadelphia **11**
Wyndham Franklin Plaza Hotel **3**

A/C MINIBAR TV TEL. $179–$209 double; $375–$750 suite. Weekend rates available. Children free in parents' room. AE, CB, DC, DISC, MC, V. Self-parking $14.50; valet parking $19.

This small, polished hotel, opened in 1990, has a terrific location in the middle of Independence National Historical Park, 3 blocks south of Ben Franklin Bridge (Chestnut St. runs one way east, so approach from 6th St.). All rooms have Independence Park views, and horse-drawn carriages clip-clop past the valet parking drop-off and an elegant glass-and-steel canopy. The lobby is classic, with current newspapers, huge vases of flowers, and a bar featuring a piano or a jazz trio nightly. Every room is cheery, with plants and original pastels of city views. State-of-the-art conveniences include voice mail, VCR, two telephones, and fax- and computer-compatible jacks. The staff here is noteworthy for its quality and knowledge of the park.

Dining/Diversions: The four-diamond Azalea is one of Philadelphia's top restaurants; founding chef Aliza Green created imaginative treatments of American regional dishes, with three-course tasting menus as an option. The restaurant is open for breakfast, lunch, brunch, and dinner. Hearty (not English) afternoon tea is served in the lobby lounge, which also features a piano trio most nights.

Amenities: 24-hour room service, concierge, valet parking. Complimentary van to Center City stops weekdays 7am to 7pm. Indoor lap pool (no lifeguard) daily 7am to 11pm; whirlpool and sauna adjoining, with Stairmaster and exercise area; Ritz five-movie theater tucked into the back corner.

Sheraton Society Hill. 2nd and Walnut sts., Philadelphia, PA 19106. ☎ **888/325-3535** or 215/238-6000. Fax 215/922-2709. www.sheraton.com/societyhill. 365 units. A/C MINIBAR TV TEL. $219–$249 double, depending on view; $450–$650 suite. Weekend rates available. Children 17 and under free in parents' room. AE, DC, MC, V. Valet parking $21 per day, self-parking $14.50 per day.

Located 3 blocks from Head House Square and 4 blocks from Independence Hall, the 1986 Sheraton Society Hill sits nestled among the tree-lined cobblestone streets of this historic district. Set on a triangular 2½-acre site between Dock and South Front streets, the building was designed in keeping with the area's Flemish Bond architecture. Its skylit, four-story atrium is entered via a circular courtyard with a splashing fountain.

The guest rooms are on the long low second, third, and fourth floors (the only Delaware River views are from the latter). They are a bit smaller than you'd expect (as are the bathrooms); half have one king-size bed, and the others have two double beds. All were renovated in winter 1998–99 in top-quality Drexel Heritage mahogany; they have four lamps, two-post headboards, an upholstered love seat and chair, and glass-and-brass coffee tables. In each bathroom, dark marble tops the vanity, and Martex bathrobes are provided. The decor is gender neutral, with American art prints on the walls.

Dining/Diversions: Hadleys, a moderately priced American bistro restaurant, features creative seasonal menus and health-conscious main dishes. The Courtyard has piano music for a cappuccino/dessert bar nightly and light fare throughout the day and evening.

Amenities: 24-hour room service, free shuttle van to Center City, concierge on duty daily 6am to 11pm. Superior meeting facilities; fourth-floor indoor pool (open daily 6am–10pm), whirlpool, and small health club with trainers; third-floor sauna.

EXPENSIVE

Holiday Inn—Independence Mall. 4th and Arch sts., Philadelphia, PA 19106. ☎ **800/843-2355** or 215/923-8660. Fax 215/829-1796. 364 units. A/C TV TEL. $160 standard with double or king bed. Excellent weekend rates available. Extra person $10 (up to five in a room).

Accommodations reserved for nonsmokers—often in blocks as large as several floors—are so common that we no longer single out hotels that offer them. However, nonsmokers should not assume that they'll get a smoke-free room without specifically requesting one. As smokers are squeezed into fewer and fewer rooms, the ones they are allowed to use become saturated with the smell of smoke, even in hotels that are otherwise antiseptic. Be sure to stress your need for a smoke-free room to avoid this disagreeable situation.

Children 18 and under free in parents' room; children 12 and under eat free. AE, DC, MC, V. Parking $10 per day. Frequent airport shuttles.

This Holiday Inn, set back from the street, is absolutely the closest you can sleep to the Liberty Bell—just turn the corner and you're at the pavilion that houses it. The continued renovation of the bedrooms and public spaces and the addition of data ports and a concierge have given it a "superior" rating within the Holiday Inn organization. Rooms are standard size and decor.

Dining: Buffet lunch is served in the renovated Benjamin's, or there's also the less expensive Café Plain and Fancy.

Amenities: Room service; laundry room; rooftop outdoor pool; game room; and children's programs in the summer.

MODERATE

Best Western Independence Park Inn. 235 Chestnut St., Philadelphia, PA 19106. ☎ 800/528-1234 or 215/922-4443. Fax 215/922-4487. www.independenceparkinn.com. 36 units. A/C TV TEL. $160 double. Rates include breakfast and afternoon tea. Children 12 and under free in parents' room; 15% AAA discount. AE, DC, DISC, MC, V. Parking $10 at nearby enclosed garage.

This top choice for bed-and-breakfast-style accommodations has a great location, 2 blocks from Independence Hall. It's a handsome 1856 former dry-goods store with renovated rooms, now a Best Western franchise. A 2001 exterior renovation shouldn't inconvenience traffic.

The guest rooms, on eight floors, are normal size, but the ceilings are nice and high. The bathrooms have big beveled mirrors, dropped ceilings, and hair dryers. Although all the windows are triple casement and double-glazed, specify an interior room if you're sensitive to noise from the traffic on Chestnut Street. A third bed can be wheeled into your room for a child at no additional charge. The Independence Park has no restaurant. However, it serves a very passable continental breakfast in a glass-enclosed garden courtyard, with the Dickens Inn (see chapter 6) supplying a complimentary afternoon tea. Special discount coupons to nearby restaurants and a nearby health club ($6) are available at the desk.

Comfort Inn Downtown/Historic Area. 100 N. Columbus Blvd. (formerly Delaware Ave.), Philadelphia, PA 19106. ☎ 800/228-5150 or 215/627-7900. Fax 215/238-0809. www.comfortinnofphiladelphia.com. 185 units. A/C TV TEL. $109–$119 double. Rates include continental breakfast. Children 18 and under free in parents' room. Ask about discounts for AAA members. AE, DC, DISC, MC, V. Parking $10 in adjacent lot.

Comfort Inn at Penn's Landing is the area's only waterfront hotel, nestled into a corner of Old City between I-95 and the Delaware River, 3 blocks from the northbound ramp off the expressway. A courtesy shuttle van to Center City stops here, and the crosstown subway line is 2 blocks away. A basic steel skeleton hung with blue-and-white concrete panels, Comfort Inn has been built to airport-area noise specifications, with insulated windows and other features to lessen the din of traffic. The eastern views of the river from the upper floors are stupendous, and 2000 saw new furniture, paint, and hall treatments. Comfort Inn has no restaurant, but a complimentary continental breakfast is served in the cocktail lounge. There's a coin laundry on the second floor, and half the rooms are designated for nonsmokers. The fitness room stocks weights and has cardio-fitness machines.

○ **Penn's View Hotel.** Front and Market sts., Philadelphia, PA 19106. ☎ **800/331-7634** or 215/922-7600. Fax 215/922-7642. www.pennsviewhotel.com. 52 units. A/C TV TEL. $145 double. Weekend rates available; $275 package includes 2 nights, champagne upon arrival, and $50 Panorama restaurant voucher. Rates include deluxe continental breakfast. Guarantee requested on reservation. AE, CB, DC, MC, V. Parking $14 at adjacent lot.

Tucked behind the Market Street ramp to I-95 in a renovated 1856 hardware store, this small, exquisite inn exudes European flair—when you enter you'll feel like you're in a private club. It was developed by the Sena family, which started La Famiglia 150 yards south (see chapter 6 for details) and has grown a small neighborhood empire. The decor is floral and rich; the main concern is traffic noise, but the rooms are well insulated and contain large framed mirrors, armoires, and efficient bath fixtures. The ceilings have been dropped for modern heat and air conditioning, and 12 new rooms with Jacuzzis and fireplaces were just added. A third bed can be wheeled into your room for $15. Ristorante Panorama offers excellent contemporary Italian cuisine at moderate prices. Next to the restaurant is Il Bar, a world-class wine bar that offers 120 different wines by the glass.

Thomas Bond House. 129 S. 2nd St., Philadelphia, PA 19106. ☎ **800/845-2663** or 215/923-8523. Fax 215/923-8504. 14 units. A/C TV TEL. $105–$175 double; $175 suite. Rates include breakfast and afternoon wine and cheese. AE, MC, V. Parking $9 at adjacent lot.

This 1769 Georgian row house sitting almost directly across from the back of Independence Park is owned by the federal government, which kept the shell and gutted the interior. The proprietors have turned the guest rooms into cheerful, comfortable, colonial-style accommodations, renovated completely in 1997. The entrance is decorated with map illustrations and secretary desks. The charming parlor has pink sofas and a replica Chippendale double chair, while the breakfast room has four tables for four. All rooms are individually decorated and feature private bathrooms and period furnishings. Fresh-baked cookies are put out each evening for bedtime snacking. The hotel is named for its first occupant, the doctor who co-founded Pennsylvania Hospital with Benjamin Franklin.

2 Center City

VERY EXPENSIVE

○ **Four Seasons Hotel.** 1 Logan Sq., Philadelphia, PA 19103. ☎ **800/332-3442** or 215/963-1500. Fax 215/963-9506. www.fourseasons.com. 380 units. A/C MINIBAR TV TEL. Doubles from $385; suites from $405. Weekend rates available. AE, DC, MC, V. Valet parking $24 weekdays, $18 weekends.

The Four Seasons, one of the two best hotels in Philadelphia, is a member of a distinguished luxury chain that includes New York's Pierre, the Four Seasons in Dallas and Washington, and London's Inn on the Park. Its luxury is refined and understated. Built in 1983, the Four Seasons is an 8-story curlicue on Logan Square. It's separated from the "partner" CIGNA headquarters by a fountain and landscaped courtyard that opens as a cafe in summer. The hotel has landscaped the Logan Circle gardens as well.

As you're waved into the porte cochere on 18th Street, your first view is of enormous masses of flowers, with stepped-stone levels, water, and honeyed woods stretching far into the distance. The lounge and promenade serve as foyers to the dining and meeting facilities and are paneled in a rare white mahogany. The guest rooms mix Federal period furniture with richer, more Victorian color schemes. There is a very direct American elegance in each room: The desk, settee, armoire, and wing chair/ottoman combinations are top-quality Henredon. All the rooms have windows that open or private verandas boasting marvelous views of Logan Circle or the interior courtyard.

Dining/Diversions: The Four Seasons restaurants regularly collect raves from local reviewers. The Fountain Restaurant, serving all three meals, continues the low-key elegance of the hotel by combining luxury (150 seats in wide, comfortable armchairs) with intimacy. Natural light streams over tapestries, fresh flowers, and walnut paneling. The Swann Lounge, closer to the lobby corridor, has marble-top tables and a colorful, civilized look like something out of a Maurice Prendergast sketch. It's open for an extensive lunch, afternoon tea, early evening cocktails, and dessert and drinks until midnight. The Courtyard Café offers light refreshments in the Summer.

Amenities: Concierge, 24-hour room service, complimentary overnight shoe shine, terry-cloth robes, and town-car service within Center City. Besides European spa weekends, the basement health center includes a heated pool (large enough for laps), a superheated whirlpool, Universal machines, Exercycles, and exercise mats—all spotlessly maintained. The hotel also has a full-service hair salon and a small sundries shop.

⊙ **Philadelphia Park Hyatt at the Bellevue.** Broad and Walnut sts., or 1415 Chancellor Court (between Walnut and Locust sts.), Philadelphia, PA 19102. ☎ **800/223-1234** or 215/893-1234. Fax 215/732-8518. www.hyatt.com. 172 units. A/C MINIBAR TV TEL. $375 standard room; $420 deluxe room; $450 executive room. Weekend packages often available. AE, DC, DISC, MC, V. Self-parking $14 at connected garage; valet parking $21.

The "grande dame of Broad Street" was the most opulent hotel in the country when it first opened in 1904, and it was fully renovated in 1989. A notch below the Four Seasons, the Rittenhouse, or the Ritz-Carlton, it's still a grand experience in a great location, and the value on weekends is substantial.

The ground floor houses internationally renowned retailers like Tiffany & Co. and Polo/Ralph Lauren, while the below-ground level features quick and easy gourmet fare and takeout from a food court. A separate elevator lifts you to the 19th-floor registration area and foyer for the hotel restaurants. The rooms, occupying floors 12 to17, are as large as ever and all slightly different, with a green-and-white

Historic Bed & Breakfasts

Many B&Bs are listed through A Bed & Breakfast Connection/Bed & Breakfast of Philadelphia. but some list themslves independently. My favorite among the latter is **Shippen Way Inn,** 418 Bainbridge St. (☎ **800/245-4873** or 215/627-7266), a tiny row house in Queen Village built around 1750 and lovingly maintained. During summer, you can wake up in a four-poster bed and have breakfast in the back herb garden for $90 to $120 per night. You might also try **Ten Eleven Clinton** (☎ **215/923-8144**), an elegant 1836 Federal townhouse (that means high ceilings!) on a beautiful tree-lined residential street. Rates run $125 to $175.

decor and wall moldings reproduced from the 1904 designs. The makeover has added to each room extra large goose-down pillows, three two-line phones with data ports, a VCR, a large bed, a writing desk, a round table, and four upholstered chairs. Closets have built-in tie racks and automatic lighting. The bathrooms are dated but have amenities like hair dryers, TVs, and illuminated close-up mirrors.

Dining/Diversions: Founders (see chapter 6), voted one of the top 50 restaurants in the nation by *Condé Nast Traveler,* has two spectacular semicircular windows draped with dramatic swags of brown and cream. The Library Lounge is quiet and a bit precious. With a copy of a Gilbert Stuart full-length portrait and a collection of books by and about Philadelphians, the lounge is open all day but serves 11am to 1am. The Ethel Barrymore Room serves afternoon tea with a view of the Philadelphia skyline, Wednesday to Friday 2 to 4:30pm, and Saturday 2 to 5pm. At night, the Ethel Barrymore Room features live music: cabaret performances, musical theater, or the hotel's house swing band. On the 12th floor is the equally impressive Conservatory, at the base of a dramatic 80-foot atrium carved out of the original hotel. It has a wonderful, whimsical cafe ambience, with trellises, an oval cloud mural, porch swings, and two-story-high palms. It serves generous breakfast and lunch buffets on weekdays.

Amenities: 24-hour room service, concierge, complimentary glass of champagne or hot drink upon arrival, full-day child-care facility at the Sporting Club. A fourth-floor skywalk from the hotel at the ballroom level leads directly to the garage on the other side of Chancellor Court. It also goes to the Sporting Club, a Michael Graves–designed facility that boggles the eye with 93,000 square feet of health space, including a half-mile jogging track; a four-lane, 25-meter junior Olympic pool; and corridors of squash and racquetball courts. The club is open daily 6:30am to 10pm and is available only to members and hotel guests (no charge).

✪ **Rittenhouse Hotel.** 210 W. Rittenhouse Sq., Philadelphia, PA 19103. ☎ **800/ 635-1042** or 215/546-9000. Fax 215/732-3364. www.rittenhousehotel.com. 98 units. A/C MINIBAR TV TEL. Doubles from $320. Weekend rates and packages including health club, dinners, and other amenities usually available. AE, DC, MC, V. Parking $24.

Among Philadelphia's luxury hotels, the Rittenhouse has the fewest and largest rooms, the most satisfying views, and the most homegrown Philadelphia feel. Built in 1989, it's a jagged concrete-and-glass high-rise off the western edge of Philadelphia's most distinguished public square. The lobby is truly magnificent, with inlaid marble floors and a series of frosted-glass chandeliers and sconces. The Rittenhouse and the Four Seasons (see above) are the only AAA Five-Diamond Award winners in the state.

The Rittenhouse Hotel has guest rooms on floors five to nine; the other floors contain condominium residences. The rooms, with new carpeting and bedding, have bay windows, reinforced walls between rooms, and solid-wood doors. All have great views: The park is wonderfully green most of the year, but the western view of the Schuylkill and the Parkway is even more dramatic. Spirited renderings of city scenes by local artists decorate the walls; amenities include VCRs and in-room fax machines.

Dining/Diversions: Radio personality and executive chef James Coleman oversees the cuisine in the upscale all-American Tree Tops, a sun-filled cafe overlooking the park offering regional cuisine for breakfast, lunch, and dinner. Smith & Wollensky, the classic New York steakhouse, has an outpost on the second floor, and the more casual Wollensky's Grill has a late night bar with separate entrance on the Square. Completing the picture is the ground floor's Cassatt Tea Room and Lounge, which serves traditional afternoon tea and cocktails daily. The site was the original town house of the painter Mary Cassatt's brother, and an ingenious trellised private garden triangle is adorned with three drypoints by this American master.

Amenities: 24-hour room service, one Clef d'Or concierge (the ultimate accolade in the world of luxury hotels), turndown service with written weather report for the next day, radio tuned to soft classical music, twice-daily room service. Many cooking classes and/or lunch events are held for children. The third floor boasts the Adolf Biecker spa/salon and fitness club, a *Condé Nast Traveler* 1997 awardee with five-lane indoor pool, a sundeck, and Cybex weight machines and aerobic equipment. Sauna, steam room, and spalike amenities such as massages, facials, and body wraps are also offered. The floor above is devoted to an executive business center. There's an ATM in the building.

✪ **The Ritz-Carlton Philadelphia.** 10 Ave. of the Arts, Philadelphia, PA 19102. ☎ **800/241-3333** or 215/735-7700. Fax 215/568-0942. www.ritzcarlton.com. 331 units. A/C MINIBAR TV TEL. $320 double. Weekend rates available. AE, MC, V. Self-parking $21; valet parking $25.

The Ritz-Carlton, spanking new in fall 2000, has electrified the city for the painstaking and glorious resuscitation of an important site, the corner between City Hall and the Avenue of the Arts. The Ritz-Carlton has incorporated a 120-foot neoclassical domed structure designed by McKim, Mead, and White, dating from 1908, and its 30-story marble-clad neighbor. The tower has been converted into the hotel, a meeting and ballroom space, and a fitness facility on the 3rd floor. The Rotunda Dome houses an eye-popping atrium and set of three restaurants (full-service, power grill, and grill/bar) and a downstairs ballroom. Many architectural details have been preserved, including marble flooring and a bank teller desk.

The hotel rooms occupy floors 4 to 29; the top three are reserved for Club members, with a spectacular concierge/club area on the 30th floor. In guest rooms, you'll find more space than normal allotted to generous baths with a tub/shower alcove, and less to the snug bedrooms, decorated with stippled paper in peach and warm ochres. The furnishings are exquisite, from the old Philadelphia prints and engravings to the high-speed Internet access for laptops. Lighting is excellent.

Dining: Pantheon, in a setting of magnificent marble Ionic columns on the side facing the Rotunda and 18-foot high windows on the other, serves sophisticated brasserie-style Italian fare all day long. The ✪ **Paris Bar and Grille,** a clubby space on the City Hall side, features an open kitchen, with Andrew Hewson supervising light sauces and fresh ingredients for too-cutely named but wonderfully prepared dishes. The downstairs Vault is a snug, tobacco-heavy lounge with warm woods and tapestries.

Amenities: Full concierge service, room service second to none, complimentary overnight shoeshine, turndown service, fitness center with massage rooms, sauna/steam room.

Westin Philadelphia. 17th and Chestnut sts. (at Liberty Place), Philadelphia, PA 19103. ☎ **800/228-3000** or 215/563-1600. Fax 215/564-9559. www.westin.com. 290 units. A/C MINIBAR TV TEL. $295 double. Weekend rates available. AE, MC, V. Self-parking $21; valet parking $25.

The Westin opened with great fanfare as a Ritz-Carlton in 1990 as part of Liberty Place. Although it's been fumbled a bit by its owner, Starwood Hotels, this wonderful place seems to be emerging with an intact blend of luxury amenities and service and is just steps away from the best in urban life.

A small porte cochere and a ground-floor lobby on 17th Street lead to a series of smaller, almost residential rooms that contain the front lobby and concierge desks, the dining areas, and the elevators on the second floor. The guest rooms feature bedside walnut tables, desks, beds with spindle-top headboards (with four pillows!), and Wedgwood or Sandwich glass lamps. Large walnut armoires house TVs, clothing drawers, and minibars. All rooms are provided with two phone lines and data ports. The modern bathrooms are outfitted with black-and-white marble, silver plate fixtures, magnifying mirrors, and lots of toiletries. The hotel runs frequent packages in tandem with museum exhibitions or other events.

Dining/Diversions: The mahogany-paneled and period-furnished Grill and Grill Bar are turning out superb contemporary American dishes in currently under-populated rooms. The Lobby Lounge, with a constantly crackling fireplace, has expanded its offerings to a continental breakfast, a formal tea, and hors d'oeuvres and desserts. Classical and jazz music accompany afternoon and evening service.

Amenities: 24-hour room service, 24-hour concierge, nightly turndown, complimentary morning newspapers, transport to and from airport, and car-rental arrangements. There is a small exercise and sauna facility, superb business meeting rooms, and a fully equipped business center, but the most impressive extra is the internal connection to the 70 Shops at Liberty Place (see chapter 9).

EXPENSIVE

Doubletree Hotel Philadelphia. Broad St. at Locust St., Philadelphia, PA 19107. ☎ **800/ 222-8733** or 215/893-1600. Fax 215/893-1663. www.doubletreehotels.com. 427 units. A/C TV TEL. $129–$243 double. Weekend packages available. AE, DC, DISC, MC, V. Self-parking $15 in adjoining garage; valet parking $19.

Although the location of this hotel is less than ideal for business travelers, it is prime for tourists and families, and the weekend packages are quite affordable. The garage entrances ingeniously keep traffic flows separate for three floors of meeting facilities. You'll probably enter through the corridor connecting the lobby to the garage on the block's southern side. The decor features rich paisleys and Degas-style murals alluding to the orchestral and ballet life at the Academy of Music across the street. Thanks to the saw-toothed design of the building, the guest rooms, all completely renovated in the last 6 years, each have two views of town. Obviously, the higher floors afford the better views; views of the Delaware River (eastern corner) or City Hall (northeastern corner) are the most popular. One tinny note: the small Magnavox clock radio.

Dining: If you dine at the Academy Cafe, an informal 220-seat restaurant and lounge that serves breakfast, lunch, and dinner, ask for one of the tables overlooking the action outside. The decor is colonial-meets-California. Jack's Center City Tavern serves until midnight.

Amenities: Boxes of great chocolate-chip cookies are delivered to your room upon arrival. Quick breakfasts are guaranteed. A guest services desk is staffed 16 hours daily. Budget will deliver rental cars to the hotel door. The fifth-floor Racquet and Health Club is free to all guests. You can tan, steam, swim in an indoor pool, whirlpool, or work out on CAM II exercise machines, Lifesteps, or Schwinn Airdynes. A racquetball court can be reserved for $10 per hour, with no equipment charge. A small jogging track circles a huge rooftop deck, and summer brings many hotel parties and parade views.

✪ **Embassy Suites Center City.** 1776 Benjamin Franklin Pkwy. (at Logan Square), Philadelphia, PA 19103. ☎ **800/362-2779** or 215/561-1776. Fax 215/963-0122.

www.embassysuites.com. 288 units. A/C TV TEL. $174 suite. Excellent weekend packages available. Rates include full breakfast. AE, CB, DC, DISC, MC, V. Parking $21 per day in underground garage.

The big 28-story cylinder of marble and glass on the Parkway at 18th Street has had its ups and downs; it's feeling a bit shabby at the moment, but the all-suite structure coupled with the location and the price makes this a fine trade-off choice. In 1993, $10 million was put into a refurbishment.

The hotel has an interesting set of strengths and weaknesses. It was designed in the 1960s as luxury apartments radiating out from a central core—the Kelly family had the last penthouse here—but the quality of views varies widely, and the basic shape is weirdly disorienting. It's evident that the elevators and lobby weren't equipped to handle this volume. On the other hand, amenities such as the full breakfast at TGI Friday's (the connected restaurant), the fitness room, and the nightly manager's reception exceed expectations. The suites themselves have a sleek severity, with black matte and putty surfaces for TV stands and a spare walnut inset bedroom armoire. The kitchenette includes microwave, under-the-counter refrigerator, and coffeemaker (no oven or dishwasher); dishes and silverware are provided upon request. An especially nice 48-inch round table with four chairs overlooks the small balcony terrace with sliding door. Bathrooms have large Italian marble tiles, plush white towels, and hair dryers. With two double beds, the bedrooms don't have a lot of extra room.

Dining/Diversions: TGI Friday's, connected on two levels, is open until 1am daily and is used for hotel breakfasts; when the hotel is full, service backs up quite a bit. The lobby lounge hosts happy hour.

Amenities: Valet parking; toiletries available at front desk upon request. The second-floor fitness center has Nordic Track, Stairmasters, rowing machine, and unisex sauna. The adjoining Please Touch Too room for children aged 2 to 7 is unfortunately a shadow of its former self, but it is clean and safe.

Hotel Sofitel. 17th and Sansom sts., Philadelphia, PA 19103. ☎ **800/SOFITEL** or 215/569-8300. Fax 215/569-1492. www.sofitelphiladelphia.com. 306 units. A/C TV TEL. $249 rooms, $269 suites. Weekend packages available. AE, CB, DC, DISC, MC, V. Parking $23 per day in underground garage.

Sofitel is the premier French luxury chain, and this urbane, sleek sanctuary of limestone and glass feels very much connected to both French and Philadelphia hospitality, even though it opened only in May 2000. The location is wonderful for business or adult tourists, tucked away between Rittenhouse Square and the Avenue of the Arts, though the long, low floors don't make for much in the way of views. Rooms are more contemporary than the norm—think of Ian Schrager watered down for local tastes—with a glass-and-chrome coffee table, two armchairs, and an opulent bed with four wall-mounted bedside lights squeezed into walls of handsome checkerboard cherrywood squares. The baths are truly sumptuous. Businessmen will find high-speed Internet jacks from the desk with easy tabletop plug-ins.

Dining: Chez Colette, a traditional French brasserie open for breakfast as well, offers classics such as onion soup and coq au vin, with surprisingly reasonable entrees at $12 to $16. The bar nearer 17th Street is a cool, New York-style lounge with a blue Brazilian granite bar, torch-style singing, and French appetizers.

Amenities: A cut rose and Evian in every room; fully equipped fitness center.

✪ **KormanSuites Hotel.** 2001 Hamilton St. (just off the Parkway), Philadelphia, PA 19130. ☎ **888/456-7626** or 215/569-7300. Fax 215/569-0584. 170 units. A/C TV TEL. $179 efficiency; $199 two-bedroom plus kitchen; $239 one-bedroom suite with connecting den.

Other options available for stays of 2 weeks or more. Children free in parents' room. Rates include continental breakfast. AE, DC, MC, V. Free parking.

The amenities and the location of this hotel make it an excellent value at rack rates; the weekend packages make it outstanding. You'll recognize it by the bright neon scribble near its roof north of Logan Circle, visible from anywhere south. Korman-Suites is really a grand hotel, but it's in separate pieces. A 28-story tower is connected by a marble-and-mahogany lobby, and a glass-enclosed corridor leads to the restaurant and lush Japanese sculpture garden and pool.

The standard rooms are unbelievably spacious, with a microwave, minibar, and coffeemaker. The suites add full kitchens with dishwashers, stoves, coffeemakers, and telephones. Each living area has a full dining table for four, TV, full couch, and three double closets. Each bedroom features a queen-size bed and another TV (in suites, with built-in VCR), and the adjoining bathroom has a stacked washer/dryer. The views are great: to the north, highlights of 19th-century manufacturing and churches; to the south, 20th-century Center City.

Dining: Catalina, the hotel restaurant, succeeds as a neighborhood favorite for moderate California-style mixtures of East Coast and West Coast. Hotel guests are offered complimentary continental breakfasts, 6 to 10am.

Amenities: Complimentary shuttle van running hourly through Center City to Independence Park, concierge, 24-hour message center, and garage attendants. Outdoor pool, Jacuzzi, two tennis and platform tennis courts, high-tech spa and fitness center, full-service hair salon, ATM on-site.

The Latham. 135 S. 17th St. at Walnut St., Philadelphia, PA 19103. ☎ **800/528-4261** or 215/563-7474. Fax 215/568-0110. www.lathamhotel.com. 139 units. A/C TV TEL. $199 double. Weekend packages from $129. One or two children free in parents' room. Rates include breakfast and parking. AE, DC, DISC, MC, V. Valet parking $20.

An apartment house until 25 years ago, the Latham now brings to mind a small, superbly run Swiss hostelry, with its charm, congeniality, and small attentions. And the weekend packages are great bargains. On weekday mornings the lobby, a high-ceilinged salon with terrazzo highlights, is filled with refreshed executives. Dealings with the reception area are quick and professional, and newsstand and lobby phones are discreetly nestled in one corner. The Latham does no convention business. The guest rooms, redone in 1998, are not huge or lavish but perfectly proportioned, with coffeemakers and hair dryers amid the cheerful striped silk. Full-wall and lighted facial mirrors, large marblelike basins, and oversize towels accentuate the white-toned bathroom interiors.

Amenities: Concierge, turndown service with Godiva chocolate mints, valet parking. Small on-site fitness room, free access to nearby fitness club with indoor pool.

Loews Philadelphia Hotel. 1200 Market St., Philadelphia, PA 19107. ☎ **800/235-6397.** www.loewshotels.com. 585 units. A/C TV TEL. $225–$250. Weekend packages available. AE, DC, DISC, MC, V. Parking $23.

The Loews, opened in spring 2000, is a great marriage of an architectural landmark and a prestigious hotel business. The PSFS tower was the nation's first skyscraper of modern design and construction, with gleaming polished stone and art deco clocks by Cartier. Loews Hotels will turn the 1932 granite and glass tower into a first-class property, directly across from Reading Terminal Headhouse and the Convention Center. The 3-story entrance hall will be preserved, and amenities will include a restaurant, fitness club with lap pool, and rooftop catering. Since this will be the second major Convention Center hotel, along with the Marriott, look for lots of group sales and weekend packages between meetings.

○ **Philadelphia Marriott.** 12th and Market sts., Philadelphia, PA 19107. ☎ **800/ 228-9290** or 215/625-2900. Fax 215/625-6000. www.marriott.com/marriott/phldt. 1,410 units. A/C TV TEL. $245 double; $260–$275 concierge-level rooms. Weekend rates available. **Courtyard by Marriott:** 13th and Filbert sts. 500 units. $155 standard, $250 suite. AE, DC, DISC, MC, V. Valet parking $23.

After more than a decade of planning and construction, the Marriott chain opened the biggest hotel in Pennsylvania in January 1995, linked by an elevated covered walkway to the Reading Terminal Shed of the Convention Center. And it's gotten bigger. In late 1999 Marriott converted the historic City Hall Annex across 13th Street at Filbert into a 500-room Courtyard by Marriott, the largest in the Courtyard division. So all together, you'll have your choice of 1,910 rooms, two fitness centers, and 10 restaurants—all linked with one another and with the Convention Center.

The hotel's major auto entrance is on Filbert Street (two way between Market and Arch sts.), with an equally grand pedestrian entrance adjoining Champions Sports Bar and retail on Market Street. The lobby is sliced up into a 5-story atrium, enlivened by a 10,000-square-foot water sculpture, a lobby bar, and a Starbucks. Setbacks and terraces provide plenty of natural light and views from the rooms on floors 6 to 23. Although tastefully outfitted with dark woods, maroon and green drapes and bedspreads, a TV armoire, club chair and ottoman, and round table plus a separate desk, the rooms are slightly less elegant than those of the top hotels. Comfortably sized bathrooms have heavy chrome fixtures and tuck sinks and counters in the corners for more dressing room space. Closets are spacious. Concierge-level rooms feature private key access and use of a special lounge. Service is impeccable, thanks to the well-trained, knowledgeable staff.

Dining/Diversions: JW's Steakhouse overlooks the lobby atrium and Market Street; Champions, a sports bar with a lot of TVs, is on the east side along Market Street; Allie's serves casual meals all day, and Starbucks fronts 12th Street. There are also three lounges. Courtyard by Marriott has a full-service restaurant, Junipers.

Amenities: The Marriott hotel offers all possible corporate and some luxury services. Concierge-floor rooms have special amenities. A complimentary 7th-floor health club is open 4:30am to midnight, with indoor lap pool, whirlpool, aerobics/fitness room, locker rooms, and wet and dry saunas. There's direct internal connection to SEPTA subways and airport train. Courtyard by Marriott has an indoor pool and fitness center as well.

Sheraton Rittenhouse Square. 227 S. 18th St. (at Rittenhouse Sq.), Philadelphia, PA 19103. ☎ **800/325-3535** or 800/854-8002. Fax 215/875-9457. www.sheraton.com. E-mail: sherarit@uscom. 192 units. A/C TV TEL. $269. Excellent weekend packages and discounts available. AE, CB, DC, DISC, MC, V. Parking $23.

This renovated apartment building—at least the 6 out of 17 floors being turned into the hotel—will bring some competition to the neighborhood, with a wonderful location and a very smart cafe right on this urbane square. This is being marketed as the first "environmentally smart" hotel in the continental United States, with fresh filtered air, organic cotton bedding, bamboo plants and recycled granite in the lobby, energy efficient lighting, and no smoking anywhere. Rooms are a spacious 400 square feet on average, with 9½-foot ceilings and state-of-the-art technology. Many have separate sitting areas.

○ **Wyndham Franklin Plaza Hotel.** 17th and Race sts., Philadelphia, PA 19103. ☎ **800/ 996-3426** or 215/448-2000. Fax 215/448-2864. www.wyndham.com. 794 units. A/C

MINIBAR TV TEL. $209 double. Excellent weekend rates available. Children 18 and under free in parents' room. AE, CB, DC, MC, V. Self-parking $16; valet parking $19.

The Wyndham has been functioning as a convenient meeting center and urban resort since 1980, and now the convention center 4 blocks away is finally filling this convention hotel. The complex uses a full city block, and the lobby, lounge, and two restaurants are beautifully integrated under a dramatic 70-foot glass roof. In terms of service and maintenance, the Wyndham has been showing signs of fatigue, but a major 1998 renovation of rooms should last for several years. Request a west view above the 19th floor for an unobstructed peek at the Parkway, but be forewarned that the cathedral bells below ring hourly from 7am.

Dining: The Terrace is a full-service cafe that serves excellent fare daily 7am to 11pm. Between Friends, the flagship, features certified Angus beef for lunch and dinner in opulent surroundings.

Amenities: Room service, travel service. The third-floor Clark's Uptown offers an indoor pool (21 by 45 ft.), a sauna, and a track—all free to hotel guests. An all-day fee of $10 gets you racquetball (three courts), squash (three courts), outdoor handball (three courts), and tennis (two courts). Around the latter is a ⅛-mile jogging track. A sundeck, whirlpool, Nautilus machine, snack bar, and superb locker and exercise facilities round out the picture.

MODERATE

○ **Alexander Inn.** 12th and Spruce sts., Philadelphia, PA 19107. ☎ **877/253-9466** or 215/923-3535. Fax 215/923-1004. www.alexanderinn.com. 48 units. A/C TV TEL. From $89–$99; $10 per additional person. AE, DC, DISC, MC, V. Garage parking $14 nearby.

The Alexander Inn, one of the smaller properties reshaped as inns south of the Convention Center since 1998, bills itself as a 4-star hotel at reasonable rates. (The *Newsweek* crew that took over all 48 rooms during the Republican National Convention had nothing but praise for its amenities and top-notch staff.) It's got all the comfort and friendliness of a bed and breakfast, with a classy 1930s art deco/cruise boat feel to the furnishings. Rooms feature DirecTV, direct dial phones with data ports, and individual artwork. Room rates include a full breakfast buffet—until noon on weekends (though there's no restaurant)—and use of the fully-equipped 24-hour fitness center. Note that the Alexander Inn is in the heart of the gay/lesbian district of Center City, and its clientele is both straight and gay.

Clarion Suites Convention Center. 1010 Race St., Philadelphia, PA 19107. ☎ **800/628-8932** or 215/922-1730. Fax 215/922-6258. www.clarionsuitesphilly.com. 96 units. A/C MINIBAR TV TEL. $99–$149 suite, for up to 4 people. Each additional person $10. Rates include continental breakfast. AE, CB, DC, DISC, MC, V. Parking $12 validated (overnight) in garage next door.

You'll find spacious and reasonable accommodations at the Clarion Suites Convention Center in the heart of Philadelphia's Chinatown. The building, dating from the 1880s, is constructed of handsome dark-red brick with lots of terra-cotta tiling and wide arches. For many years a bentwood furniture factory, it retains 13-foot ceilings, solid floors, and wood crossbeams. The hotel has a small fitness center. A couple of special advantages are offered for families. There's a very clean and well-stocked Chinese market directly across the street, and Reading Terminal Market is within 2 blocks. There is no hotel restaurant.

○ **Hawthorn Suites Philadelphia at the Convention Center.** 1100 Vine St., Philadelphia, PA 19107. ☎ **800/527-1133** or 215/829-8300. Fax 215/829-8104.

ⓘ Family-Friendly Hotels

A division of the Convention and Visitors Bureau, "Family-Friendly Philadelphia" offers special packages that include 2 nights at a number of hotels, free parking and breakfast, and free admission to attractions such as Sesame Place, the Franklin Institute, the Zoo, the Academy of Natural Sciences, the Please Touch Museum, and "The Liberty Tale Tour" run by the Historic Philadelphia people near Independence Hall. Call ☎ **800/770-5889** for details.

Embassy Suites Center City (*see p. 52*)   There's an innovative play area designed by the Please Touch Museum, with hand puppets, CD-ROM interactive "edugames," and more—perfect for kids aged 2 to 9.

Four Seasons Hotel (*see p. 48*)   The Saturday Lunch Club is a three-course meal designed for kids; it's featured on the first Saturday of the month.

The Inn at Penn (*see p. 58*)   The comfortable and safe public areas, including the Living Room with its fireplace and thousands of books, give your kids a chance to let off steam indoors—plus, it's across the street from the green swards of the U. Penn campus. Frisbee, anyone?

Rittenhouse Hotel (*see p. 50*)   The hotel intermittently offers children's cooking classes taught by Rena Coyle and also features some Saturday theme lunches for kids and their parents.

Sheraton Society Hill (*see p. 46*)   There's a special children's check-in to the right of the lobby as well as concierge treatment with free snacks, the use of the game room, and so on.

---

www.hawthorn.com. 294 units. A/C MINIBAR TV TEL. $159 suite. Rates include full hot buffet breakfast and complimentary social hour, Mon–Thurs. AE, DC, DISC, MC, V. Valet parking $15 nearby.

Opened in summer 1998, the Hawthorn Suites is directly adjacent to the Convention Center, and weekend packages make it an excellent family choice. The second floor houses a fitness center and dining area, while the 14 floors above comprise studio and one-bedroom suites, each with efficiency or full kitchens, microwaves, refrigerators, and coffeemakers. Business travelers will be happy to see data ports, a working desk, and free local phone calls.

Crowne Plaza Philadelphia Center City. 18th and Market sts., Philadelphia, PA 19103. ☎ **800/227-6963** or 215/561-7500. Fax 215/561-4484. 515 units. A/C TV TEL. $210 double; B&B packages available. Children 19 and under free in parents' room; children 12 and under eat free with parents. AE, DC, MC, V. Parking $20.

The Crowne Plaza offers solid, primarily business-oriented accommodations with no real surprises. It's very popular with conventioneers and relocating executives, but hotel policy is to leave at least 40% of the 515 rooms free for tourists.

The lobby, which dispenses coffee all day, looks like a club library in the evening with its bowls of apples and plush armchairs; it has entrances from both 18th Street and the garage. A parking garage and meeting halls occupy the next 6 floors, and rooms and several suites fill the next 17 floors. By Philadelphia standards, the rooms are large. Furnishings include coffeemakers, telephones with data ports, and plush carpeting. Bathrooms are slightly shabby. Two floors are devoted to Executive Level suites, offering upgraded decor and complimentary breakfast. The hotel restaurant, a popular English-type pub called Elephant & Castle, serves largely continental fare

6:30am to 11pm. Amenities, including the outdoor pool perched atop the garage extension's roof (open daily 10am–9pm in summer), are free to guests as is a weight room with rowing and Nautilus machines.

Rodeway Inn. 1208 Walnut St., Philadelphia, PA 19107. ☎ **800/887-1776** or 215/546-7000. Fax 215/546-7573. 25 units. A/C TV TEL. $135 double; $69–$169 standard, $119–$219 suite. Rates include continental breakfast. AE, DC, DISC, MC, V.

Robert and Thomas Manning bought this late 1800s shell in 1992 to compete with the Marriott. They've constructed seven floors of comfortable, bigger-than-average rooms with solid-core doors and private bathrooms. The front desk is attended 24 hours a day. All suites have gas fireplaces.

3 University City (West Philadelphia)

EXPENSIVE

✪ The Inn at Penn. 3600 Sansom St., Philadelphia, PA 19104. ☎ **800/809-7001** or 215/222-0200. Fax 215/222-4600. www.theinnatpenn.com. 238 units. A/C TV TEL. $179–$199 double. Children 17 and under free in parents' room. Weekend packages available. AE, DC, DISC, MC, V. Valet parking $19.

When U. Penn decides to take on a project these days, it doesn't stint—and the handsome and elegantly appointed Inn at Penn has jumped to become *the* favorite place to stay, whether west or east of the Schuylkill River. The Inn, managed by Hilton Hotels, is the keystone of the block-long Sansom Commons, an attractive 6-story brick campus neighbor that also includes the outstanding University Bookstore, collegiate trendy stores such as Steve Madden, Ma Jolie, and Urban Outfitters, and an XandO coffee bar. While the front door faces the Penn campus across Walnut Street, you'll enter through a porte cochere off Sansom Street, off the north side. Comfortable, expansive stairways and corridors connect entrances to registration and to The Living Room, where complimentary tea and coffee are dispensed until 4pm, and wine and spirits on a cash basis thereafter, amid a fully stocked library in The Living Room. Artwork and bas-reliefs of U. Penn's athletic triumphs from decades past adorn the Mission-style walls. The rooms are done in warm olive and beige tones, with top-quality furnishings, firm beds, and individual temperature controls. The academic flavor translates into efficient lighting and laptop amenities such as dual-line phones, voice mail, and coffeemakers.

Dining: The Ivy Grille, still working out opening kinks as of this writing, serves all meals in an American bistro atmosphere. The futuristic Asian-themed Pod, with a highly creative menu and exciting decor, opened in late fall 2000 within the Sansom Commons complex. And don't forget that University City is rich in ethnic restaurants within a block of the inn.

Amenities: concierge desk; 24-hour exercise room; daily newspaper delivery; Living Room lounge open until midnight, with coffee until 4pm and cash bar starting at 4:30.

Penn Tower Hotel. Civic Center Blvd. at 34th St., Philadelphia, PA 19104. ☎ **800/356-7366** or 215/387-8333. Fax 215/386-8306. www.upenn.edu/penntower. 74 units. A/C TV TEL. $169 double; $115 for relatives of patients in University and Children's Hospitals. Packages available. AE, DC, MC, V. Parking $9.

Penn Tower is a greatly improved version of a former Hilton, built with a direct skywalk to University Hospital and within steps of the University of Pennsylvania, 30th Street Station, the Civic Center, Drexel University, and a direct train to the airport. The hotel part of the tower comprises floors 17 to 20, as well as an enclosed garage and ground-floor restaurants and shops. U. Penn takes over more floors every year for medical offices. You'll have to get used to spirited displays of red and blue, Penn's colors, and a long lobby corridor of rough-textured concrete that leads to the reception desk.

Dining: P. T.'s serves breakfast; Franklin's serves lunch and dinner.

Amenities: Complimentary van service to Independence Park/historic district; limo service to and from the airport. Penn Tower is fully accessible to travelers with disabilities. It offers complimentary guest passes to Penn's nearby Hutchinson Health Complex for its track and rowing machines and makes tennis reservations at courts one block away. The ground floor also contains a newsstand and florist shop.

INEXPENSIVE

Gables. 4520 Chester Ave. (at S. 46th St.), Philadelphia, PA 19143. ☎ **215/662-1918.** Fax 215/662-1918. www.gablesbb.com. 10 units (8 with bathroom). A/C TV. $80–$115 double. Rates include full breakfast. AE, DISC, MC, V. Free parking.

This 1889 Victorian mansion, a boardinghouse until a few years ago, was one of West Philadelphia's first and finest. The location is about 8 blocks west of the University of Pennsylvania's main campus. It's right at the SEPTA trolley line stop into Center City and 5 minutes from 30th Street Station or 15 minutes from the airport. It's an excellent choice for visiting academics, parents of students, prospective applicants, and relaxed tourists.

Eight formal areas are filled with antiques. There are sitting rooms, a breakfast room, and a wraparound porch; five bedrooms with private bathrooms and four bedrooms with shared bathrooms are on the top two floors. All rooms have gorgeous inlaid wood floors, and three have charming corner turrets; closets, armoires, lamps, and desks also fit the period, with recently added private baths for many. Home-baked muffins, breads, fresh fruit, and casseroles fill out breakfasts.

International House. 3701 Chestnut St., Philadelphia, PA 19104. ☎ **215/387-5125.** Fax 215/895-6535. www.ihousephilly.org. 370 units (most with shared bathroom). A/C. Academic affiliation required. $60 single; $75 double (private bathroom). Full payment for stay required at registration. No children allowed. MC, V. No parking arrangements; garages nearby.

A residence during the academic year for U.S. and foreign students and academics, International House is a tremendous value if you're not looking for a formal hotel. Some (under 100) rooms for academically affiliated transients are generally available year-round, with more in summer. Related facilities and programs include a low-cost International Bazaar shop; coffee hours, concerts, and films at the student center—all at nominal cost; a full-service restaurant and bar; and a travel agent. To get here, take bus 21 on Walnut Street, or the trolley to 36th Street, from Center City. Most guest rooms will resemble your college dorm; doubles, when available, must be reserved 10 days in advance. Linen and towels are provided, but soap and cups are your own responsibility. There are plenty of sparkling-clean showers, sinks, and bathrooms on each floor and a 24-hour security staff; there is also a coin-operated laundry. Sunset Grille is a cafeteria by day, with evening table service.

University City Guest Houses. P.O. Box 28612, 2933 Morris Rd., Philadelphia, PA 19151. ☎ **215/387-3731.** A/C TEL. $50–$100 double. Children allowed in some situations. No credit cards; traveler's checks accepted.

This is basically a neighborhood collection of bed-and-breakfasts, most within walking distance of the University of Pennsylvania and University Hospital. Most hosts are academically affiliated. Parking is provided at most places.

4 Near the Airport

Hotel chain options are very well represented at the moderate to inexpensive level, including: **Holiday Inn Philadelphia Stadium,** 10th Street and Packer Avenue, Philadelphia, PA 19148 (☎ **800/424-0291** or 215/755-9500), which charges $120 for a double; **Airport Ramada Inn,** 76 Industrial Hwy., Essington, PA 19029 (☎ **800/277-3900** or 610/521-9600), with rates of $89 for a double, $69 weekends; **Four Points Hotel Philadelphia Airport,** 4101 Island Ave. (between I-95 and Pa. 291), Philadelphia, PA 19153 (☎ **800/325-3535** or 215/492-0400), with a stunning 1998 renovation and wonderful amenities but charging $160 for a double; **Comfort Inn Airport,** 53 Industrial Hwy., Essington, PA 19029 (☎ **800/228-5150** or 610/521-9800), with rates of $98 for a double; and **Red Roof Inn,** 49 Industrial Hwy., Essington, PA 19029 (☎ **800/843-7663** or 610/521-5090), at $83 for a double.

EXPENSIVE

Philadelphia Airport Marriott Hotel. Arrivals Rd., Philadelphia, PA 19153. ☎ **800/628-4087** or 215/492-9000. Fax 215/492-7464. www.marriott.com. 419 units. A/C TV TEL. $185 double; $199 concierge-level room for up to five people. Excellent weekend rates. AE, DC, DISC, MC, V. Parking free to guests in Level 2 of the airport garage at Terminal B.

Opened in 1995, this is the only hotel linked by skywalk to Philadelphia International Airport. The facility caters to business travelers, with voice mail, speakerphone, free incoming faxes, two data port jacks, and outlets set alongside oversize counter space for your laptop available in most rooms. However, it's not a bad choice for families, since the soundproof rooms are mostly angled away from the runways, and it's very convenient to I-95. When you throw in the full array of recreational activities, a reasonable restaurant, easy train or bus shuttle into Center City, and frequent weekend packages, it's well worth considering.

Dining: Riverbend Bar & Grille, with a rowing motif, serves breakfast, lunch, and dinner.

Amenities: Indoor lap pool, whirlpool, exercise room (open daily 5:30am–11pm).

Sheraton Philadelphia Airport. 4101 Island Ave., Philadelphia, PA 19153. ☎ **800/325-3535** or 215/365-6600. Fax 215/492-9858. www.sheraton.com. 251 units. A/C TV TEL. $175 double. Weekend and seasonal specials available. Children 18 and under free in parents' room. Rates include full buffet breakfast. AE, DC, DISC, MC, V. Free parking.

The occupancy rates at the Sheraton are among the highest in town. For first-class prices you get deluxe suites of beautifully furnished bedrooms and living rooms that encircle a dramatic eight-story atrium. A 1998 rehab replaced greenery with severe pavilions over the cafe and lounges, and suites were redecorated in taupe and olive, with cherrywood furniture. The outer room contains a business desk and chair, convertible sofa bed, multi-port speakerphone, and armoire with TV. The bedroom, with choice of king or two twin beds, has another TV and phone. There is a wet bar with coffeemaker and small refrigerator in the kitchenette, and the bath has a marble-topped vanity. Airport noise is minimal.

Dining: The Atrium Lounge and Café serves contemporary cuisine and drinks.

Amenities: *USA Today* delivered to door; complimentary coffee machines; Ambassador car rental in lobby; complimentary shuttle to and from airport. Complimentary indoor pool, whirlpool, sauna, and steam bath.

MODERATE

Philadelphia Airport Hilton. 4509 Island Ave., Philadelphia, PA 19153. ☎ **800/HILTONS** or 215/365-4150. Fax 215/937-6382. www.hilton.com. 331 units. A/C TV TEL. $159 double. Children 18 and under free in parents' room. Weekend packages available. AE, CB, DC, DISC, MC, V. Free parking, with courtesy transport to and from the airport.

The Philadelphia Airport Hilton is out of the way of flight patterns and features a lobby and cocktail lounge built around a lushly planted indoor pool. Like all airport hotels, business travelers predominate during the week, and reservations are recommended. The guest rooms, with baths redone in 2000, are classically American— spacious, comfortable, and anonymously elegant. Facilities include a restaurant and lounge, an indoor pool, whirlpool, sauna, and health club (open daily 6am–11pm).

Philadelphia Renaissance Hotel Airport. 500 Stevens Dr., Philadelphia, PA 19113. ☎ **800/468-3571** or 610/521-5900. Fax 610/521-4362. www.renaissancehotels.com. 402 units. A/C TV TEL. $169 double. Excellent weekend rates available. Children 17 and under free in parents' room. AE, DC, DISC, MC, V. Free parking.

Opened in 1991 as a Radisson, the Renaissance is trading on its sleek 12-story glass atrium and corporate clout, even while rates have dropped to match the competition. The design is ingenious, with northward balcony views of Center City expanded by a second enclosed atrium overlooking a pool and health club. The guest rooms, completely refurbished in a $10 million 2000 job, have two phones (one a speakerphone). To get here, drivers should take Route 291, 1 mile west of the airport, and follow the signs over a winding road. There are two lounges, a restaurant, and a coffee shop. Courtesy vans are provided to and from the airport and room service is available. Facilities include an indoor pool and health club.

5 City Line & Northeast

City Line Avenue (U.S. 1) just off the Schuylkill Expressway is a good jumping-off point for West Philadelphia, Bucks County, or Lancaster County. Its retail outlets are struggling with the emergence of the huge King of Prussia mall, so nearby Saks Fifth Avenue and Lord & Taylor have frequent sales.

Thoroughly comfortable national chains dot this area, including: **Holiday Inn City Line,** 4100 Presidential Blvd. (City Line Ave. at I-76), Philadelphia, PA 19131 (☎ **800/465-4329** or 215/477-0200) and the **Best Western Philadelphia Northeast,** 11580 Roosevelt Blvd., Philadelphia, PA 19116 (☎ **800/528-1234** or 215/464-9500).

MODERATE

Adam's Mark Philadelphia. City Ave. and Monument Rd., Philadelphia, PA 19131. ☎ **800/444-2326** or 215/581-5000. Fax 215/581-5069. www.adamsmark.com. 515 units. A/C TV TEL. $144 double; $164 executive room. Weekend packages and promotions available. AE, DC, DISC, MC, V. Free parking in front lots or rear-connected garage; valet parking $12.

The Adam's Mark looks like an airport control tower, but there's also an extensive brick complex of connected restaurants and function rooms. Eighty percent of the hotel's business is convention, and the lower levels contain 50,000 square feet of meeting space. But the friendly service, good value, and individual touches such as customized safe keys make up for the hotel's somewhat ungainly size. Rooms are on the large size.

The Adam's Mark's food and beverage operation really shines. The gardenlike Appleby's is several notches above your average coffee shop, with all-you-can-eat meals, 30-foot ziggurat skylights, and local antiques. Lines start forming early at the Marker, an improbable re-creation of French château orangerie, paneled English library, and Western ranch that's somehow relaxing. It seats 150 on three levels, and evenings bring American regional cuisine. Quincy's, with some of the city's best hors d'oeuvres (complimentary until 7pm), offers nightly backgammon, big-band dancing, or jazz. There's no cover Monday to Thursday, $10 Friday and Saturday (open 8pm–2am). Players, a sports bar, serves until 2am.

Amenities include budget car rental in lobby; Barclay unisex hair salon; Squires travel service; extensive sundries shop. There is a excellent health-club operation, open 7am to 10pm, includes indoor and outdoor pools with sunken whirlpool in a comfortable, high-ceilinged room. Two racquetball courts rent for $10 for a 45-minute session. Stairmasters, treadmills, Lifecycles, a rowing machine, and eight-station Nautilus and sauna round out the area.

6 Hostels

Students or travelers on tight budgets might consider staying at one of the area's hostels. A $25 annual membership with **American Youth Hostels,** 733 15th St. NW, No. 840, Washington, DC 20005 (☎ **202/783-6161**), will give you discounts on hostel rates.

Bank Street Hostel. 32 S. Bank St. (between 2nd and 3rd sts. and Market and Chestnut sts.), Philadelphia, PA 19106. ☎ **800/392-4678** or 215/922-0222. 70 beds (shared bathroom). $16 for AYH members; $19 for nonmembers; $2 sheet charge. No credit cards. Check in before 10am or after 4:30pm; curfew at 12:30am. SEPTA station 3 blocks east from 5th and Market. Parking $10 at nearby garages.

This 140-year-old former factory and its two neighbors offer Spartan accommodations for travelers on a budget, in a very convenient part of town. The dormitory-style rooms are spread over four floors of the complex. Extras include free coffee and tea, use of kitchen facilities, a pool table, and a lounge with a large-screen TV. Bathrooms are shared in clean dorm-style areas. Discounts for food and other items at area merchants are available.

Chamounix Hostel Mansion. W. Fairmount Pk., Philadelphia, PA 19131. ☎ **800/ 379-0017** or 215/878-3676. Fax 215/871-4313. $11 AYH members; $14 nonmembers; $2 sheet charge. MC, V. Closed Dec 15–Jan 15. By car: Take I-76 (Schuylkill Expressway) to Exit 33, City Line Ave., turn right (south) on City Ave. to Belmont Ave., left on Belmont to first traffic light at Ford Rd., left on Ford, through stone tunnel to stop sign, then a left onto Chamounix Dr. and follow to the end. By bus: Take SEPTA route 38 from John F. Kennedy Blvd. near City Hall to Ford and Cranston sts. (a 30-min. ride), then walk under the overpass and left onto Chamounix Dr. to the end.

The oldest building offering accommodations in town, this renovated 1802 Quaker farmhouse is also the cheapest. Chamounix Mansion is a Federal-style edifice constructed as a country retreat at what is now the upper end of Fairmount Park. It has 6 dormitory rooms for 44 people, with limited family arrangements, and another 37 spots in a fully renovated adjoining carriage house. Guests have use of the newly renovated self-serve kitchen. Write or call ahead for reservations, since the hostel is often 90% booked in summer by groups of boat crews or foreign students. You can check in daily between 4:30pm and midnight and show an American Youth Hostel card or IYHF card for member rates. Checkout is 8 to 11am. Call **AYH** directly at ☎ **215/925-6004** for information on hostel trips in the area.

Where to Dine

6

Like so many things in Philadelphia, the city's restaurants are a reflection of its 300-year history—from rediscovered colonial favorites, to early 1900s Italian cuisine, to the new spots constantly opening. In a recent *Condé Nast Traveler* readers' poll, seven Philadelphia restaurants were ranked among America's top 50, including Le Bec-Fin and The Fountain at the Four Seasons Hotel. Beyond this top tier, dozens of young culinary entrepreneurs have chosen Philadelphia as their home, reinventing the dining scene and further blurring the line between special-occasion restaurants and more casual, moderately priced bistros.

Compared to New York, Philadelphia restaurants set a higher standard for quality and attention, at prices that are up to one-third less (particularly at the high end).

This chapter unfortunately cannot include many renowned Main Line and other suburban restaurants. If you're heading out that way, many of the volunteers who staff the desk at the **Convention and Visitors Bureau,** 16th Street and Kennedy Boulevard (☎ **215/568-1666**), hail from those parts and have crackerjack knowledge of the dining options there. For Web surfers, the best site I've seen for metro Philadelphia is **www.netscape.digitalcity. com/philadelphia/dining**, which combines its own breezy synopses about 1500 locations with uncensored comments from the public.

One persistent irritant: All those new hotels and restaurants make good service from experienced waitstaff a rare thing.

This chapter will categorize **very expensive** restaurants as those charging $55 or more per person for dinner without wine; **expensive** as $40 to $55 per person; **moderate** as $20 to $40; and **inexpensive** as under $20. Meal tax is 7%, and standard tipping is 15% (the latter is occasionally included on the tab).

Note: For most restaurants I have given only summer hours; you can expect plenty of 9pm (as opposed to 10pm) closings in other seasons.

1 Restaurants by Cuisine

AMERICAN

Azalea (p. 69)
Bookbinder's 15th Street (p. 76)
Circa (p. 80)
City Tavern (p. 69)
Cutters (p. 80)
Friday Saturday Sunday (p. 77)
Jack's Firehouse (p. 78)
Jim's Steaks (p. 91)
Johnny Rockets (p. 73)
Judy's Cafe (p. 71)
Le Bus Main Street (p. 91)
Lee's Hoagies (p. 92)
Marathon on the Square (p. 82)
New Deck Tavern (p. 88)
Old Original Bookbinder's (p. 65)
Painted Parrot Café (p. 72)
Pat's King of the Steaks (p. 92)
Philadelphia Fish & Company
  (p. 72)
Society Hill Hotel (p. 74)
Sonoma (p. 91)
White Dog Cafe (p. 87)
Wichita Steak + Brews (p. 72)

BRAZILIAN

Brasil's (p. 73)

CHINESE

Golden Pond (p. 89)
Harmony Vegetarian Restaurant
  (p. 89)
Imperial Inn (p. 89)
Joe's Peking Duck House (p. 89)
Ray's Coffee Shop (p. 90)
Shiao Lan Kung (p. 90)
Susanna Foo (p. 81)

CONTEMPORARY

Jack's Firehouse (p. 78)

CONTINENTAL

Dickens Inn (p. 70)
Fork (p. 71)
Founders (p. 74)
Friday Saturday Sunday (p. 77)
The Garden (p. 77)

Palladium (p. 86)
The Saloon (p. 85)
Zanzibar Blue (p. 82)

ECLECTIC

Circa (p. 80)
The Restaurant School (p. 88)

ENGLISH

Dickens Inn (p. 70)

CONTINENTAL/FRENCH

Beau Monde (p. 73)
Brasserie Perrier (p. 76)
Ciboulette (p. 76)
Dock Street Brasserie (p. 82)
La Terrasse (p. 86)
Le Bec-Fin (p. 75)

FUSION

Buddakan (p. 68)
Pasion! (p. 78)

GREEK

Zesty's (p. 91)

INDIAN

Café Spice (p. 73)
New Delhi (p. 88)

INTERNATIONAL

The Fountain (p. 74)

IRISH

Downey's Pub (p. 70)
New Deck Tavern (p. 88)

ITALIAN

Bertucci's (p. 82)
La Famiglia (p. 68)
Marra's (p. 85)
Pizzeria Uno (p. 92)
Ralph's Italian Restaurant (p. 85)
Rex Pizza (p. 84)
Ristorante Panorama (p. 72)
The Saloon (p. 85)
Sonoma (p. 91)
Strolli's (p. 86)

Tacconelli's (p. 93)
Toto's (p. 79)
Triangle Tavern (p. 86)
Victor Cafe (p. 85)
Zesty's (p. 91)

JAPANESE
Hikaru (p. 90)
Meiji-en (p. 71)

LATIN AMERICAN
Pasion! (p. 78)

MEDITERRANEAN
Sawan's Mediterranean Bistro
  (p. 84)
Tangerine (p. 69)

MEXICAN
Zocalo (p. 88)

SEAFOOD
Bookbinder's 15th Street (p. 76)
Chart House (p. 68)
DiNardo's Famous Crabs (p. 70)

Old Original Bookbinder's (p. 65)
Philadelphia Fish & Company
  (p. 72)
Sansom Street Oyster House (p. 81)
Striped Bass (p. 79)
Walt's King of the Crabs (p. 74)

STEAK
Chart House (p. 68)
Kansas City Prime (p. 90)
Morton's of Chicago (p. 78)
Ruth's Chris Steak House (p. 80)
Wichita Steak + Brews (p. 72)

THAI
Thai Palace (p. 74)

VEGETARIAN
Harmony Vegetarian Restaurant
  (p. 89)

VIETNAMESE
Capital (p. 89)

2 Historic Area

VERY EXPENSIVE

Old Original Bookbinder's. 125 Walnut St. ☎ **215/925-7027.** www.oldbookbinders.com. Reservations recommended. Main courses $17–$40. AE, DC, MC, V. Mon–Sat 4:30–10pm, Sun 3–9pm. SEAFOOD/AMERICAN.

Old Original Bookbinder's, as the name implies, is an institution. Back when Sam Bookbinder opened this seafood restaurant in 1865, his wife would announce lunch by ringing a bell. The restaurant was considered the *only* place to dine in town for decades. In the 1930s the family sold the restaurant to the Taxins (now operating it for the third generation) and opened a new branch on 15th Street (see Bookbinder's 15th Street, under "Center City," below). Over the years, this Bookbinder's has expanded to encompass almost the entire block across from the Sheraton Society Hill. The complex includes cigar-store Indian sentries, a ship's wheel, and a gift shop that sells pies and cans of the most popular soups—snapper with sherry, New England clam chowder, and Manhattan clam chowder. To the right, the rooms stretch on and on—three bars and seven dining rooms, served by 185 staff members.

Bookbinder's, now open for dinner at breathtaking prices, is renowned for its old-style cuisine such as live-from-Maine lobsters and baked imperial crabmeat, although the new, more casual oyster bar shows a glimmer of the 21st century. The dinner menu and portions are huge, with all sizes and varieties of shellfish, as well as fish, steaks, and veal. The shortcake, strawberry cheesecake, and apple-walnut pie have all won gastronomic awards. The wine list is fairly standard.

Philadelphia Dining

Azalea **47**
Beau Monde **31**
Bertucci's **27**
Bookbinder's 15th Street **23**
Brasil's **42**
Buddakan **46**
Café Spice **50**
Capital **6**
Chart House **37**
Ciboulette **24**
Circa **19**

City Tavern **41**
Cutters **14**
Dickens Inn **39**
DiNardo's Famous Crabs **55**
Dock Street Brasserie **3**
Dock Street Terminal
  Brew Pub **13**
Downey's Pub **36**
Food Court at the Bourse **48**
Food Court at the
  Gallery **12**

Food Court at Liberty
  Place **15**
Fork **54**
The Fountain **2**
Founders **24**
Friday Saturday Sunday **28**
The Garden **30**
Golden Pond **6**
Harmony Vegetarian
  Restaurant **10**
Imperial Inn **11**

Jim's Steaks **33**	Painted Parrot Café **44**	Sawan's Mediterranean
Joe's Peking Duck House **8**	Pasion! **22**	Bistro **16**
Johnny Rockets **32**	Philadelphia Fish &	Shiao Lan Kung **7**
Judy's Cafe **34**	Company **43**	Society Hill Hotel **45**
La Famiglia **51**	Pizzeria Uno **33**	Striped Bass **21**
Le Bec-Fin **18**	Ray's Coffee Shop **9**	Susanna Foo **20**
Marathon on the Square **29**	Reading Terminal Market **5**	Tangerine **53**
Meiji-en **56**	Ristorante Panorama **52**	Thai Palace **35**
Morton's of Chicago **4**	Ruth's Chris Steak House **25**	Toto's **26**
Old Original	Sansom Street Oyster	Wichita Steak & Brews **49**
Bookbinder's **40**	House **17**	Zanzibar Blue **19**

EXPENSIVE

✪ **Buddakan.** 325 Chestnut St. ☎ **215/574-9440.** Reservations recommended. AE, DC, DISC, MC, V. Main courses $16–$26.50. Lunch $11–$19. Mon–Wed 11:30am–2pm and 5–11pm, Thurs–Fri 11:30am–2pm and 5–midnight, Sat 5–midnight, Sun 5–11pm. FUSION.

The people who help manage total environments have started to work on restaurants in a big way—and we're not talking about Chuck E. Cheese anymore, but about million-dollar treatments combined with serious cuisine. There's one Philadelphian identified with the "theme restaurant": His name is Stephen Starr, and Buddakan has captured the prize place of the genre since it opened in August 1998, followed by Blue Angel a few blocks away, Pod in West Philadelphia, and Alma de Cuba coming in 2001. What opened? Only a shimmering waterfall; Japanese river stones; luminescent walls; and a gold-coated, candle-bedecked, 10-foot Buddha who dominates the main room and the 22-seat onyx-topped community table directly under its bellybutton. It's a noisy scene, but a scene with inventive fine fare such as Indonesian jumbo shrimp, wasabi-crusted filet mignon, and sesame crusted tuna. The energy level and chance of celebrity spotting are consistently high, and the bar scene is cool and trendy until 2am nightly. The staff sometimes takes accolades from *Food & Wine* and *Travel & Leisure* too seriously.

✪ **Chart House.** 555 S. Columbus Blvd. (formerly Delaware Ave.) at Penn's Landing. ☎ **215/625-8383.** Reservations recommended. Main courses $18–$38. Sun fixed-price brunch $22. Children's menu available. AE, DC, MC, V. Mon–Thurs 5–10pm, Fri 5–11pm, Sat 4pm–midnight, Sun 4–10pm; brunch Sun 10:30am–2pm. STEAK/SEAFOOD.

The busiest restaurant in all Philadelphia has to be the Chart House, a veritable 3-story convention center right on the Delaware River with spectacular views and a tableside waterfall to boot. You may not love everything about it—expect a spirited crowd and frequent birthday celebrations. Note that the Chart House chain has been tampering with its successful formula of reasonably priced dinners with soup, fresh molasses or sourdough bread, and an unlimited salad bar; as of 2000, the salad bar and oyster bar are gone, prices are up, and all side orders are a la carte. Let's hope they respond to the disappointed recent customer. For now, stick with the New England clam chowder; prime rib or a steak of halibut or tuna; and one of their signature desserts, such as mud pie, Key lime pie, cheesecake, and ice cream.

✪ **La Famiglia.** 8 S. Front St. ☎ **215/922-2803.** Reservations required. Main courses $23–$35; lunch $20 menu. AE, CB, DC, MC, V. Tues–Fri noon–2pm and 5:30–9:30pm, Sat 5:30–10pm, Sun 5:30–9pm. ITALIAN.

The name La Famiglia refers to both the proprietors and the clientele of this refined Italian restaurant, chosen some time ago as one of the 25 best Italian restaurants in the country by *Bon Appétit* magazine and with many awards since. The Neapolitan Sena family aims for elegant dining, service, and presentation; their success here has spawned Penn's View Inn and its Ristorante Panorama (see below).

The restaurant seats 60 in a private, warm setting of hand-hammered Venetian chandeliers, majolica tiles, and fresh flowers. The chefs at La Famiglia make most of their own pasta, so you might concentrate on such dishes as *gnocchi al basilico,* which adds basil and sweet red pepper sauce to the potato pasta. There's a choice of five or six vegetables with meals; the marinated string beans and zucchini with pepper have never failed to please. The wine cellar is legendary. For dessert, try a *mille foglie,* the Italian version of the napoleon, or the profiteroles in chocolate sauce, accompanied by one of the grappas over the fireplace. People often remain here well after the closing hour, lingering over sambuca while arias play in the background. People also rave about the $19.99 full lunch special.

Tangerine. 232 Market St. ☎ **215/627-5116.** Reservations strongly recommended. Main courses $16–$28. AE, MC, V. Sun–Thurs 5–11pm, Fri–Sat 5–12pm. MEDITERRANEAN.

The theme of this Stephen Starr extravaganza is Morocco, or the Morocco of Western dreams, and Tangerine is racking up the "most trendy restaurant" awards while maintaining a solid and inventive menu of riffs off Moroccan classics. In design terms, it's a brilliant division of a long, narrow space into chambers punctuated by curtains, extensive and eclectic lighting, and wild, exotic decor. They are connected by a corridor festooned with hundreds of inset votive lights, and by a cheerful and knowledgeable staff.

To do it right, start with one of the specialty cocktails; the signature drink combines tangerine puree with vodka and club soda. The lower end of the menu offers couscous and wonderful tagine stews; the lamb and honey version is almost black with caramelizing. A pan-seared red snapper comes with spinach dumplings and toasted pepper sauce. Portions and prices are generous and can be shared. The austere, black-lighted bar area in front gets packed and noisy late at night.

MODERATE

Azalea. Omni Hotel, 4th and Chestnut sts. ☎ **215/931-4260.** Reservations recommended. Main courses $14–$28; breakfast $7–$14; lunch $9.50–$16. Fixed-price 5-course dinner $32. AE, DC, MC, V. Mon–Fri 6:30–10:30am, 11am–2pm, and 5:30–10pm (Fri until 11pm), Sat–Sun 7am–1pm and 5:30–10pm (Sat until 11pm). AMERICAN.

For imaginative interpretations of American cuisine, including local dishes, this is one of the best spots in town, with a treetop view of Independence National Historical Park. The French Provincial armchairs, arched windows, and chandeliers don't read American—but they are.

Chef Gary Flora's selections include such traditional Pennsylvania Dutch specialties as chicken-corn soup with saffron and apple fritters, shad in sorrel sauce (what saved the troops at Valley Forge), and pheasant potpie. The menus change seasonally, with surprising influences like the Chilean sea bass with lobster Bolognese sauce. Kennett Square mushrooms, Lancaster County persimmons and quinces, and elderberry preserve all make appearances. Given the way prices can add up, I'd recommend the fixed-price dinner. Desserts offer a choice of five freshly made sorbets or an old-fashioned apple-and-sour-cherry pie.

✪ **City Tavern.** 138 S. 2nd St., near Walnut St. ☎ **215/413-1443.** Reservations recommended. Main courses $18–$26; lunch $9.75–$17. AE, CB, DC, DISC, MC, V. 11:30am–9pm daily. AMERICAN.

If the hunger to relive those good old 1780s overcomes you in Independence Park, there's at least one authentic restaurant that will let you use that newfangled credit card to pay for colonial fare: City Tavern—the same tavern that members of the Constitutional Convention used as coffee shop, ballroom, and club some 200 years ago. The U.S. government now owns the building, which is operated by a concessionaire, Walter Staib. He's pumped in $500,000 to completely renovate and open up 10 dining areas plus garden and veranda, all serviced by a discreet state-of-the-art kitchen (well, almost—true to its roots, the only freezer space is for the ice cream!). Chef Peter Chan puts out menus tending toward the meaty—roast duckling, tenderloin tips, and a bow toward turkey potpie. The taproom features microbrewery and custom beers and ales, and the "shrub" (a kind of punch) also packs a wallop. Service can be undistinguished.

✪ **Dickens Inn.** 421 S. 2nd St. ☎ **215/928-9307.** Reservations recommended. Main courses $14–$25; lunch $5–$10. AE, DC, DISC, MC, V. Tues–Sun 11:30am–3pm, Tues–Sat 5:30–10pm, Sun 3–9pm; brunch Sun 11:30am–3pm. Pub only Mon 4–10pm. ENGLISH/ CONTINENTAL.

This three-story Federal town house on Head House Square has proved to have real staying power. Opened in 1980 by the owners of the famous Dickens Inn by the Tower of London, the American version simulates a friendly English pub and restaurant.

The atmosphere is all paneling, wooden tables, exposed beams, and frosted-glass lamps; lithographs of scenes from Dickens novels and framed Dickensiana adorn the walls. Main courses are extremely generous, tasty, and attractive, served on large speckled crockery. Chef Jeff Thomas offers traditional beef Wellington and prime rib with Yorkshire pudding along with lighter dishes. The seafood choices, displayed raw on a cart, include bay scallops poached with basil, tomatoes, and Muscadet. To finish, select a dessert from the restaurant's own bakery or sample the English Stilton cheese with fresh fruit. Lunch is a less ambitious affair, with Cornish pasty (traditional pastry filled with lamb, carrots, and potatoes and flavored with fresh herbs), shepherd's pie, trout fillet, and a wild-mushroom-and-vegetable crepe. There are four bars, with 14 English imported beers.

✪ **DiNardo's Famous Crabs.** 312 Race St. ☎ **215/925-5115.** Reservations required for six or more. Crabs $3–$5 each; other main courses $15–$25; lunch $6–$10. AE, DC, V. Mon–Thurs 11am–10pm, Fri–Sat 11am–11pm, Sun 3–9pm. SEAFOOD.

DiNardo's Famous Crabs, celebrating its 25th anniversary in 2001, springs to mind as the best moderately priced spot in the area around the Betsy Ross House and Elfreth's Alley. The door nearest 3rd Street is the real entrance. Only the DiNardo family mixes the secret crab seasonings.

DiNardo's is notable for three things: its site, its reasonable prices, and the staggering collection of fish lures. The building was an inn for Tory soldiers in 1776 and would later serve as an Underground Railroad stop and Prohibition-era brothel.

Prime catches from the Gulf of Mexico are flown up daily to the restaurant, where experienced hands season the crabs with the house blend of 24 spices and steam them to perfection. If you're not in a crabby mood, there are at least 30 other succulent items on the menu, from raw-bar oysters to seafood platters. Monday is all-you-can-eat crab night. Service is especially patient with families with small kids.

Downey's Pub. Northwest corner of Front and South sts. ☎ **215/629-9500.** Reservations recommended. Main courses $7–$20; lunch $8–$13. AE, DC, DISC, MC, V. Mon–Fri 11:30am–4pm and 4:30–10:45pm, Sat 11:30am–4pm and 4:30pm–12:30am, Sun 10:30am– 4pm and 4:30–9:45pm. IRISH.

Two hundred fifty years ago, Front Street from Race to Fitzwater streets was a jumble of docks, shops, and public houses that reminded English and Irish seamen of home. Downey's Pub has succumbed to such modern blandishments as electricity and quiche, but it's still a place any Irish person would be proud to frequent. Much of the ground floor was lifted from a Dublin bank built in 1903; the upstairs is from a pub in Cork City, and don't expect spotlessness.

In summer, cafe tables grace both the South Street and the river patios. Upstairs, with its wraparound deck, it's tonier still. Lunch and dinner retain some Irish dishes with American embellishments, along with Italian and lighter fare. The soups are strong; roast beef and turkey are carved on your order; and the fish of the day, done any way you like, is served with a fresh vegetable. But most popular are the crab cakes.

Live music is a staple of Downey's, both at the weekend brunches and in the upstairs Piano Bar on Friday and Saturday 8pm to 1am.

✪ **Fork.** 306 Market St. ☎ **215/625-9425.** Reservations recommended. Main courses $13–$18.50; lunch $6.50–$10. AE, CB, DC, DISC, MC, V. Mon–Wed 11:30am–2:30pm and 5–10:30pm, Thurs–Fri 11:30am–2:30pm and 5–11:30pm, Sat 5–11:30pm, Sun 11:30am–2:30pm and 5–10:30pm. Midday menu 2:30–5pm daily. CONTINENTAL.

Fork is possibly the best example in Old City of an affordable, stylish bistro, fairly priced and centrally located. Since it seats only 68 and is in the flush of a wave of rave reviews, make sure you call beforehand to get a table. The restaurant features a hip circular bar, open rear kitchen, supersize banquette walls, and glorious lighting. Most of the ingredients come from organic farms and Amish purveyors; the menu is changed and reprinted daily. New executive chef Dave Ballentine, with experience from Odeon and La Terrasse, will incorporate more classic French techniques in the service of an American bistro cuisine; look for pan-seared duck breast with ginger-anise sauce and mashed sweet potatoes, for example.

Judy's Cafe. 3rd and Bainbridge sts. ☎ **215/928-1968.** Reservations recommended for parties of 4 or more. Main courses $12–$21. AE, CB, DC, MC, V. Mon–Thurs 5:30–11pm, Fri–Sat 5:30pm–midnight, Sun 10:30am–3pm and 5:30–10pm. AMERICAN.

An agreeable bistro that's long outgrown its countercultural beginnings, Judy's is one of the finest examples of the South Street renaissance. Judy herself is gone, but owner Eileen Plato maintains a neighborhood feeling, though it's not really a family place. The regulars banter with the waiters, who dine here on their nights off, and the well-stocked bar gets an assortment of gays and straights settling into a relaxing ambience.

The main courses are eclectic. A Monday-to-Thursday special includes your choice of stir-fried duck, lamb stew, or the catch of the day, with soup and coffee. Whatever seafood is on the menu will undoubtedly be fresh. The very, very chocolate cake is almost fudgelike; the mocha or amaretto cheesecakes are likewise superb. *Note:* Local papers often advertise two-for-one weeknight specials.

Meiji-en. Upstairs at Pier 19, on the Delaware River at Callowhill St., 4 blocks north of the Benjamin Franklin Bridge. ☎ **215/592-7100.** Reservations recommended. Main courses $14–$28. AE, DC, DISC, MC, V. Mon–Fri 11:30am–2:30pm, Mon–Thurs 5–9:30pm, Fri–Sat 5–11pm, Sun 5–9pm; brunch Sun 10:30am–2:30pm. JAPANESE.

Meiji-en is an indoor theme park, with separate areas for sushi, tempura, teppanyaki (or stove top at table), and regular table seating (the latter two feature river views to the east), as well as a bar with live jazz Friday and Saturday and a lavish jazz brunch Sunday. There's something for everyone here, from romantic couple to large family. Everything is scrupulously clean, though I've heard mixed messages in the past year about the service and lag time for meals. The decor features lots of hanging rice-paper globes, blond-wood screens and seats, and comfortable black-and-red cushions.

Many of Meiji-en's dishes have the same basic ingredients—fillets of fish and chicken—prepared in different ways, from boiled to quick grilled to diced in gyoza dumplings. Many dishes are marked as especially health conscious. The teppanyaki dishes are cheapest and most fun; your group will sit around horseshoe-shaped tables with granite-and-steel stovetops while you're served seared meat and greens. If you're ordering regular service, expect beautifully presented fish steaks or marbled beef.

Be sure to call ahead to request a water view, and don't be deterred by the slightly forbidding Delaware Avenue approach. Valet parking nearby is $6.

☼ Painted Parrot Café. 211 Chestnut St. ☎ **215/922-5971.** Reservations recommended. Main courses $12.50–$17.50; lunch $5–$7.50. AE, DC, DISC, MC, V. Tues–Fri 11:30am–2:30pm, Sat–Sun noon–3pm, Tues–Thurs 5–10pm, Fri–Sat 5–11pm, Sun 5–10pm; dessert menu until midnight. AMERICAN.

There's something delectable about a restaurant where the dessert choices outnumber the entrees. But beyond the signature desserts, this cafe offers innovative and reasonable American-based fusion meals. You can basically get anything all day long, in a pretty but not precious space steps away from Independence Historical National Park.

Lunch brings standards like turkey and wild mushroom burgers and a grilled salmon club. Evening dishes center on imaginative pastas or simple roasted or grilled chicken or fish. Presentations are colorful, and the soup of the day is always superb. Most Philadelphians associate this spot with the amazing $13.95 fixed-price dinner on Tuesday night and the delightful $5 desserts—showcased in an all-you-can-savor $6.95 dessert buffet on Wednesday starting at 5pm. Fudge torte, mousse torte, old-fashioned apple pie—the list goes up to 17 most nights, including a token low-fat choice. The La Colombe roast coffee is excellent day and night.

Philadelphia Fish & Company. 207 Chestnut St. ☎ **215/625-8605.** Reservations recommended. Main courses $17–$24; lunch $7–$10. AE, DC, MC, V. Mon–Thurs 11:30am–10pm, Fri 11:30am–4pm and 5pm–midnight, Sat noon–3pm and 5pm–midnight, Sun 3–10pm. SEAFOOD/AMERICAN.

It's inevitable that you'll pass Philadelphia Fish & Company, given its location next to Independence National Historical Park. The restaurant offers a selection of fresh fish that's served with warmth and flair: Roasted sea bass, crab-pesto pancakes and vegetable are typical menu choices. The $8.25 executive lunch is a great deal: a cup of soup, the fish special, vegetable, green salad, and beverage. And the $5 dinner special at the bar (often a blackened tilapia over cheddar grits) was rated the best tavern deal in the city by *Philadelphia* magazine. The wine list, skewed toward whites, is of a good quality and very reasonable for Philadelphia. There's outdoor dining when seasonable.

☼ Ristorante Panorama. Front and Market sts. ☎ **215/922-7800.** Reservations recommended. Main courses $16.50–$24. AE, CB, DC, MC, V. Daily noon–midnight, with dinner service Mon–Thurs noon–2pm and 5:30–10pm, Fri noon–2pm and 5:30–11pm, Sat 5:30–11pm, Sun 5–9pm. ITALIAN.

Although the Ristorante Panorama is on the waterfront, its "view" is a colorful mural of the Italian countryside, and the vast majority of the staff is from the Naples area. A wonderful, choice list of lighter Italian dishes composes the menu. Pasta, salads, and fish predominate, with a few veal and beef favorites. The bread is served not with butter, but with a tiny bowl of pesto. Favorite appetizers are pasta with garlic, prosciutto, and topped with cheese, all beautifully arranged; and croquettes of shrimp and lamb served on a bed of arugula. Fish courses are usually grilled and lightly seasoned with garlic and tomatoes. The tiramisu, with its triple-cream mascarpone cheese drizzled with chocolate, needs either an espresso or a dessert wine as an accompaniment.

Panorama is also the city's best wine bar, with 120 wines (not just Italian) served to a sophisticated, lively crowd. You can order "flights," or a series of 3.5-ounce glasses of complementary wines.

Wichita Steak + Brews. 22 S. 3rd St. ☎ **215/627-4825.** Reservations recommended for dinner. Main courses $10–$16. AE, DC, MC, V. Mon–Fri 11:30am–11:30pm, Sat–Sun 11:30am–12:30am. Bar and dancing Thurs–Sat until 2am. AMERICAN/STEAKHOUSE.

David Cohen has transformed this 1837 Greek Revival church into a relaxed and improbably good combination of restaurant, bar, and nightclub, just steps from Franklin Court. The first-floor restaurant has been reborn as a self-conscious steakhouse, billed as "the home of the $10 steak." The menu now concentrates on cheesesteaks at the low end and filet mignon at the high. Original emphasis on microbrews has been succeeded by a choice of draft beers. Chef Rowland Butler also serves simple, quickly braised or baked fish and poultry. If you come for dinner, you can stay for the dancing upstairs Thursday to Saturday ($5–$10 cover charge; see chapter 10).

INEXPENSIVE

Café Spice. 35 S. 2nd St. ☎ **215/627-6273.** Main courses $8–$14. AE, DC, DISC, MC, V. Mon–Thurs 11:30am–3pm and 5pm–10:30pm, Fri 11:30am–3pm and 5pm–11:30pm, Sat 11:30am–4pm and 5pm–11:30pm, Sun 11:30am–4pm and 5–10:30pm. INDIAN.

There may be more style than substance when it comes to putting cool into curry. But Café Spice, opened in April 2000 by Sushil Malhotra (owner of Dawat in New York), gives at least a taste of what a contemporary Indian restaurant could look like, while the menu tours the subcontinent in a fairly standard way. The interior features textured beige walls with recessed display boxes for spice jars, hanging lanterns and cut-out windows—very dramatic and soothing at once. All main courses include fragrant basmati rice, nan bread, and several vegetable dishes; I find the vegetarian entrees most satisfying for their size and complex textures. And don't worry about the hours; the doors stay open until 2am most nights.

✪ **Beau Monde.** 624 S. 6th St. (at the corner of Bainbridge, 1 block south of South St.). ☎ **215/592-0656.** Reservations accepted for six or more. Crepe main courses $2.50–$9.75. AE, DC, DISC, MC, V. Tues–Fri noon–11pm, Sat–Sun 10am–11pm. FRENCH.

Americans love calzones, pita sandwiches, and dough wraps of all kinds—so why not these Breton pancakes? This pretty (but noisy) 65-seat restaurant prepares two kinds: a savory, made with buckwheat flour and filled with anything from herbs to roasted chicken or shrimp; and a sweet wheat flour dessert crepe, filled with sliced fruits or berries. Appetizers and salads are also offered, but they don't hit the spot as nicely.

✪ **Brasil's.** 112 Chestnut St. ☎ **215/413-1700.** Reservations recommended. Main courses $8–$14. AE, DC, MC, V. Tues–Thurs 5–10pm, Fri–Sat 5–11pm, Sun 5–9pm. BRAZILIAN.

This warm, welcoming bistro in the heart of the historic district has gotten positive press for all-you-can-eat feijoada Sundays and churrasco Tuesdays. The former is the Brazilian national stew of black beans, sausage, seafood, and orange garnish; the latter a spicy grilled beef. There are plenty more standard meat and poultry offerings, along with live jazz on Sunday. I can't say enough about the spirited salsa dancing upstairs on weekends—great crowd, great music.

Johnny Rockets. 443 South St. ☎ **215/829-9222.** Sandwiches and burgers $3–$5. AE, DC, DISC, MC, V. Sun–Wed 11am–11pm, Thurs 11am–midnight, Fri–Sat 11am–1am. AMERICAN.

Johnny Rockets, a national chain, is a harmless enough place—retro for the kids and comforting for their parents. Clean red-and-white booths surround an open grill. Burgers and sandwiches predominate, along with fries, onion rings, excellent malts and milkshakes, gooey desserts and pies—it's all here. Every so often, the staff even bursts into song.

Society Hill Hotel. 301 Chestnut St. ☎ **215/925-1919.** Reservations not required. Main courses $7–$15. AE, CB, DC, MC, V. Daily 11am–1am; brunch Sun 11am–1:30pm. AMERICAN.

This is a very pleasant, lively spot opposite Independence National Historical Park, with outdoor bar service during the summer. The light menu includes burgers and club sandwiches, along with omelettes and salads. Ted Gerike makes this one of the city's top piano bars.

Thai Palace. 117 South St. ☎ **215/925-2764.** Reservations recommended. Main courses $8–$15. AE, DC, MC, V. Daily 5:30–10pm. THAI.

Thai Palace boasts all the sweet and hot pastes and spices you'd expect. It isn't much to look at, so start right in on the satay, a highly spiced and marinated meat kebab. For something hot that doesn't sear the taste buds, try the chicken ka prow (chicken with fried hot pepper) cooked in an unusual basil-and-lemongrass sauce. The desserts here are not the strong point. If you're drinking, it's BYOB.

Walt's King of the Crabs. 804–806 S. 2nd St. ☎ **215/339-9124.** Reservations not accepted. Main courses $8–$14. No credit cards. Mon–Sat 11am–12:30am, Sun 2–10pm. SEAFOOD.

Walt's makes no bones (or shells?) about the house specialty, and this unpretentious little storefront hangout has acquired a fanatical following. Owner Ted Zalewski is an extremely nice, beefy guy who cares about serving lots of people well. Unless your taste includes both bizarre ocean-scene murals and Patti Page records, ignore the ambience and dig in.

The platters include truly tasty coleslaw and french-fried potatoes. The deviled crab comes in a great minced patty, fried but never greasy. Last I checked, chicken lobsters were offered for $12 each. The house specialty features two jumbo shrimp stuffed with crabmeat. Draft beer costs $1 a glass or $6 a pitcher. Take-out costs 25¢ extra. Call ahead to find out about waiting time, because the lines in summer and on weekends are fierce.

3 Center City

VERY EXPENSIVE

✪ **Founders.** Broad and Walnut sts. ☎ **215/893-1776.** Reservations recommended. Main courses $26–$34. AE, CB, DC, MC, V. Mon–Sat 7–10am, 11:30am–2:30pm, and 5:30–10pm (Sat until 10:30pm), Sun 5:30–9pm. CONTINENTAL.

Founders is the keystone of the Bellevue Hotel's restaurants, and its 19th-floor location makes it attractive for fans of views, as well as romantic dinner and dancing on weekends. The elegant dining room features arched windows, flourishes and swags of draperies, and plush armchairs. It's another winner in the 1994 *Condé Nast Traveler*'s readers' poll for America's top 50 restaurants. The "founders" are the statues of Philadelphia luminaries that surround you. At these prices, you will get fine preparations and large portions of dishes such as filet of beef with marrow, chateaubriand for two, and baked chicken breast with berries.

✪ **The Fountain.** The Four Seasons Hotel, 1 Logan Sq. (between 18th St. and the Franklin Pkwy.). ☎ **215/963-1500.** Reservations required. Main courses $18–$32; lunch $9–$20; fixed-price four-course menu $54. AE, CB, DC, MC, V. Mon–Fri 6:30am–2:30pm and 6–11pm, Sat–Sun 7am–11am, 11:30am–2:30pm, and 6–11pm; brunch Sun 10am–2:30pm. Fri–Sat dessert and dancing in Swann Lounge. INTERNATIONAL.

The Fountain and Le Bec-Fin (see below) are Philadelphia's two most nationally acclaimed restaurants. *Food & Wine* magazine chose the Fountain as one of

America's top 25. The views partially explain why, with unparalleled plumes from the Swann Fountain in Logan Circle on one side, and the hotel's own courtyard cascade on the other. The cuisine, under legend Jean Marie Lacroix (who has spread the wealth by mentoring many chefs at other listings here!), is expertly prepared and quietly served in expansive surroundings. If you're pulling out all the stops, it's $200 a couple without wine—but worth every penny.

The menu is complicated and understated, and my recommendation is to take the $54 fixed-price menu rather than pay 35% more for à la carte. After a complimentary canapé or two, you might have fillet of skate with capers, a mesclun salad with pear and purple potato, sautéed lamb tenderloin and veal kidneys with mustard-seed sauce, a cheese tray, and fresh fruit pastry. A favorite à la carte starter is the pirogi of foie gras in Savoy cabbage with truffles. The main courses include salmon fillet and pheasant with bacon and more Savoy cabbage.

✪ **Le Bec-Fin.** 1523 Walnut St. ☎ **215/567-1000.** Reservations required a week ahead for weeknights, months ahead for Fri–Sat. Fixed-price lunch $38; fixed-price dinner $120. AE, DC, MC, V. Lunch seatings Mon–Fri at 11:30am and 2pm; dinner seatings Mon–Thurs at 6 and 9pm, Fri–Sat at 6 and 9:30pm. Bar Lyonnais downstairs serves food and drink Mon–Fri 11:30am–midnight, Sat 6pm–1am. FRENCH.

Le Bec-Fin—can it really be 30 years old?—is unquestionably the best restaurant in Philadelphia and certainly one of the top 10 in the country. Owner/chef Georges Perrier hails from Lyon, France's gastronomic capital, and commands the respect of restaurateurs on two continents for his culinary accomplishments.

Le Bec-Fin looks exactly as it should: elegant and comfortable, with deep red silk over acoustic panels. Candles set in mirrored wall brackets add to the warm lighting—seeing your food can only enhance your meal. The table settings include bountiful bouquets, Christofle silver, and the same 18th-century Limoges pattern Paul Bocuse uses in his Lyon restaurant. In addition to the main dining room, the Blue Room (seating 25) may be reserved for private parties. As review after review has noted, it is virtually impossible not to enjoy yourself here, even before your meal begins.

With leisurely timing, an evening at Le Bec-Fin waltzes through hors d'oeuvres, a fish course, a main course, a salad, cheese, a dessert, and coffee with petits fours. Since most of the menu changes seasonally—and your special orders are welcome as well—dishes listed are illustrative. A roast lobster in a butter sauce infused with black truffles is unbelievably flavorful. The terrine of three fish contains a layer of turbot mousse, then a layer of salmon mousse, then one of sole mousse, each with its own dressing; the total effect, with shallots, couldn't be more subtle. The escargots au champagne are renowned as a first course, as the garlic butter also includes a touch of chartreuse and hazelnuts.

The main dishes give you the opportunity to try some rarities—pheasant, venison, and pigeon. The last (stuffed with goose liver, leeks, and mushrooms) comes in a truffle sauce. So does the mouth-watering dish of four fillets of venison, covered by a thick milk-mustard sauce. The desserts become grand opera, with trays, tables, and ice cream and sherbets (in the little aluminum canisters they were churned in) zooming from guest to guest. With the addition of pastry chef Bobby Bennett, the dessert tray looks and tastes like Dante's Paradiso, especially the 18-inch-high Mont Blanc with sides of sheet chocolate. The finest coffee in the city, served in Villeroy & Boch flowered china, makes those petits fours you really don't need easier to take. Cigars, cordials, liqueurs, and marcs and other fortified spirits gild the lily.

The basement **Le Bar Lyonnais** offers more affordable snacking and champagne toasts. Open until midnight, it has only four tables and bar stools, but trompe l'oeil pilasters and paisley wallpaper give it a bigger feel. Expect to spend about $10 a nibble and $7 for a glass of house wine. The later it gets, the more likely dishes from upstairs are to arrive—and M. Perrier himself, for that matter. In 1997, Perrier opened the more relaxed **Brasserie Perrier** down the street (see below), and has just brought the spirit of Provence to the Main Line with **Le Mas Perrier** (☎ **610/ 964-2588**), at 503 W. Lancaster Ave. in Wayne.

EXPENSIVE

Bookbinder's 15th Street. 215 S. 15th St. ☎ **215/545-1137.** Reservations recommended for Fri lunch and for dinner. Main courses $16–$32; lunch $6–$15. Occasional fixed-price dinners from $28. AE, CB, DC, DISC, MC, V. Mon–Fri 11:30am–10pm, Sat 4–11pm, Sun 3–10pm. Dinner served from 3pm. AMERICAN/SEAFOOD.

A trip to Philadelphia once automatically meant a seafood meal at Old Original Bookbinder's (see "Historic Area," above). But the restaurant has long since expanded and moved downtown. The 15th Street Booky's is less self-congratulatory and has its own solid clientele, though some feel it's coasting on its reputation. The high ceilings leave plenty of room for the mounted fish, nautical chandeliers, oak paneling, and captain's chairs. The heavy wood tables hold goblets of croutons for chowder.

You might start with the famous snapper soup laced with sherry. All the seafood but the smoked fish comes from Chesapeake Bay—the smelts get especially high marks for freshness. You can get that basket of clams you've been pining for, or a large box of Chincoteague oysters; the lobsters start at $23. The mussels in red sauce are probably the best known among Philadelphians. To adapt to modern tastes, more sauces are being served on the side and new imports, such as mako shark, have been added.

Brasserie Perrier. 1619 Walnut St. ☎ **215/568-3000.** Reservations usually required. Main courses $18–$25, lunch $9–$16 or prix-fixe 3-course for $26. AE, DC, MC, V. Mon–Sat 11:30am–2:30pm and 5:30–11pm, Fri–Sat 5:30–11:30pm, Sun 5–9pm. FRENCH.

Proprietor George Perrier rules the food scene in Philadelphia, so it was big news when he opened this brasserie in 1997, especially with top chef Francesco Martorella as sidekick. It's more a French restaurant with international influence than a bistro, although there's a brasserie dining menu throughout the day alongside scheduled lunch and dinner menus; if you like a place that aims to make a serious stir, with prices to match, this is a good choice. The art deco–style venue is decorated with plush banquettes, silver leaf ceilings, light cherry wood and dramatic lighting. It's built around a retro-cubist version of Marcel Duchamp's *Nude Descending a Staircase,* hanging across town at the Art Museum. Don't expect the hearty or casual here—we're talking exquisite yellowfin sashimi with wasabi-spiced greens; or a crispy black bass with Asian sticky rice, Chinese eggplant, and ginger sauce. The wine list features small, quality-oriented French, Italian, and U.S. varietals in the $26 to $65 range, with specially priced gems from southern France.

✪ **Ciboulette.** 200 S. Broad St. ☎ **215/790-1210.** Reservations recommended. Tasting menus $65 and $45. AE, DC, MC, V. Mon–Thurs 5:30–9pm, Fri–Sat 5:30–10:30pm. FRENCH.

Ciboulette, French for "chives," has been applauded by *Gourmet* magazine's readers as a "Top 10 Table" in town and by *Esquire* and *Travel/Holiday* for its elegance and service.

You'll enter a suite of French Renaissance rooms with an ornate fireplace, marble columns, and gilt-framed ormolu mirrors. Proprietor Bruce Lim walks a tightrope between high quality and affordable prices; he tinkers with the menu pricing, and right now is offering two prix-fixe tasting menus as well as a 3-course pretheater deal for $29, although this may change in 2001. You have a choice of up to eight dishes per course. Virtually no butter or cream is used, just fresh reductions and mostly organic meat and poultry, vegetables, and herbs. Look for tender, seared slices of squab or duck, or sea bass steamed in olive oil with organic artichokes and fennel. A dessert cart contains over twenty choices, and the lemon galette and crème brûlée are flawless. A nice surprise is the affordability of the interesting wine list.

Friday Saturday Sunday. 261 S. 21st St. (between Locust and Spruce sts.). ☎ **215/546-4232.** Reservations accepted. Main courses $14.50–$23.50. AE, CB, DC, MC, V. Tues–Fri 11:30am–2:30pm, Mon–Sat 5:30–10:30pm, Sun 5–10pm. AMERICAN/CONTINENTAL.

There's a lot to be said for a restaurant that installed a window on Rittenhouse Street for the kitchen staff. A romantic survivor of Philadelphia's early restaurant renaissance, Friday Saturday Sunday has adapted to the times by offering informality, a renovated bar upstairs, and a relaxed, confident cuisine. It's a bargain for the location, too, and the markup for the wine list is the lowest in town.

Recently renovated, Friday Saturday Sunday is classy but unostentatious: The cutlery and china don't match, flowers are rare, and the menu is a wall-mounted slate board. Pin lights frame a row of rectangular mirrors set in wood paneling. An aquarium bubbles behind the upstairs Tank Bar. Dress is everything from jeans to suits, and the service is vigilant but hands-off.

Try the fairly spicy Thai green salad with chicken breast, served over a marinade of soy, honey, and sesame; or a colorful Szechuan salad with sweet red peppers and wok-fried beef slivers. Portions of fish, such as grilled salmon with a creamy side of minced artichokes and red peppers, are enormous. You're advised to split an appetizer and even a dessert between two. The double-baked and mildly curried half duck is excellent. The wine card lists about 30 vintages. The desserts change often.

☼ The Garden. 1617 Spruce St., near Rittenhouse Square. ☎ **215/546-4455.** Reservations recommended. Main courses $15–$26; lunch $11–$23. AE, CB, DC, MC, V. Mon–Fri 11:30am–1:45pm and 2:30–5:30pm, Mon–Sat 5:30–10pm. Closed Sat–Sun July–Aug. CONTINENTAL.

Kathleen Mulhern's place captures the city's understated style better than any other spot I know. In September 1998, *Bon Appétit* magazine saluted it as one of America's "Top 10 Tried & True Restaurants." In this former music academy, the tables and bar are antiques, set off by the many 19th-century prints of fruit and animals. The three softly lit dining areas—Swan Room, with wooden decoys; Print Room, a floral back parlor; and the Main Room, a former concert hall with practice rooms—can become noisy when crowded. The gaily bedecked back garden is a fragrant and spectacularly quiet enclave; weather permitting, it's the preferable dining locale, either for candlelit evenings or for sun-shaded luncheons. Potted flowers vie with the yellow umbrellas for brightness. It's a fascinating wine list, with 20 Cruvinet choices by the glass.

The restaurant specializes in high-quality, comfortable dishes like breaded Dover sole, calves' liver with fried potato and shallots, and chateaubriand with Roquefort sauce. Spinach gnocchi made by "Aunt Diddy" is feather light with a sweet Gorgonzola sauce. All main courses include vegetables. The French chocolate cake has been called the best dessert in Philadelphia by *Food & Wine,* and the chocolate sampler plate is also frighteningly good. The Garden offers valet parking and reduced rates in a nearby garage.

✪ **Jack's Firehouse.** 2130 Fairmount Ave. ☎ **215/232-9000.** Reservations recommended. Main courses $17–$23; fixed-price menus $45 and $52. Bar service available; sandwiches from $7. AE, DC, MC, V. Mon–Sat 11:30am–10:30pm, brunch Sun 11am–3pm. Bar open nightly until 2am. CONTEMPORARY/AMERICAN.

This is one of the most imaginative, and hotly debated, restaurants now operating in Philadelphia. Chef Jack McDavid has taken a turn-of-the-century firehouse and incorporated contemporary (and rotating) art by Philadelphia artists, a beautiful rowing shell, and a glass-and-walnut island bar. He rode a cuisine featuring dramatic juxtapositions of American ingredients and flavors to his own celebrity, but service and food took a dive by 1999. I'm counting on Trish Morrisey of Philadelphia Fish & Co. to supervise a second wave, with special emphasis on the rare, the endangered, and the inheritances of immigrant cultures.

The game is outstanding, and the dressing and preparation of gopher, bear, bison, and beaver tail (to name a few) makes this a national pilgrimage of sorts. The ingredients and cooking methods of dishes such as Pennsylvania shad and bacon are historically grounded, and McDavid is fanatical about organic ingredients. A typical menu starts with a basket of buttermilk muffins. Main courses include suckling pig with a slightly sweet reduction, garnished with lettuce and Granny Smith tempura; shrimp with fennel in a lime-pepper sauce; or thick medallions of venison in a succulent berry-and-meat stock, served with haricots and baby carrots and a red-bean-and-wild-rice mélange. Desserts might be a smooth peanut-butter-and-chocolate cake or sweet pecan pie.

The extensive all-American wine list ranges from $16 to $90 per bottle. Quality beer, on tap or in the bottle, includes microbrews such as Stoudt's of Pennsylvania.

To save a bundle, try a simple meal of the black-eyed pea soup, the cornmeal crepe, or a hearty sandwich for under $20 with your drink at the bar.

✪ **Morton's of Chicago.** 1411 Walnut St., 2nd floor. ☎ **215/557-0724.** Reservations accepted for 5:30–7pm only. Jacket and tie required for men. Main courses $19–$33. AE, CB, DC, MC, V. Mon–Sat 11:30am–2:30pm and 5:30–11pm, Sun 5–10pm. STEAK.

Looking for sirloin? Morton's of Chicago has become a staple for both business lunches and celebratory evenings. Don't kid yourself about the specialty—the double-cut filets, sirloins, and T-bones come in aged, well-marbled tender masses. The house porterhouse ($31) weighs in at 24 ounces; if you wish, the server will bring your raw cut of meat or fish to your table for precooking inspection. The cauliflower soup is highly touted, and the Sicilian veal chop with garlic breadcrumbs is a "hometown" hit. If you must stray further, sample the crab cocktail or the smoked salmon served on dark bread with horseradish cream, capers, and onions.

Morton's looks as sedate as you'd expect, with glass panels between the tables and booths and dim lighting that makes the brass glow. The art deco bar has a wall lined with wine bottles, and the wine-by-the-glass list has a good selection of California cabernets.

✪ **Pasion!** 211 S. 15th St. ☎ **215/875-9895.** Reservations recommended. Main courses $18–$29; lunch $9–$15, 3-course lunch $26. AE, DC, MC, V. Mon–Thurs 11:30am–2:30pm and 5–10pm, Fri 11:30am–2:30pm and 5–11pm, Sat 5–11pm, Sun 5–9pm. LATIN AMERICAN/FUSION.

Pasion!, which opened at the end of 1998, has a double claim on its hot status. Chef Guillermo Pernot is a young star, named as one of *Food and Wine*'s ten best new

American chefs. The restaurant is the first and foremost of Philadelphia's Nuevo Latino cuisine, an exciting blend of authentic Latin ingredients, exotic presentation, and cuisine styles (though you might check out the swanky new Alma de Cuba or moderate tapas-based Cibucan in this arena). It's a no-miss hit for a date, and may expand along 15th Street to cope with demand.

Pasion! has taken a pedestrian sun-baked room seating 60 and given it warmth and mystery, with stone walls and louvered windows and candlelit sconces. Floral prints and stripes, sea grass cloth, and bamboo details evoke a tented tropical court-yard. The twelve stools at a granite and weathered wood bar in the rear—my favorite dining spot—perch over the unhurried spotless open kitchen. Cuisine itself is passionate and intense; many start and end with one of five ceviche courses (marinated fresh fish) offered daily (3 for $27), and move on to cumin-crusted roasted salmon, Argentinean sirloin, or unusual grilled or baked root vegetables. Desserts feature sweet pastries and custards, and wines are the expected California and South American vintages.

✪ **Striped Bass.** 1500 Walnut St. ☎ **215/732-4444.** Reservations almost always neces-sary. Main courses $17–32; lunch $13.50–$20. Chef tasting menu $90. AE, DC, MC, V. Mon–Thurs 11:30am–2:30pm and 5–11pm, Fri 11:30am–2:30pm and 5–11:30pm, Sat 5–11:30pm, Sun 5–10pm; brunch Sat–Sun 11am–2:30pm. SEAFOOD.

Bon Appétit, Town & Country, Esquire, and *Gourmet* have called this one of the hottest seafood restaurants in the country. The setting and ambience are absolutely spectacular: A 16-foot steel sculpture of a leaping bass poised over the exhibition kitchen sets the tone. With rows of plateaued banquettes, warm lighting, and car-peted floors to soak up the din bouncing off marble walls, you'll experience a rare and exotic sense of theater here. No one doubts that it can set you, or your expense account, back by $100 per person for dinner; most people find the quality and value well worth it.

The kitchen delivers simple, creative preparations of seafood, with emphasis on fresh herbs and clean flavors. Appetizers include a potato mousseline caske with Sevruga caviar and dill egg salad. The signature entree—wild striped bass with gar-lic mash, spring onions, and vegetables—is firm and flavorful. But take chances; this is the type of restaurant where you can feel comfortable asking the wait staff for advice—or the owners, who are religious about stopping by tables. Rising star Ter-ence Fuery, late of New York's Le Bernardin, has instituted an opulent tasting menu of seven courses. An extensive raw bar features oysters from the East and West coasts, clams, shrimp, and caviars. Desserts and ice creams are extravagant. A mostly domestic wine list starts at $22.

✪ **Toto's.** 1407 Locust St. ☎ **215/546-2000.** Reservations recommended. Main courses $19–$29; lunch $11–$15. AE, DC, MC, V. Mon–Fri 11:45am–2pm and 5:30–10pm, Sat–Sun 5:30–10pm. ITALIAN.

This wonderful Italian restaurant close to the Academy of Music and theaters has undergone a change of management and style, from opulent grandeur to a lighter, more reasonable Italian bistro. A huge copper antipasto cart, enlarged copies of impressionist and expressionist works, and a brighter new look in the series of booths separated by etched glass and ebonied wood, define the space.

Unless you opt for the "cicetti," or samplings of delightful tapas-sized plates avail-able at the bar, begin a meal with an antipasto—sautéed buffalo-milk mozzarella slices, marinated pepperoni, sun-dried tomatoes, or a seafood terrine or mousse. Italian meals of this quality demand a small first course of pasta; followed by a second course of fish, meat, or poultry with vegetables; and finally optional fruit, sweets, and coffee. If you feel like splurging, try the fazzoletti de mare, pasta triangles filled with savory shrimp and scallops. Main courses include thin-sliced fresh monkfish in lemon sauce and three slices of veal loin sautéed, then baked after a slow marinade in rosemary and garlic. If you order a grilled dish, be aware that many Americans perceive the Italian style as underdone. You'll want to finish with an espresso and some dessert. Toto's produces its own gelato, with ground fruits or beans and a splash of spirits.

MODERATE

❍ **Circa.** 1518 Walnut St. ☎ **215/545-6800.** Reservations recommended. Main courses $13.50–$25; lunch $7–$15. AE, CB, DC, MC, V. Mon 5–10pm, Tues–Wed 11:30am–2:30pm and 5–10pm, Thu–Sat 11:30am–2:30pm and 5–11, Sun 4–9:30pm. Dancing Fri–Sat 10:30pm–2:20am, Labor Day to Memorial Day. AMERICAN/ECLECTIC.

This is one of Philadelphia's hottest spots: It serves great food on a great restaurant block; it combines dinner with a sophisticated dance club; it's impressive yet engaging and comfortable; and it's cheaper than you think, though new chef Tom Harkin has upped the ante since his 2000 arrival.

The former bank building provides Circa with great beaux arts columns and windows along the east wall's long bar, opening up to a square, pleasant room upstairs, and original steel-and-brass vault fittings downstairs. Chef Harkin likes strong, congenial, flavorful food. You'll find such choices as duck ravioli, goat cheese, and sundried cherries or roast salmon osso buco with scallop marron—cleverly chosen dishes that won't suffer from the complicated trip upstairs. The wines are well chosen, starting at $18.

At 11pm Friday and Saturday (except in summer) the ground floor and mezzanine turn into a jammed dance floor, and the line to get in extends around the block.

Cutters. Commerce Square building, 2005 Market St. at 20th St. ☎ **215/851-6262.** Reservations recommended. Main courses $12–$26. AE, DC, DISC, MC, V. Mon–Fri 11:30am–4pm and 5–9pm (Fri until 10pm), Sat 5–10pm, Sun 5–9pm. AMERICAN.

This place is what you'd expect from a restaurant in a big, impressive skyscraper, with modern, cool lighting, and a huge bar (120 seats) for singles. (If you know Kinkaid's in Carmel or Washington, or Palomino's in Seattle, it's the same family.) But it's also an impeccable, convenient, 180-seat restaurant that's surprisingly warm for a romantic dinner.

The 20-foot bar is noted for its huge selection. The bottles are stacked vertically, forcing bartenders to scamper up and down ladders like gymnasts. Look for highly polished surfaces in wood and stone and handblown glass chandeliers. Fortunately the high ceilings soak up much of the din.

Cutters showcases American edibles, from Nebraska beef to pastas of all ethnicities, but its Seattle roots show through in the popular fillet of salmon (flown in fresh from the West coast daily) grilled over mesquite wood. Pizza, lamb chops, steaks, herb-crusted beef, and chicken fill out the extensive menu, with delicious flat bread to nibble on while you wait. The desserts are as good as you'd expect, with lots of chocolate and wonderful crème brûlée and pear bread pudding. The validated garage parking is complimentary after 5pm.

❍ **Ruth's Chris Steak House.** 260 S. Broad St. ☎ **215/790-1515.** Reservations recommended. Main courses $17–$39. AE, CB, DC, DISC, MC, V. Mon–Sat 5–11:30pm, Sun 5–10:30pm. STEAK.

Ruth's Chris Steak House, perfectly situated for the new Kimmel Center or any performance on the Avenue of the Arts, has gotten rave reviews since 1989. Ruth's Chris serves only U.S. prime beef that's custom aged, never frozen, and rushed to Philadelphia by the New Orleans distributor for the chain. The rib-eye steak in particular is presented lovingly, almost ritually, in a quiet and respectful setting, and with almost no garnishes. The portions are so large that you might want to skip the side dishes, although Ruth's Chris boasts nine ways of cooking potatoes. Several fish and chicken choices are also available. The desserts, mostly Southern recipes with lots of sugar and nuts, average $5. Several tables are partially in the hallway; make sure you request to avoid these.

Sansom Street Oyster House. 1516 Sansom St. ☎ **215/567-7683.** Reservations not accepted. Main courses $13.50–$20; lunch $6–$12.50. Four-course fixed-price dinner $19. AE, CB, DC, DISC, MC, V. Mon–Sat 11am–10pm. SEAFOOD.

Chef David Mink knows everything there is to know about oysters—where they come from, how their flavors differ, and how to prepare them. The ambience here was altered in 1999 from a traditional seafood parlor with a tile floor to a colorful, light-filled space; some of the regulars regret it. Nobody regrets the arrival of inventive chef Cary Neff, with Asian and contemporary notes added to a traditional tune of fresh seafood. Blackboards listing the daily specials perch beside a large collection of antique oyster plates and nautical lithographs.

You'll probably want an appetizer of several different types of oysters: metallic belons; cooler, meatier Long Island half-shells; the new, fruity Westcott hybrids from Washington state; and larger, fishier box oysters. All are opened right at the raw bar. For dinner, most people choose one of the daily selection of 8 to 10 fresh fish—local shad or tilefish, for instance. The homemade bread pudding is the most reliable dessert. The liquor prices are moderate and draft Samuel Adams beer is $2.25. The brewpub upstairs with its mahogany bar and exposed hardwood floors and (of course) copper brewing tanks, was the first brew pub in town; it's no longer theirs, but it's hitting new heights as the Nodding Head Brewery and Restaurant. Free parking after 5pm at 15th and Sansom with a $20 minimum.

✪ Susanna Foo. 1512 Walnut St. ☎ **215/545-2666.** Reservations recommended for dinner. Main courses $18–$35; lunch $14–$25. AE, MC, V. Mon–Fri 11:30am–2:30pm and 5–10pm (Fri until 11pm), Sat 5–11pm, Sun 5–9pm. CHINESE.

Susanna Foo has been touted in *Gourmet* and *Esquire* magazines and just about everywhere else for one of the best blends of Asian and Western cuisines in the country. It's enhanced by the space, a crisp, clean, fragrant garden of stone, glass, and silks, incorporating her collection of Chinese art and textiles.

The cuisine is the main thing, but be forewarned: If you're the type that finds exquisite but small portions at high prices off-putting, choose something heartier. Appetizers feature such delicacies as curried chicken ravioli with grilled eggplant, slightly crispy but not oily. Noodle dishes, salads, and main courses similarly combine East and West: water chestnuts and radicchio, savory quail with fresh litchi nuts, smoked duck and endive, grilled chicken with Thai lemongrass sauce, and spicy shrimp and pear curry. The Asian technique is to sear small amounts of ingredients, combining them just before service. Ms. Foo does include French caramelizing of certain dishes but no butter-based sauces or roux. The wine list, designed to complement these dishes, specializes in French and California white wines. Desserts such as the ginger crème with strawberries and the hazelnut meringue are light and delicate. My only complaint is the spotty service.

In the dim-sum cafe and bar upstairs, diners choose from up to 30 choices of exquisite tidbit platters, including pork-stuffed jalapeños, lamb wontons, and tiny spring rolls.

Zanzibar Blue. 200 S. Broad St. ☎ **215/732-5200.** Reservations not required. Main courses $18–$28; Sun brunch $22. Fixed-price 3-course pretheater dinner $22. AE, DC, DISC, MC, V. Daily 5:30pm–2am; Sun jazz brunch 11am–2pm. CONTINENTAL.

Philadelphia's premier venue for live jazz is also a great place to have dinner—witness the many pretheater and symphony diners who gladly take the Bellevue's escalator downstairs for the glamorous surroundings and the mixed, sophisticated group of patrons. The menu changes quarterly, but you can expect some Creole and Latin spices and seafood, along with basic steaks and fish. How about Southern fried catfish, stuffed with crab and lobster and accompanied by impeccable hush puppies and collard greens with Asian spices? Many people make a meal of the appetizers around a jazz set.

INEXPENSIVE

Bertucci's. 1515 Locust St. ☎ **215/731-1400.** Main courses $9–$15; average large pizza $14. AE, DC, MC, V. Mon–Thurs 11am–10pm, Fri 11am–11pm, Sat 11am–11:30pm, Sun noon–9pm. ITALIAN.

I grew up with the original Bertucci's and its bocce lanes in Cambridge—since they went national, what remains is a thin-crust pizza baked in a brick oven. Be open; locals love the barbecued chicken pizza, for example. What's added are antipasti of meats and vegetables, pasta, and now panini. The ambience is busy and noisy, but completely smoke-free and quite convenient to concerts and theaters.

✪ **Dock Street Brasserie.** 2 Logan Sq. (corner of 18th and Cherry sts.). ☎ **215/496-0413.** Reservations recommended. Main courses $9–$20; lunch $8–$14. Fresh-brewed tap beer $4.25 per 12-oz. glass. AE, CB, DC, DISC, MC, V. Mon–Fri 11:30am–2:30pm and 5–10pm (Fri until 11pm), Sat 5–11pm, Sun 5–10pm. Bar menu until midnight. FRENCH.

The spotless on-premises microbrewery is a definite draw to this relaxed, contemporary brew pub and popular restaurant. At any time, six or more fresh beers, ales, stouts, and porters will be on tap (Dock St. products only). Sample the subtle distinctions in hops, yeast, temperature, length of fermentation, and filtration. You can even take a tour.

The 200-seat restaurant features a 40-foot bar, a billiard room to the rear, spacious banquettes, and high ceilings. A 1999 renovation brought art deco–style: French photographs, softer lighting, black leather booths, and a 20-foot landscape mural above the bar. The menu under executive chef Olivier De Saint Martin centers on brasserie fare such as Alsatian choucroute, fisherman's cassoulet, and codfish with caramelized onions and red butter sauce. Try the crab cake sandwich for lunch. Live jazz Friday and Saturday night with no cover charge.

In May 2000, Dock Street opened the **Dock Street Brew Pub–Terminal** at 12th and Filbert streets, right in the Convention Center's restored Headhouse (☎ **215/922-4292**). The all-day menu specializes in European thin-crust pizzas, grilled items in the $13 to $18 range, and spectacular sundaes—and, of course, six or more fresh types of beer on tap. The atmosphere is woody and comfortable, with attention centered on the brewing tanks.

Marathon on the Square. 1839 Spruce St. ☎ **215/731-0800.** Reservations not accepted. Main courses $6–$14. AE, DC, DISC, MC, V. Daily 8:30am–2am. AMERICAN.

Fans of the late 24-hour Diner on the Square, with its comforting soups and deli food, take heart. Now there's Marathon on the Square, the flagship restaurant for

A Taste of Ethnic Philly: Reading Terminal Market

The ✪ **Reading Terminal Market,** at 12th and Arch streets (☎ 215/ 922-2317), has been a greengrocer, snack shop, butcher, fish market, and sundries store for smart Philadelphians since the turn of the century. The idea was to use the space underneath the terminal's tracks for food vendors so that commuters and businesspeople could stock up easily and cheaply. Half of the stalls make up an English-style covered market with cool brick floors and the scent of fresh provender and baked bread; the other half is a gourmet grocer/charcuterie.

Scrapple, mangoes, clam chowder, pretzels—you name it, if it's fresh and unpackaged, you can find it here. The northwest corner (12th and Arch sts.) is where most of the "retail"(as opposed to restaurant or institutional) Amish farm products come to market. You can still see the Amish in the big city on their market days (Wed and Sat), and you can buy sticky buns at **Beiler's Pies,** soft pretzels made before your eyes at **Fisher's,** and individual egg custards (75¢) and chicken potpies ($5.75) at **The Dutch Eating Place.** If you're in the market for meat, **Harry Ochs** and **Halteman Family** have the most extensive selections, with great country hams and local honey as well. **Reading Terminal Cheese Shop and Salumeria** offers gourmet cheeses and tinned goods, while **Margerum's,** now in its fourth generation, sells flours, spices, and coffee beans from barrels and kegs. The best coffee is sold at **Old City Coffee.**

If your stomach is rumbling uncontrollably by now, **Termini Brothers Bakery** will calm it with terrific bagels (50¢) or **Braverman's** will fill it with an egg challah ($3.50), Danish, or other pastry. For more protein, **Pearl's Oyster Bar** practically gives away six cherrystone clams for $4, and a shrimp platter with french fries, bread, and coleslaw goes for $6.95. Or try **Coastal Cave Trading Co.,** which has great clam chowder ($2.95), oyster crackers, and smoked fish. Just inside 12th Street, ✪ **Bassett's** (see "Best Restaurant Bets," in chapter 1) purveys Philadelphia's entry in the best American ice-cream contest at $1.90 a cone. The shakes ($3.50) are no less enticing, and the turkey sandwiches ($4.95) are simply the best anywhere. **Old Post Road Farm** makes a delicious cherry pie.

The 1993 renovation of the market has left it with more seating. The ✪ **Down Home Diner** (see "Best Restaurant Bets," in chapter 1) is an excellent choice for breakfast or lunch. **Jill's Vorspeise** has a great selection of hearty soups for starters. A lunch like linguine with clam sauce will cost $4.75 at **By George Pasta & Pizza; Spataro's,** an old-time favorite, vends buttermilk, cottage cheese, and huge slabs of fresh pies. The **12th Street Cantina** sells not only tasty enchiladas and burritos, but also authentic ingredients, like blue cornmeal. Some consider **Rick's Philly Steaks**—a third generation of Pat's down in South Philly—the best in town. And the **Beer Garden** can draw pints of Yuengling Porter and Dock Street Beer, among other more mass-market brews.

The market is open Monday to Saturday 9am to 6pm, but many vendors close at 5pm. Prices vary by vendor, and about half accept cash only. There are public rest rooms here.

the Borish family's Best of Philly–winning soups, grilled chicken and fish, Caesar salad, wrap sandwiches, and burgers. The space now seats about 60 at clean, crisp tables with lots of glass surfaces. The late hours and flexible menu make this a focal point for posttheater meals on the way back to Rittenhouse Square.

ⓘ Family-Friendly Restaurants

Ben's Restaurant (*see p. 106*)   In the Franklin Institute at Logan Circle (see chapter 7, "What to See and Do"), Ben's is well set up for kids, serving cafeteria food, hamburgers, and hot dogs. You can enter without museum admission.

Bertucci's (*see p. 82*)   An excellent thin-crust pizza and more, served within steps of the Avenue of the Arts and a no-nonsense attitude to service.

Chinatown   Between 9th and 11th streets and Race and Vine streets are lots of family-oriented places.

Cutters (*see p. 80*)   Lunch and dinner menus for children feature a $3.50 peanut butter and jelly sandwich, $5 fettuccine Alfredo, grilled cheese sandwiches, and fish-and-chips. Try for a window banquette.

Dave and Buster's   A playground on the Delaware waterfront (Pier 19, 325 N. Delaware Ave.) for kids of all ages. Dave and Buster's is a destination rather than a stop, since it's so far north of Independence National Historical Park and Penn's Landing. Arcade and carnival games are played in the Fun Factory from 11:30am daily.

Food Court at Liberty Place (*see p. 94*)   Kids have their choice of cuisines from among 25 stalls, and they can wander without getting out of your sight.

Johnny Rockets (*see p. 73*)   The location at 5th and South is convenient to South Street or the pedestrian walk from Penn's Landing, and the cheerful 1950s diner theme (red-and-white vinyl, indestructible booths) goes well with the very reasonable prices. The milkshakes are just what the doctor ordered.

Rex Pizza. 20 S. 18th St. ☎ **215/564-2374.** Reservations not accepted. Pizza $5–$10; hoagies from $4.75. No credit cards. Mon–Sat 11am–1am. ITALIAN.

For those self-indulgent moments when nothing but a large pepperoni pizza or a tuna hero will do, one of the most convenient and unexpectedly good spots in the city is Rex Pizza. They do a fine, nongreasy, thick-crust pizza for about $7.95 and a full-scale submarine sandwich for $4.75. Even when they're busy, your wait will rarely exceed 10 minutes.

Sawan's Mediterranean Bistro. 114–116 S. 18th St. (near Sansom St.). ☎ **215/568-3050.** Reservations recommended. Main courses $7–$15. AE, MC, V. Mon–Thurs 11am–10pm, Fri 11am–11pm, Sat noon–11:30pm, Sun 5–10pm. MEDITERRANEAN.

I like to sit closer to the front of this narrow room and plunge into a selection of dips such as baba ghanouj and tzadziki, a yogurt laced with dill and a bit of garlic; three or four of these with pita bread makes a great light meal in itself. Though they do have some American choices on the menu, stick to the ethnic entrees such as kebabs. Service is wonderful.

4 South Philadelphia

South Philly is the best place on earth to find south and central Italian dishes adapted to American ingredients and meal sizes. You can always tell by the unmistakable decor, menu, and music what decade a particular restaurant is frozen in.

EXPENSIVE

✪ The Saloon. 750 S. 7th St. ☎ **215/627-1811.** Reservations required. Main courses $19–$34. AE, MC, V. Mon 5–11pm, Tues–Fri 11:30am–2pm and 5–11pm (Fri until midnight), Sat 5pm–midnight. ITALIAN/CONTINENTAL.

The Santore family has been serving its fresh, quality cuisine here since 1965; it's probably better known for the man-size herbed and marinated steaks than for the classic Italian dishes, but new chef Clark Gilbert is someone to watch. The decor is solid wood paneling; soft, uplit sconces; antiques; and Tiffany lamps. The Saloon has a long menu and daily specials to consider as you savor the pesto tapenade, Parmesan, and olive oil delivered automatically with your bread. The Santores favor standards such as clams casino and crabmeat salads but also serve sautéed radicchio with shiitake mushrooms and superb salads. Heavy artillery includes the 12-ounce prime sirloin, the 26-ounce porterhouse with greens and roasted potatoes, or the lightly breaded veal slices with sweet and hot peppers. The wines are expensive, the desserts exquisite and high in cholesterol.

MODERATE

✪ Victor Cafe. 1303 Dickinson St. (follow Broad St. 15 blocks south of City Hall to Dickinson, then 2 blocks east). ☎ **215/468-3040.** Reservations recommended. Main courses $13–$20. AE, MC, V. Mon–Thurs 5–10pm, Fri–Sat 4:30pm–12am, Sun 4:30–9:30pm. ITALIAN.

Victor's is a South Philly shrine to opera, with servers who deliver arias along with hearty Italian classics. Opened in the 1930s by John Di Stefano, who covered the walls with photos of Toscanini, local Mario Lanza, and the like, the restaurant still has more than 45,000 classical recordings from which to choose and hires the best voices it can find. The food has received some quizzical comments recently, though; it's best to stick to basics like the cannelloni Don Carlos, with its two enormous shells filled with beef and veal and covered in marinara sauce, or the cutlet Baron Scarpia, a chop with wild mushrooms and marsala served over roasted garlic mashed potatoes.

INEXPENSIVE

✪ Marra's. 1734 E. Passyunk Ave. (between Morris and Moore sts.). ☎ **215/463-9249.** Reservations not necessary. Main courses $5–$12. Basic pizza $5.75 small, $7 large. No credit cards. Tues–Sat 11:30am–midnight, Sun 2–11pm. ITALIAN.

Marra's wins the "Best Pizza" award hands down. It's in the heart of South Philadelphia (supposedly the oldest surviving restaurant here, in fact), and the brick ovens give these thin-crust versions (and the walls) a real Italian smokiness. Marra's has a large Italian menu too and is noted for its homemade lasagna, its tomato sauce, and its squid on Friday. There's a real local attitude when it comes to service.

Ralph's Italian Restaurant. 760 S. 9th St. ☎ **215/627-6011.** Reservations recommended. Main courses $9–$16; pasta $8.25. No credit cards. Sun–Thurs noon–9:45pm, Fri–Sat noon–10:45pm. ITALIAN.

This two-story restaurant a few blocks north of the Italian Market is the epitome of the "red gravy" Italian style: unpretentious, comfortable, reasonable, and owned by the same family for decades. The baked lasagna, spaghetti with sausage, and chicken Sorrento have fans all over the city, and the extensive menu is long on veal and chicken dishes. The service is friendly and attentive. A parking tip: Try the Rite Aid lot nearby, but don't get caught without buying something.

Strolli's. 1528 Dickinson St. (follow Broad St. south to Dickinson, then walk 2 blocks west). ☎ **215/336-3390.** Reservations required. Main courses $6–$9; pasta $4. No credit cards. Mon–Sat 11:30am–1:30pm and 5–10pm, Sun 4–9pm. ITALIAN.

With all the Italians in South Philly, you'd expect to find at least one extremely inexpensive, wholesome, family restaurant here, right? Right—and the place is Strolli's. It used to look like a burned-out storefront at the corner of Mole Street—now there's a sign and an identifiable side door. Implacable, pipe-puffing John Strolli presides over two plain rooms, with plywood paneling and bare plaster enlivened by an ancient cigarette machine and a life preserver dedicated to Strolli's wife, Carmela. Music emanates from a corner radio. You'll make your own atmosphere, and any description of the size, taste, or pricing of the dishes wouldn't be believed.

You'll want to start with an antipasto; a medium-size one is a full 10 by 4 inches, so the large size would suit three fine. All seafood platters come with tomato, lettuce, and coleslaw—would you believe a scallop-crammed plate for $6? The veal-cutlet platter is an extraordinary piece of sautéed red veal. While you're making reservations, you might ask for the special stuffed shells—they're legendary.

Triangle Tavern. 10th and Reed sts. (intersection with E. Passyunk Ave.). ☎ **215/467-8683.** Reservations requested for 6 or more. Main courses $6–$10. No credit cards. Mon–Sat 11am–2pm and 4pm–midnight, Sun 3pm–midnight. ITALIAN.

Inexpensive, heaping dishes of homemade pasta and bowls of mussels are served in a steamy, good-humored atmosphere here. You'll enter through the neighborhood bar, complete with large-screen TV (keep pushing toward the back). Nothing costs more than $10, and most items (chicken cacciatore, gnocchi, spaghetti in white clam sauce) are closer to $6. The mussels in red sauce are famous. Friday and Saturday nights, a steady guitar trio plays old favorites, with a good dose of audience participation. Be prepared to wait for a table.

5 University City (West Philadelphia)

MODERATE

La Terrasse. 3432 Sansom St. ☎ **215/386-5000.** Reservations recommended. Main courses $18–$25; lunch $6.75–$13; fixed-price dinner $45 and Sun brunch $20. AE, DC, MC, V. Mon–Fri 11:30am–2:30pm and 5:30–10pm (Fri until 11pm), Sat 5:30–11pm, Sun 5–9pm; late suppers to 2am daily; brunch Sun 11am–3pm. CONTINENTAL/FRENCH.

After years of closure, David Grear brought La Terrasse back to life to general relief in 1997. The look is slightly more sleek and sophisticated, but it still has the interior clubby spaces and wraparound covered terrace, one with a tree (not the old fat one, but a black-olive sapling) growing right through it. La Terrasse is one of the area's pioneers in great dining and atmosphere; its cuisine is an imaginative mix of Southern French standards and ingredients like polenta and mahi-mahi. The $45 full dinner is regarded as an excellent value. Salads are spectacular in their variety and crispness, and wines are reasonable finds from smaller vineyards. Weekdays between 4:30 and 6:30pm bring half-price drinks and $4 wines by the glass, with complimentary hors d'oeuvres at the popular bar. Live piano music is offered most evenings.

Palladium. 3601 Locust Walk. ☎ **215/387-3463.** Reservations recommended. Main courses $10–$20; lunch $6.50–$11.50. AE, CB, DC, DISC, MC, V. Mon–Fri 11:30am–2:30pm and 5–9pm, Sat 5–9pm; late suppers daily. Closed Sat and Sun. June–Aug. CONTINENTAL.

In the heart of the University of Pennsylvania campus (Wharton, specifically) is Palladium, an elegantly appointed full-service restaurant and bar. It's reminiscent of an old-time faculty club—chesterfields and wing chairs with footstools face an old stone fireplace, while leaded-glass windows, oak wainscoting, and an ornate ceiling add the final touches. The atmosphere is similar, if slightly less cozy, in the spacious dining room. Prices here are a little high to make the Palladium a student hangout, but they're reasonable for this quality, with à la carte dishes, a fixed-price menu, and a pretheater special.

Menus change completely four times a year, ranging from Tunisian grilled shrimp to French classic lamb chops. Most main dishes are accompanied by potatoes au gratin (good enough to be a meal in themselves) and a mélange of fresh vegetables. Watch the (largely student) service, which is at best uneven, and sometimes downright slow.

Downstairs is **The Gold Standard,** a cafeteria that heats up with comedy, dinner theater, and the like.

✪ **White Dog Cafe.** 3420 Sansom St. ☎ **215/386-9224.** Reservations recommended. Main courses $14–$19; lunch $8–$16. AE, DC, DISC, MC, V. Mon–Fri 11:30am–2:30pm and 5:30–10pm (Fri until 11pm), Sat 5:30–11pm, Sun 5–10pm; brunch Sat–Sun 11am–2:30pm. Grill open until midnight. Frequent theme dinners and parties. AMERICAN.

Judy Wicks is one of Philadelphia's great citizens: She led the fight against the University of Pennsylvania to save this block of Sansom Street and has evolved into a smart, tough, and fun-loving entrepreneur. She and her partner/chef Kevin von Klause have even written a cookbook.

You'll enter two row houses with the dividing wall knocked out and with sophisticated kitchen equipment and electronics concealed behind an eclectic mélange of checkered tablecloths, antique furniture and lights, and white dogs galore. The friendly pups are everywhere—on the menu, holding matchbooks, pouring milk, and in family photographs.

From Sansom Street, the three-counter bar specializes in such all-American beers as McSorley's Ale, New Amsterdam, and Anchor Steam, as well as inexpensive American wines by the glass or bottle. Several dining areas lie to the rear and right, and there's a new glassed-in porch across the rear.

The staff offers frequently changing menus as well as "theme" dinners based on the season or a particular American region. They buy produce locally, which eliminates the middleman and results in dishes that underprice the market by $3 to $5. Starters include a lemon pepper grilled calamari salad and black olive crostini, or freshly made ravioli with European mushrooms, braised with white truffle oil and herbs. The grilled yellowtail fillet with sweet-and-sour eggplant relish is delicious, and pastry chef Heather Carb turns out signature rolls and cakes.

The White Dog attracts everyone, from Penn students to the mayor. Just next door at 3424 Sansom St., **The Black Cat** (☎ **215/386-6664**) offers more of Judy's antiques and crafts. It's open Tuesday to Thursday 11am to 11pm, Friday and Saturday 11am to midnight, and Sunday and Monday 11am to 9pm.

Food to Cure What Ails You

The name White Dog Cafe is indebted to the theosophist and mystic Madame Blavatsky, who resided here a century ago. Blavatsky was about to have an infected leg amputated when a white dog in the house slept on the leg and cured it.

INEXPENSIVE

New Deck Tavern. 3408 Sansom St. ☎ **215/386-4600.** Reservations recommended. Main courses $6–$12. Daily 11am–2am. IRISH/AMERICAN.

Virtually next door to the White Dog (see above), the New Deck Tavern is less of a restaurant than a relaxed watering hole, with real Irish beers and bartenders and a 37-foot solid cherrywood bar. The Tavern specializes in crab cakes, homemade soups, and Irish fare such as shepherd's pie. Specials abound during the 5 to 7pm happy hour. Try to catch Dottie Ford, a secretary in Penn's physics department, at the piano nightly between 7 and 9pm; she knows thousands of show and other tunes, an amazing range built up over the past 50 years.

New Delhi. 4004 Chestnut St. ☎ **215/386-1941.** Reservations not required. Main courses $4.95–$10; all-you-can-eat lunch buffet $5.95 daily; dinner buffet $8.95 Mon–Thurs only. AE, MC, V. Mon–Thurs noon–10pm, Fri–Sat noon–11pm. INDIAN.

New Delhi is a fairly good Indian restaurant near the U. Penn campus, with a 26-item all-you-can-eat buffet. It boasts quality ingredients, a tandoor clay oven, and friendly service. Look for discount coupons in student tabloids.

The Restaurant School. 4207 Walnut St. ☎ **215/222-4200.** Reservations required on weekends, accepted after 3pm. $35 fixed price for formal restaurant; at more casual student-run rooms, $15 fixed price for appetizer and main course, with extra $3 for desserts. AE, CB, DC, MC, V. Tues–Sat 5:30–10pm. ECLECTIC.

Housed in an elegant Victorian building, the Restaurant School is a major institution among Philadelphia restaurateurs. After 8 months of instruction, teams of students plan a menu and kitchen protocol, then take over the ground floor for eight weeks at a time.

There's also a formal restaurant, Great Chefs of Philadelphia, in a totally renovated parlor dining room. The $35 fixed-price menu was designed by the city's premier chefs, who serve as mentors to student staffers. Two casual restaurants—one American, one Italian—will continue the student-run tradition. Since the students are paying for the right to cook your meal, the prices are extremely low. The restaurant has acquired a liquor license and offers a fine selection of apéritifs, wines, and cocktails. You can count on at least one soup, one salad, and five main courses.

✪ **Zocalo.** 36th St. and Lancaster Ave. (1 long block north of Market St.). ☎ **215/895-0139.** Reservations recommended. Main courses $13–$19. AE, DC, DISC, MC, V. Mon–Fri noon–2:30pm and 5:30–10pm (Fri until 11pm), Sat 5:30–11pm, Sun 4–9pm. MEXICAN.

This restaurant, four blocks from the U. Penn campus, offers contemporary Mexican cuisine from all the provinces. Chef Jackie Pestha has returned to the kitchen she founded 12 years ago, to everyone's benefit. It's grown to sprawl through four or five separate dining areas, so it's quiet and civilized. It's undoubtedly the best Mexican place around, and its food is priced accordingly, though some would say overpriced, from such traditional dishes as carne asada to such modern classics as fresh shrimp in chile sauce. They pat out the tortillas by hand before your eyes using

Good to Go

Dozens of vendors have permits to operate on the streets around the University of Pennsylvania campus. I like **Bento Box** and **Quaker Shaker** at 37th and Walnut streets, or **Aladdin** at 34th and Spruce near University Museum.

fresh-flown or -grown ingredients. There's lively Latin music on most nights, with a pleasant deck in back for use in summer.

6 Chinatown

MODERATE

Golden Pond. 1006 Race St. ☎ **215/923-0303.** Reservations recommended. Main courses $8–$16; lunch special $6. AE, DC, MC, V. Mon–Fri 11:30am–10pm, Sat–Sun noon–11pm. CHINESE.

This very stylish Hong Kong–style place on three floors costs a bit more than others in the neighborhood, but the impeccable service and the obviously fresh preparation are worth it. Wing Ming Tang, the chef, is a survivor of the 1989 Tiananmen Square riots. The cuisine features potato dishes, chicken, duck, and seafood, but no pork or beef. It's one of the few places that serves brown rice.

INEXPENSIVE

✪ **Capital.** 1008 Race St. ☎ **215/925-2477.** Reservations recommended. Main courses $4.50–$9. AE, CB DC, DISC, MC, V. Daily noon–11pm. VIETNAMESE.

The positive restaurant reviews placed at every table are well deserved: Capital is one of the best spots in town for Vietnamese cuisine. Look for ground pork, sweet or pungent herbs and greens, and slight French touches. *Bun thit nuong* is a small, savory serving of pork with garlic flavor over rice noodles. No alcohol is served, but you may bring your own.

✪ **Harmony Vegetarian Restaurant.** 135 N. 9th St. ☎ **215/627-4520.** Reservations recommended. Main courses $7–$13. AE, MC, V. Sun–Thurs 11am–10:30pm, Fri–Sat 11am–midnight. VEGETARIAN/CHINESE.

Despite the menu listings for meat and fish, absolutely everything here is made with vegetables (no eggs or dairy either). George Tang makes his own gluten by washing the starch out of flour; this miracle fiber is then deep-fried and marinated to simulate beef, chicken, even fish. The decor is intimate and candlelit, and there's no smoking. Raves go to the hot-and-sour soup and the various mushroom dishes. BYOB.

Imperial Inn. 142–6 N. 10th St. ☎ **215/627-5588.** Reservations recommended. Main courses $8–$14. AE, CB, DC, MC, V. Sun–Thurs 11:30am–midnight, Fri–Sat 11:30am–2am. CHINESE.

This longtime citizen of Chinatown serves an enormous variety of Szechuan, Mandarin, and Cantonese dishes.

Lunch here features dim sum: appetizer-size dishes trundled around on carts that you can take or leave as you like; each dish is $2 or so. It's a great form of instant gratification. For dinner, the lemon chicken features a sautéed boneless breast in egg batter, laced with a mild lemon sauce. You can order a full-course dinner, which includes a choice of soup, rice, a main course, and a dessert for about $3 more than the main course alone.

Joe's Peking Duck House. 925 Race St. ☎ **215/922-3277.** Reservations recommended. Main courses $6–$13. No credit cards. Daily 10:30am–11:30pm. CHINESE.

This place still churns out Chinatown's best Peking duck, Szechuan duck, and barbecued pork with consistent quality. Recent menus have more low-fat items like steamed sea bass with light black-bean sauce. The decor is unassuming. Former chef and owner Joe Poon has started up Joseph Poon around the corner at 1002 Arch St., with a much more ambitious and expensive fusion menu; entrees there are $10 to $28.

Ray's Coffee Shop. 141 N. 9th St. ☎ **215/922-5122.** Reservations not required. Main courses $9–$19; coffee $3.50–$8. AE, MC, V. Mon–Thurs 10am–9:30pm, Fri 9am–10:30pm, Sat 9:30am–noon, Sun noon–9pm. CHINESE/COFFEE BAR.

This unlikely precursor of the city's penchant for coffee bars, with 30 seats in a pleasant room located near the Convention Center, features an unusual combination of subtle Taiwanese cuisine (the dumplings are especially touted) and dozens of exotic coffees, each smartly priced and brewed to order in little glass siphons. The iced coffee and house special noodle soup here are great.

✪ **Shiao Lan Kung.** 930 Race St. ☎ **215/928-0282.** Reservations not necessary. Main courses $6–$11. AE, CB, DC, MC, V. Sun–Thurs 4pm–3am, Fri–Sat 4pm–4am. CHINESE.

This modest place close to the Convention Center unassumingly turns out fresh and adventuresome dishes like jellyfish, along with most standards. The Pa-chen tofu in hot pot throws together ham, barbecued pork, fish balls, and several vegetables with unusual subtlety. You won't find many other restaurants in town open this late.

7 Manayunk

This neighborhood, 8 miles up the Schuylkill from the Art Museum and Center City, has soared in popularity over the past decade, with some of Philadelphia's hippest restaurants and shops (see chapter 9 for the latter). Manayunk has lots of long, thin, energetic bistros, as well as off-the-street venues for snacks and appetizer-size dishes. Getting there is simple: From the Belmont Avenue exit (north, crossing the Schuylkill River and its adjoining canal) off I-76 or 1 block south of the Green Lane SEPTA stop on the R6 line, just follow Main Street east alongside the river from the 4400 to the 3900 addresses. A cohesive local development group runs a continuous series of weekend festivals and events to attract business. Parking is plentiful, and store hours tend to run late to match dinner reservations.

EXPENSIVE

Kansas City Prime. 4417 Main St. ☎ **215/482-3700.** Reservations recommended. Main courses $18–$24; $64 porterhouse for two. AE, CB, DC, DISC, MC, V. Mon–Thurs 5:30–11pm, Fri–Sat 5:30pm–midnight, Sun 5–10pm. STEAK/SEAFOOD.

Derek Davis is the entrepreneur most associated with Manayunk as a restaurant destination, and this (along with Sonoma and Arroyo Grille, which operate on the banks of the canal) was a real surprise—I mean, a 140-seat steakhouse for yuppies? Well, it's a steakhouse with a difference. It's creamy, curving, and unclubby, deliberately attractive to couples. The cuisine has all the classics (rib-eye steak, at least five choices of fish/lobsters), but the side dishes throw in unusual combinations like spinach with raisins and pine nuts. Sauces such as a reduced-cream béarnaise and condiments such as sweet onion marmalade are superb. And if you're up for a splurge, try the Kobe beef from Japan—at $100 per order.

MODERATE

Hikaru. 4348 Main St. ☎ **215/487-3500.** Reservations recommended. Main courses $7–$15. AE, DC, MC, V. Mon–Thurs noon–2:15pm and 5–10:30pm, Fri–Sat noon–2:15pm and 5pm–midnight, Sun 5–10:30pm. JAPANESE.

This restaurant has added a top-notch Japanese element to Manayunk, with its high, elegant greenhouse and more traditional tatami room. With other branches in Queen Village and Rittenhouse Square, Hikaru is known for its sushi selection, but the teppan grill is great fun for its tabletop drama, with a server searing meat, fish, or vegetables before your eyes.

Le Bus Main Street. 4266 Main St. ☎ **215/487-2663.** Reservations accepted only for 6 or more. Main courses $10–$17; lunch $6–$9. AE, MC, V. Mon–Thurs 11am–3pm and 5–10pm, Fri 11am–3pm and 5–10:30pm, Sat 9:30am–3pm and 5–10:30pm, Sun 9:30am– 3pm and 5–10pm. AMERICAN/ECLECTIC.

Le Bus dishes out fresh, affordable, homestyle cuisine featuring American classics. Homemade breads and pastries are baked fresh daily, and the weekend brunch features omelettes, frittatas, and pancakes. The menu—from meat loaf to great pasta—and the wholesomeness of the place make it especially attractive to families. There's outdoor seating, weather permitting. Word has it they're negotiating for a cafe spot in Center City at 17th and Market streets. Watch out for lines at peak hours.

✪ **Sonoma.** 4411 Main St. ☎ **215/483-9400.** Reservations recommended. Main courses $12–$19. AE, CB, DC, DISC, MC, V. Sun–Thurs 11am–11pm, Fri–Sat 11am–midnight, late bar. AMERICAN/ITALIAN.

In 1992, Sonoma was the original hot Manayunk restaurant, and its Italian/ California cuisine and service have only gotten stronger. A renovation of the dining room and bar took place in 1999. Set in a double storefront with 35-foot windows, three levels of seating, and a decor of black-and-brushed steel as a backdrop, this restaurant is always crowded, with a hectic exposed kitchen and thin wait staff. The second-floor bar serves 87 varieties of vodka. The food is wonderful, with Italian specialties like risotto and American standards such as roasted chicken. With this noise level, kids won't be noticed.

Zesty's. 4382 Main St. ☎ **215/483-6226.** Reservations not necessary. Main courses $13–$28; lunch $6–$10. AE, DC, DISC, MC, V. Tues–Sat 11am–11pm, Sun 3–11pm. GREEK/ ITALIAN.

This spot is an agreeable upgraded cafe (one respondent called it the "anti-Sonoma") featuring gourmet grilled fish and meat along with Italian and Greek dishes such as pastas and moussaka. (I personally regret the loss of pizzas.) Don't rule out the meatier stuff like grilled lamb chops and giant Portobello mushrooms—delicious. The enormous espresso and cappuccino machine in the center of the room complements sweet desserts as well.

8 Local Favorites: Cheesesteaks, Hoagies & More

CHEESESTEAKS & HOAGIES

Philadelphia cheesesteaks are nationally known. Preparing a cheesesteak is an art here—ribbons of thinly sliced steak are cooked quickly (with onions if you like) and then slapped onto a roll on top of overlapping slices of provolone or a thick smear of Cheez Wiz. Hoagies are the local name for the sandwiches known variously throughout the Northeast as submarines, grinders, or torpedoes.

✪ **Jim's Steaks.** 400 South St. ☎ **215/928-1911.** Reservations not accepted. Lunch and main courses $4.75–$5.75. No credit cards. Mon–Thurs 10am–1am, Fri–Sat 10am–3am, Sun noon–10pm. AMERICAN.

The best practitioner of the fine art of "hoagistry" in this area is Jim's Steaks in Queen Village, which also offers the mightiest steak sandwiches in town. Jim's has a certain art deco charm, with a black-and-white enamel exterior, tile interior, and omnipresent chrome. Containers and ovens take up most of the ground floor, but there is a counter with bar stools along the opposite wall. Take-out is highly recommended in pleasant weather.

Proper hoagie construction can be debated endlessly, but Jim's treatment of the Italian hoagie with prosciutto is a benchmark. A fresh Italian roll is slit before your eyes and layers of sliced salami, provolone, and prosciutto are laid over the open faces. You choose your condiment: mayonnaise or oil and vinegar. Salad fixings—lettuce, tomatoes, and green peppers, with options of onion and hot peppers—come next, with more seasoning at the end. The result may not be subtle, but it's pungent, filling, and delicious. The steak sandwiches aren't as succulent as they used to be, but they're cheaper, at $4 (melted cheese—or Cheez Wiz—additional). Beer and soft drinks are sold in cans and bottles.

Lee's Hoagies. 44 S. 17th St. ☎ **215/564-1264.** Sandwiches $4.50–$8. No credit cards. Mon–Sat 10:30am–8pm, Sat 10:30am–6pm. AMERICAN.

For more than 30 years, Lee's hoagies have captured the hearts and mouths of many native Philadelphians, at a low-slung complex between Market and Chestnut streets. The regular hoagie (basically an elongated spicy cold-cuts sandwich) measures about 8 inches long, the giant about twice as long. The various combinations include the Italian (four meats and provolone) and the turkey (with provolone and mayonnaise). Lee's minors in steak sandwiches, served with fried onions and sauce.

✪ **Pat's King of the Steaks.** 1237 E. Passyunk Ave. (between 9th and Wharton sts.). ☎ **215/468-1546.** $4.25–$10. No credit cards. Always open. AMERICAN.

Pat's, so its adherents claim, serves the best steak sandwiches this side of the equator. The location and hours make for an interesting mix at the take-out counter. The 24-hour competition with Geno's just across the street creates one of Philadelphia's liveliest late-night scenes.

PRETZELS
Soft, salted pretzels served warm with a dollop of mustard are an authentic local tradition, dating from the German settlers of the early 1700s. The best in town continue to be made by the Amish farmers who bring them to Reading Terminal Market. But you can make your own at the new **Pretzel Museum** at 211 N. 3rd St., open 10am to 3pm Monday to Saturday. If you're outdoors, check out the vendor stand in front of the Franklin Institute.

PIZZA
I think **Marra's** (see "South Philadelphia," above) is the best of Philadelphia's hundreds of pizza parlors and restaurants, and **Bertucci's** (ditto) is a good bet for pizza and more. The following are good bets as well.

Pizzeria Uno. 509 S. 2nd St. ☎ **215/592-0400.** Pizzas $8.45 and up. AE, CB, DC, MC, V. Sun–Thurs 11:30am–midnight, Fri–Sat 11:30am–1am. ITALIAN.

This national chain of dark-green bar/cafes serves a reliable deep-dish Chicago pizza that's more like a meal-on-bread than a traditional pizza. The old 1721 Locust Street location is being converted into an American comfort food station with burgers and brews, part of the new Sheraton Rittenhouse.

⭐ **Tacconelli's.** 2604 E. Somerset St. at Aramingo Ave. ☎ **215/425-4983.** Reservations required; place pizza orders in advance. Pizzas $10.50–$12. MC, V. Wed–Thurs 4–9pm. Fri–Sat 4:30–9:30pm. Sun 4–8:30pm. ITALIAN.

A real insider recommendation for pizza is Tacconelli's—not, as you'd think, in South Philly, but north of the new discos along Christopher Columbus Boulevard (formerly Delaware Ave.). The greatly expanded Tacconelli's is open until whenever the crusts run out (about 9pm). It's imperative to call ahead to reserve the type of pizza you want, which is prepared in a brick oven. The white pizza with garlic oil and the spinach and tomato pies are particularly recommended. To get here, take the Frankfort subway line from Market Street to Somerset Street, then walk 8 blocks east. If you drive from Society Hill, take Front Street north, make a right onto Kensington Avenue, then another right onto Somerset.

COFFEE BARS

In the last few years, Center City has been transformed with the addition of dozens of coffee bars serving everything from inky espresso to mocha café (chocolate milk for grown-ups). Depending on where you are, you can blow in for a 2-minute respite at a stand-up counter, or linger for an hour at a window seat.

My wife, who is a true addict (and to whom this section is dedicated), adores **Torreo Coffee & Tea Company,** 130 S. 17th St., near Liberty Place (☎ **215/988-0061**), open daily, which roasts all its own coffees from light to full-bodied and has a selection of premium loose teas. It also has a full espresso bar and excellent muffins, scones ($1.75), and biscotti. The top restaurateurs in town all plump for **La Colombe,** both as a supplier of beans for New York's best, such as Daniele, and as its own shop at 130 S. 19th St. **Old City Coffee,** at 221 Church St., behind Christ Church (☎ **215/629-9292**), and at Reading Terminal Market (☎ **215/592-1897;** see "A Taste of Ethnic Philly: Reading Terminal Market," on p. 83), is relaxed to the point of somnolence and somewhat expensive, but the coffee selection is rich, varied, and strong. The Church Street location has eclectic acoustic acts during Old City's "First Friday" festivals. **XandO** (as in "hugs and kisses") has become the local cafe of choice with a chatty, *Friends*-like ambience during the day at four locations, including 235 S. 15th St. at Locust Street (☎ **215/893-9696**); 1720 Walnut St. near Rittenhouse Square; near Independence Hall at 4th and Chestnut streets (☎ **215/399-0214**); and by U. Penn at Sansom Commons. All XandOs add cocktails (see chapter 10) to the mix after 4pm and have recently teamed up with the equally hip sandwich chain Cosi. Everyone has heard of Seattle-based **Starbucks,** which has set up outposts at 1528 Walnut St. (☎ **215/732-0708**) and in the Convention Center Marriott at Market and 11th streets (☎ **215/569-4223**). Don't forget about the cafes inside the bookstores of **Borders** at 1727 Walnut St. (☎ **215/568-7400**) and **Barnes & Noble** at 1805 Walnut St. (☎ **215/665-0716**); the former is lauded for its café au lait. In Manayunk, try **Péché** at 4436 Main St. (☎ **215/925-2855**), with a sinful selection of desserts along with the standard blends.

FOOD COURTS & MARKETS

The **Reading Terminal Market,** 12th and Arch streets (☎ **215/922-2317**), in the space underneath the terminal, has served Philadelphians since the turn of the 20th century. For a full description, see "A Taste of Ethnic Philly: Reading Terminal Market," on p. 83.

The Bourse Food Court. 111 S. Independence Mall E. (just east of the Liberty Bell). Mon–Sat 10am–6pm, Sun 11am–5pm summers only.

This location has 11 snack/restaurant operations, all moderately priced and designed for takeout to be eaten at the tables that fill this cool and stunning restoration of the 1895 merchant exchange. Representative stalls include **Sbarro's** for pizza and pasta, **Bain's Delicatessen** for turkey sandwiches, and **Grand Old Cheesesteak** for sandwiches.

Downstairs at the Bellevue. The Bellevue Hotel, S. Broad and Walnut sts. Mon–Fri 10am–6pm. Sat 10am–5pm.

This is a sparkling 1993 effort to attract a clientele less willing to pay upscale prices. It's usually very quiet, with bright tiles, great lighting, and public rest rooms. Quiet center tables surround food-court vendors such as **Montesini Pizza, Saladworks,** and **Rocco's Italian Hoagies** ($5 and up).

⭕ **The Food Court at Liberty Place.** Second level (accessible by escalator or elevator) of Liberty Place between Chestnut and Market sts. and 16th and 17th sts. Mon–Sat 9:30am–7pm, Sun noon–6pm.

This court, in a gleaming urban mall in the heart of Center City, hosts Reading Terminal alumni like **Bain's Deli, Bassett's Original Turkey,** and **Original Philly Steaks,** along with **Mandarin Express, Montesini Pizza and Pasta Gourmet, Sbarro,** and **Chick-Fil-A.** The prepared sandwiches at **New World Coffee** are outstanding. It's spotless, large, and reasonably priced, with full lunches from $3.50. You'll find it easy to keep your eyes on the kids as they wander.

The Food Court. The Gallery, Market St. at 9th St. Mon, Tues, Thurs, and Sat 10am–7pm; Wed and Fri 10am–8pm; Sun noon–5pm.

Throngs of people parade up and down four floors of shops under a massive glass roof at The Gallery. The lowest level near Gimbels houses an enclave of oyster bars, ice-cream stands, and stalls with baked potatoes, Greek snacks, and egg rolls.

Italian Market. 9th St. between Christian and Federal sts. Daily, dawn to dusk. Bus: 47 or 64.

While touring South Street or South Philadelphia, be sure to visit the Italian Market for fresh produce, pasta, seafood, and other culinary delights. This is what shopping used to be before supermarkets and malls. It's vibrant, if often crowded to near immobility. Purists (not I) bemoan the $2.5 million project to repave the streets and add new building facades, new awnings, and night lighting. It's most interesting to head for the market from South Street, which has been gentrified from Front to Ninth streets. Only a couple of blocks filled with notable Italian restaurants—Ralph's, Felicia's, and Palumbo's—separate South Street from the market proper. Fast-talking vendors, opera-singing butchers, and try-it-before-you-buy-it cheese merchants hawk their wares here. The Market is also a great place to pick up ultra-cheap clothing, if you're willing to wade through racks of items. **Fante's Cookware** is famous nationally, and **DiBruno Bros. House of Cheese** combines a great selection with upscale savvy.

Exploring Philadelphia

7

Consider Philadelphia's sightseeing possibilities—the most historic square mile in America; more than 90 museums; innumerable colonial churches, row houses, and mansions; an Ivy League campus; more Impressionist art than you'd find in any place outside of Paris; and leafy, distinguished parks, including the largest one within city limits in the United States. Philadelphia has come a long way since 1876, when a guidebook recommended seeing the new Public Buildings at Broad and Market streets, the Naval Yards, the old YMCA, and the fortresslike prison.

Most of what you'll want to see within the city falls inside the original grid plan, between the Delaware and Schuylkill Rivers and South and Spring Garden streets. In fact, it's possible to organize your days into walking tours relatively easily—see chapter 8 for suggestions. Even if you ramble on your own, nothing is that far away. A stroll from City Hall to the Philadelphia Museum of Art takes about 25 minutes, although you'll undoubtedly be sidetracked by the flags and flowers along the Parkway. A walk down Market or one of the "tree" streets (Chestnut, Spruce, Pine, Locust) to Independence National Historical Park and Society Hill should take a little less time—but it probably won't, since there's so much to entice you on the way. If you'd rather ride, the spiffy PHLASH buses loop past most major attractions about every 10 minutes, and the all-day fare is $4. SEPTA also has an all-day $5 fare for city buses, but the two systems do *not* accept each other's passes.

The city is trying to wrap some of its attractions together in packages in various ways. The Convention and Visitors Bureau has two "package priced" offers. The first is the **combined ticket** for Independence Seaport Museum, the Camden Aquarium, and the ferry between them; prices are $18.50 adults, $16 seniors, and $13.50 children 3 to 11. The second is **Philadelphia Citypass,** which offers admission to six major attractions, including the Philadelphia Museum of Art, the Franklin Institute, the Zoo, and the Seaport Museum; prices are $28.50 adult, $23.75 seniors, and $21.25 children 3 to 11, and they may be purchased in advance on www.citypass.net/philly or at any one of the attractions. Tickets are good for up to 9 days from first use, and they represent about a 50% discount from full admissions to all of them.

Philadelphia Attractions

Academy of Music **9**
Academy of Natural Sciences **5**
Afro-American Museum **24**
Army-Navy Museum **18**
Arch Street Meeting House **23**
Betsy Ross House **26**
City Hall **7**
Edgar Allen Poe National
   Historic Site **28**

Elfreth's Alley **27**
Franklin Court **20**
Franklin Institute Science
   Museum & Science Park **4**
Free Library of Philadelphia **3**
Graff House **22**
Independence Hall **14**
Kimmel Performing Arts
   Center **11**

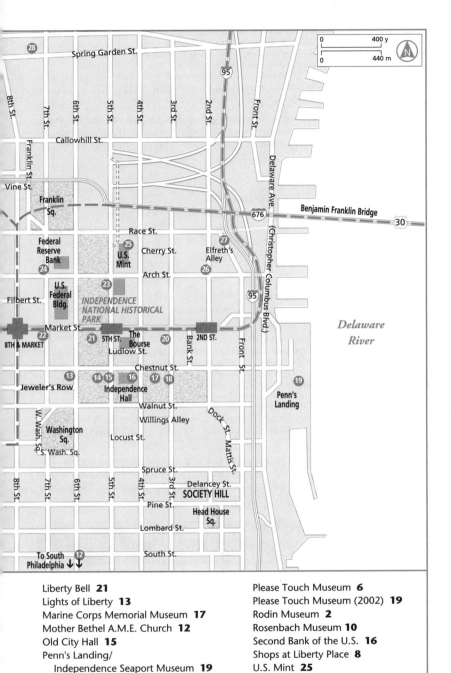

Liberty Bell **21**
Lights of Liberty **13**
Marine Corps Memorial Museum **17**
Mother Bethel A.M.E. Church **12**
Old City Hall **15**
Penn's Landing/
    Independence Seaport Museum **19**
Philadelphia Museum of Art **1**
Philadelphia Zoo **1**

Please Touch Museum **6**
Please Touch Museum (2002) **19**
Rodin Museum **2**
Rosenbach Museum **10**
Second Bank of the U.S. **16**
Shops at Liberty Place **8**
U.S. Mint **25**

Suggested Itineraries

If You Have 1 Day

Start at the Liberty Bell in Independence National Historical Park, then move south through Independence Hall and on to residential Society Hill, which is steeped in U.S. history. In the evening, if you've still got the history bug, stay for the multimedia "Lights of Liberty" show that uses the Park as backdrop. If not, see what's on at the Academy of Music or Kimmel Center, the Annenberg Center at the University of Pennsylvania, or the CoreStates Spectrum for sports.

If You Have 2 Days

Day 1   Follow the itinerary given above.
Day 2   Starting at City Hall, walk up the Benjamin Franklin Parkway to Logan Circle and spend the afternoon at Franklin Institute or the Philadelphia Museum of Art. Try to circle back to Rittenhouse Square and the Liberty Place complex before closing.

If You Have 3 Days

Days 1–2   Follow the itinerary given above.
Day 3   Spend the morning in Old City viewing its Christ Church and Elfreth's Alley, then explore the expanding Delaware River waterfront attractions and the Independence Seaport Museum at Penn's Landing. Finally, either visit the New Jersey State Aquarium by ferry to Camden or continue shoreward to eclectic South Street.

If You Have 5 Days or More

Days 1–3   Follow the itinerary given above.
Day 4   Explore the Rittenhouse Square/South Broad Street area, with a visit to the Pennsylvania Academy of Fine Arts, winding up with a stroll through Reading Terminal Market (it closes at 5pm) and Chinatown.
Day 5   Fairmount Park's Zoo and many restored colonial mansions beckon. Further out, Franklin Mills or King of Prussia Court and Plaza have become magnets for millions of tourists who want to save on clothing from America's finest stores, retail and discounted, with no state sales tax.

1 Independence National Historical Park: America's Most Historic Square Mile

Is there anyone who doesn't know about the Liberty Bell in Independence Hall? It may not be there anymore, but you get the point: The United States was conceived on this ground in 1776, and the future of the young nation was assured by the Constitutional Convention held here in 1787. The choice of Philadelphia as a site was natural because of its centrality, wealth, and gentility. The delegates argued at Independence Hall (then known as the State House) and boarded and dined at City Tavern. Philadelphia was the nation's capital during Washington's second term, so the U.S. Congress and Supreme Court met here for 10 years while awaiting the construction of the new capital in Washington, D.C. From the first penny to the First Amendment, Philadelphia led the nation.

The ✪ **Independence National Historical Park** comprises 40 buildings on 45 acres of Center City real estate (see the map on the inside back cover of this guide, as well as Walking Tour 1 in chapter 8). Independence Hall and the Liberty Bell in its glass pavilion lie between 5th and 6th streets. The Visitors Center, at the corner of 3rd and Chestnut streets, is well equipped to illustrate the early history of this country, and will be joined in 2002 by the even more explanatory new Gateway Center across from Independence Hall.

This neighborhood ranks as a superb example of successful revitalization. Fifty years ago, this area had become overgrown with warehouses, office buildings, and rooming houses. The National Park Service stepped in, soon followed by the Washington Square East urban-renewal project now known as Society Hill. To the east, gardens replaced edifices as far as the Dock Street food market, which was replaced by Society Hill Towers in 1959. Graff House, City Tavern, Pemberton House, and Library Hall all were reconstructed on the original sites; Liberty Bell Pavilion, Franklin Court, and the Visitors Center are contemporary structures that were erected for the Bicentennial of the Declaration of Independence celebrations. The most questionable project was the condemnation and destruction of 3 blocks' worth of commercial buildings to create Independence Mall, a wide swath of greenery opposite Independence Hall; the Park is trying to rectify this now through the proposed National Constitution Center construction and new landscaping for the home of the Liberty Bell around it.

Since 1998, you must get a free, same-day reserved ticket to tour Independence Hall before 3pm, and pay $2 if you wish to take one of the frequent interior tours of the Second Bank of the United States, Bishop White House, and the Todd House. The **Visitors Center,** 3rd and Chestnut streets (☎ **215/597-8974** voice, or 215/597-1785 TDD; www.nps.gov.inpe), should be your first encounter with the park. Here, you can pick up a map of the area and information in any of 13 languages. The modern bell tower houses a 6-ton bell given by Queen Elizabeth II of England to this country in 1976, and it rings at 11am and 3pm. The gift shop sells mementos and park publications, and every 30 minutes the center shows a John Huston feature, *Independence,* free of charge.

Independence Hall is open daily 9am to 5pm, often later in the summer. As mentioned, visiting some of the park's building interiors requires a reservation, and other adjacent historic buildings have separate admissions. Historic Philadelphia is a nonprofit organization dedicated to bringing the city's rich past to life; it presents many scripted walking tours beginning here.

To get here, you can take the SEPTA Market-Frankford Line to 5th and Market streets or 2nd and Market streets. By bus, take the PHLASH, 76, or any Chestnut Street Transitway bus from Center City.

If you're driving, from I-76, take I-676 east to 6th Street (last exit before the Ben Franklin Bridge), then turn south (right) along Independence Mall. From the Ben Franklin Bridge, make a left onto 6th Street and follow the same directions as above. From I-95 southbound, take the Center City exit to 2nd Street. From I-95 northbound, use the exit marked "Historic Area." Turn left on Columbus Boulevard (formerly Delaware Ave.) and follow it to the exit for Market Street (on right). There's metered parking along most streets, as well as parking facilities (all $12 per day) at 2nd and Sansom streets, at Independence Mall between Arch and Market streets, and at the corner of Dock and 2nd streets.

✪ INDEPENDENCE HALL

Independence Hall is on Chestnut Street between 5th and 6th streets, flanked by Old City Hall to the left and Congress Hall to the right. It is open daily 9am to 5pm. Free but mandatory tours are led by park rangers every 15 minutes between

9am and 3pm. Arrive as early as you can after 8:30am at 5th and Chestnut streets, across from Old City Hall, to pick up time-reserved tickets, so you won't have to wait all day to get inside. You can get here by PHLASH or bus 76.

Even if you knew nothing about Independence Hall, you could guess that noble and important events took place here. Although these buildings are best known for their national role, they also functioned as the seat of government for the city of Philadelphia and for the state of Pennsylvania both before and after Philadelphia was the capital of the U.S. From an architectural standpoint, the ensemble is graceful and functional; from the standpoint of history and American myth, it's unforgettable. Independence Square sets you thinking about the bold idea of forming an entirely sovereign state from a set of disparate colonies and about the strength and intelligence of the representatives who gathered here to do it. For some on-line context, try the wonderful Web site of the **Independence Hall Association** at www.ushistory.org.

When the French and Indian War (1754–63) required troops that in turn required money, King George III believed the colonists should pay for their own defense through taxes. The colonists disagreed, and the idea that the king harbored tyrannical thoughts swept through the colonies. Philadelphia, as the wealthiest and most cultured of the seacoast cities, was leery of radical proposals of independence, as was Franklin himself, in his role as an American agent in London at the time. But the news that British troops had fired on citizens defending their own property in Concord pushed the most moderate to reconsider what they owed to England and what they deserved as free people endowed with natural rights.

The Second Continental Congress convened in May 1775, in the Pennsylvania Assembly Room, to the left of the Independence Hall entrance. Each colony had its own green baize-covered table, but not much of the original room's furnishings escaped use as firewood when British troops occupied the city in December 1777. The Congress acted quickly, appointing a tall Virginia delegate named George Washington as commander of the Continental Army. After the failure of a last "olive branch" petition, the Congress, through John Adams, instructed each colony's government to reorganize itself as a state. Thomas Jefferson worked on a summary of why the colonists felt that independence was necessary. The resulting Declaration of Independence, wrote noted historian Richard Morris, "lifted the struggle from self-interested arguments over taxation to the exalted plane of human rights." Most of the signatories used Philip Syng's silver inkstand, which is still in the room. The country first heard the news of the Declaration on July 8 in Independence Square.

Before and after the British occupied the city, Independence Hall was the seat of the U.S. national government. Here the Congress approved ambassadors, pored over budgets, and adopted the Articles of Confederation, a loose and problematic structure for a country composed of states. Congress moved to New York after the war's end, and it grudgingly allowed delegates to recommend changes.

The delegates who met in the Assembly Room in Philadelphia in 1787 did more than that—they created a new Constitution that has guided the country for more than 200 years. Jefferson's cane rests here, as does a book belonging to Franklin. Washington, as president of the convention, kept order from his famous "Rising Sun Chair." Delegates were mature, urbane (24 of the 42 had lived or worked abroad), and trained to reason, and many had experience drafting state constitutions and laws. They decided on approaches to governance that are familiar today: a bicameral Congress, a single executive, an independent judiciary, and a philosophical belief in government by the people and for the people. No wonder John Adams called the convention "the greatest single effort of national deliberation that the world has ever seen."

Across the entrance hall from the Assembly Room, the courtroom served as Pennsylvania's Supreme Court chamber. Like the court at Williamsburg, Virginia, this room exemplifies pre–Bill of Rights justice. For example, your ranger guide will probably point out the tipstaff, a wooden pole with a brass tip that was used to keep onlookers subdued. Other period details include little coal-burning boxes to keep feet warm on chilly days. This is one of the first courtrooms in America to hear the argument that disagreement with a political leader isn't sedition, one of the great concepts in modern Anglo-American law.

The stairwell of Independence Hall held the Liberty Bell until 1976. The ranger will conduct you upstairs to the Long Gallery. Now it's set up as a banquet hall with a harpsichord (some of the guides even play) and a rare set of maps of the individual 13 colonies. Its view of Independence Mall is superb.

Two smaller rooms adjoin the Long Gallery. To the southwest, the royal governors of Pennsylvania met in council in a setting of opulent blue curtains, silver candlesticks, and a grandfather clock. Beneath a portrait of William Penn, governors met with foreign and Native American delegations, in addition to conducting normal business. On the southeast side, the Committee Room fit the whole Pennsylvania Assembly while the Second Continental Congress was meeting downstairs. More often, it stored the assembly's reference library or arms for the city militia.

As you descend the stairs, look at leafy, calm **Independence Square,** with its statue of Commodore John Barry. The clerk of the Second Congress, John Nixon, first read the Declaration of Independence here, to a mostly radical and plebeian crowd. (Philadelphia merchants didn't much like the news at first, since it meant a disruption of trade, to say the least.)

✪ THE LIBERTY BELL

You can't leave Philadelphia without seeing the Liberty Bell at Chestnut Street between 5th and 6th streets. At the stroke of midnight on January 1, 1976, it was taken out of Independence Hall and put in its own glass Liberty Bell Pavilion by the park across the street, once the site of the Executive Mansion. Admission is free; you can see the bell daily in summer 9am to 8pm, and the rest of the year, daily 9am to 5pm.

The Liberty Bell, America's symbol of independence, was commissioned in 1751 to mark the 50th anniversary of a notable event: William Penn, who governed Pennsylvania alone under Crown charter terms, decided that free colonials had a right to govern themselves, so he established the Philadelphia Assembly under a new Charter of Privileges. The bell, cast in England, cracked while it was being tested, and the Philadelphia firm of Pass and Stow recast it by 1753. It hung in Independence Hall to "proclaim liberty throughout the land" as the Declaration of Independence was read aloud to the citizens, and survived a trip to an Allentown church in 1777 so the British wouldn't melt it down for ammunition. The last time it tolled was to celebrate Washington's birthday in 1846. The term *Liberty Bell* was coined by the abolitionist movement, which recognized the potency of its inscription in the fight against slavery.

You can no longer touch the bell, but you can photograph it. You can even see it through the glass walls at night.

Note that a new home for it on the Mall, angled near 6th and Chestnut streets, is now under construction and will be completed in late 2001 or so; it will allow you to see the bell against the backdrop of Independence Hall, without the brutal Penn Mutual tower in the background. North of the Bell, a new $170 million National Constitution Center and Gateway Visitor Center with lovely landscaping is also taking shape, and will be completed in 2002.

✪ FRANKLIN COURT

Franklin Court, on Chestnut Street between 3rd and 4th streets, with another entrance at 316–318 Market St., may just be the most imaginative, informative, and downright fun (and free) museum run by the National Park Service. Designed by noted architect Robert Venturi, it was very much a sleeper when it opened in April 1976, because the Market and Chestnut streets' arched passages give little hint of the court within and the exhibit below.

Franklin Court was once the home of Benjamin Franklin, who had resided earlier with his family in smaller row houses in the neighborhood. Like Jefferson at Monticello, Franklin planned many of the time-savers and interior decorations of the house, but he spent the building period as colonial emissary first to England, then to France. His wife, Deborah, oversaw the construction, as the engraved flagstones show, while Ben sent back continental goods and a constant stream of advice. Unfortunately, they were reunited only in the family plot at Christ Church Burial Ground, since Deborah died weeks before the end of Ben's 10-year absence. Under the stewardship of his daughter Sarah and her husband, Richard Bache, Franklin Court provided a gentle home for Ben until his death in 1790.

Since archaeologists have no exact plans of the original house, a simple frame in girders indicates its dimensions and those of the smaller print shop. Excavations have uncovered wall foundations, bits of walls, and outdoor privy wells, and these have been left as protected cutaway pits. It is all very interesting—but enter the exhibition for the fun part. After a portrait and furniture gallery, a mirrored room reflects Franklin's almost limitless interests as a scientist, an inventor, a statesman, a printer, and so on. At the Franklin Exchange, dial various American and European luminaries to hear what they thought of Franklin.

The middle part of the same hall has a 15-minute series of three climactic scenes in Franklin's career as a diplomat. On a sunken stage, costumed doll figures brief you, and each other, on the English Parliament in 1765 and the Stamp Act; the Court at Versailles, when its members were wondering whether to aid America in its bid for independence; and the debates of the Constitution's framers in 1787, right around the corner at Independence Hall. Needless to say, Ben's pithy sagacity wins every time.

On your way in or out on the Market Street side, stop in the 1786 houses that Ben rented out. One is the Printing Office and Bindery, where you can see colonial methods of printing and bookmaking in action. The house at 322 Market St. is the restored office of *The Aurora and General Advertiser,* the newspaper published by Franklin's grandson. Next door, get a letter postmarked at the Benjamin Franklin Post Office (remember, Ben was Postmaster General, too!). Employees still hand-stamp the marks. Upstairs, a postal museum is open in summer.

Franklin Court is open daily 9am to 5pm, including the post office and postal museum.

✪ LIGHTS OF LIBERTY

Since the summer of 1999, the most important park sites have been the backdrop for the world's first interactive sound-and-light show, providing visitors with a high-tech immersion into the drama of the American Revolution as it happened and

Impression

The question eagerly put to me by every one in Philadelphia is, "Don't you think the city greatly improved?" They seem to me to confound augmentation with improvement. It always was a fine city, since I first knew it; and it is very greatly augmented.
—William Cobbett, *A Year's Residence in the United States of America* (1817–19)

where it happened. Five-story projections on historic buildings and wireless headsets equipped with movie-style "surround" sound make it the closest "virtual" colonial experience money can buy.

The ground floor of the PECO Energy Center, next to Independence and Congress Halls on Chestnut Street, has been transformed into a group ticketing and holding area. Try to arrive at dusk, especially with kids, since there's a maximum of 50 per tour and it's first-come, first-served. You'll pick up headsets automatically tuned to a script read by such actors as Ossie Davis and Charlton Heston, and which is triggered automatically as your group arrives at the planned Park destinations. Younger children might prefer the alternative kids' headsets, with their own Whoopi Goldberg–narrated script (mine, 8 and 10, found it too juvenile).

Led by a guide, you'll walk across the moonlit cobblestone streets to Park sites, where the Revolutionary story is compressed into five acts. Rifles crackle, cannons boom, and the founders of America argue with actual quotes interwoven into the script. They're backed with choral music and a soundtrack performed by members of the Philadelphia Orchestra. The visuals are somewhere between shadow-box projections and animation, with superb color and resolution. The finale of 1776 takes place right in back of Independence Hall, and it's irresistibly thrilling.

Lights of Liberty: One-hour tour shows depart from PECO Energy Center, 6th and Chestnut streets, ☎ **877/462-1776** or 215/LIBERTY, www.lightsofliberty. org. Admission $18 adults, $16 seniors, $12 children 6 to 12. Family pack (2 adults, 2 children) $50. AAA discount of 10%. Up to six shows per hour: shows nightly, dusk to 11:15pm, May to October. Available in Chinese, French, German, Italian, Japanese, and Spanish, as well as English.

2 The Top Museums

✪ **Barnes Foundation.** 300 N. Latch's Lane, Merion Station, PA 19066. ☎ **610/ 667-0290.** Fax 610/667-8315 for reservations. www.barnesfoundation.org. Admission $5 per person, but reservations at least a month in advance are essential. Fri–Sun 9:30–5pm Sept–June; Wed–Fri 9:30am–5pm July–Aug. Onsite parking $10. SEPTA: Take Paoli local train R5 to Merion Station; walk up Merion Rd. and turn left onto Latch's Lane. Bus: 44 to Old Lancaster Rd. and Latches Lane. Car: I-76 (Schuylkill Expressway) west to City Line Ave. (Rte. 1), then south on City Line 1½ miles to Old Lancaster Rd. Turn right onto Old Lancaster, continue 4 blocks, and turn left onto Latch's Lane.

If you're interested in art, the magnificent Barnes Foundation will stun you. Albert Barnes crammed his French provincial mansion with more than 1,000 masterpieces—180 Renoirs, 69 Cézannes, innumerable Impressionists and post-Impressionists, and a generous sampling of European art from the Italian primitives onward. The Barnes reopened in November 1995 after a world tour of more than 80 masterworks from the restored collection and a $12-million renovation of the galleries.

Barnes believed that art has a quality that can be explained objectively—for example, one curve will be beautiful and hence art, and another that's slightly different will not be art. That's why the galleries display antique door latches, keyholes, keys, and household tools with strong geometric lines right next to the paintings. Connections beg to be drawn between neighboring objects—an unusual van Gogh nude, an Amish chest, New Mexico rural icons. Virtually every first-rank European artist is included: Degas, Seurat, Bosch, Tintoretto, Lorrain, Chardin, Daumier, Delacroix, Corot, and more. Not a bad use of a fortune made from patent medicine!

The bad news is the foundation administration: They've apparently mishandled the finances of the foundation, and (with an assist from "not in my backyard" neighbors) have established restrictive visiting hours that knock out weekends during peak summer months. Call well ahead of your anticipated visit for reservations.

✪ **Philadelphia Museum of Art.** 26th St. and Ben Franklin Pkwy. ☎ **215/763-8100** or 215/684-7500 for 24-hour information. www.philamuseum.org. Admission $8 adults; $5 students, seniors, and children 5–18; free for children under 5. Free Sun 10am–1pm. Tues–Sun 10am–5pm; Wed evening hours to 8:45pm with music, talks, movies, and socializing. Bus: 7, 32, 38, 43, 48, or 76; the last is door-to-door, but runs only until 6pm. Car: From the Parkway headed west (away from City Hall), follow signs to Kelly Dr. and turn left at the first light at 25th St. to the lots at the rear entrance. Plentiful parking, free Tues–Fri and $5 Sat–Sun.

Even on a hazy day you can see America's third-largest art museum from City Hall—resplendent, huge, a beautifully proportioned Greco-Roman temple on a hill. Because the museum, established in the 1870s, has relied on donors of great wealth and idiosyncratic taste, the collection does not aim to present a comprehensive picture of Western or Eastern art. But its strengths are dazzling: It houses undoubtedly one of the finest groupings of art objects in America, and no visit to Philadelphia would be complete without at least a walk-through. Late hours on Wednesday have become a city favorite.

The museum is designed simply, with L-shaped wings off the central court on 2 stories. A major rearrangement of the collections was recently completed, and paintings, sculptures, and decorative arts are grouped within set periods. The front entrance (facing City Hall) admits you to the first floor. Special exhibition galleries and American art are to the left; the collection emphasizes that Americans came from diverse cultures, which combined to create a new, distinctly national esthetic. French- and English-inspired domestic objects, such as silver, predominate in the Colonial and Federal galleries, but don't neglect the fine rooms of Amish and sturdy Shaker crafts. The 19th-century gallery has many works by Philadelphia's Thomas Eakins, which evoke the spirit of the city in watercolors and oil portraits.

Originally controversial 19th- and 20th-century European art galleries highlight Cézanne's monumental *Bathers* and Marcel Duchamp's *Nude Descending a Staircase,* which doesn't seem nearly as revolutionary as it did in 1913. The recent gift of the McIlhenny $300-million collection of paintings is one of the last great donations of this type possible and adds French impressionist strength.

Upstairs is a chronological sweep in 83 galleries of European arts from medieval times through about 1850. The John G. Johnson Collection, a Renaissance treasure trove, has been integrated with the museum's other holdings. Roger van der Weyden's diptych *Virgin and Saint John* and *Christ on the Cross* is renowned for its exquisite sorrow and beauty. Van Eyck's *Saint Francis Receiving the Stigmata* is unbelievably precise (borrow the guard's magnifying glass). Other masterpieces include Poussin's frothy *Birth of Venus* (the USSR sold this and numerous other canvases in the early 1930s, and many were snapped up by American collectors) and Rubens's sprawling *Prometheus Bound.* The remainder of the floor takes you far away—to medieval Europe, 17th-century battlefields, Enlightenment salons, and Eastern temples.

The museum has excellent dining facilities as well. A cafeteria, open Tuesday to Friday 10am to 2:30pm and 10am to 3pm on Saturday and Sunday, dispenses simple hot lunches and salad plates for about $4. The museum restaurant down the hall is open Tuesday to Saturday 11:45am to 2:15pm, Sunday 11am to 2pm, and Wednesday 5 to 7pm.

The PMA has recently mounted shows of contemporary artists Jonathan Borofsky and Anselm Kiefer, and has brought millions into the economy with blockbuster exhibits of Picasso still lifes, Cézanne, Delacroix's late works, and van Gogh's portraits. Look for expansion with a $15 million gift in 2000—a former insurance headquarters across the way, a striking art deco site, is expected to add a huge 100,000 square feet within 5 years.

Pennsylvania Academy of Fine Arts. 118 N. Broad St. at Cherry St. ☎ **215/972-7600.** www.pafa.org. Admission $5 adults, $4 seniors and students with ID, $3 children 5–12. Tues–Sat 10am–5pm; Sun 11am–5pm. Tours are free with admission, and leave from the Grand Stairhall Sat–Sun at 12:30 and 2pm. Bus: C or 48.

Located 2 blocks north of City Hall is the Museum of American Art of the Pennsylvania Academy of Fine Arts (PAFA), the first art school in the country (1805) and at one time the unquestioned leader of American beaux arts. The museum got a healthy dose of Cinderella treatment in 1976, when its headquarters celebrated its centennial. At the end of all the scrubbing, repainting, and stuccoing, Philadelphians were once again amazed at the imagination of the Frank Furness masterpiece built in 1876. Following 6 months of further renovation in late 1994, the academy unveiled a major reinstallation of 300 works from the past 200 years.

The ground floor houses an excellent bookstore, a cafe, and the academy's classrooms. A splendid staircase, designed by Furness, from the archways to the light fixtures, shines with red, gold, and blue. Each May the annual academy school exhibition takes over the museum. The school itself has moved to sparkling new quarters at 1301 Cherry St.

As is evident from the PAFA galleries, such early American painters as Gilbert Stuart, the Peale family, and Washington Allston all congregated in Philadelphia, America's capital and wealthiest city. The main galleries feature works from the museum's collection of more than 6,000 canvases, and a large exhibit of Eakins drawings is planned for 2001. The rotunda has been the scene of cultural events ever since Walt Whitman listened spellbound to concerts here. The adjoining rooms display works from the illustrious years of the mid–19th century, when PAFA probably enjoyed its most innovative period.

Franklin Institute Science Museum. Logan Circle, 20th St. and Benjamin Franklin Pkwy. ☎ **215/448-1200.** www.fi.edu. Admission charges are confusing and depend on what you want to do. Basic admission to exhibitions and Mandell Center $9.75 adults, $8.50 children; to Planetarium, IMAX, 3-D theater, and laser shows $3–$7.50; combinations of all of the above $14.75 adults, $12.50 children. Science Center, daily 9:30am–5pm; Mandell Center, Sun–Thurs 9:30am–5pm, Fri–Sat 9:30am–9pm; CoreStates Science Park, May–Oct, daily 10am–4pm. Bus: 33, 76, or PHLASH.

The Franklin Institute Science Museum isn't just kid stuff. Everyone loves it because it's a thoroughly imaginative trip through the worlds of science that shows us their influence on our lives. The complex actually has four parts. The first is the home of the Franklin National Memorial, with a 30-ton statue of its namesake and a collection of authentic Franklin artifacts and possessions.

The second part, a collection of 1940s through 1970s science- and technology-oriented exhibition areas, pioneered hands-on displays, from a gigantic walk-through heart with heartbeat recordings to ship models to the Hall of Aviation with its small planes and a chance to sit in a cockpit of a Wright brothers' biplane. For a hair-raising experience, plug into a Van de Graaff generator at the lightning gallery. On the third floor, an energy hall bursts with Rube Goldberg contraptions, noise-makers, and light shows. The nearby Discovery Theater gives afternoon shows featuring liquid air and other oddities. The fourth floor specializes in astronomy and mathematical puzzles. The basement Fels Planetarium (☎ **215/563-1363**) rounds out the picture.

The third part of the Franklin Institute is the result of an ambitious 1991 campaign to construct the Mandell Futures Center addition. It was funded by $22 million from the city and state and $36 million from private sources. Just past the Franklin National Memorial on the second floor, you'll enter an energy-charged atrium with cafes, ticket counters, and ramps and stairs leading to the new exhibits. Just beyond is a separate-admission IMAX arena, showing films ranging from undersea explorations to the Rolling Stones in spectacular 70mm format. A new 3-D theater was opened in 2000. Eight permanent interactive exhibits, including space, earth, computers, chemistry, and health, take you into the 21st century with Disney World–style pizzazz. My personal favorites are the new virtual-reality sports games—climbing a rock wall and surfing monster waves, a video driving exercise in "Future Vision," "The Jamming Room" of musical synthesizers, and the "See Yourself Age" computer program in "Future and You." The texts throughout are witty and disarming. Quite the opposite is the new Skybike, which you can ride along a 1" cable three stories above the Bartol Atrium floor.

The fourth section is the 1995 CoreStates Science Park, a collaboration with the Please Touch Museum. It uses the 38,000-square-foot lawn between the two museums—it's free with admission to either one. The imaginative urban garden is filled with high-tech and play structures, including a high-wire tandem bicycle, 12-foot tire, step-on organ, maze, and optical illusions.

Of course, you'll eventually get hungry—with a family, the institute is a full afternoon. Your choices are excellent: a vending-machine space in the **Wawa Lunchroom** on the first floor, open only to museum-goers; the new all-American-with-a-nutritional-twist **Ben's Restaurant** on the second floor, accessible without museum admission, and open Monday to Friday 8:30am to 2:30pm and Saturday and Sunday 9am to 3:30pm; and the **Omni Café** in the Mandell Center lobby, open daily 11am to shortly before museum closing, serving beer and wine. Vendors outside sell Philadelphia soft pretzels with plenty of mustard.

3 More Attractions

Reading Terminal Market is an attraction in itself, as is the Italian Market if you're exploring South Philadelphia. Both are described in detail in chapter 6, "Dining."

ARCHITECTURAL HIGHLIGHTS

Benjamin Franklin Bridge. Entrance to free bicycle/pedestrian walkway at 5th and Vine sts. 6am–dusk. Bus 50.

An old fixture on the Old City landscape has jumped into the 21st century—the Benjamin Franklin Bridge, designed by Paul Cret, one of the architects of the Parkway across town. It was the largest single-span suspension bridge in the world (1.8 miles) when it was finished in 1926. The bridge carries cars and commuter trains and also has a foot/bicycle path along its south side. For the bicentennial of the U.S. Constitution, a Philadelphia team, including Steven Izenour (of Venturi, Rauch, and Scott Brown), a leading American architect and planner, created a computer-driven system for illuminating each and every cable. At night, Philadelphians are treated to the largest lighting effects show since Ben Franklin's kite.

City Hall. Broad and Market sts. ☎ **215/686-9074.** Free admission. Daily 10am–3pm. During school year, Mon–Fri 10am–noon reserved for school groups. Last tour at 2:45pm. Interior tours daily at 12:30pm. Bus/Subway: Most lines converge beside or underneath the building.

When construction of City Hall began in 1871, it was planned to be the tallest structure in the world. But plans were scaled back, other buildings surpassed it, and the elaborate 1901 wedding cake by John McArthur Jr., with an inner courtyard straight out of a French château, immediately seemed dated. It still arouses wildly differing reactions, although Philadelphians generally love the crowning 37-foot statue of William Penn by A. M. Calder.

You may wish to wander inside the vast floors, which range from the breathtaking to the bureaucratically forlorn. Both inside and out, City Hall boasts the richest sculptural decoration of any American building. The Mayor's Reception Room (Room 202) and the City Council Chamber (Room 400) are especially rich.

The highlight of City Hall is the **tower view.** The Juniper Street entrance is most convenient, but you can take any corner elevator to the seventh floor and follow the red tape (always indicative of city government). In this case, it leads to two escalators and a waiting area for the tower elevator. The elevator up to the Penn statue's recently renovated shoestrings, at 548 feet, can hold only eight people, and the outdoor cupola cannot hold many more. On the way, notice how thick the walls are— City Hall is the tallest building ever constructed without a skeleton of steel girders, so that its recently cleaned white stone is 6 feet thick at the top and 22 feet at ground level. The simply stupefying view from the top encompasses not only the city but also the upper and lower Delaware Valley and port, western New Jersey, and suburban Philadelphia. It's windy up there, though. If you look straight down, you can see more of the hundreds of sculptures designed by Calder, the works of whose descendants—Alexander Sterling Calder (1870–1945) and Alexander Calder (1898–1976)—beautify Logan Circle and the Philadelphia Museum of Art.

Fisher Fine Arts (Furness) Library. 220 S. 34th St. (at Locust Walk on the U. Penn. campus). ☎ **215/898-8325.** Free admission. During academic year, Mon–Fri 9am–10pm; summer hours, Mon–Fri 9am–5pm. Bus: 44.

Like the Pennsylvania Academy of Fine Arts building (see above), this citadel of learning has the characteristic chiseled thistle of Frank Furness, although it was built a decade later from 1888 to 1890. The use of 1890s leaded glass here is even richer. The library now houses, appropriately, the fine arts library of the University of Pennsylvania.

Pennsylvania Convention Center. Between 11th and 13th sts. and Market and Race sts. ☎ **215/418-4728.** Public tours are free; most shows charge admission. Public tours Tues and Thurs at 11:30am, 12:30pm, 1:30pm, and 2:15pm. Enter at the northwest corner of 12th and Arch sts. Subway: Rail lines (including Airport Express) stop at Market East Station; SEPTA at 11th and Market and 13th and Market; Bus: 12, 17, 33, 44, or PHLASH. Car: Separate exit from I-676, between I-95 and I-76.

With the July 1993 opening of the Philadelphia Convention Center (PCC), Philadelphia made clear that the future of the area depends on its ability to welcome tens of thousands of visitors weekly. The statistics are staggering: With 440,000 square feet of exhibit space, it's larger than 30th Street Station. But what's really great about the $522 million Convention Center is how solid, elegant, and in keeping with its surroundings it is. Architects Thompson, Ventulett, Stainback & Associates shoehorned blocks of brick and limestone between I-76 in the back and Market Street in the front.

Unless you're one of the millions the PCC hopes to lure in for a meeting, you'll need to take the public tour for a peek inside. The highlight is a stupendous Grand Hall on the second level, evoking the Train Shed and Headhouse of the Reading Terminal it once was. Gray and black Mexican marble alternates with waterfalls, steel, and terrazzo, with huge granite pylons for heating and cooling the mammoth space. Judy Pfaff's vast, kaleidoscopic *Cirque* extends airy steel and aluminum tubes over 70,000 square feet of space. Esplanades and corridors contain a veritable museum of 52 living artists (35 from Philadelphia) in one of the most successful public art projects of our time. In 1995, the Market Street entrance, the original Reading Railroad facade, was restored, with an escalator up to the Train Shed; the Marriott next door has a skywalk into the Great Hall. The 37-foot rotating electric guitar, niched into the southwest corner outside, signals the popular advent of the Hard Rock Café, or head for the beers and burgers of the Dock Street Brew Pub. And don't forget that the incomparable Reading Terminal Market is downstairs.

Philadelphia Exchange. Walnut and 3rd sts. ☎ **215/597-8974.** Not open to the public. Bus: 21, 42, or PHLASH.

This sloped site, alongside one of the city's original creeks emptying into a Delaware cove, was used by hometown architect William Strickland from 1832 to 1834 as a forerunner of a stock-and-trading market. It's a pity that the building, once obviously central to city life, isn't open to the public, because the exterior is fascinating—a Greek semicircular front end on the river side and a strong coffer of a building with a portico facing the city. The tower was built to provide instant information on arriving ships.

CEMETERIES

Christ Church Burial Ground. 5th and Arch sts. ☎ **215/922-1695.** Closed to the public. Bus: 48, 50, or PHLASH.

This 1719 expansion of the original graveyard of Christ Church (see below) contains the graves of Benjamin Franklin and his wife, Deborah, along with those of four other signers of the Declaration of Independence and many Revolutionary War heroes. It's a remarkably simple and peaceful place, visible through an openwork fence. There are always pennies on Ben's grave; tossing them there is a local tradition that is supposed to bring good luck.

Laurel Hill Cemetery. 3822 Ridge Ave., East Fairmount Park. ☎ **215/228-8200.** Entrance may be restricted, since it's still in use as a private institution. Grounds open Mon–Fri 8am–4pm, Sat 9:30am–1:30pm. The Friends of Laurel Hill arranges tours (☎ 215/228-8817); $10 donation per person. Bus: 61. Car: Go north on East River Dr.; make a right on Ferry Rd., go 1 block to Ridge Ave., and turn right. The entrance is a half mile down on the right. Free parking.

How come you find Benjamin Franklin buried in a small, flat plot next to a church (see above), while Civil War General George Meade is buried in a bucolic meadow? Basically, the view of death and contemplation of nature changed as the 19th-century romantic movement grew, and Laurel Hill reflects that romanticism. Laurel Hill, designated a National Historic Landmark in 1998, was the second American cemetery (after Mount Auburn in Cambridge) to use funerary monuments—some are like small Victorian palaces. Set amid the rolling, landscaped hills overlooking the Schuylkill, its 100 acres also houses plenty of tomb sculpture, pre-Raphaelite stained glass, and art nouveau sarcophagi. People picnicked here a century ago, but only walking is allowed now.

Mikveh Israel Cemetery. Spruce St. between 8th and 9th sts. ☎ **215/922-5446** (synagogue number). Summer Sun–Thurs 10am–3pm; off-season, contact synagogue or park service. Bus: 47 or 9.

Philadelphia was an early center of American Jewish life, with the second-oldest synagogue (1740) organized by English and Sephardic Jews. While this congregation shifted location and is now adjacent to the Liberty Bell, the original cemetery—well outside the city at the time—was bought from the Penn family by Nathan Levy and later filled with the likes of Haym Solomon, a Polish immigrant who helped finance the revolutionary government, and Rebecca Gratz, the daughter of a fine local family, who provided the model for Sir Walter Scott's Rebecca in *Ivanhoe.*

CHURCHES

Arch Street Meeting House. 4th and Arch sts. ☎ **215/627-2667.** Guided tours year-round. Mon–Sat 10am–4pm. Services Thurs 10am and Sun 10:30am. Bus: 17, 33, 48, 50, or PHLASH.

This plain brick building dates from 1804, but William Penn gave the land to his Religious Society of Friends in 1693. In this capital city of Quakers, the Meeting House opens its doors to 12,000 local Friends for worship during the last week in March each year. Quakers believe in direct, unmediated guidance by the Holy Spirit; individuals publicly search their souls during "threshing sessions" in a Spartan chamber with no pulpit, only hand-hewn benches that face one another. Other areas of the meetinghouse display Bibles, clothing, and implements of Quaker life past and present, along with a simple history of the growth of the religion and the life of William Penn.

Christ Church. 2nd St. ½ block north of Market St. ☎ **215/922-1695.** Donations welcome. Mon–Sat 9am–5pm, Sun 1–5pm. Sun services at 9 and 11am. Closed Jan–Feb. Open Wed–Sun except for major holidays. Bus: 5, 17, 33, 48, or PHLASH.

The most beautiful colonial building north of Market Street has to be Christ Church (1727–54). Its spire gleams white from anywhere in the neighborhood, now that the buildings to the south have been replaced by a grassy park and a subway stop. The churchyard also has benches, tucked under trees or beside brick walls.

Christ Church, dating from the apex of English Palladianism, follows the proud and graceful tradition of Christopher Wren's churches in London. As in many of them, the interior spans one large arch, with galleries above the sides as demanded by the Anglican church. Behind the altar, the massive Palladian window—a central columned arch flanked by proportional rectangles of glass—was the wonder of worshipers and probably the model for the one in Independence Hall. The main chandelier was brought over from England in 1744. As in King's Chapel in Boston, seating is by pew instead of on open benches—Washington's seat is marked with a plaque.

With all the stones, memorials, and plaques, it's impossible to ignore history here. William Penn was baptized at the font, sent over from All Hallows' Church in London. Penn left the Anglican church at age 23 (he spent most of his 20s in English jails because of it), but his charter included a clause that an Anglican church could be founded if 20 residents requested it, which they did. Socially conscious

Philadelphians of the next generations adopted Anglicanism, then switched to Episcopalianism after the Revolution.

Gloria Dei (Old Swedes' Church). 916 Swanson St., near Christian and Delaware aves. ☎ **215/389-1513.** Apr–Oct, daily 9am–5pm. By appointment in the off-season. Bus: 5, 64, or 79. By foot or car: Take Swanson St. under I-95 at Christian St. in Queen Village, opposite Pier 34 and the four-masted schooner-turned-restaurant docked there, then a turn onto Water St.

The National Park Service administers this oldest church in Pennsylvania (1700). Inside the enclosing walls, you'll think you're in the 18th century, with a miniature parish hall, a rectory, and a graveyard amid the greenery. The one-room museum directly across from the church has a map of the good old days.

The simple church interior has plenty of wonderful details. Everybody loves the ship models suspended from the ceiling: The *Key of Kalmar* and *Flying Griffin* carried the first Swedish settlers to these shores in 1638. And note the silver crown in the vestry; any woman married here wears it during the ceremony.

Mother Bethel African Methodist Episcopal Church. 419 S. 6th St. ☎ **215/925-0616.** Donations welcome. Tues–Wed, Fri–Sat, 10am–3pm, Sun noon–1pm. Sun service 10:45am.

This National Historic Landmark site is the oldest piece of land continuously owned by blacks in the United States. Richard Allen, born in 1760, was a slave in Germantown who bought his freedom in 1782, eventually walking out of St. George's down the street to found the African Methodist Episcopal order. The order today numbers some 2.5 million in 6,200 congregations, and this handsome, varnished-wood-and-stained-glass 1890 building is their mother church. Allen's tomb and a small museum, featuring his Bible and hand-hewn pulpit, are below the church floor; open by appointment only.

Old St. Joseph's Church. Willings Alley, near 4th and Walnut sts. ☎ **215/923-1733.** Mon–Fri 11am–3pm, Sat 11am–6:30pm, Sun 8:30am–3pm. One daily mass Mon–Fri, two on Sat, three on Sun. Bus: 21, 42, or 50.

At its 1733 founding, St. Joseph's was the only place in the English-speaking world where Roman Catholics could celebrate mass publicly. The story goes that Benjamin Franklin advised Father Greaton to protect the church, since religious bigotry wasn't unknown even in the Quaker city. That's why the building is so unassuming from the street, a fact that didn't save it from damage during the anti-Catholic riots of the 1830s. Such French allies as Lafayette worshipped here. The present building (1838) is Greek Revival merging into Victorian, with wooden pews and such unusual colors as mustard and pale yellow, but the interior has preserved a colonial style unusual in a Catholic church.

St. Peter's Episcopal. 3rd and Pine sts. ☎ **215/925-5968.** Tues–Sat 9am–noon, Sun 1–4pm. Guided tours Sat 10am–noon and 1–3pm, Sun 1–3pm. Bus: 50, 90, or PHLASH.

St. Peter's (1761) was originally established through the bishop of London and has remained continuously open since. So like all pre-Revolutionary Episcopal churches, St. Peter's started out as an Anglican shrine. But what was wrong with Christ Church at 2nd and Market? In a word: mud. As a local historian put it, "the long tramp from Society Hill was more and more distasteful to fine gentlemen and beautiful belles."

Robert Smith, the builder of Carpenters' Hall, continued his penchant for red brick, pediments on the ends, and keystoned arches for gallery windows. The white box pews are evidence that not much has changed. Unlike in most churches, the wineglass pulpit is set into the west end and the chancel is at the east, so the minister had to do some walking during the service. George Washington and Mayor Samuel Powel sat in pew 41. The 1764 organ case blocks the east Palladian window. The steeple outside, constructed in 1842, was designed by William Strickland to house a chime of bells, which are still played.

Seven Native American chiefs lie in the graveyard, victims of the 1793 smallpox epidemic. Painter C. W. Peale, Stephen Decatur of naval fame, Nicholas Biddle of the Second Bank of the United States, and other notables also are interred here.

HISTORIC BUILDINGS & MONUMENTS

Betsy Ross House. 239 Arch St. ☎ **215/627-5343.** Suggested contribution $2 adults, 50¢ children. Tues–Sun 10am–5pm. Bus: 5, 17, 33, 48, or PHLASH.

One colonial home everybody knows about is this one near Christ Church, restored in 1937, and distinguished by the Stars and Stripes outside. Elizabeth (Betsy) Ross was a Quaker needlewoman who, newly widowed in 1776, worked as a seamstress and upholsterer out of her home on Arch Street. Nobody is quite sure if no. 239 was hers, though. And nobody knows for sure if she did the original American flag of 13 stars set in a field of 13 red-and-white stripes, but she was commissioned to sew ship's flags for the American fleet to replace the earlier Continental banners.

The house takes only a minute or two to walk through. The wooden stairwell was designed for shorter colonial frames—certainly not Washington's! The house is set back from the street, and the city maintains the Atwater Kent Park in front, where Ross and her last husband are buried. The upholstery shop (now a gift shop renovated in 1998) opens into the period parlor. Other rooms include the cellar kitchen (standard placement for this room), tiny bedrooms, and model working areas for upholstering, making musket balls, and the like. Note such little touches as reusable note tablets made of ivory; pinecones used to help start hearth fires; and the prominent kitchen hourglass. Flag Day celebrations are held here on June 14 (see "Philadelphia Calendar of Events," in chapter 2).

Carpenters' Hall. 320 Chestnut St. ☎ **215/925-0167.** Free admission. Tues–Sun 10am–4pm; Wed–Sun in Jan–Feb. Bus: 9, 21, 42, 76, or PHLASH.

Carpenters' Hall (1773) was the guildhall for—guess who?—carpenters. At the time the city could use plenty, for 18th-century Philadelphia was the fastest-growing urban area in all the colonies and perhaps in the British Empire outside of London. Robert Smith, a Scottish member of the Carpenters' Company, designed the building (like most carpenters, he did architecture and contracting as well). He also designed the steeple of Christ Church, with the same calm Georgian lines. It's made of Flemish Bond brick in a checkerboard pattern, with stone windowsills, superb woodwork, and a cupola that resembles a salt shaker.

You'll be surprised at how small Carpenters' Hall is given the great events that transpired here. In 1774, the normal governmental channels to convey colonial complaints to the Crown were felt inadequate, and a popular Committee of Correspondence debated in Carpenters' Hall. The more radical delegates, led by Patrick Henry, had already expressed treasonous wishes for independence, but most wanted to exhaust possibilities of bettering their relationship with the Crown first.

What's here now isn't much—an exhibit of colonial building methods; some portraits; and Windsor chairs that seated the First Continental Congress. If some details seem to be from a later period, you're right: The fanlights above the north and south doors date from the 1790s, and the gilding dates from 1857. Hours are short because the Carpenters' Company still maintains the hall.

Declaration House (Graff House). 7th and Market sts. ☎ **215/597-8974.** Free admission (part of Independence National Historical Park). Varies by season; daily 9am–5pm in summer, shorter hours off-season. Bus: 17, 33, 48, 76, or PHLASH.

Bricklayer Jacob Graff constructed a modest 3-story home in the 1770s, intending to rent out the second floor for added income. The Second Continental Congress soon brought to the house a thin, red-haired tenant named Thomas Jefferson, in search of a quiet room away from city noise. He must have found it, because he drafted the Declaration of Independence here between June 10 and June 18, 1776.

The 1975 reconstruction uses the same Flemish Bond checkerboard pattern (only on visible walls; it was too expensive for party walls) for brick, windows with paneled shutters, and implements that the house exhibited in 1775. Compared to Society Hill homes, it's tiny and asymmetrical, with an off-center front door. You'll enter through a small garden and see a short film about Jefferson and a copy of Jefferson's draft (which would have forbidden slavery in the United States, had the clause survived debate). The upstairs rooms are furnished as Jefferson would have seen them.

✪ **Elfreth's Alley.** 2nd St. between Arch and Race sts. ☎ **215/574-0560.** Street is public; Mantua Maker's House admission $1 adults, 50¢ children, $2.50 families. Tues–Sat 10am–4pm, Sun noon–4pm. Bus: 5, 48, 76, or PHLASH.

The modern Benjamin Franklin Bridge shadows Elfreth's Alley, the oldest continuously inhabited street in America. Most of colonial Philadelphia looked like this: cobblestone lanes between the major thoroughfares; small two-story homes; and pent eaves over doors and windows, a local trademark. Note the busybody mirrors that let residents see who was at their door (or someone else's) from the second-story bedroom. In 1700, most of the resident artisans and tradesmen worked in shipping, but 50 years later haberdashers, bakers, printers, and house carpenters set up shop. Families moved in and out rapidly, for noisy, dusty 2nd Street was the major north-south route in Philadelphia. Jews, blacks, Welsh, and Germans made it a miniature melting pot in the 18th and 19th centuries. The destruction of the street was averted in 1937, thanks to the vigilant Elfreth's Alley Association and a good deal of luck. The minuscule, sober facades hide some ultramodern interiors, and there are some restful shady benches under a Kentucky Coffee Bean tree on Bladen Court, off the north side of the street.

Number 126, the 1755 **Mantua Maker's House** (cape maker), built by blacksmith Jeremiah Elfreth, now serves as a museum and is the only house open to the public. An 18th-century garden in back has been restored, and the interiors include a dressmaker's shop and upstairs bedroom. You can also buy colonial candy and gifts and peek in some of the open windows on the street. On the first weekend in June all the houses are thrown open for inspection—don't miss this.

Masonic Temple. 1 N. Broad St. ☎ **215/988-1917.** Free admission. Tours Mon–Fri at 10 and 11am and 1, 2, and 3pm, Sat at 10 and 11am. Bus: 17, 33, 44, 48, or 76.

Quite apart from its Masonic lore, the temple—among the world's largest—is one of America's best on-site illustrations of the use of post–Civil War architecture and design—no expense was spared in the construction, and the halls are more or less frozen in time. There are seven lodge halls, designed to capture the seven "ideal" architectures: Renaissance, Ionic, Oriental, Corinthian, Gothic, Egyptian, and Norman (notice that Renaissance was the newest style that architect James Windrim could come up with!). This is the preeminent Masonic Temple of American Freemasonry; many of the Founding Fathers, including Washington, were Masons, and the museum has preserved their letters and emblems.

Pennsylvania Hospital. 8th and Spruce sts. ☎ **215/829-3971.** Free admission. Mon–Fri 9am–5pm. Guided tours are no longer obligatory; copies of a walking tour itinerary available from the Marketing Department on the 2nd floor of the Pine St. bldg. Bus: 47 or 90.

Pennsylvania Hospital, like so much in civic Philadelphia, owes its presence to Benjamin Franklin. This was the first hospital in the colonies, and it seemed like a strange venture into social welfare at the time. Samuel Rhoads, a fine architect in the Carpenters' Company, designed the Georgian headquarters; the east wing, nearest 8th Street, was completed in 1755, and a west wing matched it in 1797. The grand Center Building by David Evans completed the ensemble in 1804. The marble pilasters and arched doorway of the middle structure add curving grace to the anchorlike wings. Instead of a dome, the hospital decided on a surgical amphitheater's skylight. In spring, the garden's azaleas brighten the neighborhood, and the beautifully designed herb garden is equally popular.

✪ **Powel House.** 244 S. 3rd St. ☎ **215/627-0364** or 215/925-2251. www.ushistory.org. Admission $3 adults, $2 students and seniors; free for children under 6. Guided tours only. Thurs–Sat noon–5pm, Sun 1–5pm. Be sure to arrive at least 30 min. before closing. Bus: 50, 76, or 90.

If Elfreth's Alley (see above) leaves you hungry for a taste of more well-to-do colonial Philadelphia, head for the Powel House. Mayor Samuel Powel and his wife, Elizabeth, hosted every founding father and foreign dignitary around. (John Adams called these feasts "sinful dinners," which shows how far Powel had come from his Quaker background.) He spent most of his 20s gallivanting around Europe, collecting wares for this 1765 mansion.

It's hard to believe that this most Georgian of houses was slated for demolition in 1930, because it had become a decrepit slum dwelling. Period rooms were removed to the Philadelphia Museum of Art and the Metropolitan Museum of Art in New York. But the Philadelphia Society for the Preservation of Landmarks saved it and has gradually refurnished the entire mansion as it was. The yellow satin Reception Room, off the entrance hall, has some gorgeous details, such as a widegrain mahogany secretary. Upstairs, the magnificent ballroom features red damask drapes whose design is copied from a bolt of cloth found untouched in a colonial attic. There is also a 1790 Irish crystal chandelier and a letter from Benjamin Franklin's daughter referring to the lively dances held here. An 18th-century garden lies below.

LIBRARIES & LITERARY SITES

Athenaeum of Philadelphia. 219 S. 6th St. (Washington Sq. E.). ☎ **215/925-2688.** www.philaAthenaeum.org. Free admission. Mon–Fri 9am–5pm. Permission to enter and guided tours given on request. Bus: 21, 42, or 90.

The age when a group of private subscribers could fund the dissemination of useful knowledge in diverse fields—or even keep tabs on it—has long since passed, but a 15-minute peek into the Athenaeum will show you one of America's finest collections of Victorian-period architectural design and also give you the flavor of private 19th-century life for the proper Philadelphian. The building, beautifully restored in 1975, houses almost one million library items for the serious researcher in American architecture. Visitors are welcome to the changing exhibitions of rare books, drawings, and photographs in the recently reconstructed first-floor gallery; tours of the entire building or collections require an appointment.

Free Library of Philadelphia. Central Library, Logan Circle at 19th and Vine sts. ☎ **215/ 686-5322.** Mon–Wed 9am–9pm, Thurs–Fri 9am–6pm, Sat 9am–5pm, Sun 1–5pm. Bus: 32, 33, 76, or PHLASH.

Splendidly situated on the north side of Logan Circle, the Free Library of Philadelphia rivals the public libraries of Boston and New York for magnificence and diversity. The library and its twin, the Municipal Court, are copies of buildings in the Place de la Concorde in Paris (the library's on the left).

The main lobby and the gallery always have some of the institution's riches on display, from medieval manuscripts to exhibits of modern bookbinding. Greeting cards and stationery are sold for reasonable prices, too. The second floor houses the best local history, travel, and resource collection in the city. The local 130,000-item map collection is fascinating. The third-floor rare book room hosts visitors Monday to Friday 9am to 5pm, with tours at 11am or by appointment. If you're interested in manuscripts, children's literature, incunabula, and early American hornbooks, or just want to see a stuffed raven, this is the place.

If you're hungry, Marietta's Skyline Cafe (open Mon–Fri 9am–4pm) is a very nice location for a snack and one of the only dining options on the Parkway. There's also an active concert and film series.

Edgar Allan Poe National Historical Site. 532 N. 7th St. (near Spring Garden St.). ☎ **215/597-8780.** Free admission. Daily 9am–5pm in summer; closed Mon–Tues Nov–May. Bus: 47.

The acclaimed American author, though more associated with Baltimore, Richmond, and New York City, lived here from 1843 to 1844. "The Black Cat," "The Gold Bug," and "The Tell-Tale Heart" were published while he was a resident. Just re-opened following structural work, it's a simple place—after all, Poe was poor most of his life—and the National Park Service keeps it unfurnished. An adjoining building contains basic information on Poe's life and work, along with a reading room and slide presentation. The Park Service also runs intermittent discussions and candlelight tours on Saturday afternoon.

Rosenbach Museum and Library. 2010 Delancey Place (between Spruce and Pine sts). ☎ **215/732-1600.** www.rosenbach.org. Admission $5 adults, $3 children under 18 and seniors. Tues–Sun 11am–4pm; last tour at 2:45pm. Closed Aug. Bus: 17 or 90.

The Rosenbach specializes in books: illuminated manuscripts, parchment, rough drafts, and first editions. If you love the variations and beauty of the printed word, they'll love your presence.

You're not allowed absolute freedom in the opulent town-house galleries, or free rein among the 30,000 rare books and 270,000 documents. Some rooms preserve the Rosenbachs' elegant living quarters, with antique furniture and Sully paintings. Others are devoted to authors and illustrators: Marianne Moore's Greenwich Village study is reproduced in its entirety, and the Maurice Sendak drawings represent only the tip of his iceberg (or forest). Holdings include the original manuscript of Joyce's *Ulysses* and first editions of Melville, in the author's own bookcase. Small special exhibitions are tucked in throughout the house, and don't miss the shop behind the entrance for bargains in greeting cards and a superb collection of Sendak.

Some welcome changes are taking place, with access for people with disabilities and the option of either guided or unaccompanied visits. However, parts of the Rosenbach will be closed to visitors until December 2001 for necessary work.

MORE MUSEUMS & EXHIBITIONS

Academy of Natural Sciences. 19th St. and Benjamin Franklin Pkwy. ☎ **215/299-1000.** www.acnatsci.org. Admission $8.50 adults, $7.75 seniors, $7.50 children 3–12, free for children under 3. Mon–Fri 10am–4:30pm; Sat–Sun and holidays 10am–5pm. Bus: 32, 33, 76, or PHLASH.

Philadelphia's Oddball Museums

Philadelphia has an amazing assortment of small single-interest museums, built out of the passions of, or inspired by, a single individual. Maybe you and your family are ready for these!

- The Mummer's Parade on New Year's Day is uniquely Philadelphian; dozens of crews spend months practicing their musical and strutting skills with spectacular costumes. Talk about multicultural—mumming comes out of both Anglo-Saxon pagan celebrations and African dancing. The **Mummers Museum,** 2nd Street and Washington Avenue (☎ **215/336-3050**), is devoted to the history and display of this phenomenon. It's open Tuesday to Saturday 9:30am to 5pm and Sunday noon to 5pm.

- In the northeast district of the city, it's a schlepp, but Steve Kanya's **Insectarium,** 8046 Frankford Ave. (☎ **215/338-3000**), has taken off (mostly as a school-class destination) thanks to a write-up in the *Wall Street Journal.* Can you believe an admission of only $3 to watch more than 40,000 cockroaches, assorted bugs, and their predators (scorpions, tarantulas, and so on) scurry around? It's open Monday to Saturday 10am to 4pm.

- Also not for the squeamish is the **Mutter Museum,** 19 S. 22nd St. (☎ **215/587-9919**), a collection of preserved human oddities assembled in the 1850s by a Philadelphia physician. Skeletons of giants and dwarves and row on row of plaster casts of abnormalities inhabit this varnished, musty place. It's open Tuesday to Friday 10am to 4pm.

- What could belong more in South Philly than the **Mario Lanza Museum,** 416 Queen St. (☎ **215/468-3623**)? This tribute to the actor/tenor is on the site of his first music lessons, with a life-size bust, clippings, and telegrams. It's open September to June, Monday to Saturday 10am to 3:30pm.

If you're looking for dinosaurs, the Academy is the best place to find them. Kids love the big diorama halls, with cases of various species mounted and posed in authentic settings. A permanent display, "Discovering Dinosaurs," features more than a dozen specimens, including a huge *Tyrannosaurus rex* with jaws agape. The Dig (weekends only) gives you an opportunity to dig for fossils in a re-created field station. The North American Hall, on the first floor, has enormous moose, buffalo, and bears. A small marine exhibit shows how some fish look different in ultraviolet light and how the bed of the Delaware has changed since Penn landed in 1682.

The second floor features groupings of Asian and African flora and fauna. Many of the cases have nearby headphones that tell you more about what you're seeing. Five or six live demonstrations are given here every day; the handlers are expert in conducting these sessions with rocks, birds, plants, and animals. Several daily Eco Shows are given in the auditorium downstairs too. The Egyptian mummy, a priest of a late dynasty, seems a bit out of place.

Upstairs, "Outside In" is a touchable museum designed for children under 12, with a model campsite, fossils, minerals, shells, and other unbreakables. It stimulates almost every sense: Children can see, feel, hear, and smell live turtles, mice, bees in a beehive, and snakes (all caged) and wander around mock forests and deserts. A large bird hall and a hall of endangered species round out the picture, along with frequent films. There's a brown-bag lunchroom and vending area with drinks and snacks.

Afro-American Historical and Cultural Museum. 7th and Arch sts. ☎ **215/574-0380.** Admission $6 adults, $4 children and seniors. Tues–Sat 10am–5pm, Sun noon–6pm. Bus: 47, 48, or PHLASH.

This museum, 3 blocks northwest of the Liberty Bell, is built in five split levels of ridged concrete (meant to evoke African mud housing) off a central atrium and ramp. As you ascend, you follow a path leading from the African roots of black Americans to the role they have played in U.S. history. Specific exhibitions change.

The ground floor contains the admissions office, the gift shop, and the African Heritage Gallery. The second level, concentrating on slavery and captivity, is the most dramatic and informed part of the museum. It emphasizes that the slave trade was hardly exclusive to, or even predominant in, North America, and that it persisted in South American until 1870.

The upper three levels, dealing with black history and culture after emancipation, lose some focus. Black cowboys, inventors, athletes, spokespeople, and business-people are all presented, along with the history of such organizations as the NAACP and CORE and the civil rights movements of the 1960s.

American Swedish Historical Museum. 1900 Pattison Ave. ☎ **215/389-1776.** www. libertynet.org/ashm. Admission $5 adults, $4 students and seniors, free for children under 12. Tues–Fri 10am–4pm, Sat noon–4pm. Bus: 17. Near the Naval Hospital and Veterans Stadium, at the southern edge of the city.

Modeled after a 17th-century Swedish manor house, this small museum chronicles 350 years of the life and accomplishments of Swedish Americans. Specific rooms highlight John Ericsson, inventor of the Civil War ironclads, 19th-century opera singer Jenny Lind, and a "Hands On Swedish History" room for children. Traditional Swedish holidays are celebrated year round, including *Valborgsmässoafton* (Spring Festival) in April, *Midsommarfest* in June, and the procession of St. Lucia and her attendants in December.

Atwater Kent Museum. 15 S. 7th St. ☎ **215/922-3031.** www.philadelphiahistory.org. Admission $3 adults, $2 seniors, $1.50 children. Tues–Sat 10am–5pm. Bus: 17, 33, 42, 76, or PHLASH.

Across the street from the Balch Institute (see below), the small and newly vitalized Atwater Kent Museum occupies an 1826 John Haviland building. The Atwater Kent shows you—with more artifacts than the Visitors Center—what Philadelphia was like from 1680 to today. Atwater Kent, you may remember, built most of America's early radios, and much of his fortune benefited Philadelphia's gardens and societies. Nothing, apparently, was too trivial to include in this collection, which jumps from dolls to dioramas, from cigar-store Indians to period toyshops. Sunbonnets, train tickets, rocking horses, ship models, and military uniforms all fill out the display. A hands-on history laboratory opens in 2001.

Balch Institute for Ethnic Studies. 18 S. 7th St. ☎ **215/925-8090.** Admission $2 adults, $1 students and seniors. Free Sat. Mon–Sat 10am–4pm. Bus: 17, 33, 42, 76, or PHLASH.

The United States is virtually the only country where nearly everyone comes from someplace else, and is proud of it. The institute has a terrific library that covers everything you've always wanted to know about your roots, for more than 100 ethnicities. The exhibits change every couple of months, ranging from ethnic images in World War I posters to African crafts.

Independence Seaport Museum. Penn's Landing at 211 S. Columbus Blvd. ☎ **215/925-5439.** www.libertynet.org/seaport. Admission $5 adults, $4 seniors, $2.50 children. Combined admission to the museum and Historic Ship Zone (USS *Olympia* and USS *Becuna;* see below) $7.50 adults, $6 seniors, $3.50 children. Daily 10am–5pm except for major holidays. RiverLink tickets, including admission to the museum, the Riverbus Ferry, and the New Jersey State Aquarium at Camden, $18.50 adults, $16 seniors, $13.50 children 3–11; this will take at least 5 hours. Bus: 5, 21, 33, 76, or PHLASH.

Opposite Walnut Street, between the two dock areas, is this great new facility in the contemporary poured-concrete structure north of the Olympia jetty. The match between the 1981 state-owned building and the 1961 museum took several years to achieve, but was consummated in July 1995. Now the user-friendly maritime museum is the jewel in the crown of the city's waterfront.

The museum is beautifully laid out, blending a first-class maritime collection with interactive exhibits for a trip through time that engages all ages. Its 11,000-square-foot main gallery is the centerpiece for exhibits, educational outreach, and activities that are jazzy and eye-catching without being noisy or obtrusive. Twelve sections mix the personal with the professional—call up interviews with river pilots, navy personnel, and shipbuilders. My family loves the stories of immigrants who flooded Philadelphia between 1920 and 1970, and the rich reminiscences and memorabilia that make the past come to life. I defy anyone to ace the computer-screen quiz.

One of the museum's most attractive features is the **Workshop on the Water,** where you can watch classes and amateurs undertake traditional wooden boat building and restoration throughout the year. Classmates bid on the chance to keep the boat they build. A new permanent exhibit, "Boats Afloat," explores the basic scientific principles in boat design and building.

National Museum of American Jewish History. 55 N. 5th St. ☎ **215/923-8811.** www.nmajh.org (a great Web site!). Admission $3 adults; $2 students, seniors, and children; free for children under 6. Mon–Thurs 10am–5pm, Fri 10am–3pm, Sun noon–5pm. Bus: 17, 33, 48, 50, or PHLASH.

This is the only museum specifically dedicated to preserving and presenting Jewish participation in the development of the United States. Don't expect to walk into another colonial structure. The complex was built in the aftermath of the 1950s' clearance that allowed for Independence Mall, although the congregation connected to it, Mikveh Israel, was established in Philadelphia in 1740 (see the "Cemeteries" section). Enter close to 4th Street (passing Christ Church Cemetery, with Ben Franklin's grave) into a dark-brick lobby. The museum starts with a fascinating permanent exhibition, "Creating American Jews," combining reproductions of portraits and documents, actual diaries, letters, and oral histories from five diverse "snapshots" involving today's 6 million American Jews and their predecessors. Smaller rotating exhibitions supplement this presentation. Attracting 40,000 visitors a year, the museum is usually cool and restful and makes a good break from a hot Independence Park tour, although its proximity to the new Gateway Visitors Centers and the improved Independence Mall will bring much more traffic and possible renovations. A small gift shop is attached.

Physick House. 321 S. 4th St. ☎ **215/925-7866** or 215/925-2251. Admission $3. Thurs–Sat noon–4pm, Sun 1pm–4pm June–Aug; Thurs–Sat 11am–2pm Sept–May. Guided tours only. Bus: 50, 90, or PHLASH.

Like the Powel house (discussed earlier in the chapter), the Physick (formerly Hill-Physick-Keith) House combines attractive design and historical interest. The house is the area's most impressive—freestanding but not boxy, gracious but solid. Built during the 1780s boom, with money from importing Madeira wine, it soon wound up housing the father of American surgery, Philip Syng Physick (a very propitious name for a physician). The usual pattern of neglect and renovation has applied here, on an even grander scale.

All the cloths and wallpapers were fashioned expressly for use here, and the mansion as restored is a landmark of the Federal style from about 1815. The drawing room opens onto a lovely 19th-century walled garden and shows the excitement caused by the discovery of the buried city of Pompeii, including a Roman stool and 18th-century Italian art. Look for an inkstand tarnished by Ben Franklin's fingerprints. Dr. Physick treated Chief Justice Marshall, and Marshall's portrait and gift of a wine stand testify to the doctor's powers.

Please Touch Museum. 210 N. 21st St. ☎ **215/963-0667.** www.pleasetouchmuseum. org. Admission $6.95 adults and children. Voluntary donation Sun 9–10am. No strollers inside, but Snuglis available. Daily 9am–6pm July–Labor Day, 9am–4:30pm Sept–June. Bus: 7, 48, or 76.

This is one of the best indoor activities in town for a younger family, and the location is great—just off the Parkway, 2 blocks south of the Franklin Institute. The museum is the first in the country designed specifically for children 7 years and younger. Dedicated to a unique fun-filled educational, cultural, hands-on experience, the converted factories help bring out the creative, exuberant, and receptive in us all.

Once you're in, you can park strollers, check coats, and buy tickets at counters that cater to kids. Exciting hands-on exhibits like "Growing Up" encourage parent/child participation and focus on specific social, cognitive, and emotional areas of child development. "Studio PTM," installed in 1993, allows children to experience being behind the camera and on stage in a television studio, including sound effects and camera angles. New in 1995 was an exhibit of oversized settings and creatures from celebrated author/illustrator Maurice Sendak. My own kids love "Nature's Nursery," with toy animals revealed through various pushes and pulls; "Play in Motion," which mixes gymnastics and science; and "Foodtastic Journey," with an extensive play route from farm to supermarket to kitchen.

In 2002, the Museum will relocate to the Penn's Landing Family Entertainment Center now under construction. This will be a 130,000 square foot, $55 million project designed to be the best children's museum in the nation, and galleries will reflect its new neighbors of the River and Center City skyline, as well as a 60-seat carousel outside.

Until then, the museum collaborates with the Franklin Institute to operate the 38,000-square-foot CoreStates Science Park between May and October, on the lawn between the two institutions. It's a great playground for the mind and body.

The Please Touch Museum is not a day-care center; you cannot simply drop the kids off, and you won't want to. Educational activities like storytelling and crafts are available daily 11am to 3:30pm. It's also a great place to celebrate a child's birthday, if you care to plan ahead.

Rodin Museum. Benjamin Franklin Pkwy. between 21st and 22nd sts. ☎ **215/763-8100.** $3 donation requested. Free with same-day admission ticket from the Philadelphia Museum of Art (see above). Tues–Sun 10am–5pm. Bus: 32, 38, or 76.

The Rodin Museum exhibits the largest collection of the master's work (129 sculptures) outside the Musée Rodin in Paris. It has inherited a little of its sibling museum's romantic mystery, making a very French use of space inside and boasting

You Paid What?

47,000 hotels, 700 airlines,
50 rental car companies. And a few
million ways to save money.

Travelocity.com
A Sabre Company

Go Virtually Anywhere.

AOL Keyword: Travel

Will you have enough stories to tell your grandchildren?

©2000 Yahoo! Inc.

Yahoo! Travel

much greenery outside. Entering from the Parkway, virtually across the street from the Franklin Institute (see above), you'll contemplate *The Thinker* contemplating other things, then pass through an imposing arch to a front garden of hardy shrubs and trees surrounding a fish pond. Before going into the museum, study the *Gates of Hell.* These gigantic doors reveal an awesome power to mold metal by the force of passionate imagination.

The galleries have just reopened after a 2000 top-to-bottom renovation, and the works look superb, with a cleaned-up exterior to boot. The main hall holds autho-rized casts of *John the Baptist, The Cathedral,* and *The Burghers of Calais.* Several of the side chambers and the library hold powerful erotic plaster models. Drawings, sketchbooks, and Steichen photographic portraits of Rodin are exhibited from time to time.

U.S. Mint. 5th and Arch sts. ☎ **215/408-0114.** Free admission. Sept–Apr Mon–Fri 9am–4:30pm; May–June Mon–Sat 9am–4:30pm; July–Aug daily 9am–4:30pm. Closed New Year's Day, Christmas. Bus: 5, 48, or 76.

The U.S. Mint building was the first authorized by the government, during Wash-ington's first term. The present edifice, diagonally across from Liberty Bell Pavilion, turns out about 1.5 million coins every hour—almost enough to pay your credit card bills. This is one factory tour that's quite stingy when it comes to free samples, but a self-guided walk through the process has its own rewards.

The coinage process involves melting raw metal, rolling it to coin thinness, punching out blanks from these sheets, and pressing designs on them. Then a counting machine automatically sorts lots of 5,000 into bags, headed for Federal Reserve Banks. Points along the route have prerecorded commentary, in case you were wondering, say, how the layers in composite coins stick together.

University of Pennsylvania Museum of Archaeology and Anthropology. 33rd and Spruce sts. ☎ **215/898-4000.** www.upenn.edu/museum. Admission $5 adults, $2.50 stu-dents and seniors, free for children under 6. Tues–Sat 10am–4:30pm, Sun 1–5pm. Closed Mon, holidays, and summer Sun Memorial Day to Labor Day. Bus: 21, 30 (from 30th St. Sta-tion), 40, or 42.

The University of Pennsylvania Museum, which celebrated its centennial in 1986–87, is endowed with Benin bronzes, ancient cuneiform texts, Mesopotamian masterpieces, pre-Columbian gold, and artifacts of every continent, mostly brought back from the more than 350 expeditions it has sponsored over the years. The taller structures that surround this museum give its Romanesque brickwork and gardens a secluded feel. The museum has had spectacular special exhibitions recently, with forays into ancient Iran, Roman glass, and works from ancient Canaan and Israel.

The museum is intelligently explained. The basement Egyptian galleries, including colossal architectural remains from Memphis and "The Egyptian Mummy: Secrets and Science," are family favorites. Probably the most famous excavation display, located on the third floor, is a spectacular Sumerian trove of jewelry and household objects from the royal tombs of the ancient city of Ur. Adjoining this, huge cloisonné lions from Peking's (now Beijing's) Imperial Palace guard Chinese court treasures and tomb figures. The Ancient Greek Gallery in the classical world collection, renovated in 1994, has 400 superb objects such as red-figure pottery—a flower of Greek civilization—and an unusual lead sarcophagus from Tyre that looks like a miniature house. Other galleries display Native American and Polynesian culture and a small but excellent African collection of bronze plaques and statues.

The glass-enclosed Museum Cafe, overlooking the museum's inner gardens, serves cafeteria-style snacks and light meals 8:30am to 3:30pm on weekdays, 10am to 4pm on Saturday, and 1 to 5pm on Sunday. The Museum Shop has cards and jewelry and crafts from around the world, and the Pyramid Shop has children's items. There's also a very active schedule of events throughout the year.

A UNIVERSITY

University of Pennsylvania. 34th and Walnut sts. and surrounding neighborhood. ☎ **215/898-5000.** www.upenn.edu. Bus: 21, 30, 40, 42, or 90. Car: Market/Chestnut exit from I-76 (Schuylkill Expressway), 6 blocks west toward West Philadelphia.

This private, coeducational Ivy League institution was founded by Benjamin Franklin and others in 1740. It boasts America's first medical (1765), law (1790), and business (1881) schools. Penn's liberal arts curriculum, dating from 1756, was the first to combine classical and practical subjects. The university has been revitalized in the last 25 years, thanks to extremely successful leadership, alumni, and fund-raising drives. Under President Judith Rodin, it's starting to reshape its neighborhood positively, with the successful Sansom Commons project across the street, including the wonderful Inn at Penn, retail stores, cinemas, the massive Barnes & Noble–run university bookstore, and a second project on 40th Street in the works.

The core campus, moved to West Philadelphia in the 1870s, features serene Gothic-style buildings and specimen trees in a spacious quadrangle. More modern buildings punctuate the 20th-century expansion of the university to accommodate 22,000 students enrolled in 4 undergraduate and 12 graduate schools, in 100 academic departments. Sites of most interest to visitors include the University Museum of Archaeology and Anthropology, the Annenberg Center for the Performing Arts, and the Institute for Contemporary Art.

A ZOO & AN AQUARIUM

✪ **Philadelphia Zoological Gardens.** 34th St. and Girard Ave. ☎ **215/243-1100.** Admission $8.50 adults, $6 seniors and children 2–11, free for children under 2. Parking spaces for 1,800 cars, $4 per vehicle. Mon–Fri 9:30am–4:45pm, Sat–Sun 9:30am–5:45pm. Closed Thanksgiving, Christmas, and New Year's Day. Bus: 76. Car: Separate exit off I-76 north of Center City.

The Philadelphia Zoo, opened in 1874, was the nation's first. By the late 1970s, the 42 acres tucked into West Fairmount Park had become rundown, with few financial resources. The zoo has since become a national leader, with more than 1,500 animals, although it has had a run of bad luck: In December 1995, a fire destroyed the Primate House and killed dozens of animals. The Zoo celebrated its 125th with the opening of the PECO Primate Center, a breathtaking pavilion that blurs the line between visitors and its 11 species.

The 1½-acre Carnivore Kingdom houses snow leopards and jaguars, but the biggest attraction is the rare white lions. Feeding time is around 11am for smaller carnivores, 3pm for tigers and lions. The monkeys have a new home on four naturally planted islands, where a variety of primate species live together naturally.

In the new Jungle Bird Walk, you can walk among free-flying birds. Glass enclosures have been replaced with wire mesh so that the birds' songs can now be heard from both sides.

As part of the zoo's concern to educate visitors about animal life, a spectacular children's exhibit, the Treehouse ($1), was opened in 1985. It contains six larger-than-life habitats for kids of all ages to explore—oversize eggs to hatch from, an oversize honeycomb to crawl through, and a 4-story ficus tree to climb and see life

> ## ❷ Did You Know?
>
> - The "hex" signs that adorn barns and houses in Pennsylvania Dutch Country were a sign to travelers that German was spoken within.
> - The first public protest in America against slavery was held at the Germantown Friends (Quaker) Meeting House in 1688.
> - The Benjamin Franklin Parkway is one of the widest streets (250 feet) in the world.
> - Ben Franklin's 1752 kite-flying experiment took place at what is now the corner of 10th and Ludlow streets.
> - George Washington lived in a mansion at the corner of 5th and Chestnut streets for his entire two terms as president.
> - On July 16, 1987, at Independence Mall, the U.S. Congress held a rare session outside the Capitol for the special bicentennial celebration of the U.S. Constitution.
> - The first medical school (1765), law school (1790), and business school (1881) in the United States were established at the University of Pennsylvania.

from a bird's-eye view. The very popular Camel Rides ($1.50) start next to the Treehouse. A Children's Zoo (50¢) portion of the gardens lets your kids pet and feed some baby zoo and farm animals; this closes 30 minutes before the zoo proper. Pony rides ($1) are also given here.

Other exhibits include polar bears; the renovated Reptile House, which bathes its snakes and tortoises with simulated tropical thunderstorms; and cavorting antelopes, zebras, and giraffes that coexist on the "African Plains" exhibit. For a quick survey, consider the Monorail Safari ($2 for adults, $1.50 for children, 50¢ more on weekends; operated Apr–Nov). It circumnavigates the zoo in 20 minutes, and has a prerecorded narrative.

The zoo has a McDonald's across from the lion house. There is a Fidelity Bank MAC ATM machine at the North Gate.

✪ **New Jersey State Aquarium.** 1 Riverside Dr., Camden, NJ 08103. ☎ **609/365-3300.** www.njaquarium.org. Admission $12.95 adults, $11.45 students and seniors, $9.95 children 3–11, free for children under 3. Reserved admission through TicketMaster (800/616-JAWS) is recommended (there's a handling charge). April 15–Sept 15 daily 9:30am–5:30pm; Sept 16–April 15 Mon–Fri 9:30am–4:30pm Sat–Sun 10am–5pm. Closed Thanksgiving, Christmas, and New Year's Day. Ferry: The RiverLink ferry from Independence Seaport Museum at Penn's Landing is $5 adults, $3 children, each way (see Seaport Museum listing above for ferry/package admissions); hourly arrivals/departures. Car: From I-676 eastbound (Vine St. Expressway/Ben Franklin Bridge) or westbound from I-295/New Jersey Turnpike, take Mickle Blvd. exit and follow signs.

The aquarium opened in 1992 as a first step in reclaiming the once-vital (and now denuded) Camden waterfront with a hotel and marina, trade center, and office and commercial development. As an aquarium, it fills a true niche in the Delaware Valley.

Up to 4,000 aquatic animals live here. The main attraction is a 760,000-gallon tank, the second largest (next to Epcot Center's) in the country, with stepped seat/benches arranged in a Greek amphitheater on the first floor. Three times a day, a diver answers questions through a "scuba phone." This window wall is by far the best; parents of younger children will find few other flat edges for them to stand on for views. This "Ocean Base Atlantic" tank also contains sharks, rockfish, a ship-wreck, and a mockup of the underwater Hudson canyon off the Jersey coast. Also on the first floor is a Caribbean outpost with 1,000 new tropical fish. The second floor features interactive exhibits and strange ocean dwellers. Touch tanks are on both floors.

The Riverview Café serves basic fast food; outdoor seating is frequently windy.

4 Parks & Penn's Landing

BENJAMIN FRANKLIN PARKWAY

The Parkway, a broad diagonal swath linking City Hall to Fairmount Park, wasn't included in Penn's original plan. In the 1920s, however, Philadelphians wanted a grand boulevard in the style of the Champs Elysées. In summer, a walk from the Visitors Center to the "Museum on the Hill" becomes a flower-bedecked and leafy stroll; but all year-round, institutions, public art, and museums enrich the avenue with their handsome facades. Most of the city's parades and festivals pass this way, too.

Logan Circle, outside the Academy of Natural Sciences, Free Library of Philadelphia, and Franklin Institute, used to be Logan Square before the Parkway was built, and it was a burying ground before becoming a park. The designers of the avenue cleverly made it into a low-landscaped fountain, with graceful figures cast by Alexander Sterling Calder. From this point, you can see how the rows of trees make sense of the diagonal thoroughfare, although all the buildings along the Parkway are aligned with the grid plan. Under the terms of the city permit, the Four Seasons Hotel now landscapes and tends Logan Circle, to magnificent effect.

Bus route 76 goes both ways every 20 minutes, and the PHLASH bus goes up as far as Logan Circle every 10 minutes.

✪ FAIRMOUNT PARK

The northern end of the Benjamin Franklin Parkway leads into Fairmount Park, the world's largest landscaped city park, with 8,700 acres of winding creeks, rustic trails, and green meadows, plus 100 miles of jogging, bike, and bridle paths. In addition, this park (☎ **215/685-0000**) features more than a dozen historical and cultural attractions, including 29 of America's finest colonial mansions (most are open year-round, including weekends, and standard admission is $2.50), as well as gardens, boathouses, America's first zoo, a youth hostel, and a Japanese teahouse. Visitors can rent sailboats and canoes, play tennis and golf, swim, or hear free symphony con-certs in the summer. See the Fairmount Park map on p. 123 as a reference.

You can get here by taking bus 76 to the Museum of Art entrance, or 38 or 76 to the upper end. If you're driving, there are several entrances and exits off I-76; East and West River drives are local roads flanking the Schuylkill River.

The park is generally divided by the Schuylkill River into East and West Fair-mount Park. Before beginning a tour of the mansions, stop by the **Waterworks** (☎ **215/581-5111**). With the establishment of the 1812 Waterworks, land and machinery were combined in a 5-acre municipal park by 1822. Now finishing a $16 million restoration are the Greek Revival mill housings in back of the Art Museum and an ornamental post–Civil War pavilion connecting them. An upscale, year-round new restaurant, marketplace, stage area, and new bike path will join them in 2001. Also on the east bank, don't miss **Boat House Row,** home of the

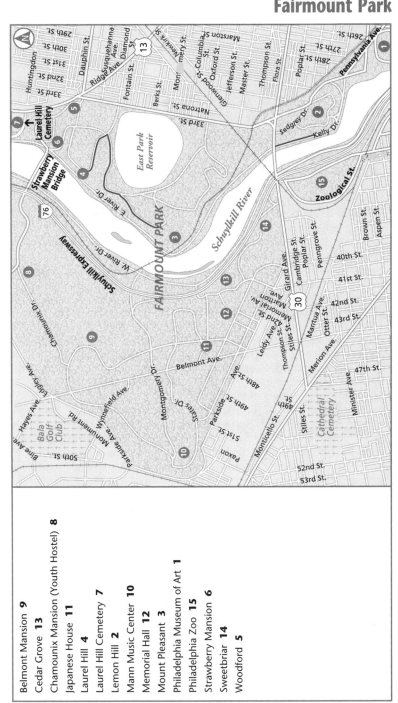

Belmont Mansion **9**
Cedar Grove **13**
Chamounix Mansion (Youth Hostel) **8**
Japanese House **11**
Laurel Hill **4**
Laurel Hill Cemetery **7**
Lemon Hill **2**
Mann Music Center **10**
Memorial Hall **12**
Mount Pleasant **3**
Philadelphia Museum of Art **1**
Philadelphia Zoo **15**
Strawberry Mansion **6**
Sweetbriar **14**
Woodford **5**

"Schuylkill Navy" and its member rowing clubs. Now you know where Thomas Eakins got the models for all those sculling scenes in the Art Museum. These gingerbread Tudors along the riverbank appear magical at night, with hundreds of tiny lights along their eaves.

The four most spectacular colonial houses are all in the lower east quadrant of the park. **Lemon Hill** (☎ 215/232-4337), just up the hill from Boat House Row, shows the influence of Robert Adam's architectural style, with its generous windows, curved archways and doors, and beautiful oval parlors. John Adams described **Mount Pleasant** (☎ 215/763-8100), built for a privateer in 1763 and once owned by Benedict Arnold, as "the most elegant seat in Pennsylvania" for its carved designs and inlays. **Woodford** (☎ 215/229-6115), the center of Tory occupation of the city in 1779, is not to be missed, both for its architecture and for the Naomi Wood Collection of colonial housewares. Along with Winterthur (see chapter 11), this is the best place to step into the full atmosphere of 18th-century home life, with all its ingenious gadgets and elegant objects. The next lawn over from Woodford is the park's largest mansion, **Strawberry Mansion** (☎ 215/228-8364), with a Federal-style center section and Greek Revival wings.

Just north of this mansion is bucolic **Laurel Hill Cemetery** (see "Cemeteries," earlier in this chapter, for a fuller description), but if you cross Strawberry Mansion Bridge, West Fairmount Park also has many charms. **Belmont Mansion** (☎ 215/878-8844), currently being restored, hosted all the leaders of the Revolutionary cause. South of this area, you'll enter the site occupied by the stupendous 1876 Centennial Exposition. Approximately 100 buildings were designed and constructed in under 2 years. Only two remain today: **Ohio House,** built out of stone from that state, and **Memorial Hall** (☎ 215/685-0000), now the park's headquarters and a recreation site. The **Japanese House and Gardens** (☎ 215/878-5097), on the grounds of the nearby Horticultural Center, is a typical 17th-century Japanese scholar's house, with its sliding screens and paper doors in place of walls and glass. It was originally presented to the Museum of Modern Art in New York. Since the Centennial Exposition had featured a similar house, it wound up here. The waterfall, grounds, and house are serene and simple and were extensively refurbished in 1976 by a Japanese team as a bicentennial gift to the city. It's open during the summer only, Tuesday to Sunday 11am to 4pm.

Two more major homes lie south of the Exposition's original concourses: **Cedar Grove** (☎ 215/763-8100), a Quaker farmhouse built as a country retreat in 1748 and moved here in 1928, and **Sweetbriar** (☎ 215/222-1333), a mixture of French Empire and English neoclassicism with wonderful river views. Continuing south past the Girard Avenue Bridge will bring you to the **Philadelphia Zoo** (see above), and then to Center City.

If you have some time and really want to get away from it all, Wissahickon and Pennsylvania Creeks lie north of the park and don't allow access by automobile—only pedestrians, bicycles, and horses. The primeval trees and slopes of these valleys completely block out buildings and noise—right within the limits of the fifth largest city in the United States! Search out attractions like the 340-year-old Valley Green Inn and the only covered bridge left in an American city.

⊙ PENN'S LANDING

Philadelphia started out as a major freshwater port, and its tourism and services are increasingly nudging it back to the water after 50 years of neglect, typified by the placement of the I-95 superhighway between the city and its port. In 1945,

155 "finger" piers jutted out into the river; today, only 14 remain. The Delaware waterfront is quite wide, and the esplanade along it has always had a pleasant spaciousness. The challenge has been to give it a unified, coherent sense of destination. Since 1976, the city has added on parts of a complete waterfront park at Penn's Landing (☎ **215/629-3200;** www.pennslandingcorp.com), on Columbus Boulevard (formerly Delaware Ave.) between Market and Lombard streets, with a wonderful new museum and an assembly of historic ships, performance and park areas, cruise facilities, and a marina. Further additions include more pedestrian bridges over I-95; a 1996 project to install wider sidewalks, lighting, and kiosks along Columbus Boulevard; more sites and transport; and now the establishment of a full-fledged Family Entertainment Center with a Hyatt hotel and other amenities. All of this has been made possible through the city's commercial partnership with the people who developed The Mall of America in Minneapolis and The Shops at Sunset Place in Miami.

You can access the Penn's Landing waterfront by parking along the piers or by walking across several bridges spanning I-95 between Market Street, at the northern edge, and South Street to the south. There are pedestrian walkways across Front Street on Market, Chestnut, Walnut, Spruce, or South streets; Front Street connects directly at Spruce Street. Buses 17, 21, 33, 76, and the purple PHLASH go directly to Penn's Landing; 42 is an easy walk from 2nd Street. If you're driving, from I-95 use the Columbus Boulevard/Washington Street exit and turn left on to Columbus Boulevard. From I-76, take I-676 across Center City to I-95 south. There's ample parking available on-site.

Walking south from Market Street, you'll see an esplanade with pretty new blue guardrails and charts to help you identify the Camden shoreline opposite and the funnels of passing freighters. The hill that connects the shoreline with the current Front Street level has been enhanced with the festive **Great Plaza,** a multitiered, tree-lined amphitheater that hosts many Visitors and Convention Bureau festivals, such as Jam on the River. This will all be changed by 2003; the 4,000-seat amphitheater replacing the Great Plaza will sit on the Center's buildings including 550,000 square feet of space for shops, and a garage holding 2,250 parking spaces. The Center will not be a traditional shopping mall with major retail "anchors"; the anchors will be entertainment venues such as an 18-screen AMC megaplex; the expanded **Please Touch Museum;** restaurants such as the local hit **Circa;** and medium-size stores by such names as Borders, Pottery Barn, Versace, and notably FAO Schwarz. Just north of the Great Plaza will continue to be the **Blue Cross RiverRink,** Philadelphia's only outdoor ice-skating rink, open night and day November to March. In the other direction is a jetty/marina complex, anchored by the new **Independence Seaport Museum** (see above), that's perfect for strolling and snacking. The sober 1987 **Philadelphia Vietnam Veteran Memorial** lists 641 local casualties, and nearby is the **International Sculpture Garden** with its new obelisk monument to Christopher Columbus.

There's also plenty to do in and near the water. The Penn's Landing Corporation coordinates more than 100 events annually, all designed to attract crowds with high-quality entertainment like Jam on the River during Memorial Day weekend, the Sunoco Welcome America! festival punctuating July 4, and many others. Even the most spontaneous visit is likely to be greeted with sounds and performances. Note that with the demolition of the Great Plaza, these activities are relocated to Pier 27 North for the 2001 and 2002 season, moving back to the site in the summer of 2003.

Several ships and museums are berthed around a long jetty at Spruce Street, and the Independence Seaport Museum is slowly consolidating management of these as a **Historic Ship Zone.** Starting at the north end, these attractions are the brig **Niagara,** built for the War of 1812 and rededicated as the official flagship of Pennsylvania in 1990; the **USS** *Becuna,* a guppy-class submarine, commissioned in 1944 to serve in Admiral Halsey's South Pacific fleet; and the **USS** *Olympia,* Admiral Dewey's own flagship in the Spanish-American War, with a self-guided three-deck tour. (Separate admission to both the *Olympia* and the *Becuna* is $3.50 for adults, $1.75 for children under 12; both are open daily 10am to 5pm.) Harbor cruise boats, *Liberty Belle II* (☎ 215/629-1131), *Spirit of Philadelphia* (☎ 215/ 923-1419), and a stop for the paddle-wheeler *Riverboat Queen* (☎ 215/ 923-BOAT), are augmented by private yachts; Queen Elizabeth docked her yacht Britannia here in 1976. Anchoring the southern end is the **Chart House** restaurant, open for lunch and dinner, and the restored **Moshulu** four-masted floating restaurant at Pier 34 (see "The Club and Music Scene," in chapter 10 for details).

Another group of boats occupies the landfill directly on the Delaware between Market and Walnut streets. The *Gazela Primiero,* a working three-masted, square-rigged wooden ship launched from Portugal in 1883, has visiting hours on Saturday and Sunday 12:30 to 5:30pm when it's in port. Adjoining are the *Barnegat Lightship* and the tugboat *Jupiter;* all of the above are operated by the Philadelphia Ship Preservation Guild (☎ 215/923-9030); admission $3 adults, $2 students.

If you want to get out onto the water, the *RiverLink* (☎ 609/364-1400), at the river's edge in front of the Independence Seaport Museum at Walnut Street, plies a round-trip route to the New Jersey State Aquarium in Camden every hour on the hour between 9am and 5pm. The trip takes 10 minutes, and the fare without museum admission on either end is $5 adults, $3 children each way. Penn's Landing also runs a free **Waterfront Shuttle** on Friday, Saturday, and Sunday evenings between 9pm and 2am in the summer. This is meant to reduce drunk driving between the many Columbus Boulevard clubs to the north of Penn's Landing, but it does stop here as well as at Pier 34 and the Moshulu. Call ☎ 215/629-3200 for more information.

5 Especially for Kids

Philadelphia is one of the country's great family destinations. It has a variety of attractions for different aged kids, and because it's so walkable and neighborhood-like, a respite or an amenity is never far away. Since so many of the family attractions are explained in more detail elsewhere in this or other chapters, I'll restrict myself to a list of the basics. See "Fast Facts: Philadelphia," in chapter 4, for baby-sitting options.

A monthly publication on what to do with kids in Philadelphia, *Metrokids,* is available at the Visitors Center, 16th Street and John F. Kennedy Boulevard. The center also coordinates and sells several packages that combine free admission to much of what follows with accommodations at hotels such as the Penn Tower, Sheraton Society Hill, and Embassy Suites Center City; call the Family Friendly Funline at ☎ 800/770-5889.

MUSEUMS & SIGHTS

In Center City, there are the **Please Touch Museum,** 210 N. 21st St. (until it moves to Penns Landing); **Franklin Institute,** Benjamin Franklin Parkway and 20th Street; **CoreStates Science Park** between these two on 21st Street; and the

Academy of Natural Sciences, the Parkway and 19th Street. The **Free Library of Philadelphia Children's Department,** across Logan Circle at Vine and 19th streets, is a joy, with a separate entrance, 100,000 books and microcomputers in a playgroundlike space, with weekend hours. Around Independence Hall are the **Liberty Bell** at Market and 5th streets; **Franklin Court,** between Market and Chestnut streets at 4th Street; the waterfront at **Penn's Landing,** off Front Street; and, of course, the guided tour of **Independence Hall.** You can also take the ferry from Penn's Landing and the great new **Independence Seaport Museum** to the **aquarium** in Camden. In West Fairmount Park you'll find the **zoo.**

PLAYGROUNDS

Rittenhouse Square at 18th and Walnut streets has a small playground and space in which to eat and relax. Other imaginative urban playgrounds on this side of Center City are **Schuylkill River Park** at Pine and 26th streets and at 26th Street and the Benjamin Franklin Parkway, opposite the art museum. Nearest Independence Hall, try **Delancey Park** at Delancey between 3rd and 4th streets (with lots of fountains and animal sculptures to climb on) or **Starr Garden** at 6th and Lombard streets. The best in Fairmount Park is the **Smith Memorial** (head north on 33rd St., then take a left into the park at Oxford Ave., near Woodford).

ENTERTAINMENT

Penn's Landing has free children's theater performances by American Family Theater on Fridays at 7pm in July and August; call ☎ **215/629-3237** for details. **Philadelphia Marionette Theater** has heavily reserved programs in Belmont Mansion in West Fairmount Park on Monday to Friday at 10:30am; call ☎ **215/879-1213** for details.

The **Philadelphia Museum of Art** has dedicated itself to producing Sunday-morning and early afternoon programs for children, at minimal or no charge. Your kids could wind up drawing pictures of armor or watching a puppet theater about dragons, visiting a Chinese court, or playing with Picasso-style cubism. Call ☎ **215/763-8100,** or ☎ 215/684-7500 for 24-hour information.

OUTSIDE PHILADELPHIA

In Bucks County, there is **Sesame Place,** based on public TV's *Sesame Street,* in Langhorne, and the restored antique carousel at **Peddler's Village** in Lahaska. To the northwest, try the 20th-century entertainment areas connected with **Franklin Mills,** and **Ridley Creek State Park** and its 17th-century working farm in Montgomery County. For Revolutionary War history in action, try Valley Forge or Washington Crossing National Historical Parks. And for fascinating real life, spend a couple of days in Lancaster County—you can even stay on a working "Plain People" farm. See chapters 11 and 12 for directions and information.

6 Organized Tours

BUS TOURS

Those double-decker buses decked out like trolleys clanging along the city streets are from **American Trolley Tours** (☎ **215/333-2119**). Tours of historic areas, conducted by guides in the climate-controlled vehicles, leave mornings and afternoons from the Visitors Center at 16th Street and John F. Kennedy Boulevard and from the Independence National Park Visitors Center at 3rd and Walnut streets. The tours cost $10 for adults, $5 for children.

Gray Line (☎ 800/577-7745) has introduced year-round, 3-hour excursions of historic Philadelphia, Philadelphia at night, and Valley Forge: $18 adults and $12 children ages 3 to 11. All tours leave from 30th Street Station, but shuttles from hotels are available.

WALKING TOURS

The next chapter will give you some guided walking tours to follow. The most spectacular, the movable-site "Lights of Liberty" show using Independence National Historic Park as a backdrop, is described as a "Top Attraction" above. There are also many specific-interest tours, such as African-American Philadelphia, architectural walks, Jewish sites in Society Hill, and the Italian Market. Check the Visitors Center (☎ 215/636-3300) for information.

CANDLELIGHT STROLLS

From May to October, evening tours of the historic area, led by costumed guides, leave from Welcome Park at 2nd and Walnut streets at 6:30pm. Tours of Old City (Fri) and Society Hill (Sat) take 90 minutes; they cost $6 for adults, $5 for seniors and children. Call ☎ 215/735-3123 for reservations with **Centipede Tours,** 1315 Walnut St. **Historic Philadelphia** (☎ 215/625-5801) offers programs such as the "Tippler's Tour" starting from the Visitor Center and the Powel House.

HORSE & CARRIAGE TOURS

To get the feel of Philadelphia as it was (well, almost—asphalt is a lot smoother than cobblestones!), try a narrated horse-drawn carriage ride. Operated daily by the **76 Carriage Co.** (☎ 215/923-8516), tours begin at 5th and Chestnut streets in front of Independence Hall 10am to 5pm, with later hours in summer. Fares range from $15 for 15 minutes to $25 for 30 minutes, with a maximum of four per carriage; additional people $5 each. Reservations are not necessary.

BOATING TOURS

Two choices are available at Penn's Landing. The *Spirit of Philadelphia* (☎ 215/923-1419) at the Great Plaza combines lunch, brunch, or dinner with a cruise on a 600-person passenger ship, fully climate controlled, with two enclosed decks and two open-air decks. Trips, which require reservations, are $25 and up for 2 or 3 hours.

The newly redecorated *Liberty Belle II* (☎ 215/629-1131) boards from Lombard Street Circle, near the Chart House restaurant at the southern end of Penn's Landing, and can accommodate up to 475 passengers on three decks.

The *RiverLink* (☎ 609/365-1400) provides a 10-minute crossing from a landing just outside the Independence Seaport Museum and the New Jersey State Aquarium. The ferry is large inside, and the views of the Philadelphia skyline are great, although the aquarium is the only destination in New Jersey. Departures from Penn's Landing are on the hour, from Camden on the half hour, 9am to 5pm daily. One-way fares are $5 for adults, $3 for children and seniors. The package admissions with the attractions are a good deal.

7 Outdoor Activities

I can't begin to make a complete list of all that you can do outdoors while in Philadelphia, so the following is merely a sample. You may also want to contact the Department of Recreation (☎ 215/686-3600).

BIKING/BLADING

Plaisted Hall, the Fairmount Park rental spot for bikes and boats, burned down in 1993, and it has yet to be reconstructed as of press time. It's a shame, because the paths along the Schuylkill on Kelly (East River) Drive, West River Drive, and off West River Drive to Belmont Avenue are pure pleasure. The lower half of West River Drive along the Schuylkill is closed to vehicular traffic most weekend hours in summer. You can rent mountain bikes or in-line skates for about $25 at **Via Bicycle** at 1134 Pine St. (☎ 215/627-3370), or the **Bike Lines** at 13th and Locust streets (☎ 215/735-1503), 226 S. 40th in University City (☎ 215/243-2453), or 1028 Arch near the Convention Center (☎ 215/923-1310). The ground is flat near the Schuylkill on either side but loops up sharply near Laurel Hill Cemetery or Manayunk. Anyone who enjoys cycling would love the outlying countryside, and you can rent bicycles in Lumberville, 8 miles north of New Hope on the Delaware (☎ 215/297-5388), and in Lancaster, the heart of Amish farmland (☎ 717/684-7226). Bicycles may be taken free on all SEPTA and PATCO trains, so you're within easy range of some nice country rides.

Call the **Bicycle Club of Philadelphia** at ☎ 215/440-9483 for specific neighborhood recommendations.

BOATING

Like cyclists, city rowers and sailors must also await Plaisted Hall's reconstruction. Outside of the city, try **Northbrook Canoe Co.,** north of Route 842 in Northbrook on Brandywine Creek (☎ 610/793-2279), or **Point Pleasant,** on Route 32, 7 miles north of the New Hope exit on I-95, with canoeing, inner tubing, and rafting on the Delaware River (☎ 215/297-8823).

FISHING

Pennypack Creek and **Wissahickon Creek** are stocked mid-April to December with trout and muskie and provide good, even rustic, conditions. A required license of $12.25 for Pennsylvania residents or $20.25 for out-of-staters is available at such sporting-goods stores as I. Goldberg or at the Municipal Services Building near the Visitors Center. Outside the city, **Ridley Creek** and its **state park** (☎ 610/566-4800) and **Brandywine Creek** at Hibernia Park (☎ 610/384-0290) are stocked with several kinds of trout.

GOLF

Your chance to find superior golf around Philadelphia actually exceeds the scene in most major cities; many of the region's 100 courses are extremely close to Center City, and the quality and variety of public access golf is wonderful. The city of Philadelphia operates five municipal courses in the region. All have 18 holes, and current fees range $13 to $25 on Monday to Friday and $19 to $29 on Saturday and Sunday. Not everyone can get onto the legendary Pine Valley or Merion, but Hugh Wilson of Merion also designed the pretty and challenging **Cobbs Creek,** 7800 Lansdowne Ave. at 72nd Street (☎ 215/877-8707). Since Meadowbrook Golf Group took over in April 1999, course conditions have improved dramatically. **Karakung** is the shorter 18-hole course, and preferred for seniors and juniors. **John F. Byrne,** Frankford Avenue and Eden Street in North Philadelphia (☎ 215/632-8666), has an Alex Findlay design with Torresdale Creek meandering through or beside 10 holes, and plenty of rolling fairways and elevations. **Walnut Lane,** Walnut Lane and Henry Avenue in Roxborough (☎ 215/482-3370), places a premium on short game skills, with 10 par-3 holes and deep bunkers set into hills and valleys. There's also a driving range in East Fairmount Park.

Among the better township courses outside the city are **Montgomeryville Golf Club,** Route 202 (☎ 215/855-6112); **Paxon Hollow Golf Club,** Paxon Hollow Road in Marple Township (☎ 610/353-0220), under 6,000 yards and demanding accuracy; and **Valley Forge Golf Club,** 401 N. Gulph Rd., King of Prussia (☎ 215/337-1776). Expect fees of $65 and up. **Tattersall Golf Club** in West Chester (☎ 610/353-0220) is a new all-daily-fee 6,800-yard course, with dramatic 200-foot elevation changes. Current greens fees are $79, cart included.

HEALTH CLUBS

The Philadelphia Marriott, Wyndham Franklin Plaza, Four Seasons, the Rittenhouse, and Sheraton Society Hill have in-house facilities free to guests but open to nonguests at an additional charge. The spectacular **Sporting Club** is free and available only to guests of the Park Hyatt at the Bellevue. Most other moderately priced hotels have at least a few Exercycles and an aerobics space; the KormanSuites, 4 blocks from Logan Circle, has a full gym room, pool, and tennis court. Near Society Hill, the top health club that admits per-day guests is **Gold's Gym** with Ron Jaworski, 834 Chestnut St. (☎ 215/592-9644). It provides an understanding staff, large Universal weight machines, free weights, and several aerobics classes daily. The cost is $10 per guest, and it's open Monday to Friday 6am to 10pm, Saturday and Sunday 8am to 5pm. Another alternative closer to midtown is the **12th Street Gym,** 204 S. 12th St. (☎ 215/985-4092), a restored 1930s men's club (women are welcome these days), with a pool, courts for squash and racquetball, and weights and aerobics rooms. It's open Monday to Friday 5:30am to 11pm, Saturday 7am to 7pm, and Sunday 9am to 7pm. The basic rate is $10 per guest.

HIKING

Fairmount Park (☎ 215/686-3616) has dozens of miles of paths, and the extensions of the park into the Wissahickon Creek area are quite unspoiled, with dirt roads and no auto traffic. Farther afield, **Horseshoe Trail** (☎ 215/664-0719) starts at Routes 23 and 252 in Valley Forge State Park and winds 120 miles west marked by yellow horseshoes until it meets the Appalachian Trail.

HORSEBACK RIDING

There are many riding trails in Fairmount Park, the Wissahickon, and Pennypack Park within city limits. Chester and Brandywine counties are famous for horsemanship, from fox hunting to the Winterthur point-to-point races. Unfortunately, insurance costs have made it unprofitable for most riding stables to allow visitors to rent horses. The only riding stable within city limits that does is **Harry's Riding Stables** (☎ 215/335-9975), 2240 Holmesburg Ave., near Pennypack Park. It's open 7 days a week 9am to 8pm, and seven or eight horses are always available, with rates of $20 per hour for guided trail rides with Western saddles. The easiest direction from Center City is via I-95 north. Take the Academy Road exit, following the exit ramp to the left onto Academy until the first light; then turn left onto Frankford Avenue and continue for 2 miles. After a hill, there's an intersection with a railroad trestle that passes above Frankford. Before going under it, take the dirt road on the left and follow 300 yards to the white barn building on the right.

ICE SKATING

One great improvement to the city has been the **Blue Cross RiverRink at Penn's Landing,** open for public skating near the intersection of Chestnut Street and

Columbus Boulevard daily, late November to early March. Admission for one 2-hour session is $4 to $6, with skate rental only $2. Call ☎ **215/925-RINK** for details; there's a nice food court, too.

RUNNING & JOGGING

Again, **Fairmount Park** has more trails than you could cover in a week. An 8.2-mile loop starts in front of the Museum of Art, up the east bank of the Schuylkill, across the river at Falls Bridge, and back down to the museum. At the north end, Forbidden Drive along the Wissahickon has loops of dirt/gravel of 5 miles and more, with no traffic. The Benjamin Franklin Bridge path from 5th and Vine streets is 1.8 miles each way.

SWIMMING

Philadelphia has 86 municipal swimming pools, and many hotels have small lap pools. Municipal pools are open daily 11am to 7pm and are free. Two of the best are **Cobbs Creek,** 63rd and Spruce streets, and **FDR Pool,** Broad and Pattison in South Philadelphia. Call ☎ **215/686-1776** for details.

TENNIS

Some 115 courts are scattered throughout **Fairmount Park,** and you can get a tourist permit to use them by calling ☎ **215/686-0152.** You might also try the University of Pennsylvania's indoor courts at the **Robert P. Levy Tennis Pavilion,** 3130 Walnut St. (☎ **215/898-4741**). Rates are $32 for two visitors until 4pm, $36 for two after 4pm.

8 Spectator Sports

Even in these days of nomadic professional teams, Philadelphia fields teams in every major sport and boasts a newly enhanced complex at the end of South Broad Street to house them all. **Veterans Stadium** (☎ **215/686-1776**) is a graceful bowl with undulating ramps that can seat 58,000 for the Phillies in baseball and 68,000 for the Eagles in football. The new $230 million, 21,000-seat **First Union Center** houses the Philadelphia Flyers pro hockey and Philadelphia 76ers basketball teams. It couples with the 17,000-seat **Spectrum,** which functions as one of the best rock-concert forums around and hosts the U.S. Pro Indoor Tennis Championships and other one-of-a-kind events.

All these facilities are next to each other and can be reached via a 10-minute sub-way ride straight down South Broad Street to Pattison Avenue ($1.60). The same fare will put you on the SEPTA bus C, which goes down Broad Street more slowly but with a bit more safety late at night.

As of this writing, there's some hubbub on finding a new Phillies stadium site on the Chinatown side of Center City, while building a new stadium for the Eagles downtown. The estimated cost is $1.2 billion, and the sources even murkier, since City administration probably can't foot even part of this bill.

Professional sports aren't the only game in town, though. Philadelphia has a lot of colleges, and **Franklin Field** and the **Palestra** dominate West Philadelphia on 33rd below Walnut Street. The Penn Relays, the first intercollegiate and amateur track event in the nation, books Franklin Field on the last weekend in April. Regat-tas pull along the Schuylkill all spring, summer, and fall, within sight of Fairmount Park's mansions.

A call to Teletron (☎ **800/233-4050**) or Ticketmaster (☎ **212/507-7171** in New York, or 215/336-2000 in Philadelphia) can get you tickets in many cases before you hit town.

BASEBALL

The **Philadelphia Phillies,** Box 7575, Philadelphia, PA 19101 (☎ **215/463-1000** for ticket information, or 215/463-5300 for daily game information), won the National League pennant in 1993 and made playoffs in 1995. They play at Veterans Stadium, Broad Street and Pattison Avenue. Day games usually begin at 1:35pm, regular night games at 8:05pm on Friday, 7:35pm on other days. When there's a twilight doubleheader, it begins at 5:35pm. The huge computerized scoreboard and the antics that follow a Phillies home run will leave you laughing and amazed.

Box seats overlooking the field are $20, and the cheapest bleacher seats are $6 to $12 if you're over 14.

BASKETBALL

Energized by young superstar Allan Iverson, the **Philadelphia 76ers,** Box 25050, Philadelphia, PA 19147, play about 40 games at the CoreStates Center between early November and late April. Call ☎ **215/339-7676** for ticket information; single tickets range $13 to $59. There's always a good halftime show, and the promotion department works overtime with special nights, especially involving 76ers T-shirts.

There are five major college basketball teams in the Philadelphia area, and the newspapers print schedules of their games. Most games are at the Palestra, with tickets going for $5 to $8. Call ☎ **215/898-4747** to find out about ticket availability.

BIKING

The **CoreStates Pro Cycling Championship,** held each June, is a top event in the cycling world. The 156-mile race starts and finishes along the Benjamin Franklin Parkway, and watching the cyclists climb "The Wall" in Manayunk is terrifying.

BOATING

April to September, you can watch regattas on the Schuylkill River, which have been held since the earliest days of the "Schuylkill Navy" a century ago. The **National Association of Amateur Oarsmen** (☎ 215/769-2068) and the **Boathouse Association** (☎ 215/686-0052) have a complete schedule of races, one of the best known being the Dad Vail Regatta.

FOOTBALL

Football is, without a doubt, Philadelphia's favorite sport, and current veteran quarterback Rodney Peete is especially popular. It will take all your ingenuity to get tickets, since 85% of tickets to **Philadelphia Eagles** games (at Veterans Stadium, Philadelphia, PA 19148) are sold to season ticket-holders. Call ☎ **215/463-5500** for ticket advice. The games start at 1 or 4pm, and tickets cost up to $75.

HORSE RACING

Philadelphia Park (the old Keystone Track) has races June 15 to February 13, Saturday to Tuesday. (Post time is 12:35pm.) Admission, general parking, and a program are free. The park is at 3001 Street Rd. in Bensalem, half a mile from Exit 28 on the Pennsylvania Turnpike. Call ☎ **215/639-9000** for information.

For more thoroughbred horse racing, try **Garden State Park,** N.J. 70 and Haddonfield Road in Cherry Hill, New Jersey (☎ **609/488-8400**), which runs Thoroughbred races in the spring and harness (Standardbred) races in the fall. Call for exact schedules, but the first post time is usually 7:30pm, Wednesday to Saturday.

Off-Track Wagering Parlor and Dining, 7 Penn Center, 1635 Market St., on the concourse and lower mezzanine levels (☎ **215/245-1556**), features 270 color video monitors and an ersatz art deco design; it brings the wagering to you in the comfort of Center City.

ICE HOCKEY

The First Union Center rocks to the **Philadelphia Flyers,** led by star Eric Lindros, from fall to spring, and tickets are even harder to get than to the Eagles—80% of tickets are sold by the season. Call ☎ **215/465-5500** for ticket information; if you can get them, they'll cost between $15 and $35.

TENNIS

Philadelphia has several world-class tournaments annually. February brings the **Comcast U.S. Professional Indoor Championships** at the Spectrum, with $600,000 in prize money; call ☎ **215/947-2530** for information. The women's invitational held at Haverford College (☎ **610/896-1000**) in late September has attracted top players, and Advanta sometimes brings the **Virginia Slims tour** to the Civic Center in November. The late-summer **USTA Senior Men's Grass Court Championships** at Germantown Cricket Club (☎ **215/438-9900**) can bring you face-to-face with former greats.

TRACK & FIELD

The city hosts the **Penn Relays,** the oldest and still the largest amateur track meet in the country, in late April at Franklin Field. There's an annual **Marathon** in November and a September **Philadelphia Distance Run,** a half-marathon; the latter is becoming a world-class event. Call ☎ **215/686-0053** for more details on any of these runs.

8

City Strolls

Philadelphia is probably the most compact, walkable major city in the United States, just as it was in 1776. On a random walk, it's fascinating to see the progress of the centuries and the many unexpected juxtapositions. Keep in mind that the nearer you are to the Delaware, the older (and smaller) the buildings are likely to be. The walking tours mapped out below are specifically designed to cover the most worthwhile attractions, allowing you to recoup your strength along the way.

Walking Tour 1:
Historic Highlights & Society Hill

Start: Visitors Center, 3rd and Walnut streets.
Finish: City Tavern, 2nd and Walnut streets; optional extension to Penn's Landing.
Time: From 6 to 7 hours.
Best Time: Start between 9 and 11am to avoid hour-long waits for Independence Hall tours.

Start your tour at the:

1. **Visitors Center** in Independence National Historical Park, 3rd and Walnut streets. This handsome brick building was built for the 1976 bicentennial celebration and maintains spotless rest rooms and cool benches as well as providing pamphlets and maps of the park, free tickets (limited in number) for the Bishop White and Todd Houses (see below), and information about special tours or special daily events. The John Huston–directed film *Independence* is shown free of charge every half hour. There is a small exhibition area and a substantial quality gift shop and bookstore.

Just opposite the Visitor Center is the:

2. **First Bank of the United States** (1795), not open to the public but a superb example of Federal architecture. As graceful as a Roman rotunda, this building is the oldest surviving bank building in America. Initially, each of the new states issued their own currency. Dealing with 13 different currencies hampered commerce and travel among the states, so Alexander Hamilton proposed a single bank (originally in Carpenters' Hall) for loans and

Walking Tour: Historic Highlights & Society Hill

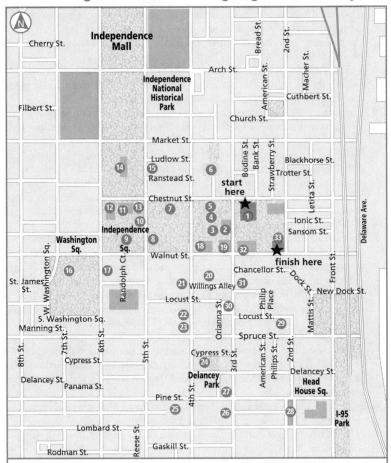

1 Visitor Center	**17** Athenaeum
2 First Bank of the United States	**18** Todd House
3 Carpenters' Hall	**19** Bishop White House
4 New Hall	**20** St. Joseph's Church
5 Pemberton House	**21** Philadelphia Contributionship
6 Franklin Court	**22** Episcopal Diocese
7 Second Bank of the United States	**23** Old St. Mary's Church
	24 Hill-Physick-Keith House
8 Library Hall	**25** Old Pine Presbyterian
9 Independence Square	**26** St. Peter's Episcopal Church
10 Philosophical Hall	**27** Kosciuszko National Memorial
11 Independence Hall	**28** Head House Square
12 Congress Hall	**29** Man Full of Trouble Tavern
13 Old City Hall	**30** Powel House
14 The Liberty Bell	**31** St. Paul's Episcopal Church
15 The Bourse	**32** Philadelphia Exchange
16 Washington Square	**33** City Tavern

deposits. The classical facade, Hamilton's inspiration, is meant to recall the democracy and splendor of ancient Greece. The mahogany American eagle on the pediment over the Corinthian entrance columns is a famous and rare example of 18th-century sculpture.

The Park Service cleared many of the non-historic structures on the block behind the First Bank (as throughout the Historic Park area), creating 18th-century gardens and lawns. To the right, a walkway leads to:

3. Carpenters' Hall, which was a newly built guildhall when the First Continental Congress met here in 1774. See chapter 7 for a more detailed description. Just north of this, you'll find:

4. New Hall, a modern copy of a hall built in 1791 for rent by the Carpenters' Company. When the federal government was provisionally based in Philadelphia, this space was used as the headquarters for the first War (now Defense) Department. The building now houses the Marine Corps Museum. (The marines were founded at nearby Tun Tavern.) You'll see lots of uniforms, swords, and medals.

A few steps north, on Chestnut Street proper, is:

5. Pemberton House, another reconstruction. Joseph Pemberton, a Quaker sugar and Madeira merchant, had just built this fine Georgian home when the Second Continental Congress, in the aftermath of the gunfire at Concord and Lexington, cut back on British imports. Pemberton went bankrupt, and the house was razed in 1862, only to be reconstructed a century later. The exhibit here shows the development of the fledgling U.S. Army and Navy. A film about the military history of the Revolutionary War plays continuously. The second floor's highlight is the model gun deck of a frigate, with instructions on maneuvering for a naval battle.

The other side of Chestnut Street features a handsome collection of 19th-century banks and commercial facades, including the 1867 **First National Bank** at no. 315 and the **Philadelphia National Bank** at no. 323. The Chestnut Street entrance to:

6. Franklin Court is nestled here. See chapter 7 for a full description of this wonderful tribute to Benjamin Franklin in his final home.

Walk west along Chestnut Street or back in the gardens, crossing 4th Street until you get to:

7. Second Bank of the United States. Its strong Greek columns have worn away somewhat, but the bank still holds interest. The Second Bank was chartered by Congress in 1816 for a term of 20 years, again at a time when the country felt that it needed reliable circulating money. The building (1818–24), designed like the Philadelphia Exchange by William Strickland, is adapted from the Parthenon, and the Greeks would have been proud of its capable director, Nicholas Biddle. An elitist to the core, he was the man Andrew Jackson and his supporters had in mind when they complained about private individuals controlling public government. "Old Hickory" vetoed renewal of the bank's charter, increasing the money supply but ruining Biddle and the bank.

The building was used as a Customs House until 1934. Now the National Park Service uses it as a portrait gallery of early Americans. The collection contains many of the oldest gallery portraits in the country, painted by Peale, Sully, Neagle, Stuart, and Allston. Admission is $2 for persons 17 or over, open daily 9am to 5pm.

☕ **TAKE A BREAK**   A **tea garden** in the adjoining holly garden, staffed by the Friends of Independence National Historical Park, provides ice cream and cool drinks from mid-May to mid-September, noon to 5pm.

Just west of the Second Bank lies:

8. Library Hall, the 1954 reconstruction of Benjamin Franklin's old Library Company, which was the first lending library of its type in the colonies. The Library Company is now at 1314 Locust St. (see the "Midtown & the Parkway" stroll, below), and this graceful Federal building now houses the library of the American Philosophical Society, across the street. The collection is fascinating, including Franklin's will, a copy of William Penn's 1701 Charter of Privileges, and Jefferson's own handwritten copy of the Declaration of Independence. The exhibits focus on the history of science in America. The library's hours follow the park schedule.

The pull of great government will lead you across 5th Street to:

9. Independence Square, where on July 8, 1776, John Nixon read the Declaration of Independence to the assembled city. You'll be at the back of the official trio of **Independence Hall, Congress Hall,** and **Old City Hall** on Chestnut Street between 5th and 6th streets.

On your right is:

10. Philosophical Hall, the home of the American Philosophical Society. The society, founded by Ben Franklin, is made up of a prestigious honor roll of America's outstanding intellects and achievers. In Franklin's day, philosophers were more often than not industrious young men with scientific and learned interests. Current members of the society include former senator Ben Bradley, violinist Itzhak Perlman, poet Rita Dove, and commentator Bill Moyers. The building's interior is not open to the public, but look for traces of old Georgian springing into new Federal architecture, such as fan-shaped and larger windows and more elaborate doorsteps.

To your left is:

11. Independence Hall, grand, graceful, and one of democracy's true shrines (see chapter 7 for a full description). Ranger-led 35-minute tours depart every 15 minutes or so. The two flanking buildings, **Old City Hall** (Supreme Court Building) and **Congress Hall,** were intended to balance each other, and their fanlighted doors, keystoned windows, and simple lines are appealing from any angle. They were used by a combination of federal, state, county, and city governments during a relatively short period. (Don't even bother to try to get them all straight.)

12. Congress Hall (1787) housed the U.S. Congress for 10 years and witnessed the inaugurations of two presidents. The wall-to-wall carpeting and venetian blinds are disappointingly anachronistic, but it's hard to get mahogany desks and leather armchairs of such workmanship now. Look for the little corners where representatives could smoke, take snuff, and drink sherry during recess. Watching the House and Senate from the balconies became a popular social activity, and if debate was boring, one could always admire the ceiling moldings.

13. Old City Hall (1790), at the corner of 5th and Chestnut streets, was home to the third branch of the federal government, the U.S. Supreme Court, under Chief Justice John Jay. From 1800 to 1870 the building was used as city hall. An exhibit here describes the first years of the judiciary.

Across Chestnut Street from this central trio is:

14. The Liberty Bell, once located in Independence Hall and moved for the 1976 bicentennial to the special glass pavilion across Chestnut Street. See chapter 7 for a full description; by 2002, the Bell should be moved to a new building on the same block that does more justice to colonial sightlines.

Just to the east of the Liberty Bell is:

15. The Bourse, a superb example of late Victorian architecture. It has been renovated as a mall in the form of two arcades surrounding an expansive skylit atrium. Built from 1893 to 1895 as a merchants exchange, the Bourse handsomely combines a brick-and-sandstone exterior with a cool and colorful interior.

🔄 **TAKE A BREAK**   The Bourse's spacious, cool ground-floor **Food Court** is open Monday, Tuesday, and Thursday 10am to 6pm; Wednesday, Friday, and Saturday until 8pm; and Sunday 11am to 6pm.

Now cut through Independence Square to the greenery at the southwest corner. This is Washington Square.

16. Washington Square seems a little unbalanced since Independence National Historical Park opened up the block to the northeast—but it's just as expansive and even more leafy than when it was the town's pasture. In the 1840s, this was the center of fashionable Philadelphia. Many handsome structures have been razed to make room for chunky offices and apartment houses. Only the 1823 southwest corner Federals, the **Meredith-Penrose House** and its neighbors, give you a sense of what was lost. It now holds the Tomb of the Unknown Soldier from the Revolutionary War, with its eternal flame. The square has also been the center of Philadelphia publishing for 150 years, with **Lea and Febiger** and **J. B. Lippincott** at no. 227. The massive white building on the north face has been redeveloped, but the Curtis Publishing Co. (now the **Curtis Center**) once sent out the *Saturday Evening Post* and other magazines from here.

The solid, Italianate Revival brownstone (1845–47) on Washington Square East is the:

17. Athenaeum, a virtually unchanged pocket of 19th-century society life (see chapter 7 for a fuller description).

You may be surprised to learn that Society Hill wasn't named after the upper crust who lived here in colonial times. Rather, the name refers to the Free Society of Traders, a group of businessmen and investors persuaded by William Penn to settle here with their families in 1683. The name applies to the area east of Washington Square between Walnut and Lombard streets. Many of Philadelphia's white-collar workers, clerics, teachers, importers, and politicos have lived and worked here over the years.

Despite the colonial facades, nobody would have considered walking through this decrepit and undesirable neighborhood a few decades ago. That's all changed now thanks to a massive urban-renewal project, which has superbly blended new housing developments in with their Georgian neighbors.

Of course, Society Hill isn't just residential. Georgian and Federal public buildings and churches, from **Head House Square** and **Pennsylvania Hospital** to **St. Peter's** and **St. Paul's,** may make you feel as if you've stumbled onto a movie set. But all of the buildings are used—and the area works as a living community today. It's a little south of where you are, but fine restaurants and charming stores cluster south of Lombard, especially around Head House Square (1803) at 2nd and Lombard streets.

Continuing on your tour, leave the Athenaeum and walk east 1 block on St. James Street, then go north on 5th Street and take a right turn onto Walnut Street for 2 blocks. As you walk down Walnut to 3rd Street, the restored row houses will catch your eye, with their paneled doors and shutters, bands of brick or stone between floors, and small lozenges of painted metal. These last are fire-insurance markers—all early American cities were terrible fire hazards, and Philadelphia, led by Benjamin Franklin, was the first to do anything about it. The plaques functioned as advertisements for the various companies and also

Architectural ABCs

You'll enjoy your stroll around Society Hill and Queen Village more if you know something about colonial and Federal architecture, especially since many homes aren't open to individual tours. Brick is the constant, clay being abundant by the Delaware's banks—but construction methods have varied over the past 150 years.

Generally, houses built before the 1750s, such as the **Trump House** at 214 Delancey St., are 2½ stories, with two rooms per floor and a dormer window jutting out of a steep gambrel roof. An eave usually separates the simple door and its transom windows from the second level. Careful bricklayers liked to alternate the long and short sides of bricks (called "stretchers" and "headers"), a style known as Flemish Bond. The headers were often glazed to create a checkerboard pattern. Wrought-iron boot scrapers flank the doorsteps.

Houses built in Philadelphia's colonial heyday soared to 3 or 4 stories—taller after the Revolution—and adopted heavy Georgian cornices (the underside of a roof overhang) and elaborate doorways. The homes of the truly wealthy, such as the **Powel House** at 244 S. 3rd St. and the **Morris House** at 235 S. 8th St., have fanlights above their arched brick doorways; the **Davis-Lenox House** at 217 Spruce St. has a simple raised pediment. Since the Georgian style demanded symmetry, the parlors were often given imaginary doors and windows to even things out. The less wealthy lived in "trinity" houses—one room on each of three floors, named for faith, hope, and charity. Few town houses stood on individual plots—the **Hill-Physick-Keith House** at 321 S. 4th St. is an exception.

Federal architecture, which blew in from England and New England in the 1790s, is less heavy (no more Flemish Bond for bricks), generally more graceful (more glass, with delicate molding instead of wainscoting). Any house like the **Meredith House** at 700 S. Washington Sq., with a half story of marble stairs leading to a raised mahogany door, was surely constructed after 1800. Greek Revival elements such as rounded dormer windows and oval staircases became the fashion from the 1810s on. Three Victorian brownstones at 260 S. 3rd St. once belonged to Michel Bouvier, Jacqueline Kennedy Onassis's great-great-grandfather.

If you're here in May, don't pass up the **Philadelphia Open House** to view the bandbox interiors of dozens of homes (volunteered by proud owners). Call ☎ **215/928-1188** for information.

---

helped firemen identify which houses they were responsible for saving. Now the houses belong to park offices and the Pennsylvania Horticultural Association, which maintains an 18th-century formal garden open to the public.

At the corner of Fourth and Walnut streets is the:

18. Todd House. Tours (for 10 persons at a time) are required, and tickets by advance reservation are available for $2 at the Visitors Center. John Todd Jr. was a young Quaker lawyer of moderate means. His house, built in 1775, cannot compare to that of Bishop White (see below), but it is far grander than Betsy Ross's. Todd used the ground-floor parlor as his law office and the family lived and entertained on the second floor. When Todd died in the 1793 epidemic of yellow fever, his vivacious widow Dolley married a Virginia lawyer named James Madison, the future president.

Farther down Walnut toward 3rd Street is the other park-run dwelling, the:

19. Bishop White House, at no. 309. Tours (for 10 persons at a time) are required; $2 tickets can be obtained at the Visitors Center. This house is on one of the loveliest row-house blocks in the city, and it's a splendid example of how a pillar of the community lived in Federal America. Bishop White (1748–1836) was the founder of Episcopalianism, breaking with the Anglican church. He was a good friend of Franklin, as you'll see from the upstairs library. Notice how well the painted cloth floor in the entrance hall survived muddy boots and 20 varnishings. In case you take the indoor "necessity" for granted, remember that outhouses provided the only relief on most colonial property. The library reveals the bishop's "modern" tastes, with Sir Walter Scott's Waverley novels, the *Encyclopaedia Britannica,* and even the Koran alongside traditional religious texts. The collection has survived intact.

Across the street, the park has purchased property and created a garden that exposes the side of:

20. St. Joseph's Church, the first Roman Catholic church in Philadelphia (see chapter 7 for a description). It's much more intriguing if you enter through the iron gate and archway on Willing's Alley, off 4th Street between Walnut and Spruce.

Not many tourists know it, but the headquarters of 18th-century fire-insurance companies are open to the public, in the heart of Society Hill. In a neighborhood as moneyed and as crowded as this one was, fire was a constant danger. Before the days of fire departments, groups of subscribers pledged to help each other in case of fire. Many companies required a complete inventory of a house's possessions before they would set premiums, and these inventories have helped in the restoration of run-down town houses. You can see the insurance plaques on the upper facades of many homes. For example, the:

21. Philadelphia Contributionship (1836), 212 S. 4th St. (below Walnut St.), has used the "Hand-in-Hand" mark since 1752. The facade of the building is Greek Revival, with a gorgeous limestone entrance, columns, and balustrades leading to the front door. Architect Thomas U. Walter also designed the dome and the House and Senate wings of the U.S. Capitol. Entrance to the building is free, and it's open Monday to Friday 10am to 3pm. The normal exhibition displays old leather fire-fighting equipment and the original policy statement and list of members. If you call ☎ 215/627-1752 ahead of time, you'll get to view two meeting rooms and a dining room, with their veined marble fireplaces and rare bird's-eye maple dining-room chairs.

Just below Locust Street on the same block is the:

22. Episcopal Diocese of Philadelphia, at no. 240, which combines two splendid row houses built in 1750 and 1826 for the Cadwallader family. Both houses are closed to the public. Just opposite the Diocese is **Bingham Court,** a 1967 adaptation of the Society Hill style of brick row houses. A few doors down 4th Street is:

23. Old St. Mary's Church, the most important Roman Catholic church during the Revolution (this was the "Sunday" church, as opposed to St. Joseph's weekday chapel). The interior is fairly prosaic, but the paved graveyard is a picturesque spot for a breather, with some interesting headstones and memorials.

The corner of Spruce and 4th streets is a good place to take a breath, with the town houses of **Girard Row** in front of you. Half a block to the west at

Impressions

It is a handsome city, but distractingly regular. After walking about it for an hour or two, I felt that I would have given the world for a crooked street. The collar of my coat appeared to stiffen, and the brim of my hat to expand, beneath its Quakery influence. My hair shrunk into a sleek short crop, my hands folded themselves upon my breast of their own calm accord, and thoughts of taking lodgings in Mark Lane over against the Market Place, and of making a large fortune by speculations in corn, came over me involuntarily.

—Charles Dickens, *American Notes* (1842)

426 Spruce St., Thomas U. Walter, the architect of the Contributionship (see above), designed a Baptist church in 1830 that has been modified as the **Society Hill Synagogue,** run by Romanian immigrants at the turn of the century and by Conservative Jews more recently.

A half block down 4th Street is the:

24. **Hill-Physick-Keith House,** at no. 321, possibly the finest residential structure in Society Hill (see chapter 7 for a fuller description). Take a few steps east on adjoining Cypress Street to reach **Delancey Park,** a delightful playground with sturdy activities and a group of stone bears that are perfect photo props.

More Georgian and Federal church facades appear at the corners of 4th and Pine streets. One is Old Pine:

25. **Old Pine Presbyterian,** with its enormous raised facade and forbidding iron fence, didn't always look like a Greek temple, but that's what makes it worth seeing (it's free and open daily 9am–5pm). The Penns granted the Presbyterians this land in perpetuity, and the first sanctuary took shape in 1768. The double Corinthian columns, inside and out, were added in 1830, after the occupying British soldiers burned most of the interior. Everything is linear at Old Pine: The portico leads into a rectangle of pews, and slim pillars support a gallery with an elaborately carved rail of flowers and dentils. The altar will surprise you—it's just a dais backed by elaborate columns and entablature. You'll find it hard to believe that this filigree is of wood and not clay or plaster.

Old Pine Community Center on the block south to Lombard Street leads to South Street's funky shopping and nightlife district just beyond. Walk east on Pine Street to:

26. **St. Peter's Episcopal Church** (1761), an example of classic Georgian simplicity (see chapter 7 for a fuller description).

Farther north, at 301 Pine St., is the:

27. **Kosciuszko National Memorial,** a double 1775 Georgian that housed this Polish engineer and soldier who turned the tide for American forces at Saratoga and West Point. It's part of the Park system and open daily. Now follow Pine Street to 2nd Street, the major north-south route through Philadelphia in colonial days. Open markets were a big part of urban life. In fact, no colonial native would recognize Market Street today without the wooden sheds that covered stalls from Front to 6th streets and its narrow cart paths on both sides. One place that would be recognizable, though, is:

28. **Head House Square,** built in 1803 in the middle of 2nd Street as a place where shoppers could congregate. Head House itself, that brick shed with a cupola that once held a fire bell, trails a simple brick arcade between Pine and South streets;

it used to house fire companies and stables. In those days, market took place at dawn on Tuesday and Friday. Butter and eggs were sold on the west side, meat under the eaves, and herbs and vegetables on the river side. Fish sellers were relegated to the far sidewalks (it isn't hard to imagine why). Now craftspeople spread out their goods here in summer, especially on weekends.

☕ **TAKE A BREAK**   **Dickens Inn,** 421 S. 2nd St., and several other Head House Square restaurants make excellent lunch or snack stopovers; Dickens Inn (open from 11:30am daily) has an English afternoon tea, as well as a tempting ground-floor bakery. For great chocolate chip cookies or brownies, go to **Koffmeyer's Bakery** on 2nd near Lombard.

Now head up 2nd Street, perhaps cutting in to Delancey Street between 2nd and 3rd streets, north on Philip Street's quaint court, and back to 2nd on Spruce Street. Across the street from the 1765 **Abercrombie House** (one of the tallest colonial dwellings in America) is the:

29. Man Full of Trouble Tavern, at 127 Spruce St. This place re-creates the life of Capt. James Abercrombie. The Knauer Foundation has restored the tavern to its original appearance with Delft tiles, a cagelike bar, and tables with Windsor chairs and pewter candlesticks. The 1760 tavern bordered Little Dock Creek then, and sailors and dockworkers ate, drank, and roughhoused here nightly. Admission is now by group appointment only.

Just up the hill are **Society Hill Towers** (1964), the I. M. Pei twins, which seemed so modern at the time, yet stick out like 30-story sore thumbs today. It's best to walk west back to 3rd Street, then north to a stunning block of row-house mansions including **Bishop Stevens** at no. 232, with its cast-iron balcony; **Atkinson House** at no. 236, which today conceals an indoor pool; and **Penn-Chew House** at no. 242, owned by the grandson of William and the last colonial governor of Pennsylvania. The mansion that you can visit is:

30. Powel House, at 244 S. 3rd St. This home of Philadelphia's last colonial and first U.S. mayor beats the Bishop White House by far (see chapter 7).

Across the street is:

31. St. Paul's Episcopal Church (1761), at 225 S. 3rd St., another church founded thanks to Philadelphia's religious tolerance. When the High Anglican Church refused to license the speech of William McClenachan, a young clergyman who preached such radical notions as the separation of church and state, St. Paul's was set up as his "bully pulpit." The money for the Georgian hall was raised through donations and lotteries. Now it houses the headquarters of the denomination's community services, inside beautiful pre-Revolutionary wrought-iron gates and marble-topped enclosing walls. If you go up to the second floor (open Mon–Fri 9am–5pm), you can still see most of the original chancel.

Standing at the corner of 3rd and Walnut streets, you can't miss the:

32. Philadelphia Exchange (1832), a masterwork by William Strickland (described in chapter 7). It's not open to the public. Heading toward 2nd Street and the river, you'll cross one of my favorite spaces, a broad area of cobblestones covering Dock Street (Dock Creek in Penn's day) and the Delaware River beyond. The **Ritz 5** movie house on your left shows fine independent fare. Soon you'll approach the reconstructed:

33. City Tavern restaurant and gardens from the rear. Built in 1773, this was the most opulent and genteel tavern and social hall in the colonies and the scene of

many discussions among the founding fathers. Unlike most of the city's pubs, it was built with businessmen's subscriptions, to assure its quality. George Washington met with most delegates to the Constitutional Convention for a farewell dinner here in 1787. The park now operates the City Tavern as a concession, which serves continuously from 11am (see chapter 6). The back garden seating is shady and cool for a midafternoon break.

If you choose to continue toward the Delaware via the pleasant pedestrian extension of Walnut Street and the staircase at its end, you'll pass between the new **Sheraton Society Hill** hotel and the famed **Old Original Bookbinder's** restaurant, winding up more or less in front of the wonderful **Independence Seaport Museum** on the waterfront. Consult the "Penn's Landing" description in chapter 7 for more details.

Walking Tour 2: Old City

Start: Visitors Center, 3rd and Walnut streets.
Finish: Market Place East, 7th and Market streets.
Time: From 3 to 5 hours.
Best Time: Start no later than 3pm to avoid museum closings. If contemporary art and socializing is your interest, the first Friday of every month brings special late hours for all galleries, all cafes, and many historic attractions.

Old City is an intriguing blend of 17th- and 18th-century artisan row houses, robust 19th-century commercial structures, and 20th-century rehabs of all of the above featuring artist lofts and galleries. See it while you can: Many property owners would rather demolish than rehab, and classics on 110–112 S. Front St., for example, were recently destroyed despite public outcry. Walk out the south entrance of the **Visitors Center** and along the narrow lane adjoining **City Tavern** to:

1. **Welcome Park,** the site of the Slate Roof House where William Penn granted the "Charter of Privileges" (now at the Library Hall off Independence Square) in 1701. The pavement bears a massive and whimsical map of Penn's City, with a time line of his life on the walls.

   Next door is the **Thomas Bond House,** a restored 1769 Georgian row house that's now a bed-and-breakfast (see chapter 5 for more information). Walk along the block-long **AMC Olde City 2** cinemas to:

2. **Front Street,** which actually lapped at the river's edge in colonial times. A walk north brings you to **Bonnie's Exceptional Ice Cream** at the corner of Chestnut Street and the possibility of exploring Penn's Landing (see chapter 7 for a description) via a beautifully terraced park. But head back to the florid **Corn Exchange Bank** at 2nd and Chestnut streets, then turn right onto one of the liveliest blocks in the historic area.

   ☕ **TAKE A BREAK**   The block of "Two Street" between Chestnut and Market contains lots of good or at least passable restaurants such as **New Mexico Grille.** My favorite is **Foodtek Market and Café,** with great hot and cold charcuterie and quiet, cool seating for 40 at the rear. It's open Monday to Friday 9am to 1am, Saturday and Sunday until 2am.

   Once you hit the newly widened sidewalks of Market Street (High St. in colonial times), you'll find a different world, where a burst of natural food stores and

[With its] streets of small, low, yet snug-looking houses . . . Philadelphia must contain in comfort the largest number of small householders of any city in the world.
—*London Times* reporter William Bussell, *My Diary North and South* (1850)

upgraded bistros like **Fork, Novelty,** and **Continental** are moving in on sharp discount clothing and wholesale toy stores. The many alleyways between Front and 5th streets, with names like **Trotter Street, Black Horse Alley, Bank Street,** and **Strawberry Lane,** testify to the activities and preoccupations of colonial residents. A particular favorite facade of mine is that of the:

3. **Norwegian Seaman's Church,** at 22 S. 3rd St. This William Strickland gem from 1837, with Corinthian columns and granite steps, is now **Wichita Steak + Brews,** a restaurant and club. If you took the first walking tour, continue right through the Franklin Court site to Market Street and Christ Church. Otherwise, go now to:

4. **Franklin Court,** between 3rd and 4th streets, Ben Franklin's final home, now a post office (see chapter 7 for a full discussion). Standing on Market Street, you can't miss the graceful spire of:

5. **Christ Church.** Urban renewal removed the unsightly buildings that hid its walls from Market Street. Christ Church, with its restful benches and adjoining cemetery, is Philadelphia's leading place of worship. See chapter 7 for a full description.

🏺 **TAKE A BREAK** It may be a bit early for another refueling stop, but the block of Church Street directly to the west of the church contains **Old City Coffee** at no. 221, a favorite place for marvelous coffee and light lunches. If the end of the day is approaching by the time you get here, duck underneath the Market Street ramp to I-95 at Front Street to reach **Panorama's** wine bar and bistro.

Walk north along Front Street for 4 short blocks to get the flavor of 1830s warehouses, such as the **Girard** at 18–30 N. Front St. and **Smythe** at 101 Arch St. If you continued north and east, you would come to the attractive new clubs and restaurants on the water, such as **Meiji-en, Rock Lobster,** and **The Beach Club.** Instead, take a left onto:

6. **Elfreth's Alley** (from 1702), the oldest continuously occupied group of homes in America. See "More Attractions," in chapter 7, for a full description of these tiny houses. Several courts are perfect for wandering, and you can enter no. 126.

Back on 2nd Street with its china and restaurant supply stores, you might detour north for a minute to look at **2nd Street Art Building,** which houses the Clay Studio and NEXUS galleries, or to visit the:

7. **Fireman's Hall Museum,** at Quarry Street. This restored century-old firehouse contains a hand pump used by Ben Franklin, who helped advance fire fighting beyond rudimentary wooden buckets. On display are 19th- and 20th-century fire wagons, along with assorted fire-fighting tools and memorabilia.

Head south now and turn right on Arch Street, where you'll come to the:

8. **Betsy Ross House,** at no. 239 (see chapter 7 for full details). The tour of the house is short, but there's a large garden. Directly opposite are the **Mulberry**

Walking Tour: Old City

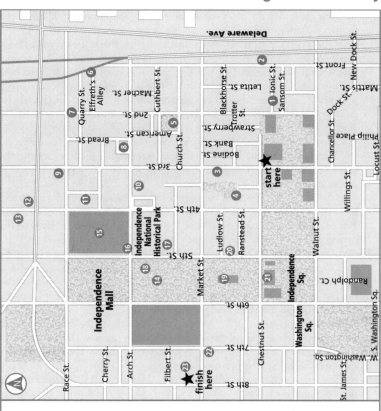

1 Welcome Park
2 Front Street
3 Norwegian Seaman's Church
4 Franklin Court
5 Christ Church
6 Elfreth's Alley
7 Fireman's Hall Museum
8 Betsy Ross House
9 Pretzel Museum
10 Arch Street Friends Meeting House
11 Old First Reformed Church
12 Old St. George's Methodist Church
13 St. Augustine's Roman Catholic Church
14 Independence Mall
15 U.S. Mint
16 Christ Church Burial Ground
17 National Museum of American Jewish History
18 The Free Quaker Meetinghouse
19 Liberty Bell
20 The Bourse
21 Independence Hall
22 Declaration (Graff) House
23 Market Place East

Market, an upscale deli with seating in the rear, and **Humphry Flags,** if you're feeling patriotic.

At the corner of 3rd Street, if you turn north (toward the Ben Franklin Bridge) you'll reach:

9. **The Pretzel Museum** at 211 N. Third St., basically a factory tour with hands-on instruction in kneading and twisting, plus a 7-minute video. Philadelphians consume 12 times the national average annually of this baked dough snack, and you'll get your samples with the $1.50 admission. Open Monday to Saturday 9am to 5pm.

Cross 3rd Street to the **Hoop Skirt Factory** at 309–313 Arch St., dating from 1875, and the charming **Loxley Court** just beyond, designed by carpenter Benjamin Loxley in 1741. (It stayed within the family until 1901.) On the south side of the street is the:

10. **Arch Street Friends Meeting House,** the largest Quaker meetinghouse in America, a simple 1805 structure with a substantial history (see chapter 7 for details). You could keep walking straight west 1 block to Independence Mall, but I recommend that you take a slightly gritty walk north on 4th Street to:

11. **Old First Reformed Church,** at 151 N. 4th St. Built in 1837 for a sect of German Protestants, the building survived a stint as a paint warehouse in the late 19th century. The church functions as a small and always full youth hostel during July and August (see chapter 5 for details). Crossing under the gloomy piers of the **Benjamin Franklin Bridge,** you'll see:

12. **Old St. George's Methodist Church,** at 235 N. 4th St., the cradle of American Methodism and the scene of fanatic religious revival meetings in the early 1770s. The bridge was built farther south to preserve the church. On the other side of the street, below Vine, is one more church:

13. **St. Augustine's Roman Catholic Church.** It's another 18th-century building, this one built for German and Irish Catholics who couldn't get to St. Joseph's south of Market Street because of muddy streets. Villanova University, and the Augustinian presence in the United States, started here. The building actually only dates from 1844; the original burned down during anti-Catholic riots. Now, keep walking west along the bridge to 5th Street, then head south along:

14. **Independence Mall,** a swath of urban renewal that bit off more than the Historical Park could chew, and which is being redressed with Gateway Visitors Center, beautiful landscaping, and a new home for the Liberty Bell by 2003. At the upper end of the Mall (Florist St.) is the bicycle and pedestrian entrance to the Benjamin Franklin Bridge; cycling or walking across the bridge makes for a thrilling but time-consuming expedition. Continuing on, head down 5th Street, stopping at the:

15. **U.S. Mint.** Of the three mints in the country (the others are in Denver and San Francisco), Philadelphia's is the oldest and the largest. (See chapter 7 for hours and description.) Just south of the Mint is:

16. **Christ Church Burial Ground** (see chapter 7), the resting place of Benjamin and Deborah Franklin and other notables (toss a coin through the opening in the brick wall for luck), and also the:

17. **National Museum of American Jewish History,** at 55 N. 5th St. The city of Philadelphia has a history of distinguished Jewish involvement in town affairs almost as long as the life of the town itself. This museum, connected to the city's oldest congregation, commemorates this story (see chapter 7 for a fuller

description). You'll notice how much lower street level used to be by looking at the statuary outside.

A small building across from the Franklin graves, in Independence Mall, is the:

18. Free Quaker Meetinghouse, run by the Park Service. "Fighting Quakers," such as Betsy Ross, were willing to support the Revolutionary War. But since this violated the tenets of pure Quakerism, they were forced to leave Arch Street Friends and establish their own meetinghouse.

Cross Market Street to see the:

19. Liberty Bell, if you haven't already visited it. Near the Liberty Bell is:

20. The Bourse, a 19th-century exchange that now contains a food court and pleasant urban mall (a "Take a Break" stop discussed in the "Historic Highlights" tour above). Reenter Independence Mall and you'll be in front of:

21. Independence Hall, with its two flanking buildings, **Congress Hall** and **Old City Hall.** (See chapter 7 for tour hours.)

Continue west along Chestnut Street to 7th Street, and turn right onto a historic block containing the **Atwater Kent Museum** of city memorabilia, the **Balch Institute of Ethnic Studies,** and:

22. Declaration (Graff) House, a reconstruction of the lodgings where Thomas Jefferson drafted the Declaration of Independence. It is run by the National Park Service, with free daily admission. (All of the above are described more fully in chapter 7.)

From the old to the new: Right behind Graff House on Market Street is a huge McDonald's designed for children; directly opposite it on Market Street is:

23. Market Place East, the converted and rehabilitated former home of Lit Brothers Department Store, a wrought-iron palace that's a block long (see the full description in chapter 9). The below-ground food area contains an **Au Bon Pain.**

Walking Tour 3: Midtown & the Parkway

Start: Visitors Center, 16th Street and John F. Kennedy Boulevard.

Finish: Logan Circle, intersection of 19th Street, Race Street, and the Benjamin Franklin Parkway.

Time: 6 hours (including stops at museums).

Best Time: No later than noon, to avoid museum closings.

Worst Time: Sunday, when many stores are closed, and Monday, when most museums are shuttered.

This tour encompasses the confident heart of 19th-century Philadelphia. If you've already sampled the charm and excitement of historic Philadelphia, the downtown area and southwest of Center City may seem anticlimactic. But there's plenty to see here, too, starting with the massive French Renaissance City Hall. Center Square and its environs were farmland or parkland during the 18th century. But as commercial buildings and loft warehouses began to dominate Old City, old Philadelphia families came to consider Rittenhouse Square the fashionable part of town. Individual dwellings, such as Hockley House (1875) at 235 S. 21st St. and the present Art Alliance Building on Rittenhouse Square, coexist with attractive row houses such as those at 18th Street and Delancey Place. Churches, the Academy of Fine Arts (at Broad and Cherry), the Academy of Music (at Broad and Locust), and such private clubs as the Union League (at Broad and Sansom) enhanced the Victorian lifestyle.

The 20th century has added skyscrapers to the business district, notably the international style Philadelphia Savings Fund Society (PSFS) Building (about to become the Loew's Hotel Philadelphia), and such postmodern structures as I. M. Pei's Commerce Square (41 stories, at Market and 21st sts.) and Helmut Jahn's One and Two Liberty Place (61 and 54 stories, respectively, 3 blocks east). This is also a wonderful shopping, cultural, and restaurant area, catering to up-to-the-minute tastes.

Start your walking tour at the:

1. **Visitors Center,** run by the Philadelphia Convention and Visitors Bureau, at 16th Street and John F. Kennedy Boulevard. The Visitors Center has it all in a shiny wedding cake of a building that's open daily 9am to 6pm. Half-price tickets to many evening events are sold here as well.

Passing by Robert Indiana's *LOVE* statue, you'll reach:

2. **City Hall.** You can't miss City Hall, at the intersection of Broad and Market streets. This fanciful, exuberant hodgepodge graced with a huge statue of William Penn has free tours and elevators to the viewing area at Penn's feet. Until Liberty Place was built, Penn's hat was generally considered to be the tallest point within city limits. (See chapter 7 for full details.)

Everyone wonders what that chiseled-looking building just north of City Hall with the single tower is—a church? No, it's the:

3. **Masonic Temple,** one of the world's largest (see chapter 7 for a full description). Continue two blocks up North Broad Street to the:

4. **Museum of American Art of the Pennsylvania Academy of Fine Arts,** founded in 1804. This 1876 building is now overshadowed by the Philadelphia Museum of Art, but it still holds an excellent blend of the best in old and new American art, in a wonderful renovated High Victorian building (see chapter 7 for details).

Now backtrack to City Hall and head east through:

5. **Lord & Taylor,** now a shadow of Wanamaker's, its former incarnation, is still an impressive department store. It features an enormous pipe organ, an atrium, and "the Iggle," a statue of our national bird that has been a rendezvous for shoppers for generations (see chapter 9 for details).

Back on Market Street, you'll pass the classic international style **Philadelphia Savings Fund Society (PSFS) Building** skyscraper at 12th Street, now a sparkling and swanky Loews Hotel. Directly opposite that is:

6. **Reading Terminal,** once a commuter terminal but now the facade of the brand-new **Pennsylvania Convention Center.** The **Reading Terminal Market,** just north of Market Street, is one of the country's great surviving urban food markets (see chapter 6 for the delicious details).

Three blocks south, Locust and 12th streets are the center for:

7. **Philadelphia's littlest streets,** a group of wonderfully charming row houses tucked into alleys and courtyards. My favorites are the art clubs of **South Camac Street,** between 12th and 13th streets and between Locust and Spruce streets, followed by **Manning, Sartain, Quince,** and **Jessup** streets, between 11th and 12th streets at the same latitude. If you care to continue 2 blocks south, you'll find **Antique Row** lining Pine Street with galleries between 9th and 12th streets.

From here, walk past the Doubletree Hotel at Broad and Locust to:

8. **South Broad Street,** once the undisputed cultural capital of the city, now picking up steam as a revitalized "Avenue of the Arts." For reasons of safety and

Walking Tour: Midtown & the Parkway

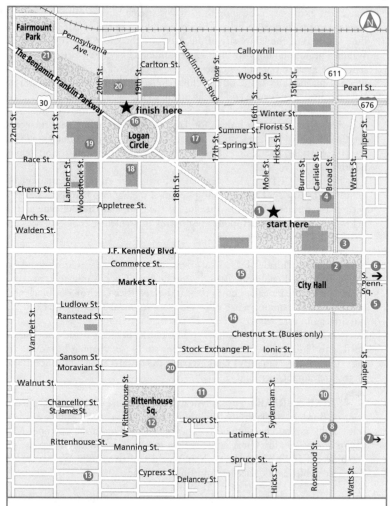

1 Visitors Center
2 City Hall
3 Masonic Temple
4 Pennsylvania Academy of Fine Arts
5 Lord & Taylor
6 Pennsylvania Convention
  Center/Reading Terminal
7 Philadelphia's littlest streets
8 South Broad Street
  ("Avenue of the Arts")
9 Academy of Music
10 Park Hyatt at the Bellevue
11 Rittenhouse Square area shopping

12 Rittenhouse Square
13 Rosenbach Museum and Library 13
14 Liberty Place
15 Penn Center (the former
  Suburban) Station
16 Logan Circle
17 Cathedral-Basilica of
  Sts. Peter and Paul
18 Academy of Natural Sciences
19 Franklin Institute Science Museum
  and Futures Center
20 Free Library of Philadelphia
21 Rodin Museum

convenience, the city is pushing to turn this stretch into an unbroken series of theaters and performance halls. The Philadelphia College of Art at Broad and Pine has become the University of the Arts, and the Clef Club, Arts Bank, and Wilma Theater buildings are all up and running. The city's chief improvement slated for a 2001 opening, in fact, is the opening of the Kimmel Center, a regional magnet and home of the Philadelphia Orchestra. The Orchestra will lease out its current venue two blocks north, the:

9. Academy of Music, modeled on La Scala in Milan, to a variety of hometown and visiting performers. It is open for daytime tours or evening performances of the Philadelphia Orchestra, one of the best ensembles in the country (see chapter 10 for details). Walk one block north (passing Philadelphia's most opulent health club) to:

10. The Philadelphia Park Hyatt at the Bellevue, the current incarnation of a grand 1901 hostelry. Thomas Edison designed the lighting fixtures; it's worth a peek at the former lobby, now the site for the **Shops at the Bellevue** and the below-ground **Food Court** (public rest rooms and refueling available). See chapters 5 and 6 for full information.

Keep walking north to the **Union League** at Broad and Sansom streets, the most evident of Philadelphia's many private clubs. This one was formed and constructed for the Republican Party in the flush of Civil War sentiment. By all means, be tempted to take a quick peek at the new **Ritz-Carlton** one block north of this, with its stunning rehab of its old bank rotunda. Then backtrack to Walnut Street and turn left to:

11. Rittenhouse Square area shopping. The blocks between Broad and 18th are lined with Philadelphia's finest independent stores (see chapter 9 for a full listing). You'll also pass the city's (and probably the country's) highest concentration of great restaurants per foot!

☕ **TAKE A BREAK**   For a physical and intellectual pick-me-up, the second floor of **Borders,** arguably the city's best bookstore, at 1727 Walnut St., has a comfortable espresso bar with racks of newspapers and magazines. It's open Monday to Friday 7am to 10pm, Saturday 9am to 9pm, and Sunday 11am to 7pm. **Starbucks** at 1528 Walnut St. or **New World Coffee** at 1809 Walnut St. both have several blends and excellent muffins and scones.

12. Rittenhouse Square was the center of social prestige in the city from roughly 1870 to 1930, when proper Philadelphians discovered they could live in the Main Line suburbs year-round. Despite the construction of apartment houses to replace such mansions as **McIlhenny House** at the southwest corner, the square still adds elegance to the city, bolstered by the **Curtis School of Music** at Locust Street and the **Rittenhouse Hotel** (though not by the latter's jagged architecture). The newest kids on the block—the Sheraton Rittenhouse and Barnes & Noble—fit well into existing 1930s structures, as do the bistro neighbors such as **Bleu, Rouge,** and **Devon Seafood Grille** jostling for sidewalk space on 18th Street. The park itself has splendid curving walks around whimsical fountains and decorative pools.

South and west of Rittenhouse Square are unusual turn-of-the-century town houses ranging from severe Georgian to fanciful neo-medieval. A favorite representative street is **Delancey Street,** between Spruce and Lombard. If you detour as far west as 20th Street, you'll be rewarded with the interiors and garden of:

13. Rosenbach Museum and Library, at no. 2010, a shrine for book collectors and lovers of literature (see chapter 7 for a full description).

From Rittenhouse Square, head north on 18th Street to Chestnut Street. Take a right and go down a block to:

14. Liberty Place, a tremendously inviting urban mall and superb family refueling stop at the second-floor food court. (See chapter 6 for the cuisine and chapter 9 for the shops.)

Walking east 1 block, then north 1 block, you'll see the Visitors Center. Look northwest and begin your stroll along Benjamin Franklin Parkway. The Parkway connects City Hall with the welcoming arms of the Philadelphia Museum of Art, just over a mile away, swirling through Logan Circle and its fountain en route. The last decade's explosive growth of new corporate headquarters in town has solidified the many grand cultural institutions built on its edges. If you visit the cultural attractions, you can pick up a "Parkway Passport" offering discounts at most local restaurants, where the passport is also available.

Walking up from the **Visitors Center** at 16th Street and John F. Kennedy Boulevard, you'll pass:

15. Penn Center (the former Suburban) Station, a compact art deco terminal whose ground floor has been transformed into the inviting **Marathon Grill.** An underground concourse linking the station to City Hall contains dozens of shops, services, and food vendors. A left turn will bring you onto the Parkway itself.

Three blocks up, past the rounded marble tower of the **Embassy Suites Hotel,** lies:

16. Logan Circle. Originally a square, it was converted with the Parkway construction. This most corporate and institutional setting of all of William Penn's original city parks has the lowest buildings surrounding it. The highlight is the 1920 **Swann Fountain,** designed by Alexander Calder, which evokes the three waters (Delaware, Schuylkill, Wissahickon) that nourish Philadelphia.

At the eastern end of Logan Circle is the:

17. Cathedral-Basilica of Sts. Peter and Paul. Built in 1846, on the heels of the anti-Catholic riots of the early 1840s, this sober Roman church with a copper dome was meant to proclaim that Catholics would recover and populate a newer part of Center City.

Continue walking clockwise around Logan Circle. The 4-story **Four Seasons Hotel** was sensitively designed not to intrude architecturally. The hotel renovated the Swann Fountain in the mid-1980s and maintains its hothouse gardens. Afternoon tea at the **Fountain Café** is a quintessential Philadelphia experience.

Just past 19th Street on Logan Circle is the:

18. Academy of Natural Sciences, displaying flora and fauna from the world over, from dinosaurs to contemporary volcanoes (see chapter 7 for details).

Next to the academy is **Moore College of Art,** with its street-level exhibition space open to the public. Taking up the whole west side of Logan Circle is the neoclassical facade of the:

19. Franklin Institute Science Museum and Futures Center, a top attraction (see chapter 7 for details). Even if you decide not to visit the museum, you can still eat at **Ben's Café.** With a detour 2 blocks south on 21st Street, you'll come to the **Please Touch Museum** (also see chapter 7).

To the north side lie both the:

20. Free Library of Philadelphia, with a wonderful Children's Library as well as research and circulating collections and an inexpensive rooftop cafeteria (again, chapter 7 has details), and the twin **Municipal Court Building.**

If you continue up toward the **Philadelphia Museum of Art** on the north side of the Parkway from the Free Library, 2 blocks up you'll come to:

21. Rodin Museum, an ancillary collection of the Museum of Art, bequeathed to the city in the 1920s and just renovated and reinstalled. It has a very pleasant out-door sculpture collection in a leafy garden (see full description in chapter 7).

Shopping 9

In colonial days, Philadelphia was one of the most interesting shopping marts in the world. Franklin's *Autobiography* tells of his surprise upon coming to breakfast one morning to find a china bowl and silver spoon in his own kitchen: "Luxury will enter families and make a progress in spite of principle." Due in part to its proximity to New York City, Philadelphia still has plenty of goods to help luxury enter your life.

1 The Shopping Scene

The best places to look for high fashion and international wares are the specialty shops around **Liberty Place** and **Rittenhouse Square.** These boutiques are virtually duplicated in one of the enormous malls to the north of the city, in **King of Prussia**—a 450-store behemoth, second only to Minnesota's Mall of America—and at **Franklin Mills,** an outlet mall that draws four times the traffic of the Liberty Bell. For more contemporary items, **Manayunk** is Philadelphia's hippest neighborhood. The new airport retail center also carries a surprising number of national names.

The once-funky area on **South Street,** just south of Society Hill, has turned into big business. Because restaurants and nightlife now line South Street from Front to 8th streets, many of the 180 stores here are open well into the evening and offer goods ranging from the gentrified to the somewhat grotesque.

There is no sales tax on clothing; other items are taxed at 7%. Most stores stay open during regular business hours, Monday to Friday, Saturday, and later on Wednesday evening. Some are also open on Sunday.

You can pick up a free *Philadelphia Loves Visa Value* booklet offering 470 discounts throughout town, at the Visitors Center at 16th and John F. Kennedy Boulevard, or at most hotels.

OUTLET MALLS & SHOPPING CENTERS

The Bellevue. Broad and Walnut sts. ☎ **215/875-8350.**

The lower floors of the Park Hyatt/Bellevue Hotel have been turned into a very upscale collection of top names in retailing. Browsing here is quite low key; it feels a little like a private club. The **Polo/Ralph Lauren** store is the third largest in the world, with three floors of mahogany-and-brass splendor. Other tenants include **Tiffany & Co.,** with its extraordinary jewelry, silver, and

Food & Shops at the Airport

If you haven't seen the Philadelphia International Airport (☎ 215/937-1200) in the past year or so, you're in for a big surprise. They've added over 30 shops and eateries in the "Philadelphia Marketplace" between Terminals B and C, including a lively and spacious food court with seating for 400. Retail includes **GAP/GAP Kids, Discovery Channel Store, Staples, Brookstone** and **Wilson's Leather,** while the **Dock Street Airport Brew Pub** headlines the food court operation. There are 70 other shopping and dining venues along the other concourses near airline gates and along every concourse.

accessories; **Williams Sonoma** for gourmet accessories; a new **Nicole Miller; Hope Chest** for intimates and lingerie; **Suky Rosan** for women's fashion; **Vigant** luggage; and **Origins** cosmetics. Dining is at **Ciboulette** on the mezzanine, the **Palm Restaurant,** or the lower-level food court.

Shops at the Bellevue are open Monday to Saturday 10am to 6pm (until 8pm on Wed).

Franklin Mills. 1455 Franklin Mills Circle. ☎ **800/336-6255** or 215/632-1500. Follow the signs from I-95 (take Exit 24 north) or from the Pa. Turnpike (take Exit 28 south).

About 15 miles northeast of Center City on the edge of Bucks County, the former Liberty Bell racetrack opened in mid-1989 as Franklin Mills, the city's largest single-story mall, with 1.8 million square feet devoted to 220 discount and outlet stores. It generates 18 million shoppers annually, and there's parking for more than 9,000 cars in four color-coded zones. More recently, Franklin Mills has become a discount shoppers' landmark, with last-call outlets from Saks Fifth Avenue, Neiman Marcus, Nordstrom, Bally Shoes, Burlington Coat Factory, and Kaspar. General Cinema has just opened a 14-screen multiplex with stadium seating. For other amusement, the **49th Street Galleria** has bowling, roller skating, miniature golf, batting cages, and rides and games (open Mon–Thurs 10am–11pm, Fri–Sat until midnight, and Sun until 9pm). If you can't stop there, two ancillary malls are a 61-checkout-lane (that's right, 61 lanes) **Carrefour** supermarket/department store, and a 30-store **Home and Design Centre.**

Franklin Mills is open Monday to Saturday 10am to 9:30pm and Sunday 11am to 6pm. SEPTA trains go right to the complex.

The Gallery at Market East. 8th to 11th and Market sts. ☎ **215/625-4962.**

The Gallery at Market East, next to the Pennsylvania Convention Center, is built on four levels accommodating more than 170 stores and restaurants around sunken arcades and a glass atrium. The JC Penney department store, at the 10th Street corner of Market Street, has fit in Gimbel's shoes, and a 2-story Kmart in the old Clover. The **food court** has more than 25 snack bars and take-out spots. The **Hardshell Café,** at the street corner of 9th and Market, offers all-you-can-eat specials. Stores offer running shoes, books, pets, cameras, jewelry, fresh produce, toys, and all the clothing you could ever need. **Strawbridge's** connects over 9th Street with merchandise of slightly higher quality and prices. You can pick up a substantial coupon discount book at the Gallery's Information Center, which also provides city maps and sells SEPTA day passes and PHLASH bus passes. It's open Monday, Tuesday, Thursday, and Saturday 10am to 7pm, Wednesday and Friday 10am to 8pm, and Sunday noon to 5pm.

✪ **King of Prussia Court and Plaza.** Near junction of U.S. 202 and Pa. 363. ☎ **610/ 337-4752.** www.shopking.com. One-half mile south of I-276; 3 miles south of Valley Forge National Historical Park via Rte. 422.

People have always been drawn to King of Prussia because of its name, though it is generally referred to as the "Court and Plaza." It's now the second largest mall in the country, impeccably designed and marketed, with 450 establishments in three connected tiers, grouped roughly by price range. The major stores include Bloomingdale's, JC Penney, Lord & Taylor, Neiman Marcus, Nordstrom, Strawbridge's, and Sears. Other top-quality boutiques include Hugo Boss, Williams-Sonoma, Hermes, Guess Home Collection, and Tiffany & Co. Choose from 59 restaurants and eateries, from a food court to the Brew Moon microbrewery, but there's no inhouse entertainment—just shopping. And with 126 acres of parking, don't forget where you left your car.

Market Place East. 701 Market St., between 7th and 8th sts. ☎ **215/592-8905.**

The century-old Lit Brothers Department Store was a sprawling assembly of wrought-iron facades that has been recently and beautifully resuscitated. The ground floor has attracted tenants including **Ross Dress for Less** and **Dress Barn.** The lower level has a food court with atrium seating. There is garage space nearby.

Market Place East is open Monday to Thursday and Saturday 10am to 6pm, until 8pm on Wednesday. Some stores are open noon to 5pm on Sunday.

The Shops at Penn. 34th and Walnut sts. and **Sansom Commons,** 36th and Sansom sts. ☎ **215/222-8595.**

There are dozens of specialty fashion, music, books and gift shops, and a nine-store food court, as part of U. Penn's urban redevelopment around the campus.

✪ **The Shops at Liberty Place.** 1625 Chestnut St. between 16th and 17th sts. ☎ **215/ 851-9154.**

The Liberty Place development is the real thing: It's the handsome 60-story tower that supplanted City Hall as the city's tallest spire, and it contains 70 stores and stalls that together achieve an ambience and a comfort level that are the finest in the city. It's beautifully designed, with many street exits and entrances that curve and converge on a soaring, glass-domed rotunda. Representative of the retailers are **Rand McNally** for maps and children's games, **Brentano's** for books, **The Coach Store** for luggage, **Country Road Australia** and **Warner Bros. Studio Store** for casual clothes, **Handblock** for high-quality Indian clothes and fabrics, **Jos. A. Bank** and **J. Crew** for traditional clothes, and a new **Victoria's Secret.** The second floor is a wonderfully convenient, reasonably priced court where you can eat on the run, with hundreds of well-kept tables and chairs around quality food stalls. Provident Bank operates an ATM inside near 17th Street, and the garage directly underneath holds 750 cars. The Shops at Liberty Place are open Monday to Saturday 9:30am to 7pm and Sunday noon to 6pm.

2 Shopping A to Z

ANTIQUES

Philadelphia sometimes seems like one big attic, full of the undervalued heirlooms and cast-offs of previous generations. Pine Street from 9th to 12th streets boasts some 25 stores, many of which do their own refinishing. Old City stores may specialize in any decade from the 1850s through the 1970s, and Germantown Avenue in Chestnut Hill also has a large concentration of shops. As in any antiques market, you'll have to bring your own expertise to the store, and you'll have to trust your dealer. There are usually dozens of antiques markets every week in the Delaware Valley. Consult the "Weekend" section of the *Philadelphia Inquirer* for details.

Calderwood Gallery. 1427 Walnut St. ☎ **215/568-7475.**

This is an international resource for French art nouveau and art deco furnishings, which are beautifully displayed. The prices are reasonable compared to those in New York City.

Freeman/Fine Arts of Philadelphia. 1808 Chestnut St. ☎ **215/563-9275.**

The dean of the nation's auction houses since 1805, Freeman's stages a full auction every Wednesday (previews on Mon and Tues), specializing in Americana. Special fully cataloged auctions for jewelry and fine furniture are held about once a month. Regular auctions include standard home furnishings and some fine silver, rugs, jewelry, and decorative arts.

✪ **Gargoyles.** 512 S. 3rd St. ☎ **215/629-1700.**

In Society Hill, my personal favorite is Gargoyles, which has everything from toothpick holders to mantels and bars. Although much of the stock is American, there's also a delightful selection of English pub signs, dart boards, top hats, polo mallets, and the like. Several large items have been salvaged from 19th-century buildings and businesses.

First Loyalty Antiques. 1042 Pine St. ☎ **215/922-5594.**

The displays of Victorian and art deco furnishings and jewelry here are remarkably uncluttered compared to others in the neighborhood.

M. Finkel and Daughter. 936 Pine St. ☎ **215/627-7797.**

Finkel is one of the true anchors of Pine Street. Look here for folk art, furniture, and painting. And if you're looking for antique needlework samplers, this is the place; they publish the scholarly journal *Samplings* twice a year. Appointments are advised.

✪ **W. Graham Arader III Gallery.** 1308 Walnut St. ☎ **215/735-8811.**

Arader has become one of the country's leading rare book, map, and print dealers in the past 20 years thanks to its aggressive purchasing (which translates into high prices). You'll find a variety of interesting items here.

ART GALLERIES

The line between museums, such as the Pennsylvania Academy of Fine Arts (PAFA), that exhibit studio artists, and galleries that promote sales is more blurred here than in many cities. The line between art and crafts is also a fine one (see "Crafts," below, for more listings). Many of the less traditional galleries are in the colonial district or on South Street.

The Eyes Gallery. 402 South St. ☎ **215/925-0193.**

Julia Zagar has presented a cheerful assortment of Latin American folk art, including santos and retablos, for 30 years now, in the same location. Also included are one-of-a-kind articles of clothing and jewelry spread over three floors. Open every day of the week.

Fleisher/Ollman Gallery. 211 S. 17th St. ☎ **215/545-7562.**

This gallery is known for carrying fine works by emerging contemporary artists and self-taught American artists such as Martin Ramirez. Style is variable.

Gross-McCleaf Gallery. 127 S. 16th St. ☎ **215/665-8138.**

Now in its 27th year, Jay Gross's gallery features exhibits of regional painting or any medium that can be hung. The focus is on painterly realism, including landscape, still life, and figurative work.

Helen Drutt. 1721 Walnut St. ☎ **215/735-1625.**

Among the private galleries, Helen Drutt English has the most influential shows of crafted objects of fiber, clay, and metal—both aesthetic and utilitarian. Winter hours are Wednesday to Saturday 10am to 5pm; summer hours are Wednesday and Thursday 11am to 5pm and Friday 11am to 4pm.

Locks. 600 Washington Sq. South. ☎ **215/629-1000.**

This is a powerhouse gallery for paintings, sculptures, and mixed-media works, hard to beat for its serenity and elegance. Gallery 1 is frequently devoted to group theme shows, and the smaller Gallery 2 usually focuses on a single artist—Frank Stella, Robert Motherwell, and Jennifer Bartlett are scheduled for 2001–2. Sueyun Locks aims "to help collectors get savvy," and there's more for the beginner than you might think.

Moderne Gallery. 111 N. 3rd St. ☎ **215/923-8536.**

Moderne is unique in specializing in vintage craft furniture. Robert Aibel offers a very good selection of American and French ironworks—furniture and decorative items. They've also added inventory from the 1940s and 1950s, along with the world's largest selection of vintage pieces by woodworker George Nakashima. Books and fabrics appropriate to 20th-century design are also available.

✪ **Newman Galleries.** 1625 Walnut St. ☎ **215/563-1779.**

The oldest gallery in Philadelphia (founded in 1865), Newman Galleries provides a strong representation of Bucks County artists and American sculptors and painters in general. Custom framing and art conservation are also available. Signed, limited edition prints from $200.

✪ **Philadelphia Art Alliance.** Rittenhouse Square, 251 S. 18th St. ☎ **215/545-4302.**

Founded in 1915 in a striking mansion on Rittenhouse Square, the Alliance now boasts exhibition space along with 30 performing/literary programs annually and the acclaimed OPUS 251 restaurant. The three floors of local talent here are chosen by the alliance's committee of laypersons and artists, so most of the material—pottery, sculpture, and hangings—already has its stamp of approval. There's a new satellite gallery on the third floor of the Rittenhouse Hotel across the square. Open Tuesday to Sunday 9am to 5pm.

The School Gallery of the Pennsylvania Academy of Fine Arts. 1301 Cherry St. ☎ **215/972-7600.**

The first art school in the country has student and faculty exhibits that change frequently during the year. Housed in a gorgeous rehab near the Convention Center, it's open daily 9am to 7pm. Admission is free.

BOOKSTORES

AIA Bookstore and Design Center. 117 S. 17th St. at Sansom St. ☎ **215/569-3188.**

This bookstore has expanded to include gardening along with architecture and design. It also offers an excellent downstairs gallery of architectural renderings, watercolors, and drawings (see below). It's a triple "Best of Philly" award winner. And the bookshelves are gorgeous!

Barnes & Noble. 1805 Walnut St. ☎ **215/656-0716.**

Going head to head with archrival Borders (see below) but open one hour later (until 11pm nightly), B&N opened this massive store with a cafe right on Rittenhouse Square next to Anthropologie. The neighborhood seems to be able to sustain both. Top sellers are discounted to 40%.

Book Trader. 501 South St. ☎ **215/925-0219.**

If you're on South Street and feel like browsing or just resting, Book Trader has a fine paperback and fiction collection, along with benches and a resident cat. It's open until midnight every night. You can also find a good selection of out-of-print books and used LPs, tapes, and CDs.

Borders. 1727 Walnut St. ☎ **215/568-7400.**

Started by the Borders brothers in Minneapolis, this was the first superstore of its kind in town, and remains a cultural center. Borders features a great staff and an even greater selection. It has an active reading series in the evening that pays attention to local writers. There's a fine children's book section with toys and storytelling hours on most Saturdays, and a second-floor espresso bar with newspapers.

The University of Pennsylvania Bookstore. Sansom Common, 3601 Walnut St. ☎ **215/898-7595.**

A 50,000-square-foot collaboration between U. Penn and Barnes & Noble, just recently opened. It's a great academic bookstore, but you'll also find excellent selections of quality fiction and nonfiction and children's books; a 100-seat Starbucks cafe; a comprehensive music department with listening stations; and even clothes and accessories suitable for that hastily scheduled job interview. Open Monday to Saturday 8:30am to 11pm, Sunday 10am to 6pm.

COLONIAL REPRODUCTIONS

Fried Brothers. 467 N. 7th St. ☎ **800/523-2924** or 215/627-3205.

Near the Edgar Allan Poe National Historical Site, Fried Brothers specializes in hardware suitable for colonial buildings and furnishings. If you admire the doorknobs in Society Hill, you'll see similar ones here.

CRAFTS

Philadelphia artisanship has always commanded respect. The tradition lingers on, in both small individual workshops and cooperative stores. The Old City section, north of Society Hill, has seen a mushrooming of contemporary crafts and design stores. The Craft Show held every November is one of the best in the country.

For outdoor crafts vendors, check **Independence Mall** during summer weekends, although flea-market items seem to predominate there. **Head House Square** becomes a bustling bunch of booths April to September, all day Saturday and Sunday afternoon.

AIA Bookstore and Design Center. 117 S. 17th St. ☎ **215/569-3188.**

This recently renovated lower-level gallery specializes in small house furnishings, lighting, and drawings. They've also added custom framing and home furnishings. In the fall it becomes a gorgeous holiday shop and features Inuit sculpture and textiles each spring. Connected to it is an excellent bookstore (see above).

✪ **The Black Cat.** 3424 Sansom St. ☎ **215/386-6664.**

Next door to the White Dog Cafe, Judy Wicks has set up a charming arts-and-crafts store that's open Monday to Wednesday until 9pm, Thursday to Sunday to 11pm. There's a small number of antiques and near antiques.

The Fabric Workshop and Museum. 1315 Cherry St., 5th floor. ☎ **215/568-1111.**

This is the only nonprofit arts organization in the United States devoted to creating new work in fabric and other materials. It operates as an education center as well as a store, in collaboration with both emerging and recognized artists. Don't miss the bags, scarves, ties, and umbrellas of Venturi and Red Grooms design. It's close to the Convention Center.

OLC. 152–154 N. 3rd St. ☎ **215/923-6085.**

OLC, in the Old City, has 6,000 feet of sophisticated lighting and furnishings displayed in a museum-quality setting that's been cited by the American Institute of Architects. It represents 30 European lighting lines and classic furniture by LeCorbusier, Bertoia, Breuer, and hard-to-get contemporaries like B&B Italia.

✪ **Thos. Moser Cabinetmakers.** 1401 Walnut St. ☎ **215/569-8848.**

Recently relocated to Rittenhouse Row is one of the country's great craftsmen of wooden furniture—or his store at least, since Tom Moser lives and works out of Maine. The beds, cabinets, desks, and chairs here are inspired by Shaker and other rural American designs, and the execution and finish are wondrous. Custom furniture inquiries are welcome.

✪ **Snyderman/The Works Gallery.** 303 Cherry St. ☎ **215/922-7775** or 215/ 238-9576.

Snyderman/The Works Gallery, where dramatic light pours through tall windows onto polished wood floors, is one of my Old City favorites. The recently merged gallery now focuses primarily on painting, sculpture, and studio artists working in wood, clay, and glass. Photography is also tucked in between rooms.

DEPARTMENT STORES

Lord & Taylor. Between Market and Chestnut and 13th and Juniper sts. ☎ **215/ 241-9000.**

As Wanamaker's, this was one of the first of the great department stores in the country, and a real city institution. Several owners later, it's a subdivision of May Department Stores, and it looks like Lord & Taylor is making this glorious building a destination again, with their updated classics of American style. The present building (1902–10), which fills a city block, is ingeniously modeled on Renaissance motifs, giving its 12 stories proportion and grace.

On the first floor, there's an Adrien Arpel salon, a chiropodist on call at the shoe salon, and an estate-jewelry counter. On the mezzanine, you'll find a service center with a post office, film developer, travel bureau, dry cleaner, and optometrist. The retail area has shrunk from eight to five floors, with 3 stories of commercial offices on top. A 5-story court presents Christmas shows with a massive 30,000-pipe organ; this court also hosts daily organ concerts at 11:15am and 5:15pm. Café Americanstyle overlooks the scene from a third floor terrace.

Strawbridge's. 8th and Market sts. ☎ **215/629-6000.**

Formerly Strawbridge & Clothier, this once family-run store quietly anchors the Market East neighborhood. Now connected to the Gallery Mall, it covers 3 stories;

Manayunk Shopping

This neighborhood, 8 miles up the Schuylkill from the Art Museum and Center City, has soared in popularity in the last decade, with some of Philadelphia's hippest restaurants and shops (see chapter 6 for the former). A wonderful hour's stroll can put you in touch with contemporary crafts, clothing, antiques, and galleries. Getting there is easy: From the Belmont Avenue exit (north, crossing the Schuylkill River) off I-76 or 1 block south of the Green Lane SEPTA stop, just follow Main Street east alongside the river from the 4400 to the 3900 addresses. A cohesive local development group runs a continuous series of weekend festivals and events to attract business. Parking is plentiful, and store hours tend to run late to match dinner reservations.

ARTS, CRAFTS & GIFTS   I like **Xcessories Inc. by Design,** 4319 Main St. (☎ **215/483-9665**), for its elegant candlesticks, updated Tiffany-style lamps, and contemporary frames; the entrance is on Cotton Street. I'm also partial to **Home Grown,** 4321 Main St. (☎ **215/483-1910**), with kitchenware, tabletop accessories, and home furnishings you'd expect to see in a whimsical, upscale country house. **Owen Patrick Gallery,** 4345 Main St. (☎ **215/482-9395**), has interesting glass and ceramics, as well as bigger furniture and sculptural art, and carries American West/Urbana upholstered pieces from California. **Artistes en Fleurs,** 4363 Main St. (☎ **215/508-9908**), specializes in hand-painted furnishings and uncommon pieces perfect for gardeners. If you're in the market for a modern watch or clock, you should definitely check out **Timeworks,** 4386 Main St. (☎ **215/482-5959**), with a large selection in every price range.

FASHION   In just 4 years, **Nicole Miller,** 4249 Main St. (☎ **215/692-7658**), has become the high priestess of high fashion, with little black dresses, cool sportswear, and whimsical men's neckties, formal wear, and boxers. Three delightful Boston sisters run **Ma Jolie Atelier,** 4340 Main St. (☎ **215/483-8850**), in a handsome 2-story cross between a boutique and a mansion. It's primarily aimed at the fashionable woman, carrying both elegant and casual wear, but they've added an adorable kids' fashion area and an upstairs cappuccino bar too. **Public Image,** 4390 Main St. (☎ **215/482-4008**), has 2 stories of designer labels such as Product, Vivienne Tam, Diesel, and Freelance; and **Touchables,** 4309 Main St. (☎ **215/487-7988**), has a very extensive selection of lingerie and night wear, including Swiss cotton and silk loungewear and peignoirs. **Neo Deco,** 4409 Main St. (☎ **215/487-7757**), sounds dated, but has a very well chosen selection of chic men's and women's fashions at reasonable prices.

FOOD   It's impossible to walk through Manayunk without being seduced, storefront after storefront, by tempting baked goods, sandwiches, coffee bars, sweets, and full-scale restaurants. If you're purchasing for future consumption, go to the **Manayunk Farmer's Market,** 4120 Main St. (☎ **215/483-0100**), a former factory near the eastern edge of the chic part of Manayunk, with a wonderful deck overlooking the river. It's got some true farm stand booths such as **Casey's Farm Fresh Rotisserie** and the wonderfully named **Hel's Kitchen,** but also elegantly packaged processed goods of all sorts. **Manayunk Brewing Company & Harry's Pub** (☎ **215/482-8220**) serves regional American cuisine alongside the brewing vats.

its prices and boutiques are moderately scaled, with frequent sales. It contains an underrated but excellent food hall.

DISCOUNT SHOPPING

Daffy's. 17th and Chestnut sts. ☎ **215/963-9996.**

Daffy's offers excellent value for name and house brands for men, women, and children. Prices are 40% to 75% off regular retail, and men's and women's Italian suits, fine leather items on the third floor, and lingerie are particular bargains.

Filene's Basement. 1610 Chestnut St. ☎ **215/864-9080.**

This Boston discounter has finally moved into Center City. Lines such as Barneys New York can be seen here, though expect more along the lines of Jones New York. You'll find great accessories here.

House of Bargains. 1939–1943 S. Juniper St. ☎ **215/465-8841.**

This South Philly institution for children's clothes stocks a remarkable assembly of brand names anywhere from 40% to 80% off retail prices. It's actually located at the intersection of South Broad Street and Passyunk Avenue, where postshopping treats abound.

Night Dressing. 2100 Walnut St. ☎ **215/563-2828.** Also at 724 S. 4th St. ☎ **215/ 627-5244.**

Locations in Rittenhouse Square and Society Hill carry Lily of France, Olga, Warners, and so forth, almost all at half price. New arrivals come in almost daily. There's a big selection of sleepwear and robes.

Ron Friedman Co. 14 S. 3rd St. ☎ **215/922-4877.**

Umbrellas of all sorts are the main selling point, but you can also save 40% to 60% on American and imported leather handbags, wallets, and briefcases.

FASHION

Look for conservative styles in the stores around Rittenhouse Square and in department stores. For more sharply styled or contemporary fashions, try South Street or the malls. Remember, there is no state sales tax on clothing.

Anthropologie. 1801 Walnut St. ☎ **215/568-2114.**

A 1992 offshoot of Urban Outfitters, this exclusive chain was founded to bring the best of other cultures into our own. Their buyers troll bazaars and artisan shops in Europe, India, and the Far East for inspiration, and they adapt or reproduce apparel, accessories, home decor (think platters and comforters, for example) and gifts exclusively in their 20 U.S. stores. This one's a gorgeous turn-of-the-century mansion on the corner of Rittenhouse Square.

Burberrys Limited. 1705 Walnut St. ☎ **215/557-7400.**

Burberrys has the traditional suits, raincoats, and accessories for both men and women.

J. Crew. Liberty Place, 1625 Chestnut St. ☎ **215/977-7335.**

This store offers a nice merging of casual with formal clothes, all brightly colored and softly styled, plus beautiful cable-knit sweaters. It's a popular rendezvous spot for high-school and college-aged students.

✪ **The Original I. Goldberg.** 902 Chestnut St. ☎ **215/925-9393.**

An army-navy paradise for three generations, I. Goldberg provides, at excellent prices, the basic goods you'll need for anything outdoors, with styles from the determinedly antifashion to the up-to-the-minute. The selection is very large, but the staff is harried.

Polo/Ralph Lauren. The Bellevue, Broad and Walnut sts. ☎ **215/985-2800.**

See The Bellevue, above.

CHILDREN'S FASHION

Born Yesterday. 1901 Walnut St. ☎ **215/568-6556.**

Right on Rittenhouse Square, this store fits babies, boys to size 8, and girls to size 10. The fashions are always current, with a good sense of style and selection of classics. This is a "Best of Philly" store for unique baby gifts. It has an attentive staff.

The Children's Boutique. 1717 Walnut St. ☎ **215/563-3881.**

This place features many all-cotton, color-coordinated outfits by local designers and a good selection of top-of-the-line traditional children's clothes. The store also has a large infant's department and stocks some toys.

Kamikaze Kids. 527 S. 4th St. ☎ **215/574-9800.**

Aggressively styled fashion wear is sold here. The stock ranges from tights to hair ornaments—everything the urban chic child needs. It also stocks incredible Halloween costumes. Not cheap.

MEN'S FASHION

Black Tie. 1120 Walnut St. ☎ **215/925-4404.**

If you find yourself suddenly in need of formal wear, sales and rentals can be found at Black Tie. They carry Lord West, After Six, Bill Blass, and other suave styles, and offer custom tailoring as well as accessories and shirts.

✪ **Boyd's.** 1818 Chestnut St. ☎ **215/564-9000.**

Under the Gushner family, Boyd's has moved "uptown" to a beautifully restored blue-and-white commercial palace. It's the largest in the city, with 65 tailors on site, and has European and American lines of all types, as well as alterations for a variety of fine designers such as Ermenegildo Zegna. Boyd's still has its valet and has added a cafe. Sale periods are January and July.

Brooks Brothers. 1513 Walnut St. ☎ **215/564-4100.**

Brooks Brothers won't steer you wrong on perfectly acceptable items for business and casual wear. Slimmer men should head for the Brooksgate section because the regular styles are cut generously.

Wayne Edwards. 1521 Walnut St. ☎ **215/563-6801.**

This stretch of Walnut Street is *the* block for fashion. Wayne Edwards sports a slightly larger selection of contemporary styles than the other stores, including Brioni, Ralph Lauren Purple Label, and the Prada collection of clothes, sportswear and shoes as of 2001. It also carries some of the finest handmade shoes in the world.

WOMEN'S FASHION

✪ **Boyd's.** 1818 Chestnut St. ☎ **215/564-9000.**

Boyd's, a superb men's fashion mansion (see above), has leapt into the women's wear game with a third-floor boutique. Look for classic suits, dresses, and casual wear by names such as Yves St. Laurent, Genny, Ungaro, Isaac Mizrahi, and Krizia. They provide free custom alterations and an in-store cafe.

Joan Shepp. 1616 Walnut St. ☎ **215/735-2666.**

The presentation is elegant, with an eclectic mix of accessories, antique jewelry, cosmetics, and home furnishings. Among the Yohji Yamamatos, Dries van Notens, and Robert Clergeries, you'll occasionally find spectacular bargains.

✪ **Knit Wit.** 1721 Walnut St. ☎ **215/564-4760.**

Now in a chic new location, Knit Wit specializes in the latest in contemporary fashions and accessories for women from designers such as Miu Miu, Paul Smith, and Bluemarine. Sales come in March and September.

Plage Tahiti. 128 S. 17th St. ☎ **215/569-9139.**

A selective store and a 1995 "Best of Philly" winner, Plage Tahiti has original separates with an artistic slant from Theory, Ghost, and Garfield + Marks. The second floor sale racks have some real steals in Betsey Johnson dresses and the like. As the name suggests, French bathing suits are a constant.

Rodier Paris. 1737 Walnut St. ☎ **215/496-0447.**

This expensive, fashion-forward retailer is now back in Rittenhouse Square, after an untimely fling at The Bourse. The sophisticated clothing offered is designed and manufactured in France.

Toby Lerner. 117 S. 17th St. ☎ **215/568-5760.** Also in Suburban Square, Ardmore. ☎ **610/642-8370.**

With an intimate setting for clothes, accessories, and shoes, this spot is in one of the most affluent neighborhoods in town, and the prices show it. Selections include the best: Armani, Calvin Klein, Versus by Versace, Jimmy Choo Shoes, Celine, TSE Cashmere, and Moschino, with lower-priced lines from Jenne Maag, Votre Nom, and others.

FOOD

✪ **The Reading Terminal Market** at 12th and Market streets, with its dozens of individual booths and cafes, has been recommended in chapter 6. Also, see the "Local Favorites" section at the end of chapter 6.

Assouline and Ting. 314 Brown St. and at Marketplace at the Airport. Caviar Assouline at Liberty Place. ☎ **215/627-3000.**

The prices and astonishing selection of oils, chocolates, fish pastes, and such make a detour to the superb gourmet market 12 blocks north of Market Street worth contemplating. There's a very active schedule of master classes with Philly's best chefs. The other locations are higher priced but much more convenient.

✪ **Chef's Market.** 231 South St. ☎ **215/925-8360.**

The premier gourmet store in Society Hill is Chef's Market, with a staggering array of charcuterie, cookbooks, and condiments. Would you believe this place stocks breads and cakes supplied by 20 bakeries?

Fresh Fields Whole Food Market. 2001 Pennsylvania Ave. ☎ **215/557-0015.**

I know, I know—a supermarket? Fresh Fields, however, has a wonderful selection of the finest natural and organic foods, including a great assortment of prepared dishes and oven-baked goods. Just north of the Ben Franklin Parkway, they are also open 8am–10pm daily, and the café seating has a relaxing view of the Philadelphia skyline at no extra charge.

Italian Market. 9th St. between Christian and Wharton sts.

The Italian Market feels like it's straight out of another era, with pushcarts and open stalls selling fresh goods, produce, and cheese from Tuesday through Saturday (the end of the week is better). Many shops are open until noon on Sunday. Particular favorites are **DiBruno's** at 930 S. 9th St. (☎ **888/322-4337** or 215/922-2876) for cheese, **Sarcone and Sons** at 758 S. 9th St. (☎ **215/922-0445**) for bread, the pound cake at the **Pasticceria** at 9th and Federal streets (no phone), and **Fante's** at 1006 S. 9th St. (☎ **215/922-5557**) for kitchenware. The Italian Market is also a great place to pick up cheap clothes: Try **Evantash** lingerie at 1022 S. 9th St. (☎ **215/413-3433**) or **Irv's** endless racks at 1118 S. 9th St. (☎ **215/468-8204**). You can always snack on fried dough or pastries as you shop. To reach the market, head 5 blocks south of South Street; SEPTA bus 47 goes south on 8th Street from Market.

R&W Delicatessen. 19th and Walnut sts. ☎ **215/563-7247.**

The deli nearest Rittenhouse Square, R&W has plenty of fixings for do-it-yourself lunches, including hearty noodle pudding.

Rago. 258 S. 20th St. ☎ **215/732-0444.**

A gem of a store just north of Spruce Street, Rago is run by the same family that operates Fratelli Rago, a fine Italian trattoria 3 blocks away.

GIFTS & SOUVENIRS

Amy & Friends. 2124 Walnut St. ☎ **215/496-1778** or 215/232-3714.

You have to put up with a fair amount of disorder to enjoy this place, but there's a truly eclectic assortment of antiques and bric-a-brac, including a boutique specializing in top-quality fountain pens.

Country Elegance. 269 S. 20th St. ☎ **215/545-2992.**

Unique gifts and home accessories, along with a great selection of fine and antique linens, are sold here.

Details. 131 S. 18th St. ☎ **215/977-9559.**

Sumptuous gifts, such as invitation cards, desktop accessories, picture frames, and stationery, are sold in this turn-of-the-century town house.

Touches. 225 S. 15th St. ☎ **215/546-1221.**

This upscale boutique stocks clothing and accessories, leather goods, boxes, perfume bottles, handmade jewelry, frames, and baby gifts. Open daily.

Urban Outfitters. 1801 Walnut St. ☎ **215/569-3131.**

Urban Outfitters was actually founded in 1970 right here in town as the People's Free Store and has about 40 stores nationwide selling casual clothing, gift items, and apartment decor to Generation Xers. They have some nice tech toys like digital camera watches, too.

Xenos Candy and Gifts. 231 Chestnut St. ☎ **215/922-1445.**

Miniature Liberty Bells? Snow globes of Independence Hall? Tea towels with the Betsy Ross story? All this and much more, just around the corner from the sites themselves.

JEWELRY & SILVER

Philadelphia is known for all types of jewelry—traditional, one-of-a-kind, heir-loom, and contemporary. Most of the city's jewelers can be found within a couple of city blocks at **Jeweler's Row,** centering on Sansom and 8th streets, which touts itself as offering 30% to 50% off retail (though I can't vouch for this).

Bailey, Banks & Biddle. 16th and Chestnut sts. ☎ **215/564-6200.**

Established in 1832, Bailey, Banks & Biddle has extraordinary silverware and sta-tionery as well as jewelry. It's a huge store (or museum, if you're not looking to spend).

I. Switt. 130 S. 8th St. ☎ **215/922-3830.**

Don't let the crotchety help scare you away; the store does beautiful traditional set-tings at reasonable prices.

Jack Kellmer. 717 Chestnut St. ☎ **215/627-8350.**

With a magnificent marble showroom, Kellmer imports diamonds by the dozen and sells unusual gold and diamond jewelry.

✪ **J. E. Caldwell & Co.** 1339 Chestnut at Juniper St. ☎ **215/864-7800.**

This is another big and traditional store, founded in 1839. It stocks watches and sil-ver as well as jewelry, carrying such lines as Waterford, Orrefors, Kosta Boda, Lalique, and Reed and Barton. It also does repairs, and the building has just been magnificently renovated.

✪ **Jeweler's Row.** Between Sansom and Walnut sts. and 7th and 8th sts. ☎ **215/627-1834.**

This area contains more than 350 retailers, wholesalers, and craftspeople. Particu-larly noted is **Sydney Rosen** at 714 Sansom St. (☎ **215/922-3500**). **Robinson Jewelers,** 730 Chestnut St. (☎ **215/627-3066**), specializes in Masonic jewelry and watch repair.

✪ **Linde Meyer Gold & Silver.** Liberty Place, 1625 Chestnut St. ☎ **215/851-8555.**

This contemporary nook on the ground floor passage to the central atrium presents contemporary designer jewelry from Niessing, Georg Jensen, and Henrich+Denzel in precious metals, along with an adjoining collection of estate jewelry and giftware. I love her taste, as well as the daily schedule.

Niederkorn Silver. 2005 Locust St. ☎ **215/567-2606.**

Antique baby items, dressing-table adornments, napkin rings, picture frames, and Judaica are featured here. Also on display is Philadelphia's largest selection of period silver, including works of such fine crafters as Jensen, Tiffany, and Spratling.

Spiros Doulis. 136 S. 11th St. ☎ **215/922-1199.**

Browsing in this small shop is like looking through your grandmother's jewelry or watch collection—there's a combination of unusual and antique settings and new pieces. They will happily customize pieces and repair watches.

✪ **Tiffany & Co.** The Bellevue, 1414 Walnut St. ☎ **215/735-1919.**

Tiffany & Co. is an American institution with an international reputation for qual-ity, craftsmanship, and design. Today, the store has an extensive collection of ster-ling and jewelry, but also offers china, crystal, timepieces, writing instruments, and fragrance. Though many items are very expensive here, there are plenty of attractive items under $100.

LUGGAGE

Robinson Luggage Company. Broad and Walnut sts. ☎ **215/735-9859.**

At this flagship of six regional locations, you'll find a great selection of leather, along with discounted travel accessories and briefcases.

Travelers Emporium. 210 S. 17th St. ☎ **215/546-2021.**

From airplane roll-ons to backpacks, adventure wear, and accessories, this Rittenhouse Square store offers a combination of outdoor necessities and the luggage you need to get where you're going.

MUSIC

✪ **HMV.** 1510 Walnut St. ☎ **215/875-5100.**

How they got zoning approval for a gleaming, two-story, double-width cube of a building on Rittenhouse Row's best block is a question best left unasked. But it's huge, with a wonderful selection across all genres and price ranges of CDs.

Jacobs Music Co. 1718 Chestnut St. ☎ **215/568-7800.**

Known primarily as a piano store (since 1900), Jacobs is Center City's best source of sheet music for serious and pop musicians alike (in the same building as Theodore Presser).

Third Street Jazz and Rock. 20 N. 3rd St. ☎ **800/486-8745** or 215/627-3366.

With 20 years of experience and 25,000 CDs in stock, Jerry Gordon has one of the finest collections of jazz in the country. Also featured are new wave, Caribbean, and African music.

✪ **Tower Records.** 610 South St. ☎ **215/574-9888.**

The Los Angeles–based Tower Records stocks virtually all current recordings at low prices, and the Tower Records Classical Annex across the street at no. 537 (☎ **215/925-0422**) is even cheaper. Walk-up service at a Ticketmaster booth open daily.

SHOES

Aldo. 1625 Chestnut St. ☎ **215/564-5736.**

This new women's shoe store in Liberty Place has classics and up-to-date fashions and great service. Also just opened at 1707 Walnut St. (☎ **215/690-9675**) around the corner.

Bottino Shoes. 121 S. 18th St. ☎ **215/854-0907.**

Look here for sharper, more avant-garde European (and particularly Italian) men's and women's fashions.

Dan's Shoes. 1733 Chestnut St. ☎ **215/922-6622.**

Fully guaranteed and tremendously discounted designer shoes are found here. It's more like a bazaar than a full-service store, but there are some real finds along with the regular stuff.

Sherman Brothers. 1520 Sansom St. ☎ **215/561-4550.**

Here more than 35 years, and recently expanding into the suburbs, Sherman Brothers has the city's best collection of fine men's shoes like Cole Haan, Allen Edmonds, and Bally, as well as difficult sizes. Everything is discounted 10% to 25% all the time.

SPORTING GOODS

City Sports. 1608 Walnut St. ☎ **215/985-5860.**

This full-service and well-designed store for the urban runner, in-line skater, swimmer, or racquet player has captured the Center City market. You can buy a second pair of athletic shoes for only $25.

✪ **The Original I. Goldberg.** 902 Chestnut St. ☎ **215/925-9393.**

See "Fashion," above.

TOBACCO

Holt's. 1522 Walnut St. ☎ **215/732-8500.**

Holt's is renowned throughout the country for its selection of pipes and tobaccos. There are enough fresh cigars here to fill every humidor on Wall Street, plus an excellent pen selection. The opulent relocation and late hours fit perfectly with the neighborhood.

TOYS

Chestnut Toybox. 1316 Chestnut St. ☎ **215/545-0455.**

This store offers a diverse selection of specialty toys for all ages, including Brio, Gund, Playmobil, Carolle and others. It has an old-fashioned atmosphere of fun and friendly service.

✪ **FAO Schwarz.** Penn's Landing Family Entertainment Center. No Phone at presstime.

Everyone knows FAO Schwarz, an American institution since 1862—and the world's third largest flagship store is coming to the Delaware waterfront in 2002.

WINE & LIQUOR

After the repeal of Prohibition, Pennsylvania decided not to license private liquor retailing but to establish a government monopoly on alcohol sales. You can only buy wine and spirits in state stores (or at a vineyard), which are usually open Monday to Wednesday 9am to 5pm and Thursday to Saturday until 9pm. The selection has improved greatly in recent years, but the system is widely regarded as an anti-consumer nuisance. Beer, champagne, wine coolers, and hard cider are exempt from the system; pick them up at a delicatessen, distributor, or licensed supermarket.

Near Independence Hall, **Old City Liquor,** 32 S. 2nd St. (☎ **215/625-0906**), looks and acts almost like a nonstate store. It's open Monday and Tuesday 11am to 7pm and Wednesday to Saturday 9am to 9pm.

Also in the Independence Hall area, try the **Bourse Building,** 5th and Chestnut streets (☎ **215/560-5504**); 32 S. 2nd Street (☎ **215/625-0906**); or **Society Hill Shopping Center** (☎ **215/922-4224**). In the City Hall area, there are state stores at 1318 Walnut St. (☎ **215/735-8464**) and 265 S. 10th St. (☎ **215/922-6497**). Around Rittenhouse Square, you might try **The Wine Reserve,** at 205 S. 18th St. (☎ **215/560-4529**), an upscale version of a state store where consumers can browse freely amid mahogany counters and shelves. In University City there's a state store at 4049 Walnut St. (☎ **215/222-3547**).

10

Philadelphia After Dark

If you ask Philadelphians to name the biggest change in their city over the last 20 years, the explosion of entertainment and nightlife possibilities will rank right up there with the decline of the manufacturing economy and the restaurant renaissance. From sound-and-light shows at Independence Hall to sound-and-light shows in the Columbus Boulevard dance clubs, there's enough pizzazz and activity in this city to fill months of idle evenings.

The city, always known for its sedate domestic pleasures, seems a little surprised with its newfound vitality. Individual initiatives on the piers along the Delaware River, Old City north of Society Hill, and the northwest quadrant of Center City have joined South Broad Street and Rittenhouse Square as lively areas for bar- or cafe-hopping and live entertainment.

Philadelphia's city government has a big economic stake in aiding these efforts, particularly in the renovation of street areas around Independence National Historical Park and the cultural heart of Center City. A project to make South Broad Street into "Avenue of the Arts" is picking up steam, with the new **Arts Bank** and **Wilma Theater** performance spaces, the revitalized **Merriam Theater,** and an impending new home for the Philadelphia Orchestra. The **Academy of Music** presents a full season of the marvelous Philadelphia Orchestra and the financially struggling but artistically vital Pennsylvania Ballet. Two or three theaters offer road productions and preliminary versions of Broadway shows, and the **Walnut Street Theatre** has been going strong since 1809.

The best sources for what's current are the "Weekend" supplement of the *Philadelphia Inquirer,* which comes out Friday, and the free tabloids *City Paper* and *Philadelphia Weekly* (I prefer the latter, on-line at **www.phillyweekly.com**), which you can find throughout Center City. Most hotel lobbies carry them, as does the Visitors Center, which is also an excellent information source. For monthly happenings, consult the back section of *Philadelphia* magazine.

If you're on-line, **www.libertynet.org** will direct you to other sites for current schedules. The Web site **www.netscape. digitalcity.com/philadelphia** is a concise and accurate location for events and destinations, and **www.phillymusic.com** provides information on musical events.

Most cultural attractions keep their box offices open until curtain time. Also check out **UPSTAGES** (☎ **215/569-9786**), the city's premier nonprofit box-office service. They take phone orders Monday to Saturday 9am to 5pm, and purchase locations are at the Visitors Center, 16th Street and John F. Kennedy Boulevard (☎ **215/567-0670**); the Arts Bank, 601 S. Broad St.; Plays and Players Theater, 1714 Delancey St.; and at the top of the escalators at Liberty Place, 1625 Chestnut St. All are open Tuesday to Saturday 10am to 5pm; the Liberty Place location also offers half-price tickets on the day of the show. There's a small service charge.

For commercial attractions from theater to pop shows, an advance call to Teletron (☎ **800/233-4050**), Tele-Charge (☎ **800/833-0080**), or Ticketmaster (☎ **215/336-2000**) is your best bet. Local ticket brokers such as **Philadelphia Ticket Office,** 1500 Locust St. (☎ **215/735-1903**), or **Ticket Warehouse** (☎ **609/786-7700**), are supposed to be limited to 25% above face value. Out-of-state brokers have no limit, so while they may have better selections, the prices could be exorbitant.

Senior citizens can receive discounts of about 10% or $5 per ticket or more at many theaters, including the Annenberg Center, American Music Theater Festival, and Wilma Theater. Concert halls generally make rush or last-minute seats available to students at prices under $10; these programs sometimes extend to adults as well. Groups can generally get discounts of 20% to 50% by calling well in advance.

1 The Performing Arts

Music, theater, and dance are presented regularly all over the city. I have restricted the venues below to Center City and West Philadelphia, where you'll be most of the time and where the quality of entertainment tends to be highest. There's really no off-season for the performing arts in Philadelphia; when the regular seasons of the Philadelphia Orchestra or Pennsylvania Ballet end at the end of May, the outdoor activities that make Philadelphia so pleasant take over.

OPERA
The **Opera Company Of Philadelphia,** 510 Walnut St., Suite 1600 (☎ **215/928-2110**), presents full stagings of four operas per year at the Academy of Music. The performances take place Monday, Tuesday, Thursday, or Friday evenings, with Sunday matinees; seating preference is given to season subscribers. Such international opera stars as Benita Valente (who lives down the street), Elena Filipova, and Vinson Cole appear in about half of the productions. The company has snagged Luciano Pavarotti to judge and host an annual International Voice Competition, with the winner receiving a role in a production the following season. Tickets cost $20 to $130; half-price amphitheater tickets are available on the day of the performance.

CLASSICAL MUSIC
All-Star Forum. 1530 Locust St. ☎ **215/735-7506.** Tickets $15–$45.

Recital soloists, chamber groups, dance troupes, and occasionally theater groups perform at the Academy of Music weekday nights at 8pm or Sunday at 3pm. The talent is world class. The All-Star Forum also presents the **Philadelphia Pops** in four series per year. Bridging symphonic and popular music under acclaimed pianist Peter Nero, the Pops sells out for most performances.

Concerto Soloists Chamber Orchestra. 338 S. 15th St. ☎ **215/545-5451** office, or 215/893-1145 box office through Upstages. Tickets $15–$35.

This orchestra, made up mostly of homegrown Curtis graduates and talent from New York, performs chamber music at the **Church of the Holy Trinity** (☎ 215/ 567-1267) near Rittenhouse Square at 19th and Walnut streets and at the **Convention Center Recital Hall,** 11th and Arch streets.

✪ **Curtis Institute Of Music.** 1726 Locust St. ☎ **215/893-5252.** www.curtis.edu.

Philadelphia has a surfeit of excellent musicians and programs, many of them springing from the world-famous Curtis Institute, led for many years by Rudolf Serkin and now headed by Gary Graffman. Curtis itself has a small hall just off Rittenhouse Square that's good for chamber works; call ☎ 215/893-5261 for a schedule of the mostly free concerts, operas, and recitals. Student recitals are Monday, Wednesday, and Friday evenings at 8pm. The Curtis Opera Theater presents full-scale productions; tickets are $20 onsite or at UPSTAGES.

Mann Music Center. George's Hill near 52nd St. and Parkside Ave. ☎ **215/878-7707** box office, or 215/567-0707 office. Amphitheater seats $18–$35.

The Mann Music Center, traditionally specializing in summer presentations of the Philadelphia Orchestra in the 6-week PNC Bank Summer Concert Series, has balanced this profile under Peter Lane to present artists such as Tony Bennett, Garrison Keillor, and Bernadette Peters. New are a Symphonic Pops series, Jazz at the Mann, a Family Series, and rock-and-roll concerts.

A Mann concert is one of the delights of summer. Special SEPTA buses travel from Center City and there's plenty of paid parking available in lots around the Mann. Concerts are Monday, Wednesday, and Thursday at 8pm. Tickets for the amphitheater seats may be purchased at the box office there, if available, or by calling ahead.

If you prefer, you can enjoy music under the stars, on the grassy slopes above the orchestra, for free. Seating is unassigned, but tickets are required. Send a request along with a self-addressed, stamped envelope to the Department of Recreation, P.O. Box 1000, Philadelphia, PA 19105. There's a limit of two tickets per request, and requests made too far in advance (more than 2 months or so) will be returned. Don't forget the blankets and insect repellent.

Philadelphia Chamber Music Society (PCMS). 135 S. 18th St. ☎ **215/569-8587.** www.pcmsnet.org. Tickets $18–$20.

Celebrating its 15th season in 2001, the PCMS is committed to bringing renowned international soloists, chamber musicians, and jazz and popular artists to the city. All 52 concerts are at the Pennsylvania Convention Center's 600-seat hall. Ticket prices are exceptionally low for the quality.

✪ **Philadelphia Orchestra.** Regular season Sept–May at the Academy of Music, Broad and Locust sts. From the 2002–3 season at the Kimmel Center, Broad and Spruce sts. ☎ **215/ 893-1999** to charge tickets, or 215/893-1900. Tickets $15–$90; student rush seats $7 at 7:30pm for all Tues and Thurs concerts. Unreserved amphitheater seats $4 at 1:30pm Fri and 7pm Fri and Sat.

For many people, a visit to Philadelphia isn't complete without hearing a concert given by the smooth, powerful Philadelphia Orchestra, under the direction of Wolfgang Sawallisch. The orchestra achieved renown under Leopold Stokowski, then was led for 44 years by the legendary Eugene Ormandy, and for 12 years by Riccardo Muti. Wooing a new conductor, taking place now, is squarely in the public eye. The ensemble has built a reputation for virtuosity and balance that only a handful of the world's orchestras can match.

Concerts are Tuesday, Thursday, Friday, and Saturday evenings and Friday and Sunday afternoons. More tickets to individual performances are available than in the past, with certain dress rehearsals open and fewer subscriptions sold. Try to buy tickets well in advance for the best seats.

In summer the orchestra moves to Mann Music Center for 6 weeks of free concerts (see above). As noted, in 2002 the ensemble is scheduled to relocate to the beautiful and acoustically excellent new Kimmel Center, 2 blocks south of its current home.

Relâche Ensemble. Various venues. Office at 715 S. 3rd St. ☎ **215/574-8246.** Tickets $10–$25.

This contemporary music group, with a particular affinity for young composers, strikes a refreshing balance between the interesting and the intellectual. Made up of a dozen or so instrumentalists, the group performs primarily at the new Arts Bank on South Broad Street and the Mandell Theatre at the Annenberg Center. Concerts are also audio-streamed into a theater at the Franklin Institute.

THEATER

At any given time there will be at least one Broadway show in Philadelphia, on its way into or out of New York. There are also student repertory productions, professional performances by casts connected with the University of Pennsylvania, small-theater offerings in neighborhoods of Center City, and cabaret or dinner theater in the suburbs.

The premier modern theater company in town has to be the ✪ **Wilma Theater,** Broad and Spruce streets (☎ **215/546-7824; www.wilmatheater.org**), which has grown to receive national acclaim. Recent seasons featured new plays by Athol Fugard, Tom Stoppard, Martin McDonagh, and Tina Howe. They've left their old quarters for a new, state-of-the-art 300-seat theater designed by Hugh Hardy in the heart of the "Avenue of the Arts."

Founded in 1984 by visionary Marjorie Samoff, the **American Music Theater Festival** has triumphantly renovated an old 450-seat picture palace as the **Harold Prince Music Theater,** 1412 Chestnut St. (☎ 215/972-1000; www. princemusictheater.org). Music theater is presented in all major forms—opera, musical comedy, cabaret, and experimental theater, along with film. *Time* magazine calls it the foremost presenter of new and adventurous music theater in the country. Tickets run between $10 and $40.

One of the city's most popular professional theaters, the **Arden Theatre Company,** 40 N. 2nd St. (☎ **215/922-1122,** or UPSTAGES at 215/893-1145), has recently relocated among the trendy galleries and restaurants of Old City. The Arden performs in an intimate 175-seat space and has mounted 34 diverse productions over the past 8 years, including 11 world premieres. Tickets run $17 to $27.

Philadelphia Theater Company, 1714 Delancey Place (tickets ☎ **215/ 735-0631** or 215/568-1920) combines fine regional talent with Tony Award–winning actors and directors. They've produced the local premieres of plays such as *True West* and *Glengarry Glen Ross,* and occasional Broadway-bound productions like *Master Class* and *Side Man.* Their Plays and Players Theater is a slightly antiquated but charming hall just off Rittenhouse Square, with some of the worst bathrooms in town. Tickets are $25 to $40.

The **Walnut Street Theatre,** 9th and Walnut streets (☎ **215/574-3550**), has been in business, incredibly, since 1809. The regional Walnut Street Company plays in this 1,052-seat theater, along with numerous local and touring attractions. The resident company presents five plays from September through June; both subscriptions and single tickets are available. Tickets run $25 to $40, with $5 student rush. Wednesday is singles night, with half-price tickets and a mixer. Same-day tickets (if available) are sold for half price between 6 and 6:30pm every day. In 1986, the company began a Studio Theater Season, presenting new and more experimental works in the 75- and 90-seat studio spaces at 825 Walnut St., adjoining the theater. Barrymore's Café is a welcome downstairs addition.

The **Philadelphia Festival Theatre for New Plays** (PFTNP), 1515 Locust St., 7th floor (☎ 215/735-1500), was founded in 1981 to help develop and produce new plays at the highest level; since 1990, they've worked on new translations, adaptations, commissions, and coproductions. They have 2,100 subscribers for a season of four plays in the Annenberg Center; tickets are $10 to $25.

The **InterAct Theatre Company,** 2030 Sansom St. (☎ 215/568-8077), was founded in 1988 as a theater mirroring today's world. All plays are new to Philadelphia audiences and bring a social consciousness of time and place, with three contemporary productions annually between September and May.

DANCE

Local troupes vie successfully with such distinguished visitors as Alwin Nikolais, Pilobolus, and the Dance Theater of Harlem. Contact the **Philadelphia Dance Alliance,** 135 S. 23rd St., Philadelphia, PA 19103 (☎ 215/564-5270), whose members (most of the performing dance companies in the city), appear at WHYY's Forum Theater.

Movement Theatre International (MTI), 3700 Chestnut St. (☎ 215/382-0600), goes well beyond modern dance to present vaudeville, clown theater, mime, circus acts, and classical dance-drama. Productions are held at a tabernacle temple near the University of Pennsylvania campus; tickets are usually $15. MTI produces an annual festival and rents its space out to outside presenters as well.

Founded in 1963, the nationally renowned ✪ **Pennsylvania Ballet,** 1101 S. Broad St. at Washington Avenue (☎ 215/551-7014; box office at Academy of Music, ☎ 215/893-1930; at the Merriam Theater ☎ 215/875-4829; www.paballet.org), almost went under in 1991 but was rejuvenated under young director Christopher d'Amboise, son of dancer/choreographer Jacques d'Amboise, and later by Roy Kaiser. The company, with current stars Jodie Gates and Jeffrey Gribler, performs at the Academy of Music, the Annenberg Center, and the Merriam Theater during the yearly season. Its Christmas-season performances of Tchaikovsky's *Nutcracker,* with the complete Balanchine choreography, are a new city tradition. Each of the company's dozens of performances September to June offers something old, something new, and always something interesting. Tickets cost $15 to $65; *Nutcracker* performances are slightly more, at $20 to $80.

MULTIUSE VENUES

In addition to musical performances held at the following major institutions, look for the many concerts presented in churches, especially around Rittenhouse Square. (The city suffers from a dearth of medium-size concert halls.)

Academy of Music. Broad and Locust sts. ☎ **215/893-1935** for general information, or 215/893-1999 for ticket availability. www.academyofmusic.org.

In the early 19th century an Academy of Music was a proposal much discussed by the cultural movers and shakers in Philadelphia. At the time, opera was the hallmark of culture, and Philadelphia lagged behind New York and Boston in the construction of a hall equipped for it. The cornerstone was laid in 1852. Modeled on La Scala in Milan, it's grand, ornate, and acoustically problematic. The academy underwent a major multimillion-dollar overhaul in 1997–99, with construction of a level extended stage, replacement of an old bowl-shaped floor with a raked one, and better seating and lighting. It remains a symphony of Victorian crimson and gold, with original gaslights still flaming at the Broad Street entrance. The marble planned for the facade has never been added, but the brick and glass seem to suit Philadelphia far better.

The Philadelphia Orchestra has been a resident since its inception, playing some 100 dates annually; however, it'll be moving in 2002 to a brand-new hall 2 blocks south. When that happens, look for many more touring orchestras to touch base here, along with local groups such as the Pennsylvania Ballet, the Opera Company of Philadelphia, and the Philly Pops.

The box office is open Monday to Saturday 10am to 5:30pm (until 8pm on event dates) and Sunday 1pm on event dates. Tickets for an event go on sale 4 weeks ahead of time at the box office; prices vary widely depending on the event. You can also request tickets by mail 1 month ahead: Write to the Academy of Music Box Office, Broad and Locust streets, Philadelphia, PA 19102; include a self-addressed, stamped envelope and charge card information. (But ask to be notified of the total cost before authorizing.) Tours of the academy (reservations required) are given for $3 (☎ **215/893-1935**).

Annenberg Center at the University of Pennsylvania. 3680 Walnut St. ☎ **215/ 898-6791,** or TDD 215/898-4939.

Located on the beautiful University of Pennsylvania campus and easily reached by bus or subway, the Annenberg Center presents a wide variety of performances by American and international companies September to June. Of the two stages, the Harold Prince Theater generally has more intimate, usually more avant-garde productions. The Zellerbach Theater can handle the most demanding lighting and staging needs.

The Annenberg Center Theatre Series includes touring and regional theater and productions by the Philadelphia Festival Theatre for New Plays, which produces a professional season by both established and emerging playwrights. Dance Celebration, copresented with Dance Affiliates, offers a wide selection of companies. Music events include concerts by major contemporary composers and musicians, from Sonny Rollins to Itzhak Perlman. For young people, the Annenberg presents Theatre for Children; Young Adult Theatre; and the Philadelphia International Theatre Festival for Children, a 5-day event that attracts a regional audience. The box office is open noon to 6pm weekdays, with extended hours during performances. Prices of $15–$48 vary depending on the performance. Discounts are available for students and seniors.

Arts Bank. 601 S. Broad St. at South St. ☎ **215/545-0590,** 215/567-0670 box office, or 215/875-4800 telecharge.

One of the cornerstones of the new Avenue of the Arts project, the Arts Bank is a gift of the William Penn Foundation, which realized that there wasn't enough quality, affordable performance space in Center City. The 230-seat theater is owned and operated by the nearby University of the Arts and serves a large, diverse constituency. The stage has a sprung (bouncy) wood floor and state-of-the-art computerized lighting and sound. Relâche, Philadanco, and University of the Arts students are just a few of the performing artists.

HMV, 1510 Walnut St. (☎ **215/875-5100**), and **Tower Records,** 610 South St. (☎ **215/574-9888**), have stacks of coupons for reduced admission to clubs and music venues.

The Forrest. 11th and Walnut sts. ☎ **215/923-1515.**

Of the commercial Philadelphia theaters, The Forrest is the best equipped to handle big musicals like *Phantom of the Opera,* and it hosts several of these during the year, along with other short-running plays and concerts. Performances are usually Tuesday to Saturday at 8pm (occasionally Sun night as well) and Wednesday, Saturday, and Sunday at 2pm.

Merriam Theater. 250 S. Broad St. at Locust St. ☎ **215/732-5446,** or 215/336-1234 telecharge.

The Merriam, belonging to the newly rejuvenated University of the Arts, hosts many of Broadway's top touring shows such as *Annie Get Your Gun* and *The Scarlet Pimpernel* in addition to popular artists like Patti LaBelle, Barry Manilow, comedians, magicians, and the Pennsylvania Ballet. It's an ornate turn-of-the-century hall with 1,668 seats, renovated to some degree for uses never foreseen during the vaudeville era.

Painted Bride Art Center. 230 Vine St. ☎ **215/925-9914.**

It's hard to know what to call the Painted Bride Art Center, near the entrance to the Benjamin Franklin Bridge. It's an art gallery catering to contemporary tastes, but it also hosts folk, electronic and new music, jazz, dance, and theater events. Tickets are $8 to $25. Although its director claims that the room can hold 300, the official seat count for the main hall is 60.

2 The Club & Music Scene

Club kids (or just interested onlookers) will be happy to learn that Philadelphia has plenty of homegrown "house" talent and enjoys frequent visits from New York artists and DJs. Most of the clubs mentioned below are within blocks of the Delaware waterfront, as opposed to mid–Center City's more "establishment" culture. The minimum legal drinking age in Pennsylvania is 21. Bars may stay open until 2am; establishments that operate as private clubs can serve until 3am.

NIGHTLIFE CENTERS
DELAWARE WATERFRONT

With their huge, open spaces and night lights shimmering off the water, the unused piers and warehouses of Delaware Avenue (aka Christopher Columbus Blvd.), both north and south of the Ben Franklin Bridge, exploded as a social scene in the early 1990s. Although many waterfront spots serve passable food (I recommend **Meijien, Moshulu on Pier 34, Rock Lobster,** and **The Chart House**), they shine most for nightlife.

If you're driving, park at Pier 24 at Callowhill Street, between **Rock Lobster** and **KatManDu,** 3 blocks north of the bridge ($5), or at Pier 34 ($3) well to the south. To help reduce drunk driving, club owners have subsidized water taxis (summer only) that run free of charge between waterfront venues every 30 minutes Friday, Saturday, and Sunday nights 9pm to 2am. Other nights, they cost $3 per ride or $5

Sleepless in Philadelphia

Philadelphia has the reputation of rolling up the sidewalks after 10pm. It seems that way only because there are so many sidewalks and so many diverse little pockets of late-night activity. The best places to start looking for entertainment after the sun goes down include:

- The Delaware Avenue pier clubs—watch the traffic, because these clubs get very, very crowded.
- The neighborhoods next to the waterfront, west along either Spring Garden Street to the north (rehabbed industrial warehouse clubs and restaurants, edging into smaller bistros in Old City to the south) or into South Street's funky to tawdry vibrancy.
- For sophisticated clubbing, the 1500 block of Walnut, between 15th and 16th streets, with Circa, Le Bar Lyonnais, and the nearby bars of the Park Hyatt at the Bellevue.
- The fringes of the University of Pennsylvania, west of the Schuylkill.
- South Philly, for those craving cheesesteak or pasta.

for an all-night pass until 11pm. Most clubs charge admission of $10 to $15 during peak hours and accept major credit cards.

The clubs are constantly changing; I've included the current favorites. Start about 3 blocks north of the intersection of Delaware Avenue and Spring Garden Street and work your way south.

Maui Entertainment Complex. Pier 53, 1143 N. Delaware Ave. ☎ **215/423-8116.**

Here you'll find lush tropical foliage like something out of "Gilligan's Island," an outdoor beach grill and volleyball court, the city's biggest dance floor, and King Sunny Ade live music at deafening levels. The crowd, up to 3,000 people, is in its 20s and 30s.

Baja Beach Club. 939 N. Delaware Ave. ☎ **215/928-9979.**

Another testosterone-fueled summer party scene with live music. There's a complimentary 50-foot hot and cold dinner buffet and no cover—so guess what the drinks cost?

Eighth Floor/Ciao. 800 N. Delaware Ave. ☎ **215/922-1000.**

This very upscale spot attracts a style-conscious 30s and 40s crowd. The wrap-around waterfront view, with rooftop summer dining to boot, is terrific. With 15,000 square feet it's usually not overwhelmingly crowded, and it's easier to get a drink than at most of the clubs. Ciao Restaurant (☎ **215/925-2700**) offers serious fresh fish, veal, and steaks. Friday happy hour cover is $5 until 8pm, $12 thereafter. On-site parking is $6 to $10.

✪ **Egypt.** 520 N. Delaware Ave. at Spring Garden St. ☎ **215/922-6500.**

Open year-round on the west side of Delaware Avenue, this is probably the city's foremost nightclub. A bilevel dance floor features concert light and sound systems in a campy "oasis" setting in the main room, with separate DJs and atmospheres in two semidetached areas. They make a special effort Tuesday to woo Asian neighbors from nearby Chinatown.

KatManDu. Pier 25, 417 N. Delaware Ave. ☎ **215/629-7400.**

Club Med in Philadelphia, anyone? KatManDu was the first and remains the most pleasant outdoor island getaway, complete with palm trees, white-sand beaches, world dance music, daiquiris, and an island "mall" with a travel agency. An enclosed 2-story addition allows it to stay open year-round, with a music stage and room for 400. There's a reasonably priced outdoor pit barbecue, plenty of secluded nooks, and dancing to classic rock or artists like Buju Banton. Cover is $8.

Dave & Buster's. Pier 19, 325 N. Delaware Ave. ☎ **215/413-1951.**

Traffic is huge for this urban country club with video arcades, virtual reality head-sets, electronic golf, billiards, and blackjack. Burgers are good at the Bridgeside Grill, and there's a murder mystery dinner theater every Saturday night in winter, at $32.95 per person. The cover is $5 Friday and Saturday after 10pm.

✪ **Rock Lobster.** 221 N. Delaware Ave. ☎ **215/627-7625.**

At the corner of Race Street, just north of Ben Franklin Bridge and on the Marina, is this blend of top nightclub/disco and good restaurant. From May to mid-September, it serves hundreds of moderately priced lunches and dinners daily in a 4,000-square-foot tent or alfresco area designed to look like a Maine yacht club. The restaurant opens for lunch at 11:30am and stays open until 2am. The crowd is in its 30s, 40s, and 50s. There's no cover until 9pm, then it's usually $5 Wednesday and Thursday, $10 Friday and Saturday. The cover is higher when national acts appear. Valet parking $8.

Moshulu, The Port Saloon, and Club 34. 735 S. Columbus Blvd. (Exit 16 off I-95). ☎ **215/923-2500.**

Apart from the rest of the waterfront night spots, at Fitzwater Street, just south of the historic ships at Penn's Landing and The Chart House, the world's largest and only four-masted restaurant sailing ship has been restored in art nouveau design. Complementing the ship are the Port Saloon, with a painstaking 1904-era look, and Club 34, a casual eatery with a fireplace lounge, pool tables, and dance area. The views are spectacular as it's the longest of all the Delaware piers and somewhat set apart. Danny Fleischmann, from the Ritz-Carlton, supervises lunch and dinner daily, with entrees in the $14 to $23 range.

OLD CITY AREA

Spurred by the Delaware riverfront boom, a number of new clubs and bars have opened in the shadow of the Ben Franklin Bridge.

The Bank. 600 Spring Garden St. ☎ **215/351-9404.**

The Bank, now 12 years old, was created by the same people who started Chestnut Cabaret. It offers one of the city's largest dance floors, situated in a shabby yet chic renovated 1872 Frank Furness–designed bank. The young but sophisticated crowd is kind of J. Crew meets Seattle. The Thursday open bar and buffet, 9pm to 2am, is a steal at $10. Cover is $10 Thursday, $7 Friday, and $5 Saturday.

Black Banana. 3rd and Race sts. ☎ **215/925-4433.**

Even though this is technically a private club, nonmembers can join for the night. You can dance to cool postmodern music until 3am. Videos are shown on the first floor, and the dance floor is on the second. American Express cards are accepted. The cover charge is a steep $55.

Silk City Lounge. 5th and Spring Garden sts. ☎ **215/592-8838.**

With lava lamps and a young, ultrahip crowd, this is what would have been called a dive before the postmodern era. Occasional nights are devoted to music of the Sinatra era, although the owner likes to change themes every six months or so. Live bands play about once a week. The attached American Diner is open all night Friday to Sunday.

Shampoo. 417 N. 8th St. ☎ **215/922-7500.**

This new spot, the former Milkbar, rides a trend of progressive music and trendy retro chic over two floors of entertainment with eight bars and three dance floors. Open Thursday, Friday, and Saturday from 9pm, it's popular with a mixed gay and straight crowd. Cover charges vary.

Sugar Mom's Church Street Lounge. 225 Church St. ☎ **215/925-8219.**

This basement lounge, next door to Christ Church, draws a diverse and hip crowd in its 20s and early 30s, with plenty of friendly chatter and a wide-ranging music selection.

SOUTH STREET AREA

Love Lounge. 232 South St., above Knave of Hearts. ☎ **215/922-3956.**

Knave of Hearts has been a long-time South Street standby for its continental menu and art deco bar. The Love Lounge attracts an artsy, sophisticated crowd in its 40s, with rosy lighting, plush couches, and informal ambience.

Monte Carlo Living Room. 2nd and South sts. ☎ **215/925-2220.**

The way to do the Monte Carlo is to dine romantically and well, then dance the night away at the piano bar and old-style disco upstairs, complete with sentimental artwork and a tinkling fountain illuminated in alternating reds and blues, all reflected in lots of mirrors. The Living Room is open Monday to Saturday 6pm to 2am. Dancing to continental crooners starts at 9:30pm, with a deejay playing Top 40 between sets. A brass plaque on the door states that proper attire is required (coats and ties for men, dresses for women). Cover is $10 Friday and Saturday, unless you've dined downstairs or are a member.

Xero. 613 S. 4th St., one-half block south of South St. ☎ **215/629-0565.**

This has been one of the most solid and successful bar/restaurant/clubs in town since the early 1990s. Thursday brings a complete food, drink, and dance package for $5, and alternative deejays set the mood on weekends. Happy hour is 7 to 9pm Friday and Saturday.

CENTER CITY AREA

✪ **Circa.** 1518 Walnut St. ☎ **215/545-6800.**

This club is absolutely the greatest: It tastes like the Mediterranean, looks like Paris, and feels like Manhattan. Thursday to Saturday, after the excellent dinner (see chapter 6), the main room is cleared to accommodate stylish throngs on a wooden dance floor until 2am. Music is deejay-spun house, pop, and 1970s disco. Cover is $5 Friday and Saturday after 9pm, $8 after 10pm. There's free admission for two if you use valet parking.

CITY LINE/MANAYUNK

Quincy's. City Line Ave. at Monument Rd., at the Adam's Mark. ☎ **215/581-5000.**

The top choice in this flashy suburban-mall area is Quincy's. Smooth sounds emanate from good bands, there's lots of wood paneling and old brass, and backgammon tables galore. Quincy's also provides one of the best happy hours anywhere, with incredible buffet tables. There's a singles dance Sunday 5 to 10pm, with no cover charge. Otherwise, cover ranges free to $10.

River Cafe. 4100 Main St., Manayunk. ☎ **215/483-4100.**

This complex, housed in a former mill with a deck overlooking the Schuylkill, mixes a great dance floor with a fine restaurant. The music tends toward current commercial hits.

ROCK CLUBS

Two firms now control the presentation of large rock concerts in town, and advance tickets are almost obligatory. The long-established local firm is **Electric Factory Concerts** (☎ **215/569-9416** or 215/568-3222; **www.electricfactory.com**), which usually books major talent into the **First Union Spectrum** (box office ☎ **215/ 336-3600**), the city's major indoor arena, in South Philly. Other venues include **The Electric Factory,** 421 N. 7th St., a plain industrial rehab with questionable acoustics, the **Tower Theater,** at 69th and Market streets in West Philadelphia, and, in the summer, the **Mann Music Center** in Fairmount Park. The **Theater of Living Arts** at 334 South St. (☎ **215/922-1011**), newly bereft of all seating, is used for smaller shows like Mary Chapin Carpenter.

Recently, Houston-based **Pace Concerts** has begun muscling in national acts such as Diana Ross, Barry Manilow, and George Benson through their exclusive contract with the spanking new, 25,000–seat, outdoor amphitheater or 1,600–seat concert hall **Blockbuster–Sony Music Entertainment Centre at the Waterfront** in Camden. Locally, try the box office at ☎ **856/365-1300,** or in advance through **Tele-Charge** (☎ **800/833-0800**).

Chestnut Cabaret. 38th and Chestnut sts. ☎ **215/382-1201.**

The Chestnut Cabaret, in the heart of University City, is committed to bringing the best in local, regional, and even national acts in rock, pop, jazz, reggae, blues, and R&B on Tuesday to Saturday nights. It does not serve food. Cover varies, but there's no minimum.

J. C. Dobbs. 304 South St. ☎ **215/925-4053.**

Dobbs features rock bands, both crude and smooth, every night until 2am. The upstairs serves food until 1am. It's a hard-drinking, hard-smoking place, with lots of energy when the band is good. Cover is $5 or less.

The Khyber. 56 S. 2nd St. ☎ **215/238-5888.**

This is one of the most popular spots to hear jazz, funk, and rock nightly. There's live entertainment 9:30pm until 1 or 2am, depending on the crowd and the day. Khyber Pass is named after the route the British took to get through Pakistan, and this is somebody's version of what a British overseas officers' club would look like. It does have a certain atticlike charm, nevertheless. English ales and Irish stout are served. Cover is usually $5.

North Star Bar. 27th and Poplar sts. ☎ **215/235-7827.**

North Star, located near the Philadelphia Museum of Art, has photo exhibits and poetry readings. Rock groups perform 5 nights a week in a recently glassed-in courtyard. You'll see an older bar as you enter. It's a very comfortable place to drink, and the spicy chicken wings are tasty. Cover ranges $3 to $10.

✪ JAZZ & BLUES

Philadelphia is one of the great American hothouses for jazz, from John Coltrane to the current sax phenomenon Grover Washington Jr., who still lives in the city, and new bassist Christian McBride. May brings Jam on the River, and the Mellon PSFS Jazz Festival is held in June (see "Philadelphia Calendar of Events," chapter 2). The new Philadelphia Clef Club on the "Avenue of the Arts" has given jazz a legitimate performance home. Increasingly, major cultural venues like the Philadelphia Museum of Art are also getting into the act, and The Electric Factory presents stars like Gato Barbieri at the Ballroom of the Park Hyatt at the Bellevue. For specific information, write or call Mill Creek Jazz and Cultural Society, 4624 Lancaster Ave., Philadelphia, PA 19131 (☎ **215/473-2880**).

The Khyber. 56 S. 2nd St. ☎ **215/238-5888.**

See "Rock Clubs," above.

Liberties. 705 N. 2nd St., above Fairmount Ave. ☎ **215/238-0660.**

A carved walnut bar and high-backed booths highlight this pub with a changing schedule of jazz trios. It's a favorite haunt of local artists and musicians. Live music is featured nightly 8:30pm to 12:30am.

Ortlieb's Jazzhaus. 847 N. 3rd St. at Poplar St. ☎ **215/922-1035.**

The expansion of Delaware riverfront life has caught up with this longtime hangout of quartets headed by Shirley Scott and Mickey Roker. There's a terrific seven-piece house band that performs nightly at 9:30pm, and there's no cover charge to enjoy the smoky, down-home ambience.

Philadelphia Clef Club of Jazz & Performing Arts. 736–738 S. Broad St. ☎ **215/893-9912.**

The first of its kind in the country, the nonprofit Clef Club is dedicated solely to the preservation and promotion of jazz. In its handsome building on the "Avenue of the Arts" it presents jazz workshops and instrumental training as well as concerts in a 250-seat performance hall.

✪ Warmdaddy's. Front & Market sts. ☎ **215/627-2500.**

Run by the Bynum brothers, who made a success of Zanzibar Blue, this wine-colored, sophisticated entrant to the historic district features authentic live blues from Koko Taylor, Murali Coryell, and the like, and excellent traditional Southern cuisine, with entrees ranging $11 to $17. The stage and sound system are first rate, and the ambience is simultaneously sexy and familial. A cover of $8 after 8pm is waived with dinner. Closed Monday.

Zanzibar Blue. 200 S. Broad St. ☎ **215/732-5200.**

This place, down the escalator at the Bellevue, features the best of the city's—and increasingly the nation's—jazz bands. The ambience is elegant, so you may want to dress up for a visit. Zanzibar is open until 2am nightly; there's also a jazz brunch ($20) on Sunday. Cover is $8 to $10.

FOLK & COUNTRY

Boot N Saddle. 1131 S. Broad St. ☎ **215/336-1742.**

In the heart of South Philly, this cash-only place features live country music every Friday and Saturday night, with seating at tiny tables in the back. There's a large island bar in the front. It's open Monday to Saturday until 2am.

Bronko Bill's. Grant Ave. and Bluegrass Rd. (near Rte. 1 across from the Northeast Airport). ☎ **215/677-8700.**

This unlikely and immense spot highlights its reincarnation as a home for country-and-western line dancing with foam mountains outside. Inside is a 4,000-square-foot dance floor, crowded with Texas-style boots and genteel five-steps. Once you work up a sweat, repair to the Ranch Lounge or the American Indian area.

Tin Angel Acoustic Cafe. 20 S. 2nd St. ☎ **215/928-0770.**

This very conveniently located 105-seat club above Serrano restaurant/bar (see below) is riding the unplugged wave with artists like John Wesley Harding, Livingston Taylor, and Maria Muldaur. Open Wednesday to Saturday. There's no cover for Wednesday's open-mike evenings; other nights run $8 to $15.

DANCING

Brasil's. 112 Chestnut St. ☎ **215/413-1700.**

Following a warm feast of feijoada or steak, people rave about the spirited salsa dancing upstairs on weekends—the music and crowd are both great.

The Social Club. 2009 Sansom St., 2nd floor. ☎ **215/564-2277.**

While there's no live entertainment, the sound system is programmed with mambos, fox-trots, and swing. Most attendees are members, but nonmembers are welcome. Admission is $10.

That's Amore: Italian Crooning in South Philly

There's a tremendous history of Italian crooning in South Philadelphia. Operatic training was applied to American popular singing. The style of Frank Sinatra in the 1940s and 1950s led to other jazz-influenced singers like Vic Damone, and in turn to the smooth harmonics of singers like Frankie Avalon and groups like the Persuasions. Here are three places where you can get a good handle on this history in rambunctious action:

On Friday and Saturday, Dave Morris and his band bring the otherwise sedate **D'Medici Restaurant,** 824 S. 8th St. (☎ 215/922-3986), in South Philadelphia, to life with renditions of Sinatra, Mel Tormé, Tony Bennett, and other neighborhood favorites. There's no cover charge.

Deep in the heart of South Philly, **The Saloon,** 7th and Catharine streets (☎ 215/627-1811), features a fine Italian restaurant decorated with Victorian antiques. If you want to hear mellow music, head upstairs by the glossy mahogany bar. The Saloon bar is open Wednesday to Saturday until 12:30am. The drinks average $2.50 and admission is free.

If you're in search of the kind of place where Rocky Balboa would go to sing along with the band, look no further than the **Triangle Tavern,** 10th and Reed streets (☎ 215/467-8683). The staff really participates, and the place couldn't be cheaper.

Wichita Steak & Brews. 22 S. 3rd St. ☎ **215/627-4825.**

This beautiful 1837 church is now a temple of techno, house, and alternative music, with a large dance floor, Monday to Saturday nights. The first floor has a fine restaurant (see chapter 6). Cover ranges $1 to $10, for ages 21 and over. Major credit cards are accepted.

A COMEDY CLUB
The Laff House. 211 South St. ☎ **215/440-4242.**

This Abbott Square lounge has writers and performers from Comedy Central, among other breeding grounds. Shows are Wednesday to Sunday evenings, and admission is $10–$25.

3 The Bar Scene
BREWERIES & PUBS
Bridgid's. 726 N. 24th St. ☎ **215/232-3232.**

This tiny, very friendly horseshoe-shaped bar near the Philadelphia Museum of Art stocks a superb collection of Belgian beers, including an array of fruit- to hops-originated brews. A tapas menu is also available at the bar.

Continental Restaurant and Martini Bar. 138 Market St. ☎ **215/923-6069.**

This Old City vintage diner, aluminum siding and all, turned bar is one of the coolest spots of the moment. Snacks include filet mignon brochettes and miniature spring rolls.

Dock Street Brasserie. 2 Logan Sq., 18th and Cherry sts. ☎ **215/496-0413.**

This comfortable, moderate place brews and sells only its own beers. Up to six varieties of beer at $2.50 per glass (or a sampler of all six for $4), painstakingly brewed within the last month, are offered at two bars. You can even inspect the spotless fermenting vats to the right of the bar. There's live jazz and Latin music Friday and Saturday.

Irish Pub. 1123 Walnut St. ☎ **215/925-3311.** Also at 2007 Walnut St. ☎ **215/568-5603.**

With one located across from the Forrest Theatre and the other off Rittenhouse Square, both Irish Pubs pack in hundreds of good-natured professionals, both men and women of all ages. There is Irish and American folk music in the front, but you can escape it if you wish. Both pubs are open until 2am nightly.

Nodding Head Brewery and Restaurant. 1516 Sansom St. ☎ **215/569-9525.**

The brew house was opened in the late 1980s as an offshoot of the Sansom Street Oyster House downstairs, but now has its own identity. Three beers are regularly brewed right here: a light ale, an amber ale, and a dark porter. The restaurant menu features burgers, tuna steak, and chicken sandwiches as well as vegetarian choices.

Serrano. 20 S. 2nd St. ☎ **215/928-0770.**

Serrano, along with the Tin Angel Acoustic Cafe (see above), offers a wonderful collection of brews in an intimate setting, along with eclectic world cuisine. It's also on one of the Historic District's nicest blocks. The old wooden bar has antique stained glass behind it, and a spiced wood fire burns in the fireplace. If you can't get out to Stoudt's own brew pub in Adamstown (see chapter 12), try their unpasteurized beer here ($5.95 per bottle).

Saint Jack's. 45 S. 3rd St. ☎ **215/238-9353.**

Fascinating, friendly and funky: Think two floors of exotic comfort in the heart of the historic district, with deep reds and beads decor and a long bar. Owner Louis DeMaise boasts a mixed clientele of college students, club-hoppers, artists, and professionals. The restaurant/bar menu is Asian-American and reasonable (I like the vegetarian dumplings); no cover charge, and weekday $2 drink specials.

XandO. 325 Chestnut St. ☎ **215/928-0770.** Sansom Commons, 3601 Walnut St. ☎ **215/222-4545.**

XandO—as in "hugs and kisses"—operates bustling cafes serving coffee throughout the day and drinks starting at 4:30pm, with two more locations in the works. The lively 325 Chestnut site, possibly the largest cafe in the city, takes care of the throngs emerging from the two Ritz theaters nearby with comfortable armchairs and seats. The 235 S. 15th St. (☎ **215/893-9696**) venue has the same ambience; service tends to be slow at both locations. As of this writing, they are also expanding into the former IHOP at 1740 Walnut near Rittenhouse Square.

PIANO BARS & LOUNGES
Bridget Foy's South Street Grill. 200 South St. ☎ **215/922-1813.**

Newly renovated and with a fine open-style grill at reasonable prices, Bridget Foy's offers a nice, mellow atmosphere. There's no pressure to socialize if you don't feel like it, but plenty of company to keep you entertained if you do. Situated at the lower corner of Head House Square, the establishment features a lively sidewalk cafe in summer. It's open every evening until 1am.

Cutters. 2005 Market St. ☎ **215/851-6262.**

This is the quintessential 1990s bar: long, high, massively stocked, with businesslike high-tech systems, and a friendly and elegant atmosphere. The location, in the IBM building at Commerce Square, makes it a fine postbusiness meeting place. (See also chapter 6.)

Downey's. Front and South sts. ☎ **215/625-9500.**

Downey's is a terrific Irish pub with a contemporary flair. Many of the local professional athletes head here to relax after a game. There's piano upstairs, sometimes with accompaniment, Friday and Saturday 8pm to 1am. At Sunday brunch (11:30am–3pm) a strolling string quartet punctuates the atmosphere. A beautiful wraparound second-floor deck offers waterfront views for dining or cocktails.

Le Bar Lyonnais. 1523 Walnut St. ☎ **215/567-1000.**

Downstairs from the famed Le Bec-Fin Restaurant (see chapter 6) is this crowded, intimate, smoky bar, a favorite hangout of those with high bank balances, hormones, or hopes.

Le Colonial. 1623 Walnut St. ☎ **215/851-1623.**

The restaurant downstairs is a sultry evocation of colonial Vietnam in the 1950s. Upstairs at the Salon, the amber glow, soft sofas, potted palms, and light fare will make you think of Jane Russell asking Robert Mitchum for a light.

The Lounge at the Omni. 4th and Chestnut sts. ☎ **215/925-0000.**

This lounge is a very posh spot, with dark woods and Oriental carpets, a crackling fireplace, a piano trio, and large picture windows surveying Independence National

Historical Park across the street. Good if you're looking for a quiet, sophisticated backdrop to conversation. It stays open past midnight on weekends.

Society Hill Hotel. 3rd and Chestnut sts. ☎ **215/925-1919.**

The Society Hill Hotel, a renovated 1832 shell, has a dozen rooms upstairs—but the bar has all of Society Hill excited. It's one of the few modern bars in town that's sophisticated but not glitzy, and the outdoor cafe makes it even more charming on a summer eve. (Why don't more places follow their lead and screw hooks into the undersides of tables and counters so that women can hang their purses safely but conveniently?)

TGI Friday's. 18th St. and the Parkway. ☎ **215/665-8443.**

It's hard to believe that a place with such a deliberately corporate atmosphere could make it, but TGI Friday's has become a favorite of the younger crowd that populates Logan Circle's new office towers. There's standing room only at the outdoor terrace on summer evenings for the happy-hour buffet and socializing.

A WINE BAR

Panorama. 14 N. Front St. at Market St. ☎ **215/922-7800.**

Panorama is at the rear of Penn's View Hotel but separate from the moderately priced Italian restaurant. Its curving wine bar features 120 different selections by the glass, most around $5. There's piano entertainment. Panorama is open Sunday to Thursday until midnight, Friday and Saturday to 1am.

4 The Gay & Lesbian Scene

The area between Walnut and Locust streets south of the Convention Center—roughly from 9th Street to 13th Street—is the heart of gay and lesbian Philadelphia, and it's filled with social services, bookstores and clubs, bars and restaurants. You can leaf through a copy of *Philadelphia Gay News* for suggestions of places that cater to a variety of niches and sub-niches. What follows is a brief selection of the most mainstream spots.

Judy's Café. 627 S. 3rd St. at Bainbridge. ☎ **215/928-1968.**

I've mentioned Judy's as a simple, very affordable Queen Village neighborhood restaurant with great meatloaf and fish. If you're looking for a friendly place just to hang out, it's also a haven for gay and lesbian singles and couples in the front bar area.

Rodz. 1418 Rodman St. ☎ **215/546-1900.**

Rodz has a cute piano bar along with excellent, affordable eclectic American cuisine for a primarily male clientele.

Sisters. 1320 Chancellor St. ☎ **215/735-0735.**

This preeminent lesbian center, sporting three bars over 3 floors with over 5000 square feet, is close to City Hall and the Convention Center. It features Saturday "Liquid Sex" events, Sunday vinyl dance parties, and Thursday karaoke.

12th Air Command. 254 S. 12th St. ☎ **215/545-8088.**

The former Hepburn's now caters to a primarily male clientele nightly until 2am, and the crowds tend to spill outside on nice nights, which can be intimidating. Downstairs there's a lounge bar and game room; Italian cuisine is served Wednesday to Saturday and there's a Sunday brunch. There's another bar and a crowded disco upstairs. No credit cards are accepted. There's a $5 cover for dancing only Friday and Saturday.

The 2-4 Club. 1221 St. James St. ☎ **215/735-5772.**

The Weiss family who transformed the Eighth Street Lounge in Old City and Grape Street Pub in Manayunk, cleaned up this cavernous after-hours bar and dance club in 1999. Fabrics abound, from the neon zebra fake fur to baroque red velvet and chandeliers. It's got three floors, and the third is filled with couches and multimedia screens; altogether the space holds nearly 1,000 people and hosts topname DJs and drag hostesses.

Woody's. 202 S. 13th St. ☎ **215/545-1893.**

Woody's' party atmosphere also attracts a straight clientele. The original bar is downstairs, and a sandwich counter with cyberbar (and free internet access) has been added alongside. The disco adjoining the upstairs lounge features trompe l'oeil atlases holding up a roof of stars. Line dancing, with free two-step lessons, Thursday nights. Cover Friday and Saturday ranges $5 to $10.

5 More Entertainment

BOWLING

Philadelphia is not much of a bowling town; no lanes are found not in Center City, but there are lanes out along the northern routes leading out of it, or across the Delaware in New Jersey. Many lanes have adapted to a younger social crowd by offering special "cosmic" or "extreme" bowling nights on the weekend—same lanes, but loud music, black-lighted rooms.

Boulevard Lanes. 8011 Roosevelt Avenue. ☎ **215/332-9200.**

"Cosmic" evenings are Friday and Saturday.

Thunderbird Lanes. 5830 Castor Avenue. ☎ **215/743-2521.**

Thunderbird gets high marks from devotees and daters alike; Saturday evenings are "cosmic bowling," and the wait for a lane can be up to an hour unless you're there early.

READINGS

Borders Book Shop and Espresso Bar, 1727 Walnut St. (☎ **215/568-7400**), runs one of the country's top series of author readings in an elegant setting steps away from Rittenhouse Square. Readings are usually at 7:30pm weekdays and 2pm weekends.

Going head to head with Borders is the new **Barnes & Noble,** 1805 Walnut St. (☎ **215/665-0716**), with 7pm readings. **City Book Shop,** 1129 Pine St. (☎ **215/592-1992**), features poetry readings in a comfortable setting every Friday night.

SALONS

Several spots around town have started catering to the large pool of intellectually curious singles in Philadelphia. Judy Wicks at the **White Dog Cafe,** 3420 Sansom St. (☎ **215/386-9224**), has instituted salon meals, calling on local academics, artists, and her own contacts to address issues such as domestic and foreign policy, the arts, and social movements. Dinner talks include a three-course meal for $30 per person, and reservations are recommended.

SPECTACLES

The **Benjamin Franklin Bridge** has been outfitted with special lighting effects by the noted architectural firm Venturi, Rauch, and Scott Brown. The lights are triggered into mesmerizing patterns by the auto and train traffic along the span. As of 2000, permanent lighting was installed to play on most of the major monuments and bridges leading in and out of Center City and on City Hall as well.

May to October, dusk until 11:15pm, Independence Historic National Park becomes the backdrop for the mesmerizing **Lights of Liberty** show. Wearing special headsets you hear 3-D stereophonic sound and see 50-foot projections and surprising special effects that witness the struggle toward America's independence. See "Top Attractions" in chapter 6 for details.

CINEMA

The biggest movie news in Philadelphia is that Robert Redford is teaming up with the University of Pennsylvania to bring a Sundance Film Center with independent theaters, a coffeehouse, and dining spots to the edge of the U. Penn campus, at 40th and Walnut streets. Redford was impressed with Penn's efforts to integrate the community into the campus, and this looks to be a smash hit economically and culturally. Sundance will be opening in late 2001.

In the historic district, **Ritz 5 Movies,** 214 Walnut St. (☎ **215/925-7900/1**), is the best choice for independent releases. It has five comfortable screening rooms and shows sophisticated, often foreign, fare. The first daily matinee performance is $4.

The five-screen **Ritz at the Bourse,** 4th and Ranstead streets (☎ **215/925-7900**), behind The Bourse and the new Omni Hotel, has the advantage of a superb espresso/cappuccino bar replete with long leather sofas.

In Center City, standard studio releases only are offered at the four-screen **United Artists Sameric,** 1908 Chestnut St. (☎ **215/567-0604**).

In University City, **International House,** 3701 Chestnut St. (☎ **215/387-5125**), presents a fine series of foreign films, political documentaries, and work from independent filmmakers. Admission is $3.50. **Cinemagic 3 at Penn,** 3925 Walnut St. (☎ **215/222-5555**), screens intelligent releases from the U.S. and abroad. The popcorn is outstanding.

6 Late-Night Bites

Twenty years ago, this section wouldn't have been envisioned; the fact is, Philadelphia does stay up late, but until recently it was private about it. As the city becomes more oriented to tourism and service professions, hours are adapting to fit the clientele.

Bleu. 227 S. 18th St. ☎ **215/545-0342.** Dinner served to 1am Mon–Sat and midnight Sun.

Bleu, the Rittenhouse Square creation of notable Neil Stein, has simple, contemporary food with a modern twist, and the location is perfect for a summer evening.

Dock Street Brewpub at the Terminal. 1150 Filbert St. ☎ **215/922-4292.** Open to 2am daily.

If you don't want to venture far from the Convention Center in taste or size, you can't do better than this huge, attractive space with a great selection of freshly brewed beers.

Downey's. 526 S. Front St. (corner of South St.). ☎ **215/629-0526.** Open until 2am nightly.

Earthy, comfortable Irish and American fare in a very central late-night location.

Melrose Diner. 1501 Snyder St. (intersection of 15th St., Passyunk Ave., and Snyder St., 1 block west of S. Broad St.). ☎ **215/467-6644.** Reservations not accepted. No credit cards. Always open.

The Melrose's logo of a coffee cup with a clock face and knife-and-fork hands, like the place in general, is somewhere between kitsch and postmodern. The Melrose dishes out scrapple (a local fried combination of pork, herbs, and cornmeal) and eggs, creamed chipped beef, and the like 10 blocks north of the sporting stadiums in South Philly. If you hanker for the type of place where you'll be called "Hon," this is for you. They bake pies three times a day to ensure freshness and turn out wonderful butter cookies and a great buttercream layer cake.

Silk City Diner. 435 Spring Garden St. ☎ **215/592-8838.** Open to midnight Sun–Thurs, 24 hours Fri–Sat.

Silk City is what happens when a 1950s diner is given a real postmodern twist; in particular, the pastel pinks and grays in the decor mix with an eclectic song selection and the hip couture. Menu runs from the gourmet aspirant to chocolate bread pudding and huevos rancheros.

Tangerine. 232 Market St. ☎ **215/627-5116.** Open until 1am.

This is the closest you'll come to playing out a sophisticated fantasy of entering the Casbah for swank, exotic Moroccan fusion cuisine. The over-the-top, low-wattage decor varies from room to room; somewhat pricey but service is excellent.

Side Trips from Philadelphia

The same boats that brought Penn's Quakers also brought the pioneers that fanned out into the Delaware Valley to the south, Bucks County to the north, and what is now Pennsylvania Dutch Country to the west. This chapter covers Bucks and Brandywine counties; the next chapter guides you through the Amish heartland of Lancaster County.

Much of this area remains lush and unspoiled, although development-versus-environment struggles are becoming pointed. The major attractions of the Bucks and Brandywine countryside are historical: colonial mansions and inns, early American factories and businesses, and Revolutionary and Civil War battlegrounds.

1 Bucks County & Nearby New Jersey

Bucks County, at most an hour by car from Philadelphia, is bordered by the Delaware River to the east and Montgomery County to the west. Historic estates and sites, along with the antiques stores and country inns they've spawned, abound. Many artists and authors, including Oscar Hammerstein II, Pearl Buck, and James Michener, have gained inspiration from the natural beauty here, which has survived major development so far. A new interest is ecotourism—the area is great for gentle outdoor activities. Nearby New Jersey offers scenic routes for bicycling and walking as well as fine restaurants.

ESSENTIALS

GETTING THERE   The best automobile route into Bucks County from Center City is I-95 (north). Pa. 32 (which intersects I-95 in Yardley) runs along the Delaware past Washington Crossing State Park to New Hope, which connects to Doylestown by U.S. 202. By train, the R5 SEPTA commuter rail ends at Doylestown, with connections to New Hope and Lahaska.

From New York, take the New Jersey Turnpike to I-78 west; follow to Exit 29 and pick up Route 287 south to Route 202, which crosses the Delaware River at Lambertville, straight into New Hope.

VISITOR INFORMATION   To find out more about the hundreds of historic sites, camping facilities, and accommodations here, contact the **Bucks County Tourist Commission,** 152 Swamp Rd., Doylestown, PA 18901 (☎ **800/836-2825** or 215/345-4552). You

Where Washington Crossed the Delaware

A trip along the Delaware via Route 32 through Morrisville and Yardley will bring you to **Washington Crossing State Park,** 500 acres that are open year-round. Most people know that Washington crossed a big river in a small boat on Christmas Eve of 1776, and many people are familiar with the heroic painting depicting this event, with Washington standing in the boat, his eyes on the farther shore (the painting is by Emanuel Leutze, a German, who trained as an artist in Philadelphia). This was the spot, although the Durham boats Washington and his troops used, which are on display in the boat barn, were hardly tiny—they held 30 soldiers.

The state park, located at the intersection of Pa. 532 and Pa. 32 (River Rd.), 3 miles north of I-95 from Exit 31, is divided into an upper and a lower section separated by 3 miles; Washington left from the lower park. You can sip a glass of punch at the low-ceilinged **Old (McKonkey's) Ferry Inn** (1752), where he ate before the assault, and tour the bird sanctuary and the Memorial Building at the point of embarkation. The 30-minute film in the Visitors Center (closed Mon) is dated and not worth sitting through—just start exploring on your own.

The **Wild Flower Preserve** in the upper park is really an 100-acre arboretum, flower garden, and shrub preserve rolled into one; it contains 15 different paths, each emphasizing different botanical wonders. The **Thompson-Neely House** was intact when General Washington, Brigadier General Stirling, and Lt. James Monroe decided on the year-end push into New Jersey. Next to the Wild Flower Preserve is the stone **Bowman's Hill Tower;** it will reward you (or the children) with a view of this part of the Delaware Valley, which would probably still belong to the British Commonwealth if Washington's troops hadn't routed the Hessians in 1776.

An annual reenactment of the historic crossing takes place here at Christmas. For more information, contact the park at P.O. Box 103, Washington Crossing, PA 18977 (☎ 215/493-4076).

A combination ticket, including a walking tour, Thompson-Neely House, Boman's Hill and Tower, costs $4 for adults, $3 for seniors, and $2 for children ages 6 to 12. The buildings are open Monday to Saturday 9am to 5pm, Sunday noon to 5pm. The grounds are open daily 9am to 8pm or sunset.

can also write to or stop by the **New Hope Information Center,** South Main and Mechanic streets, Box 141, New Hope, PA 18938 (☎ 215/862-5880); open Monday to Friday 9am to 5pm, Saturday and Sunday 10am to 6pm.

Along with specific accommodations listed below, you might want to contact the **Association of Bed & Breakfasts,** P.O. Box 562, Valley Forge, PA 19481 (☎ 800/344-0123 or 610/783-7838; fax 610/783-7783; open 9am to 9pm); they have dozens of charming rooms in Philadelphia, Bucks and Lancaster counties, and the Valley Forge and Brandywine Valley areas in the $45 to $100 range. Most of these have fewer than five rooms and don't advertise.

ATTRACTIONS IN BUCKS COUNTY

✪ **Sesame Place.** 100 Sesame Rd., Langhorne, PA 19047. ☎ **215/752-7070.** Admission $31.95 ages 3–55, $28.75 seniors over 55. Second-day tickets at discounted $16.95 rate with validated first-day ticket. Parking $6 per day. Note: Many hotels in the area offer discount tickets in their package rates. May to mid-June, Mon–Fri 10am–5pm, Sat–Sun 10am–7pm; late June–Aug, daily 9am–8pm; Sept–Oct, Sat–Sun 10am–5pm. Junction of Route 1 and I-95.

Bucks County

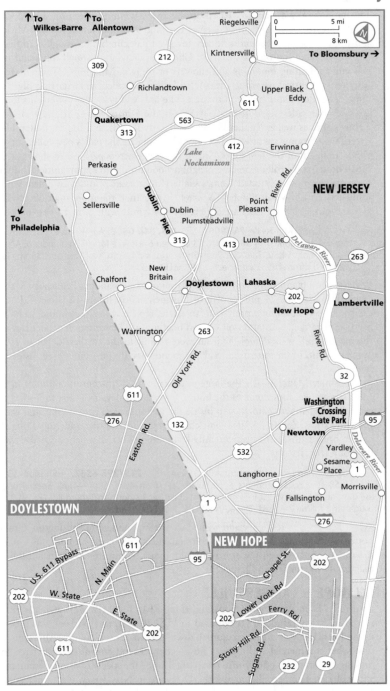

Riegelsville

0 ━━━ 5 mi
0 ━━━ 8 km

To Bloomsbury →

↑ To
Wilkes-Barre

↑ To
Allentown

Kintnersville

212

309

Richlandtown

Upper Black
Eddy

611

Quakertown

563

313

*Lake
Nockamixon*

412

Erwinna

Perkasie

NEW JERSEY

Sellersville

Dublin Pike

Point
Pleasant

To
Philadelphia

Dublin

Plumsteadville

313

413

Lumberville

Delaware River

263

Chalfont

New
Britain

Doylestown

Lahaska

202

New Hope

Lambertville

Warrington

263

Old York Rd.

River Rd.

32

611

Washington
Crossing
State Park

276

Easton Rd.

132

95

Newtown

Yardley

Sesame
Place

1

532

Delaware River

Langhorne

Morrisville

1

Fallsington

276

DOYLESTOWN

U.S. 611 Bypass

611

N. Main

202

W. State

E. State

202

611

NEW HOPE

95

Chapel St.

202

202

Lower York Rd.

Ferry Rd.

Stony Hill Rd.

Sugan Rd.

232

29

The nation's only theme park based on the award-winning television show *Sesame Street* is located 30 minutes from Center City and 90 from New York City. My kids and millions of others spend a totally involved day climbing through 3 stories of sloping, swaying fun on the Nets and Climbs or crawling through tubes and tunnels amid splashing fountains and showers of spray at Mumford's Water Maze. A daily festive musical parade is a fun-filled interactive celebration starring Big Bird, Elmo, Zoe, Bert and Ernie, and the rest. The kids will want their swimsuits for 15 age-safe water rides; these include Sky Splash, the 5-story water adventure in Twiddlebug Land, as well as Rubber Duckie, Runaway Rapids, and Big Bird's Rambling River (locker rooms are provided). Older kids will love the park's new roller coaster, Vapor Trail. All of the best-loved *Sesame Street* characters perform in shows at Big Bird Theater and stroll on Sesame Neighborhood for photo opportunities. Indoors, there are the air-conditioned Games Gallery and Sesame Studio complete with a simulated TV show for young "TV stars." Altogether, the more than 60 physical play stations and water rides are perfect for any family with 3- to 15-year-olds.

Pennsbury Manor. Morrisville, PA 19067. ☎ **215/946-0400.** Admission to buildings (by guided tour only) $5 adults, $4.50 seniors, $3 children 6–12, free for children under 6. Admission to grounds only $4.50. Tues–Sat 9am–5pm, Sun noon–5pm. Last tour at 3:30pm. Take Pa. 9 (Tyburn Rd.) from U.S. 1 (intersects I-95) or U.S. 13.

William Penn planned his very English plantation and manor at Pennsbury Manor, along the Delaware, 24 miles north of Philadelphia on Route 32 (River Rd.). He designed a self-sustaining, pre-Georgian estate, replete with smokehouse, icehouse, barn, herb garden, plantation office, and boathouse. The various dependencies and the manor itself were demolished but were rebuilt to the smallest detail in 1939. Taking a tour, given four times daily, is mandatory if you want to see inside the buildings.

Pennsbury Manor boasts the largest collection of 17th-century antiques in the state, spread over four floors of the house. On a sunny day, it's a treat to inspect the carefully labeled herb garden, step inside the icehouse for a cool respite, and watch the guinea fowl (more popular than chickens in the 1600s) wandering along the golden brick paths. Sundays frequently bring events such as a period Quaker wedding or a farm festival.

Fallsington. Tyburn Rd., Fallsington, PA 19054. ☎ **215/295-6567.** Admission $3.50 adults, $2.50 seniors, $1 students 6–18. Mon–Sat 10am–4pm, Sun 1–4pm. Special open-house days on the second Sat in May and Oct. Take Pa. 13 north to Tyburn Rd. (Pa. 9), then turn right and follow the road. Or south off U.S. 1 at Tyburn Rd.

When Penn was in residence and wished to worship, he'd go to Fallsington, 6 miles north of Pennsbury Manor. This colonial village, grouped around the Quaker meetinghouse, has been preserved virtually intact. Again, tours, given hourly, are mandatory to enter the buildings.

NEW HOPE & LAMBERTVILLE

Four miles from Washington Crossing, along River Road (Pa. 32), which is punctuated by lovely farmland (as opposed to U.S. 202's factory outlets), you'll come upon New Hope, a former colonial town turned artists' colony. Although it's somewhat commercial and touristy now—the weekend crowds can get fierce and parking is cramped—once you're there you'll enjoy the specialty stores, restaurants, and galleries. Lambertville, across the Delaware in New Jersey, has rather pedestrian architecture but more scenic routes along the river and, many say, better restaurants.

NEW HOPE AREA ATTRACTIONS

Bucks County Playhouse. 70 S. Main St. (P.O. Box 313), New Hope, PA 18938. ☎ **215/862-2041.** Tickets $18–$25. Apr–Dec Wed–Sun evenings and Wed and Thurs matinees.

This is the center of New Hope entertainment with summer theater that features Broadway hits and musical revivals. It's a former gristmill with a seating capacity of almost 500.

New Hope Mule Barge. New and S. Main sts., New Hope, PA 18938. ☎ **215/862-2842.** Admission $7.50 adults, $6.75 seniors, $5.50 students, $4.75 children under 12. May 1– Oct 15, six launchings daily. Apr and Oct 16–Nov 15, reduced launchings on Wed, Sat–Sun.

For a while in the early 1800s, canals were thought to be the transport revolution in England and the eastern United States. Coal was floated down this one in the 1830s from mines in the Lehigh Valley, with barges pulled by mules. The barges, still pulled by mules, run April to November and leave from New Street.

Parry Mansion Museum. Main and Ferry sts., New Hope, PA 18938. ☎ **215/862-5652.** Admission $4 adults, $3 seniors, $1 children under 12. May–Dec, Fri–Sun 1–5pm.

One of the loveliest old homes in town, this mansion was erected in 1784 by the elite of New Hope. The Parry family lived in this 11-room Georgian until 1966, and the rooms are decorated in different period styles ranging from 1775 (white-wash and candles) to 1900 (wallpaper and oil lamps).

Peddler's Village. U.S. 202 and Rte. 263, Lahaska, PA 18931. ☎ **215/794-4000.** Most stores Mon–Thurs and Sat 10am–6pm, Fri 10am–9pm, Sun 11am–6pm. Year–round festivals and events.

Five miles south of New Hope, on Route 202, Peddler's Village looks antique, but only the heavily marketed appeal to customers is classic—most of the merchandise is contemporary. It's not a country market—the prices are marked up considerably—but the ambience and convenience are attractive. **Carousel World** can spin the family on a 1922 restored carousel, along with other fine examples of this art (museum admission is $3 for adults, $2.75 for seniors, $2 for children 3–13; rides cost $1.50 each). Among the ten restaurants, **Jenny's** on Route 202 at Street Road (☎ **215/794-4020**) offers elegant continental dining in an atmosphere of brass and stained glass. The specialties of the **Cock 'n' Bull** (☎ **215/794-4010**) include a massive buffet on Thursday, an unlimited Sunday brunch, and beef burgundy served in a loaf of bread baked in the hearth. The 66 rooms in the **Golden Plough Inn** (☎ **215/794-4063**) are scattered throughout the village, all with private bathrooms and complimentary champagne from $115 per night.

COUNTRY WALKING & BICYCLING

Walking or riding along the Delaware River or along the canals built for coal hauling on either side can be the highlight of a summer. The following two routes are particularly convenient.

The first is between Lumberville and the point, 3 miles south, where Route 263 crosses the Delaware into New Jersey. The towpath along the canal on the Pennsylvania side is charming, and Lumberville has a quaint general store.

The **Lumberville Store Bicycle Rental Co.** (Rte. 32, Lumberville, PA 18933; ☎ 215/297-5388) has all kinds of bicycles for rent at moderate day rates. It's open April to mid-October 8am to 6pm daily.

The second route, also just south of Lumberville, follows River Road (Rte. 32) south and west to Cuttalossa Road, which winds past an alpine chalet, creeks, ponds, and grazing sheep clanking their antique Swiss bells. **Cuttalossa Inn,**

Cuttalossa Road, Lumberville, PA 18933 (☎ 215/297-5082), offers high-class cuisine in a spectacular setting.

More Outdoor Activities

Other transport-based attractions of the New Hope area are a **covered-bridges tour** (☎ 215/345-4552 for information about this self-guided free tour); **river tubing** at Point Pleasant Canoe, up the Delaware from New Hope at upper Black Eddy and Riegelsville (☎ 215/297-8181), for relaxing family fun; and a **steam railway** out of New Hope (☎ 215/862-2707).

SHOPPING

Rice's Sale & Country Market. 6326 Greenhill Rd., New Hope, PA 18938. ☎ 215/297-5993. Admission $1 Tues, free on Sat. Tues and Sat, 6am–1pm. One mile north of Peddler's Village on Greenhill Rd., just off Route 263 in Lahaska.

Rice's Market is the real thing—a quality market of country goods and crafts since 1860. Amish wares are sold in the main building, along with antiques and collectibles; more than 1,000 outdoor stalls have vendors. New features include indoor bathrooms and paved walkways for strollers and wheelchairs. There's an ATM on the premises. Get there early.

WHERE TO STAY

New Hope and its New Jersey neighbor across the Delaware River, Lambertville, have well-deserved reputations for their country inns and restaurants. All used to require 2-day stays and frown on children, but Sesame Place's success is changing this. The listings here only scratch the surface; other choices might include the romantic **Inn at Phillips Mill** in New Hope (☎ 215/862-2984), the newly opened and fashionable **Auldridge Mead** in Tinicum Township (☎ 215/847-5842), or the tranquil **Bucksville House** in Kintnersville (☎ 215/847-8948).

Country Inns

✪ **Centre Bridge Inn.** P.O. Box 74, Intersection of Rte. 32 and Rte. 263, New Hope, PA 18938. ☎ 215/862-2048 or 215/862-9139. 9 units. A/C. $85–$135 weekday; $110–$160 weekend. Rates include continental breakfast. AE, MC, V.

Situated beside the Delaware River 3½ miles north of New Hope, the current building is the third since the early 18th century. Many of the elegant guest rooms have canopy, four-poster, or brass beds; wall-high armoires; modern private bathrooms; outside decks; and views of the river or countryside. Five rooms have TVs. The inn also has a pretty restaurant overlooking the river and the adjoining canal (and the mule-drawn barges coasting on it) serving lunch, dinner, and a $20 fixed-price Sunday brunch.

Evermay-on-the-Delaware. River Rd., Erwinna, PA 18920. ☎ 610/294-9100. Fax 610/294-8249. 16 units, 1 carriage house suite. A/C TEL. $85–$95 single; $100–$185 double; $260 suite. Rates include continental breakfast and 4pm tea. MC, V.

Thirteen miles north of New Hope on River Road in Erwinna lies this gracious historic inn, now under the ownership of William and Danielle Moffley. Evermay once hosted the Barrymores for croquet weekends. Combining privacy with a romantic setting overlooking the Delaware, the inn offers rooms with luxurious antique furnishings. The formal dining room offers an excellent $56 fixed-price six-course dinner at a 7:30pm seating on Friday, Saturday, Sunday, and holidays; it's open to the public as well as guests, so reserve well in advance.

✪ **Whitehall Inn.** 1370 Pineville Rd., New Hope, PA 18938. ☎ 215/598-7945. 5 units. A/C TEL. $140–$210 single or double. Rates include 4-course breakfast and 4pm high tea. Two-night minimum. AE, CB, DC, DISC, MC, V.

Four miles outside New Hope is this 18th-century manor house on a former horse farm, complete with a pool. Mike and Suella Wass serve magnificent four-course breakfasts, and their "innsmanship" is nationally known, with such touches as fresh fruit bowls, a bottle of mineral water in every room, and afternoon tea concerts.

Hotels & Motels

✪   **Comfort Inn.** 3660 Street Rd., Bensalem, PA 19020. ☎ **800/228-5150** or 215/245-0100. 141 units. A/C TV TEL. $79–$135. Rates include continental breakfast. Children under 18 free in parents' room. AE, DC, DISC, MC, V.

For moderate lodgings in Bucks County, this is one of the best choices, off I-95 about 20 miles from Washington Crossing and 5 miles from Sesame Place. The inn is a bright, modern 3-story property; each room has two double beds, queen-size bed plus sofa bed, or a king-size bed. There's also an exercise room. There's only one elevator, so get used to the stairs.

✪   **New Hope Motel in the Woods.** 400 W. Bridge St., New Hope, PA 18938. ☎ **215/ 862-2800.** 28 units. A/C TV. $59–$89 double. AE, DISC, MC, V.

Just a mile west of town is this motel tucked in a peaceful woodland setting off Route 179. For more than 30 years it has offered modern ground-level rooms with private bathrooms and standard motel amenities. It's open all year, with a swimming pool in the summer.

Sheraton Bucks County Hotel. 400 Oxford Valley Rd., Langhorne, PA 19047. ☎ **800/ 325-3535** or 215/547-4100. 167 units. A/C TV TEL. $155–$165 double. Sesame Street packages $139–$169 include free shuttle and free room and board for children. AE, DC, DISC, MC, V.

This festive, modern, 14-story hotel is right across the street from Sesame Place. The soundproof guest rooms have oversize beds and quilted fabrics, many with extra sofa beds. Other facilities include a health club, an indoor swimming pool and sauna, and a full-service restaurant.

WHERE TO DINE

Karla's. 5 W. Mechanic St., New Hope, PA 18938. ☎ **215/862-2612.** Reservations recommended for dinner. Main courses $13–$22; lunch $3.95–$8.95. AE, DC, MC, V. Sun–Thurs 11am–10pm, Fri–Sat 11am–4am. INTERNATIONAL.

In the heart of New Hope, next door to the Information Center, this lively and informal restaurant offers three settings: a sunlit conservatory with ceiling fans, stained glass, and plants; a gallery room with local artists' works; and a bistro with marble tabletops. The eclectic menu offers grilled rib-eye steak, veal à la française, and chicken breast with Thai ginger sauce. Lunch items are tamer.

✪   **Odette's Fine Country Dining.** S. River Rd. and Route 32, New Hope, PA 18938. ☎ **215/862-2432.** Reservations recommended. Main courses $16–$26; lunch $7–$10. AE, DC, MC, V. Mon–Sat 11:30am–3pm and 5–10pm; Sun 4–10pm; brunch Sun 10:30am–1:30pm. INTERNATIONAL.

Surrounded by the river and the canal on the southern edge of town, this elegant restaurant has been an inn since 1794. The previous owner, Odette Myrtil, was a Ziegfeld Follies girl whose memorabilia adorns the place. The menus are seasonal and change three times a year, providing nice twists on steak, seafood, duck, and veal. There is also a weekend cabaret.

DOYLESTOWN

The intersection of U.S. 202 (west of New Hope), Pa. 313 (south of Scranton), and U.S. 611 (N. Broad St. in Philadelphia) defines Doylestown, the county seat; the

R5 commuter rail from Center City ends here. It's a pleasant town just to walk around, but three interesting collections invite you indoors. All were endowed by Dr. Henry Chapman Mercer (1856–1930), a collector, local archaeologist, and master of pottery techniques.

DOYLESTOWN AREA ATTRACTIONS

✪ **Fonthill Museum.** E. Court St., off Swamp Rd. (Rte. 313), Doylestown, PA 18901. ☎ **215/348-9461.** Admission $5 adults, $4.50 seniors, $1.50 children. Mon–Sat 10am–5pm, Sun noon–5pm. Closed Thanksgiving, Christmas, and New Year's Day. Guided tours only; reservations recommended.

Not many people can call their home a castle, but Dr. Mercer could. The core of this castle, built from reinforced concrete in Mercer's own design, is a 19th-century farmhouse, with towers, turrets, and tiles piled on beyond belief. All the rooms are different shapes, each with tiles from Mercer's collection set into the floors and walls.

Moravian Pottery and Tile Works. Swamp Rd., Doylestown, PA 18901. ☎ **215/345-6722.** Admission $3 adults, $1.50 youths, $2.50 seniors. Daily 10am–4:45pm. Tours available every 30 min. until 4pm. Closed major holidays.

Down the road on Pa. 313, the Moravian Pottery and Tile Works was Dr. Mercer's next big project. If you go to the State Capitol in Harrisburg, you can see more than 400 mosaics from here that illustrate the history of Pennsylvania. The ceramists working at the pottery turn out tiles and mosaics available through the museum shop; prices range from $5 to $1,800.

✪ **Mercer Museum.** Pine St. at Ashland St., Doylestown, PA 18901. ☎ **215/345-0210.** www.mercermuseum.org. Admission to the museum and library $5 adults, $4.50 seniors, $1.50 children 6–17, free for children under 6. Mon–Sat 10am–5pm, Sun noon–5pm, Tues 10am–9pm. Spruance Library (Bucks County history), Tues 1–9pm, Wed–Sat 10am–5pm. Closed Thanksgiving, Christmas, and New Year's Day.

Mercer Museum displays thousands of early American tools, vehicles, cooking pieces, looms, and even weather vanes. Mercer had the collecting bug in a big way, and you can't help being impressed with the breadth of the collection and the castle that houses it. It rivals the Shelburne, Vermont, complex for Americana—and that's 35 buildings on 100 acres! The open atrium rises 5 stories, suspending a Conestoga wagon, chairs, and sleighs as if they were Christmas-tree ornaments. During the summer, a log cabin, schoolhouse, and other large bits of American life are open for inspection. The museum recently added six hands-on stations for children to build a log house, try on period clothes, and drive a buggy. The old library is a functional reading room.

WHERE TO DINE

✪ **Sign of the Sorrel Horse Country Inn.** 4424 Old Easton Rd., Doylestown, PA 18901. ☎ **215/230-9999.** Reservations required. Jackets recommended for men. Main courses $18–$28. AE, CD, DC, MC, V. Wed–Sat 5:30–9:30pm. FRENCH.

Led by the indefatigable team of Jon Atkin and Monique Gaumont, this is the best restaurant in the Doylestown area, and it's housed in a 200-year-old inn. I prefer the new Cafe Room to the original low-ceilinged Escoffier Room, but the cuisine remains superb in both. The menu is rich, with smoked sea scallops, lobster, and filet mignon—all served with fresh reductions and mousses. Salads are abundant with their own herbs. The ice cream is homemade with honey.

2 Valley Forge

Montgomery County is a region of rivers, hills, fall foliage, and Main Line suburban development. It's best known for Valley Forge, Washington's winter headquarters at the nadir of the Revolutionary War, and the enormous King of Prussia mall, the second largest in the nation.

The **Valley Forge Convention and Visitors Bureau,** 600 W. Germantown Pike, Plymouth Meeting, PA 19462 (☎ **800/345-8112** or 610/834-1550), has particulars on sites, recreation, annual events, and campgrounds.

EXPLORING VALLEY FORGE NATIONAL HISTORICAL PARK

Only 30 minutes from central Philadelphia today, Valley Forge was hours of frozen trails away in the winter of 1777–78. The Revolutionary forces had just lost the battles of Brandywine and Germantown. While the British occupied Philadelphia, Washington's forces repaired to winter quarters near an iron forge where the Schuylkill met Valley Creek, 18 miles northwest. A sawmill and gristmill were supposed to help provide basic requirements, but they had been destroyed by the British. Some 12,000 men and boys straggled into the encampment, setting up quarters and lines of defense.

Unfortunately, the winter turned bitter, with 6 inches of snow and iced-up rivers. Critical shortages of food and clothing, along with damp shelters, left nearly 4,000 men diseased and unfit for duty. Almost 2,000 perished, and many others deserted. Congress, which had left Philadelphia hurriedly, couldn't persuade the colonies to give money to alleviate the conditions. Nevertheless, the forces slowly gained strength and confidence, thanks in part to the Prussian army veteran, Baron von Steuben, appointed by Washington to retrain the Continental Army under his revised and distinctly American "Manual of Arms." By springtime the Continentals were an army on which their new allies, the French, could rely. Replicas of their huts, some of the officers' lodgings, and later memorials dot the park today.

Admission to the park is free. Start your visit at the **Visitors Center** (☎ **610/ 783-1077**) at the junction of Pa. 23 and North Gulph Road. If you're driving, access is from Exit 24 of the Pennsylvania Turnpike or Exit 25 of the Schuylkill Expressway (I-76) to Route 363—follow the signs. From Philadelphia, you can take bus 45 from the Visitors Center at 16th Street and JFK Boulevard to King of Prussia Plaza, then take the hourly 99 bus to the park. A 15-minute film depicting the encampment is shown at the Visitors Center every half hour. Also at the Visitors Center is a museum containing Washington's tent, an extensive collection of Revolutionary War artifacts, and a bookstore.

Highlights within the park include the **National Memorial Arch;** an 1865 covered bridge; the **Isaac Potts House** (1770), which Washington commandeered as his headquarters; and the 1993 Monument to Patriots of African Descent. Admission to Washington's headquarters is $2 for adults, $1.50 for children April to November, and includes admission to the Historical Society (see below, and note that the Historical Society does not offer the same package).

If you're here in late April or early May, you'll see the magnificent dogwood blossoms. Herds of cute deer also proliferate annually, to the chagrin of park officials and neighbors—imagine how Washington's army would have made short work of that nuisance as venison!

That Gothic chapel (1903) houses the **Washington Memorial Chapel** (it's free, with Sunday carillon recitals in the bell tower at 2pm), next to the Valley Forge Historical Society Museum (see below). Like the Memorial Arch, the chapel seems to honor an American hero in a peculiarly European way, with flags and stained-glass medievalism.

Next to the chapel is the **Valley Forge Historical Society Museum** (☎ **610/ 783-0535**), with a large collection of Washingtoniana and other historical artifacts. Admission is $2 for adults, $1.50 for seniors and children ages 6 to 18. It's open Monday to Saturday 10am to 5pm, Sunday 1 to 5pm; closed major holidays.

An audiotape tour costs $8 for 2 hours; there's also tour bus service from the Visitors Center, which costs $5.50 for adults, $4.50 for ages 5 to 16. The park is open daily 9am to 5pm, later in summer.

A WILDLIFE SANCTUARY

Mill Grove. Audubon and Pawlings rds., P.O. Box 7125, Audubon, PA 19407. ☎ **610/ 666-5593.** Admission by donation. Museum, Tues–Sat 10am–4pm, Sun 1–4pm. Grounds, dawn to dusk. Closed Mondays and major holidays. Take Audubon Rd. directly, or Rte. 422 west to Rte. 363 north, then a left onto Audubon Rd. at traffic light.

Situated 2 miles north of Valley Forge, the Audubon Wildlife Sanctuary preserves 170 acres around the home of the young John James Audubon. The fieldstone mansion with Georgian touches and a kitchen wing is decorated with 1950s murals of bird life and Audubon's observations. Audubon's drawing studio and taxidermy workplace have been restored. Outside, you can walk for miles listening to the calls and chirps of nature—it's easy to linger all afternoon. Picnicking is not allowed.

SHOPPING

King of Prussia Court and Plaza. Near the junction of U.S. 202 and Pa. 363, ½ mile south of I-276; 3 miles south of Valley Forge National Historical Park via Route 422. ☎ **610/ 265-5727.** Mon–Sat 10am–9:30pm, Sun 11am–6pm.

With 450 establishments in three connected tiers, grouped roughly by price range, this is now the second largest mall in the country. It's a fantastic experience; see chapter 9 for specific retailers and tips.

WHERE TO STAY

Comfort Inn Valley Forge/King of Prussia. 550 W. DeKalb Pike, King of Prussia, PA 19406. ☎ **800/222-0222** or 610/962-0700. Fax 610/962-0218. 121 units. A/C MINIBAR TV TEL. $92 single, $102 double Mon–Thurs; weekend specials available. Rates include continental breakfast. AAA and CAA discounts. AE, CB, DC, DISC, MC, V.

This five-floor inn is only a mile from the Valley Forge National Park, which makes it good for families. It's 30% to 40% cheaper than similar hotels in the area, even after 1997 renovations. There's a coin-operated laundry and a fitness center on the premises, and rooms on the top two floors have VCRs.

Sheraton Valley Forge Hotel. North Gulph Rd. and 1st Ave., Valley Forge, PA 19406. ☎ **800/325-3535** or 610/337-2000. Fax 610/768-3222. 399 units. A/C MINIBAR TV TEL. $169–$189 double; $185–$250 suite. AE, CB, DC, DISC, MC, V.

This is a busy high-rise complex with rooms, suites, five restaurants, and two lounges that are all of primary interest to getaway weekenders. The fantasy suites (Caveman, Wild West, Pre-Raphaelite, Futurist) are remarkably popular. The health club is open 24 hours, with Nautilus machines, racquetball courts, a whirlpool, a tanning bed, and a steam room. There is also an outdoor pool and no-smoking floors.

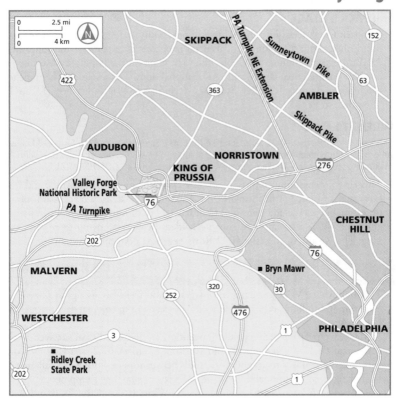

WEST OF VALLEY FORGE
RIDLEY CREEK STATE PARK

Ridley Creek State Park, on Route 3 (West Chester Pike), is about 15 miles west of Center City, 17 miles from the Valley Forge interchange, and 7 miles north of Media and I-95 via Pa. 352. It has two unusual attractions: the bona fide **Colonial Pennsylvania Plantation,** handed down straight from William Penn's charter; and a **superb park** with miles of picnic areas, playgrounds, and hiking and cycling trails. The plantation is the best example in the area of how a "yeoman," or common family, lived in virtual self-sufficiency on a colonial farm. It's staffed mostly by talented schoolteachers who come summer after summer to build wood fences, garden and grow corn, tend pigs and shear sheep, and weave cloth for clothes. Children love it.

The park (☎ **610/566-4800**) is 3 miles past Newtown Square, Sycamore Mills Road, Media, PA 19063. You can contact the Colonial Pennsylvania Plantation, within the park, at P.O. Box 150, Edgemont, PA 19028 (☎ **610/566-1725**). Park admission is free, and plantation admission is $3 for adults, $2 for seniors and children ages 4 to 12. The park is open daily 8am to dusk. The plantation is open April to June and October, Friday to Sunday, 10am to 5pm; July and August, Thursday to Sunday, 10am to 5pm; weekends only during winter months, 10am to 4pm.

SKIPPACK VILLAGE

Skippack Creek feeds into the Schuylkill near Mill Grove, and entrepreneurs have refurbished about 40 colonial and Federal mansions as restaurants and shops here. As you'd expect, antiques and collectibles rate high on the popularity list, but you can also pursue casual clothes and international dolls. The restaurants here include the moderately priced **Trolley Stop** (☎ **610/584-4849**). To get here, follow Pa. 363 north to Pa. 73.

WHERE TO DINE

Skippack Roadhouse. 4022 Skippack Pike (Rte. 73), Skippack. ☎ **610/584-4231.** Reservations recommended. Main courses $8–$12 at lunch, $17–$30 at dinner. AE, MC, V. Mon–Sat 11:30am–2:30pm; Mon–Thurs 5–9pm, Fri 5–10pm. Jazz Fri–Sat. CONTINENTAL.

This elegant, charming country roadhouse with a white tile bar, mirrors, and fresh flowers is composed of six intimate dining rooms. The extensive blackboard specials of seasonal items include game and fresh fish and traditional meals of veal, chicken, and lamb. *Wine Spectator* magazine has lauded their selections for three years running. They've also opened the **4022 Rotisserie** next door for reasonable deli fare.

3 Exploring the Brandywine Valley

The Brandywine Valley, bridging Pennsylvania and Delaware, is a great 1- or 2-day excursion into rolling country filled with Americana from colonial days through the Gilded Age.

Many of the farms that kept the Revolutionary troops fed have survived to this day. There are 15 covered bridges and 100 antique stores in Chester County alone, with miles of country roads and horse trails between them. Spring and fall are particularly colorful seasons, and don't forget Delaware's tax-free shopping.

The valley is particularly rich in history. Without the defeat at Brandywine, Washington would never have ended up at Valley Forge, from which he emerged with a competent army. When the Du Pont de Nemours family fled post-Revolutionary France, they wound up owning powder mills on the Brandywine Creek. Every pioneer needed gunpowder and iron, and the business grew astronomically, expanding into chemicals and textiles. The Du Ponts controlled upper Delaware as a virtual fiefdom, building splendid estates and gardens. Most of these, along with the original mills, are open to visitors. Winterthur houses the finest collection of American decorative arts ever assembled, and artists like Pyle and Wyeth left rich collections now on public view.

---

❷ Did You Know?

- The Brandywine Valley has inspired three generations of Wyeths, America's foremost family of artists.
- According to the 1990 census, Pennsylvania has the largest rural population in the nation: 32%.
- Almost a quarter of all mushrooms produced in the U.S.—some 330 million pounds a year—are grown within a 50-mile radius of Kennett Square, in the Brandywine Valley.

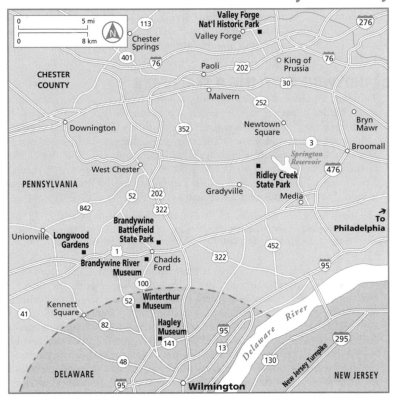

ESSENTIALS

GETTING THERE   I-95 South from Philadelphia has various exits north of Wilmington marked for specific sites, most of which are off Exit 7 to Pa. 52 North. If you have time, Pa. 100 off Pa. 52 North, linking West Chester to Wilmington, passes through picturesque pastureland, forest, and crops. From New York, take Exit 2 off the New Jersey Turnpike onto Route 322 West over the Commodore Barry Bridge into Pennsylvania, and continue on Route 322 to Route 452; take Route 452 north 4 miles to Route 1, the main artery of the valley.

VISITOR INFORMATION   For more information, call the **Brandywine Valley Tourist Information Center,** just outside the gates of **Longwood Gardens,** at ☎ **800/343-3983** or 610/388-2900. For motorists on I-95, Delaware maintains a Visitors Center just south of Wilmington, between Routes 272 and 896. It operates 8am to 8pm.

CHADDS FORD

Land where a Native American trail (now U.S. 1) forded the Brandywine Creek was purchased from William Penn by Francis Chadsey, an early Quaker immigrant. The present **Chadds Ford Inn,** at the junction of U.S. 1 and U.S. 100 (☎ **610/388-7361**), filled one of the village's first needs—a tavern. For small villages in the middle colonies, taverns served as mail depots, law courts, election hustings, and occasionally prisons. Before the Battle of Brandywine, Washington's officers stayed at the inn; afterward, British troops slaughtered the cattle before marching on Philadelphia. There's a small shopping area next to the premises.

BRANDYWINE BATTLEFIELD STATE PARK

This park, 2 miles east of Chadds Ford on Route 1, has no monuments, since the actual battle, according to the guides, was fought outside park borders. But Washington's and Lafayette's reconstructed headquarters mark the site. The grounds and Visitor Center, which are excellent for picnicking and hiking, are open free Memorial Day to Labor Day until 8pm. For information, call ☎ **610/459-3342.** House tour admission is $3.50 for adults, $2.50 for seniors, $1.50 for children ages 6 to 17, free for children under 6. Open Tuesday to Saturday 9am to 5pm, Sunday noon to 5pm; last house tours are at 3pm.

✪ **Brandywine River Museum.** Rts. 1 and 100, Chadds Ford, PA 19317. ☎ **610/ 388-2700.** www.brandywinemuseum.org. Admission $5 adults, $2.50 children 6–12, free for children under 6. AAA 2-for-1 discount. Daily 9:30am–4:30pm. Self-service restaurant open 11am–3pm.

Across the road from the Brandywine Battlefield State Park, a 19th-century grist-mill has been restored and joined by a dramatic spiral of brick and glass. The museum showcases American painters of the Brandywine school and others. A newer wing contains a gallery devoted to paintings by Andrew Wyeth. Howard Pyle, painter and illustrator of adventure tales in the late 19th century, established a school nearby; his students included N. C. Wyeth, Frank Schoonover, and Harvey Dunn. Three generations of Wyeths, from N. C., Carolyn, and Andrew to Jamie, have remained here, and the museum is particularly strong in their works. Many of the museum's exhibits display the art of book and magazine illustration at its pre-television zenith.

✪ LONGWOOD GARDENS

Simply one of the world's great garden displays, Longwood is on Route 1, 30 miles west of Philadelphia and just west of the junction with Pa. 52 (☎ **610/388-1000;** www.longwoodgardens.org). Pierre S. Du Pont devoted his life to horticulture. Here he bought a 19th-century arboretum and created the ultimate estate garden on 1,050 acres. You should plan a half day here.

A Visitors Center has a multimedia briefing of the gardens. Most people head to the left, toward the Main Fountain Garden, which has special fluid fireworks shows on Tuesday, Thursday, and Saturday evenings from June to September, usually preceded by hour-long garden concerts. Wrought-iron chairs and clipped trees and shrubs overlook the jets of water, which rise up to 130 feet. A topiary garden of closely pruned shrubs surrounds a 37-foot sundial.

The 4 acres of massive bronze-and-glass conservatories, renovated in 1996–97, are among the finest and largest in the United States. Orangery displays are breathtaking. African violets, bonsai trees up to 400 years old, hibiscus, orchids, and tropical plants are among the specialties, but expect anything from Easter lilies to scarlet begonias. Special collections display silver desert plants, plants of the Mediterranean, and roses, among others. The plants are exhibited only at their peak and are constantly replaced from the extensive growing houses.

A parquet-floor ballroom was added later, connected to the greenhouses, along with a 10,000-pipe organ, a magnificent instrument played during the year and on Sunday afternoon in winter.

Ahead and to the right of the Visitors Center, more gardens and fountains await, along with the Longwood Heritage Exhibit inside the Peirce-Du Pont House, the founder's residence. This exhibit, opened in 1995, shows the history of the property, from 2,000-year-old Native American spear points to Du Pont family movies. The restaurant offers cafeteria-style dining year-round and full-service dining in mid-April to December, with surprisingly good meals.

Admission is $12 for adults ($8 Tues), $6 for ages 16 to 20, $2 for ages 6 to 15, free for children under 6. It's open April to October daily 9am to 6pm (conservatories 10am–6pm); November to March, daily 9am to 5pm. The grounds and conservatories are frequently open late for special events and holiday displays.

✪ WINTERTHUR MUSEUM, GARDEN AND LIBRARY

The later home of the Du Ponts now provides the setting for America's best collection of native decorative arts. Winterthur (☎ **800/448-3883** or 302/888-4600; www.winterthur.org) is 6 miles northwest of Wilmington, Delaware, on Route 52.

Henry Francis Du Pont, a great-grandson of E. I. Du Pont, was a connoisseur of European antiques. But when he turned his attention to a simple Pennsylvania Dutch chest in 1923, he realized that no study had illustrated how American pieces are related to European ones or how the concepts of beauty and taste differed on the two continents. Du Pont collected first American furniture, then decorative objects, then the interior woodwork of entire homes built between 1640 and 1840. Finally, he added to his home more than 200 rooms for the display of his collection. Because the museum started out as a private home, the rooms have a unique richness and intimacy.

In 1992, Winterthur opened the Galleries, a new building adjacent to the existing period rooms. On the first floor the exhibition, *Perspectives on the Decorative Arts in Early America,* focuses on the social, functional, and other meanings of objects in everyday lives. The second floor features three areas of various aspects of American craftsmanship, with changing exhibitions. The Main Museum, open for specific guided tours, displays the bulk of the collection and includes complete interiors from every eastern seaboard colony. Special landmarks include the famous Montmorenci Stair Hall, two Shaker Rooms, fine examples of Pennsylvania Dutch decorative art, and the Du Pont dining room. The Campbell Soup Tureen collection, with 125 items currently on display, is housed in the Dorrance Gallery, between the museum and research building.

In spring the extensive Winterthur Gardens explode into an abundance of cherry and crabapple blossoms, rhododendrons, Virginia bluebells, and azaleas. The lush, carefully planned gardens are well worth viewing any season. Garden tram rides through the grounds are available when weather permits. There are two superb gift shops selling a selection of licensed reproductions, gifts, books, jewelry, and plants. The Visitor Pavilion Restaurant cooks breakfast, lunch, brunch, and tea to order and seats 350; the Cappuccino Cafe next to the museum offers lighter fare.

There are four admission options: The **General Admission ticket** ($8 adults, $6 seniors and students, $4 children 5–11) available year-round includes the Galleries, the Dorrance Gallery, a self-guided garden walk, and the garden tram. The **Highlight Introduction to Winterthur** tour (an additional $5) adds a 1-hour guided tour of a selection of 175 period rooms. **Decorative Arts tours** (an additional $9 for 1 hr. or $13 for 2 hrs.) offer in-depth guided tours in small groups for ages 12 and up; reservations are required. You can go on a **Guided Garden Walk** for $5 plus general admission. Winterthur is open Monday to Saturday 9:30am to 5pm, Sunday noon to 5pm; it's closed on major holidays.

✪ HAGLEY MUSEUM: THE STORY OF THE DU PONTS

The northern part of Delaware saw early skirmishes among the Swedes, Dutch, and English, and the Revolution was never far away. Since the early 1800s this has been Du Pont country, and the Hagley Museum shows how and when they got their start. It's a wonderful illustration of early American industrialism and manufacturing. The museum (☎ **302/658-2400;** www.hagley.lib.de.us) is located on Route 141 in Wilmington; take Route 52 to Route 100, go to the junction of Routes 100 and 141, then follow directions on Route 141. The museum is open March 15 to December, daily 9:30am to 4:30pm; January to March 14, Saturday and Sunday, 9:30am to 4:30pm. The Upper Eleutherian Mills Residence is open seasonally in spring and fall; the last jitney leaves at 3:30pm. Admission is $9.75 for adults, $7.50 for seniors and students aged 14 to 20, $3.50 for children 6 to 14, free for children under 6.

Hagley has three parts: the museum building, the reconstructed grounds, and the Upper Residence. The museum building covers the harnessing of the Brandywine River, originally for flour mills. The Du Ponts, who made their first fortune in gunpowder, needed waterpower and willow charcoal—both were here—and the raw materials a barge ride away. E. Irénée Du Pont, the founder, lived in the Upper Residence. He had experience in France with gunpowder and supervised the delicate production process. Nonetheless, explosions happened every decade or so.

On Blacksmith Hill, part of the workers' community has been restored. A visit through the Gibbons House reveals the lifestyle of a typical family, from foods to furniture. Nearby is the school the children attended, complete with lesson demonstrations. At the base of Blacksmith Hill a restored 1880s machine shop offers an exciting picture of change in the workplace. Volunteers demonstrate how the din of power tools with whirring belts and grinding metal replaced the quiet, painstaking hand-tooling of the earlier artisans.

Jitneys traverse the tour of the powder yard, but it's just as easy to walk the part of the 240 acres lying between the private family roads on the Upper Residence and the burbling Brandywine. A restored New Century Power House (1880) generates electricity here. Next to the electrical generator, a waterwheel, steam engine, and water turbine show improvements in power through the decades.

The wisteria-covered Georgian residence of the Du Ponts was renovated by a member of the fourth generation, Mrs. Louis Crowninshield, who lived here until her death in 1958. Empire, Federal, and Victorian periods of furniture are highlighted in various room settings. As with all Du Pont residences, the gardens and espaliered trees are superb, and there are flowers throughout the year.

The Belin House on Blacksmith Hill offers light lunches and drinks.

WHERE TO STAY

Abbey Green Motor Lodge. 1036 Wilmington Pike (Rte. 202), West Chester, PA 19382. ☎ **610/692-3310.** 18 units. A/C TV TEL. $57–$67 double. AE, DISC, MC, V.

This excellent budget choice is close to the battlefield site at scenic Routes 52 and 100. The family-run motel is designed with a courtyard with its own picnic tables, gazebo, and outdoor fireplace, all set back from the road. All rooms have double beds and a refrigerator, and six units have individual fireplaces.

✪ **Brandywine River Hotel.** Rts. 1 and 100, P.O. Box 1058, Chadds Ford, PA 19317-1058. ☎ **610/388-1200.** Fax 610/388-1200, ext. 301. 44 units. A/C TV TEL. $130 double; $159–$179 suite. Rates include continental breakfast and afternoon tea. Children under 12 stay free in parents' room. AE, CB, DC, DISC, MC, V.

Built in 1988 and completely renovated by its new owners in 1995, this hotel blends into a hillside, with a facade of brick and cedar shingle, steps away from Chadds Ford Inn. Several rooms have working fireplaces and Jacuzzis. The lobby has a huge open stone fireplace and friendly service, and guest rooms are decorated with Queen Anne cherry-wood furnishings, brass fixtures, chintz fabrics, and local paintings. Breakfast is served in an attractive hospitality room with a fireplace.

✪ **Hamanasett Bed & Breakfast.** P.O. Box 129, Lima, PA 19037. ☎ and fax **610/459-3000.** 9 units, 7 with private bathroom. TV. $100–$130 double. MC, V only through reservation service. No children under 14.

Built in 1856, this farmhouse now functions as one of the most impressive bed-and-breakfasts in the state—the house itself has been in the hands of Evelene Dohan's family since 1870. Mrs. Dohan's mother was director of the University of Pennsylvania Museum, and her father was a Philadelphia lawyer. The inn and its 48 acres reflect these ties to the world-class travels and achievements of the local "aristocracy." All rooms are beautifully furnished in family antiques; the first floor has a conservatory, 2,000-book and 500-video library, and magnificent foyer stairway. Breakfast is opulent; afternoon tea and evening coffee are available. Smoking is not allowed. Mrs. Dohan has an encyclopedic knowledge of the history and attractions of the county—in her youth she covered it all on horseback.

Meadow Spring Farm. 201 E. Street Rd., Kennett Square, PA 19348. ☎ **610/444-3903.** 7 units, 5 with private bathroom. A/C TV. $80–$90 double. Rates include full country breakfast. $10 per child in parents' room. No credit cards. Two-night minimum on weekends; reservations recommended 2 months in advance.

Anne Hicks operates this working 1936 farmhouse, situated on 125 acres traversed by walking paths. Rooms come with Amish quilts, and common areas display family antiques and dolls. Families are welcome; children may collect eggs, feed the animals, swim in the outdoor pool, or fish in the pond. There's also a hot tub in the solarium and a game room. Countryside carriage rides and picnic lunches are easily arranged.

WHERE TO DINE

Of the many inns with connecting restaurants, try the **Chadds Ford Inn,** Routes 1 and 100, Chadds Ford (☎ **610/388-7361**), with its Wyeth paintings; **Dilworthtown Inn,** Old Wilmington Pike and Brinton's Bridge Road, Dilworthtown (☎ **610/399-1390**), for homegrown vegetables and game birds; and **Longwood Inn,** 815 E. Baltimore Pike (Rte. 1), Kennett Square (☎ **610/444-3515**), showing off this area's position as the mushroom capital of the world.

12

Lancaster County: The Amish Country

Drive about 50 miles west of Philadelphia along Route 30, and you will come to a quietly beautiful region of rolling hills, winding creeks, neatly cultivated farms, covered bridges, and towns with picturesque names like Paradise and Bird-in-Hand. Amish, or Pennsylvania Dutch, Country is an area of 7,100 square miles centered around Lancaster County in the heart of the state. Pennsylvania Dutch Amish, Mennonites, and Brethren (see "Meet the Amish," below, for an explanation of the differences) represent 70,000 of Lancaster County's 422,000 residents. It's a small group that quietly and steadfastly continues to live a life of agrarian simplicity centered around religious worship and family cohesiveness. As the economic, social, and technological pressures on their lives mount, the preservation of their world evokes feelings of curiosity, nostalgia, amazement, and respect. Not all of these feelings are legitimate or welcomed by the Pennsylvania Dutch. But they are a rare yardstick for us to measure the distance that our own "outside" world has come over the last 2 centuries.

Pennsylvania Dutch Country has many special qualities for the visitor. The area is relatively small, with good roads for motorists and bicyclists alike. There are plenty of opportunities to get to know the Amish, and tourism has, perhaps surprisingly, promoted excellence in quilt making, antiques, and farm-based crafts. There are historical sites, pretzel and chocolate factories, covered bridges, and wonderful farmer's markets, as well as modern diversions such as movie theaters, amusement parks, and great outlet mall shopping. And, of course, the family style, smorgasbord, all-you-can-eat, or gourmet Pennsylvania Dutch restaurants are experiences in themselves.

1 Introducing the Pennsylvania Dutch Country

This land has been a major farming region since German settlers came across its limestone-rich soil and rolling hills 3 centuries ago. Lancaster County boasts the most productive nonirrigated farmland in the United States, and it's the country's fifth-largest dairy-producing county. The natural abundance of the region, the ease of getting goods to market in Philadelphia, and the hard work of its residents have all preserved major portions of the land for farming,

Lancaster & the Pennsylvania Dutch Country

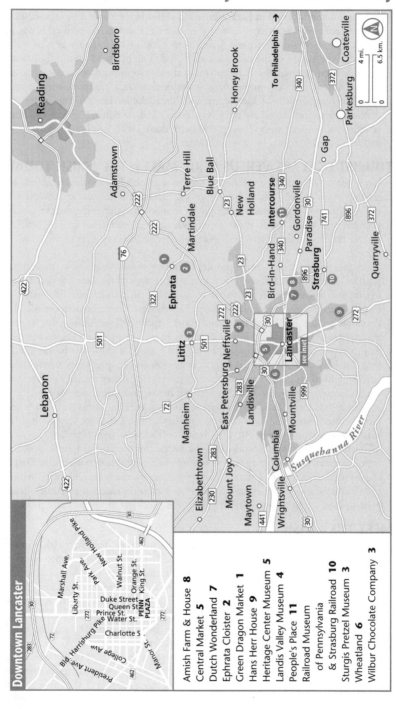

Reading

Birdsboro

Adamstown

Honey Brook

To Philadelphia →

Coatesville

Parkesburg

Terre Hill

Blue Ball

New Holland

Martindale

Gap

Ephrata

Intercourse

Gordonville

Paradise

Bird-in-Hand

Strasburg

Quarryville

Litz

Neffsville

East Petersburg

Lancaster
see inset

Lebanon

Manheim

Landisville

Mountville

Columbia

Susquehanna River

Elizabethtown

Mount Joy

Maytown

Wrightsville

Downtown Lancaster

New Holland Pike

Harrisburg Pike

President Ave.

College Ave.

Manor St.

Marshall Ave.

Liberty St.

Park Ave.

Walnut St.

Orange St.

King St.

Duke Street
Queen St.
Prince St.
Water St.

PENN
PLAZA

Charlotte S.

Amish Farm & House **8**

Central Market **5**

Dutch Wonderland **7**

Ephrata Cloister **2**

Green Dragon Market **1**

Hans Herr House **9**

Heritage Center Museum **5**

Landis Valley Museum **4**

People's Place **11**

Railroad Museum
of Pennsylvania

Sturgis Pretzel Museum **3**

Railroad **10**
& Strasburg

Wheatland **6**

Wilbur Chocolate Company **3**

although manufacturing in Lancaster, York, and other towns is also important. In its day, Lancaster was a major center of commerce, culture, and politics. It was the largest inland city in the United States from 1760 to 1810, and was even a contender in the choice of the new nation's capital. The balance between factory and farm has been threatened in this century by the development of the automobile and the construction of such major roads as the Pennsylvania Turnpike, which turned farmland into suburbs of Harrisburg and Philadelphia. The buildup of housing developments and attendant schools, services, and strip malls for an exploding population competes with lovely, placid fields dotted with farmhouses, barns, silos, and small creeks crossed by covered bridges.

TOURIST DOLLARS VERSUS STRIP MALLS: THE AMISH TODAY

Until about 40 years ago, the Amish were not especially a tourist attraction. But starting in the mid-1950s, with the growing incursion of technology into all areas of life in the rest of the country, the Amish tenacity in maintaining their traditional customs and values made them seem both unusual and alluring. For better or worse, the Amish have spawned a major tourist industry over the last several decades.

As this process began, most people, including many Amish, saw tourism as a positive development. Money flowed into the county, and the Amish found a growing market for such goods as quilts, metalwork, crafts, and foodstuff—with customers literally appearing at their doors. But the less benign consequences of this development are becoming more and more apparent. The Amish population is about 20,000 and growing, but as outsiders move to Lancaster County, the non-Amish population has grown to 400,000. Their need for affordable housing is driving up land prices and attracting strip developers. In past years when Amish families looked for land to buy for their children's farms, they turned to other, non-Amish farmers. Today, those farmers can get better prices from developers.

This means many Amish have been forced to leave their farms and set up non-farming businesses. The local construction business in Lancaster County includes many Amish workers who have to travel to Delaware and Maryland to work. Women who traditionally worked in the home and on the farm are increasingly running restaurants and shops or overseeing quilting and craft enterprises. Despite the injunction to remain separate from wider society, many families offer "Amish-style" dinners at their homes, and aggressively exploit the cachet that "Amish-made" gives to foods, craft objects, clothing, hex signs, and other souvenirs and products.

MEET THE AMISH

William Penn's "holy experiment" of religious tolerance, together with word of mouth about the region's fertile farmland, drew thousands of German-speaking immigrants to Pennsylvania in the early 18th century. They were lumped together as Pennsylvania "Dutch"—a corruption of *Deutsch,* or German. The most famous and long-lasting immigrants were the Mennonite sects, particularly the Amish, but the colonial period also saw a mixture of Scotch-Irish Presbyterians, French Protestants, English from Maryland, and Jews from Iberia settle the region. The ethnic makeup of this part of the country has changed very little since 1796.

The religious sects that make up the Pennsylvania Dutch are part of the Anabaptist strand of the Protestant Reformation. A Christian faith that emerged during the 16th century, Anabaptism believes in the literal interpretation of the Bible, in baptism only for people adult enough to choose this rite of transformation, and in remaining separate from larger society. Menno Simons, a Catholic priest from

Holland, joined the Anabaptists in 1536 and united the various groups, who became known after him as Mennonites. In 1693, Jacob Amman, a Mennonite bishop who found the Mennonite Church too tolerant of lax sinners, broke with his followers to establish the Old Order Amish church.

The three major sects in Lancaster County, the Amish, the Mennonites, and the Brethren as well as another sect, the Schwenkfelders, share many beliefs, including those concerning baptism, nonresistance, and basic Bible doctrine. They differ in matters of dress, use or avoidance of technology, literal interpretation of the Bible, and form of worship. For example, the Amish worship in home services, the Mennonites in churches. The Amish do not proselytize, while Mennonites have a strong tradition of missionary work.

Today, the Amish live in settlements in 20 states and in Ontario, Canada. In Lancaster County they center around Intercourse, Bird-in-Hand, and Lancaster; Mennonites center around Terre Hill and Martindale, a few miles to the northeast. The majority of Amish live and work on farms growing corn, wheat, tobacco (though most will not smoke it, and some won't grow it), and alfalfa. But an increasing number earn their incomes at other jobs, either in crafts, a sideline out of the home, or in the nonfarm economy of the region. They are a trilingual people, speaking Pennsylvania Dutch (essentially a dialect of German) at home, High German at worship services (the German of Luther's Bible translation), and English with members of the larger society.

The family is the most important social unit among the Amish, and large families with 7 to 10 children are the norm. Not surprisingly, the Amish population is growing—it has more than doubled since the 1970s—and more than half the Amish in Lancaster County are under the age of 18. You will see dozens of mailboxes marked with the names Zook, Stoltzfus, and Zinn—a testimony to the proliferation of extended families. The Old Testament–sounding practice of "shunning"—complete excommunication from family relations for Amish who marry outsiders or violate basic tenets—seems to have relaxed in recent decades. Even so, about 80% of the Amish end up spending their entire lives within the community—dying in the same house in which they were born.

Children attend school in one-room schoolhouses, built and maintained by the Amish, through the eighth grade. There are approximately 150 such schools in Lancaster County, and new ones are still being built. Amish schools teach only the basics; students have special exemptions from the standard state curriculum and are allowed to leave school at the age of 16 if they choose. There is no formal religious instruction in school; this is kept within the family.

To the visitor, the two most distinctive characteristics of the Amish are their clothing and their use of horse and buggies rather than cars. Both these features are linked to their religious beliefs. The distinctive clothing worn by about 35,000 "Plain People" in Lancaster County is meant to encourage humility and modesty as well as separation from larger society. Amish men and boys wear dark-colored suits, straight-cut coats without lapels, broadcloth trousers, suspenders, solid-colored shirts, black socks and shoes, and black or straw broad-brimmed hats. Men wait to grow beards until they are married, and do not grow mustaches. Women and girls wear modest, solid-colored dresses with long sleeves and long full skirts, covered by a cape and an apron. They never cut their hair, but gather it in a bun on the back of the head, concealed by a white prayer covering. Amish women do not wear jewelry or printed fabric. Single women in their teens and 20s wear black prayer coverings for church services. After marriage, a white covering is worn.

The Amish are reluctant to accept technology, which could weaken the family structure. Their horse-drawn buggies help keep them close to home by limiting distances that can be traveled in a day. Most use no electricity or telephones. As new ideas emerge, each district congregation of about 100 families evaluates them and decides what to accept and what to reject. The fundamental criterion is that an innovation should not jeopardize the simplicity of their lives and the strength of the family unit. The 1998 arrest of two young Amish for drug trafficking, while hardly an everyday occurrence, has prompted wide reexamination of how much "outside" exposure is too much.

There are a number of excellent books on the Amish way of life. The classic is John Hostetler's *Amish Society.* A more impassioned if ideological New Age take is *After the Fire: The Destruction of the Lancaster County Amish* by Randy-Michael Testa. Children's books include *Growing Up Amish* by Richard Ammon, and Raymond Bial's *Amish Home,* with wonderful photographs. Since Amish do not permit photography, any film depiction is bound to be compromised; this is unfortunately the case with *Witness* (1985), in which Harrison Ford goes undercover in the region as a Philadelphia cop.

2   Essentials

The heart of Pennsylvania Dutch Country centers on wedges of land to the east and (to a lesser extent) west of Lancaster. It is bordered on the west by the Susquehanna River, and to the south by the Maryland border and the Mason-Dixon line.

GETTING THERE

Lancaster County is 57 miles and 90 minutes west of Philadelphia, directly on Route 30. From the northeast, the easiest route is to take I-95 south from New York City onto the New Jersey Turnpike, then take Exit 6 onto the Pennsylvania Turnpike (I-76), following this to Exit 21 or 20 on either side of Lancaster. You'll still be about 10 miles north of the town: From Exit 21, you'll follow Route 222 into the city; from Exit 20, Route 72. Travel time is $2\frac{1}{4}$ hours, and tolls amount to $6 from New York City. From the south, follow I-83 north for 90 minutes from Baltimore, then head east on Route 30 from York into the county. If you're in Brandywine County or Longwood Gardens, you're only minutes from Amish farms in Gap, via Routes 41 and 741.

By train, Amtrak (☎ 800/872-7245) takes 70 minutes from 30th Street Station in Philadelphia to the great old Lancaster station, 53 McGovern Ave. (☎ 717/291-5080), 10 blocks from Penn Square. The fare is $16 one way, and eight trains run daily. Three buses run daily from Philadelphia ($13) and take 2 hours from the Convention Center Trailways Terminal to the Capitol Trailways Bus Terminal, 22 W. Clay St., in Lancaster (☎ 717/397-4861).

VISITOR INFORMATION

Before you set out you should get in touch with the **Pennsylvania Dutch Convention & Visitors Bureau,** 501 Greenfield Rd., Lancaster, PA 17601 (☎ 800/PA-DUTCH, ext. 2405, or 717/299-8901). The Web site **www.800padutchcountry. com** has links to most of the attractions listed below. The office itself is off the Route 30 bypass east of Lancaster, Greenfield Road exit. They provide an excellent detailed map and visitors' guide to the region, along with answers to specific questions and interests. They also have a wealth of brochures, direct telephone links to many local hotels, and a multi-image slide show, a good 14-minute overview of the county. The bureau is open daily 9am to 5pm except for major holidays.

The **Mennonite Information Center,** 2209 Millstream Rd., Lancaster 17602 (☎ 717/299-0954), has a lot of the same information but specializes in linking you with Mennonite guest houses and church worship. Every half hour they show a film featuring a Mennonite family at home on their farm. They will also provide Mennonite tour guides who will travel the back roads with you in your car to farm stands and local crafters and quilters—expect a dose of religious dialogue. The center is open Monday to Saturday 8am to 5pm.

Many towns such as Intercourse, Strasburg, and Lancaster have local information centers, and the **Exit 21 Tourist Information Center** (☎ 717/336-7482), on Route 272 just south of I-76, is open 10am to 2pm daily. It's next to **Zinn's Diner** (☎ 717/336-2210; www.zinnsdiner.com), which looks suspect with its statue of "Big Amos," batting cages, and miniature golf, but the menu, portions, and clientele are very typically Pennsylvania Dutch. The diner is open daily 6am to 11pm.

GETTING AROUND

Lancaster County's principal artery is Route 30, which runs from Philadelphia to York and Gettysburg. But beware: Major roads like Route 30 and Route 222 at Lancaster, and Route 340 from Intercourse to Lancaster, can be crowded, especially in the summer with the onslaught of bus tours. The 25,000 horse-drawn vehicles in the county tend to stick to quieter back roads, but some highways cannot be avoided. Traffic is much lighter in spring and autumn. And please be careful; the past few years have seen several horrible rear-end crashes in which tourists killed Amish families in buggies. If you're in a jam, you can reach AAA service at ☎ 717/397-6135.

Red Rose Transit Authority, 45 Erick St. (☎ 717/397-4246), serves Lancaster County, with a base fare of $1. The Route 13 bus leaves from the Old Courthouse on Duke Street in Lancaster and goes through Bird-in-Hand and Intercourse.

ORGANIZED TOURS

Amish Country Tours, Route 340 in Intercourse (☎ 717/768-3800), offers guided back-road bus and minivan tours during high season at 10:30am and 1, 2, and 2:30pm daily (10:30am and 2pm only on Sun), which last 2 hours and include stops at Amish farms and one-room schoolhouses. The fee is $16 for adults and $11 for children. A 4-hour version is offered Monday to Saturday at 9am and costs $25 for adults and $15 for children. Tours leave from Plain and Fancy Farm on Route 340 in Intercourse, and you can buy tickets at local hotels or at the farm. The Visitors Center can recommend several tours with private guides who will take you in their vans or ride in your car. They generally run in the range of $30 per hour with a 2-hour minimum. Among the best are **Brunswick Tours,** at the National Wax Museum, 2249 Lincoln Highway, Route 30 East (☎ 717/397-7451), and **Red Rose Excursions** (☎ 800/296-7337), which provides guides on Monday to Saturday 9am to 9pm to any Lancaster County location. The **Mennonite Information Center** (see above) can also provide local guides. Finally, **Lancaster Bicycle Touring,** 3 Colt Ridge Lane in Strasburg (☎ 717/396-0456), offers maps and an active schedule of tours.

A NOTE ON ETIQUETTE

There aren't too many settings in the world where an entire native population is a tourist attraction. Pennsylvania Dutch country is one of them, but that doesn't mean that the Amish are there as theme park characters. They are hardworking people leading busy lives. Your courtesy and respect is especially vital because their lifestyle is designed to remove them as much as possible from your 20th-century fast focus on visiting the area.

First, *do not trespass* onto Amish farms, homesteads, or schools in session. We've listed several settings where you can visit a working farm, take a carriage ride, or even stay on a farm. Although these are necessarily not operated by the most orthodox Amish, they are near enough in letter and spirit.

Second, if you're dealing with Pennsylvania Dutch directly, *don't even think of photographing them, and ask before taking any photographs at all.* The Amish have a strongly held belief that photographic images violate the biblical injunction against graven images and promote the sins of personal vanity and pride. Taking pictures of their land and animals is permissible; taking pictures of them is not.

Third, *watch the road.* What passes for moderate suburban speed in a car can be life-threatening in this area. Roads in Lancaster County have especially wide shoulders to accommodate horses, carriages, and farm tractors, and these are marked with red reflective triangles and lights at night. It's much preferable, if only to better see the sights, to slow down to Amish paces. And honking disturbs the horses. If you have the time, this is superb walking and bicycling country, punctuated by farm stands for refreshment and quiet conversations with Amish families.

3 Exploring Amish Country

LANCASTER

While Lancaster (pronounced *lank*-uh-stir) is still the most important city in the region, it hit its peak in the colonial era and as an early 20th-century urban beehive; this is reflected in the architecture and attractions. The basic street grid layout is copied from Philadelphia centers at Penn Square: the intersection of King (east-west) and Queen (north-south) streets. You won't see too many Plain People venturing into town anymore, since they can buy provisions and equipment more easily at regional stores, but they still sell at the **Central Market.** Erected just off Penn Square in 1889 but operating since the 1730s, this is the nation's oldest farmer's market, with more than 80 stalls. You can savor and select regional produce and foods, from sweet bologna and scrapple to breads, cheeses, egg noodles, shoofly pie (a concoction of molasses and sweet dough), and *schnitzel* or dried apple. The market is open Tuesday and Friday 6am to 4:30pm and Saturday 6am to 2pm.

Beside the Market is a **Heritage Center Museum** (☎ 717/299-6440) in the old City Hall, with a moderately interesting collection of Lancaster County crafts and historical artifacts. It's free and open Tuesday to Saturday 10am to 5pm; closed January to March. On the western edge of town is **Wheatland,** 1120 Marietta Ave. (Rte. 23; ☎ 717/392-8721), the gracious Federal mansion of the 15th U.S. president, James Buchanan. It features costumed guides and is open April to November, daily 10am to 4:15pm; admission is $5.50 for adults, $4.50 for seniors, $3.50 for students, and $1.75 for children 6 to 12.

Five miles south of town near Willow Street rests the 1719 **Hans Herr House,** 1849 Hans Herr Dr., off Route 222 (☎ 717/464-4438), the oldest building in the county. Now owned by the Lancaster Mennonite Historical Society, it's been restored and furnished to illustrate early Mennonite life, with a historic orchard and outdoor exhibit of agricultural tools. You can visit April to December, Monday to Saturday 9am to 4pm; admission is $4 for adults and $1.50 for children 7 to 12.

The eastern side of town peters into a welter of faux Amish attractions and amusements like Dutch Wonderland and Running Pump Mini-Golf, fast-food restaurants, and outlet stores on Route 30 near where Route 340 splits to the north toward Intercourse. The **Amish Farm & House,** 2395 Lincoln Highway (☎ **717/ 394-6185**), offers guided tours of a 10-room Amish house, with live animals and exhibits including a waterwheel outside. A Dutch Food Pavilion provides local treats. It's open June to September, daily 8:30am to 6pm; October to May, 8:30am to 4pm; admission is $5 for adults and $2.50 for children 5 to 11.

INTERCOURSE

Intercourse's suggestive name refers to the intersection of two old highways, the King's Highway (now Rte. 340 or Old Philadelphia Pike) and Newport Road (now Rte. 772). The King's Highway was used by the Conestoga wagons invented a few miles south—the unusually broad and deep wagons that became famous for transporting homesteaders all the way west to the Pacific.

The town, in the midst of the wedge of country east of Lancaster, is now the center of Amish life in the county. Unfortunately, there are about as many commercial attractions, from the schlocky to good quality, as there are places of genuine interest along Route 340. One thing not to miss is **The People's Place,** 3513 Old Philadelphia Pike (☎ **717/768-7171**), an interpretive center with a 30-minute documentary on the Amish, an excellent hands-on museum exhibit, an exhibit of antique quilts, and a bookshop/gallery. It's open April to October, Monday to Saturday 9:30am to 9pm; November to March, 9:30am to 5pm; admission is $5 for

---

The Bridges of Lancaster County

Forget about the Midwest and Clint Eastwood—Pennsylvania is the birthplace of the covered bridge, with some 1,500 built between the 1820s and 1900. Today 219 remain, mostly on small country roads, and you can actually drive (slowly!) through most of them. Lancaster County has the largest concentration, with 28, including one on the way to Paradise, a small village east of Lancaster City (see below). Bridges were covered to protect the trusses from the weather, and more are lost through floods and hurricanes than anything else. Does kissing inside one bring good luck? Well, they're protected from rain, and their one-lane width means a certain amount of privacy—not to mention those evocative wooden planks. The Lancaster County Visitors Bureau map indicates all covered bridge locations; call ☎ **800/723-8824,** extension 2435, for a copy.

Of the 28 county bridges, the following three are interesting and relatively easy to get to:

- **Hunsecker Bridge:** This is the largest covered bridge in the county, built in 1975 to replace the original, which was washed away in Hurricane Agnes. From Lancaster, drive 5 miles north on Route 272. After you pass Landis Valley Farm Museum, turn right on Hunsecker Road and drive 2 miles.
- **Paradise/Leaman Place Bridge:** This bridge is in the midst of Amish cornfields and farms. A truck that couldn't fit through the bridge put it out of commission in the 1980s, but it has been restored. Drive north 1 mile on Belmont Road from Route 30, just east of the center of Paradise.
- **Kauffman's Distillery Bridge:** Drive west on Route 772 from Manheim, and make a left onto West Sunhill Road. The bridge will be in front of you, along with horses grazing nearby.

adults and $2.50 for children. Of the commercial developments, try **Kitchen Kettle Village,** also on the Old Philadelphia Pike (Rte. 340; ☎ **800/732-3538** or 717/768-8261). You'll find 32 stores selling crafts from decoys to fudge here, grouped around Pat and Bob Burnley's 1954 jam and relish kitchen. Their Lapp Family Farms ice-cream store, with 20 all-natural flavors, is much more convenient than the original farm stand near New Holland.

EPHRATA

Ephrata, near Exit 21 off I-76 northeast of Lancaster, combines a historic 18th-century Moravian religious site with some pleasant country and the area's largest farmer's market and auction center. **Ephrata Cloister,** 632 W. Main St. (☎ **717/ 733-6600**), near the junction of Routes 272 and 322, was one of America's earliest communal societies, known for its *fraktur*—an ornate, medieval German lettering you'll see on inscribed pottery and official documents. Ten austere wooden 18th-century buildings (put together without nails) remain in a grassy park setting. The cloister is open Monday to Saturday 9am to 5pm and on Sunday noon to 5pm; admission is $5 for adults, $4 for seniors, and $3 for children 6 to 17. Saturday evenings in summer bring "Vorspiel" performances that feel like Bach live.

The main street of Ephrata is pleasant for strolling and includes an old rail car where the train line used to run. **Doneckers** (see below) has expanded from a single inn north of town into a farmer's market, gourmet restaurant, and shopping complex. On North State Street 4 miles north of town is the wonderful ✪ **Green Dragon Market & Auction** (☎ 717/738-1117), open Friday 6am to 7pm. Two auction houses make up the heart of Green Dragon—one for antiques and bric-a-brac, one for farm animals. You'll see goats and cows changing hands in the most elemental way, and children are allowed total petting access in the process. Summer brings fresh corn, fruit, and melons. A flea market and arcade have sprung up around the auctions, with plenty of cotton candy, clams on the half shell, and fresh corn.

LITITZ

Founded in 1756, this town, 6 miles north of Lancaster on Route 501, is one of the state's most charming. The cottage facades along East Main Street haven't changed much in the past 2 centuries. One of the most interesting is the **Linden Hall Academy,** founded in 1794 as the first school for girls in the United States. There are several Revolutionary War–era churches and buildings on the grounds. Lititz was once known as "the Pretzel Town," and across the street from Linden Hall is the **Julius Sturgis Pretzel House,** 219 E. Main St. (☎ **717/626-4354**). Founded in 1861, it's the oldest such bakery in the country. At the conclusion of the 20-minute guided tours you can try your own hand at rolling, twisting, and sprinkling the dough with coarse salt. Summer tours are given Monday to Saturday 9:30am to 4:30pm for $1.50; the store is open Sunday noon to 5pm.

At the junction of Route 501 and Main Street is **Wilbur Chocolate Company's Candy Americana Museum & Store,** 48 N. Broad St. (☎ 717/626-3249). Famous for its Wilbur buds, the factory offers a brief look at the process and history, with samples and sales in a country store atmosphere. Next door is the **Lititz Springs Park,** with a lovely duck-filled brook emanating from the 1756 spring, fields, and playgrounds, and the historic **General Sutter Inn.**

STRASBURG

This little town, named by French Huguenots, southeast of Lancaster on Route 896 is a paradise for rail buffs. Until the invention of the auto, railroads were the major

> ### ❷ Did You Know?
>
> - The Pennsylvania Dutch Country hosts three to four million visitors a year.
> - Lancaster was the nation's capital for a day, when Congress fled from Philadelphia on September 27, 1777.
> - In-line skating is considered an acceptable form of transportation among the Amish.

mode of fast transport, and Pennsylvania was a leader in building and servicing thousands of engines. The **Strasburg Rail Road** (☎ 717/687-7522), as it has since 1832, winds 9 miles of preserved track from Strasburg to Paradise and back; wooden coaches and a Victorian parlor car are pulled by an iron steam locomotive. It's on Route 741 east of town and is open April to October daily, and on weekends only November to March; the fare is $8 for adults and $4 for children. Other attractions include the **Railroad Museum of Pennsylvania** (☎ 717/687-8628), with dozens of stationary engines right across the street; the **National Toy Train Museum** (☎ 717/687-8976), on Paradise Lane off Route 741, with five huge push-button operating layouts; and **Choo Choo Barn** (☎ 717/687-7911), a 1,700-square-foot miniature county landscape filled with animated trains, figures, and activities such as parades and circuses. It recently linked up with the inevitable authorized Thomas Trackside Station store.

4 Especially for Kids

With the exception of beaches, Pennsylvania Dutch Country has everything for families, including rainy-day alternatives. In addition to the suggestions below, try the above-mentioned **Julius Sturgis Pretzel Museum** in Lititz, **People's Place** in Intercourse, and the various **railroad attractions** in Strasburg.

BUGGY RIDES

Driving for a couple of miles along a country lane in a horse-drawn carriage not only sounds irresistible but fits right in with the speed of Amish life. Of the half-dozen outfits, the most reliable are **Abe's Buggy Ride** (☎ 717/664-4888), Route 340, one-half mile east of the Route 896 junction, with 20-minute, 2-mile jaunts, and **Ed's Buggy Rides** (☎ 717/687-0360), on Route 896, 1½ miles south of Route 30 in Strasburg, with 3-mile rides leaving from the Red Caboose Motel. Jack Meyer of Abe's is slightly more expensive ($10 for adults and $5 for children versus $8 and $4); both are open Monday to Saturday until dusk. Jack Meyer, his wife, Dee Dee, and their six children are Mennonite and are open to inviting guests to their home for dinner; the meal is $15 for adults and $7.50 for children. Call them at ☎ 717/664-4888 for reservations or information.

DUTCH WONDERLAND

That ersatz castle (☎ 717/291-1888; www.dutchwonderland.com) you see heading east on 2249 Lincoln Highway (Rte. 30) out of Lancaster is the headquarters for a 44-acre amusement park with gardens and shows like high diving. There's a moderately wild roller coaster, but most of the 24 rides are easy to take for young families. Unlimited rides cost $20 for adults, $15 for children 3 to 5 and seniors. The park is open May to mid-October, with peak hours of 10am to 7pm daily during high season and weekends only in the spring and fall.

HERSHEY

Hershey is technically outside the county, 30 minutes northwest of Lancaster on Route 422, but the assembly of rides, amusements, and natural scenery in a storybook setting makes this sweetest town on earth worth the trip. Milton Hershey set up his town at the turn of the century to reflect his business and philanthropy; in 1998 alone the company poured $50 million into local attractions and lodgings. Start with the Web site (www.800hershey.com) or in person with **Hershey's Chocolate World,** Park Boulevard (☎ **717/534-4900**), a free tour that takes you from cacao beans to wrapped samples.

Hersheypark is a huge theme park at the junction of Routes 743 and 422 (☎ **800/HERSHEY** or 717/534-3090), with more than 50 rides and attractions including water rides, 4 roller coasters, 5 theaters with periodic music, and 20 kiddie rides. The park also includes the 11-acre **ZooAmerica,** with more than 200 animals native to this continent. Hersheypark is open mid-May to September, and all summer until 10pm Monday to Thursday, and until 11pm Friday to Sunday. Admission is $30 for adults (defined as ages 9–54), and $17 for children 3 to 8; admission to just ZooAmerica is much less.

The logical place to stay is the **Hershey Lodge,** West Chocolate Avenue and University Drive (☎ **717/534-8600**), with miniature golf, tennis courts, and its own movie theater. And if you're tempted to sneak away without the kids, Hershey does have superb gardens, 72 holes of championship golf, and the palacelike **Hotel Hershey** (☎ **717/533-2176**) up the mountain.

LANDIS VALLEY MUSEUM

Following Oregon Pike (Rte. 272) north from Lancaster for 5 miles, you'll come to Landis Valley, 2451 Kissel Hill Rd. (☎ **717/569-0401**), a large outdoor museum of Pennsylvania German culture, folk traditions, decorative arts, and language. George and Henry Landis established a small museum here to exhibit family heirlooms in the 1920s; when the state acquired it in the 1950s it mushroomed into a 21-building "living arts" complex. The costumed practitioners—clock makers and clergymen, tavern keepers and tinsmiths, storekeepers, teachers, printers, weavers, and farmers—are expert in their fields and generous with samples, which are also for sale in the shop. The museum is open Tuesday to Saturday 9am to 5pm and on Sunday noon to 5pm; admission is $6 for adults and $4 for children 6 to 17.

5 Shopping

There are three reasons to keep that credit card handy in Lancaster County. Quilts and other craft products unique to the area are sold in dozens of small stores and out of individual farms. The thrifty Pennsylvania Dutch have been keeping old furniture and objects in their barns and attics for 300 years, so antiquing is plentiful here. Fine pieces tend to migrate toward New Hope and Bucks County for resale, where you compete directly with dealers at the many fairs and shows. If antiques aren't your bag, a dozen outlet centers provide name-brand items at discounts of 30% to 70% along Route 30 east of Lancaster and in central Reading.

QUILTS

Quilts occupy a special place in Lancaster County. Quilting is a time for fun and socializing, but it also affords an opportunity for young girls to learn the values and expectations of Amish life from their elders. German immigrant women started the tradition of reworking strips of used fabric into an ever-expanding series of pleasant, folkloric designs. Popular designs include *Wedding Ring,* interlocking sets of four circles; the eight-pointed *Lone Star* radiating out with bursts of colors; *Sunshine and Shadow,* virtuoso displays of diamonded color; and herringbone *Log Cabin* squares with multicolored strips. More contemporary quilters have added free-form picture designs to these traditional patterns. The process is laborious and technically astounding—involving choosing, cutting, and affixing thousands of pieces of fabric, then filling in the design with intricate needlework patterns on the white "ground" that holds the layers of the quilt together. Expect to pay $500 or more for a good-quality quilt, and $25 and up for pot holders, bags, and throw pillows.

The People's Place in Intercourse, 3513 Old Philadelphia Pike, is a good place to start looking for quilts; their Old Country Store (☎ 717/768-7171) has a knowledgeable sales staff and excellent inventory. **The Quiltworks at Doneckers,** located at The Artworks complex, 100 N. State St. in Ephrata (open daily), has collected more than 100 traditional Amish and contemporary quilts from the area. Emma Witmer's mother was one of the first women to hang out a shingle to sell quilts 30 years ago, and she continues the business with more than 100 patterns at **Witmer Quilt Shop,** 1070 W. Main St. in New Holland (☎ 717/656-9526). The shop is open 8am to 6pm on Tuesday to Thursday and Saturday and until 8pm on Monday and Friday.

Most of the county's back roads will have simple signs indicating places where quilts are sold; selections tend to be more limited but prices are slightly lower. Rosa Stoltzfus operates **Hand Made Quilts** at 102 N. Ronks Rd. in Ronks (no telephone) out of a room in her Amish home in the middle of cornfields. **Hannah Stoltzfoos** has a similar selection on 216 Witmer Rd. (no telephone), just south of Route 340 near Smoketown.

OTHER CRAFTS

Amish and Mennonites have produced their own baskets, dolls, furniture, pillows, toys, wall hangings, and hex designs for centuries, and tourism has led to a healthy growth in their production. Much of this output is channeled into the stores lining Route 340 in Intercourse and Bird-in-Hand, such as the Amish-owned **Country Barn Quilts and Crafts,** 2808 Old Philadelphia Pike (no telephone; www.castyournet.com/quilts), and **Dutchland Quilt Patch,** 4361 Old Philadelphia Pike (☎ 800/411-03221 or 717/687-0534). The **Weathervane Shop** at Landis Valley Museum (see "Especially for Kids," above) has a fine collection produced by their own craftspeople, from tin and pottery to caned chairs. On the contemporary side, no one works harder than **The Artworks at Doneckers,** 100 N. State St., Ephrata (☎ 717/738-9503), which combines crafts with designer clothing and contemporary needs.

ANTIQUES

Two miles east of Exit 21 off I-76, Route 272 in Adamstown, just before it crosses into Berks County to the northeast, is the undisputed local center of Sunday fairs, with six or seven competitors within 5 miles. The largest are **Stoudt's Black Angus Antique Mall,** with more than 350 permanent dealers, and **Renninger's Antique and Collectors Market,** with 370 dealers. At Renninger's, check out stall 52½A for Tiffany glass, 89 for children's clothes, or 32A for antique linens and hooked rugs. For weekday stocks, try the 125 dealers at **White Horses Antiques Market,** 973 W. Main St. (Rte. 230; ☎ 717/653-6338), in Mount Joy, a pleasant town north of some covered bridges.

FARMER'S MARKETS

Most farmer's markets in Lancaster County today are stable shedlike buildings with stalls at which local farmers, butchers, and bakers vend their fruits and vegetables, eggs and cheese, baked goods and pastries, and meat products like turkey sausage and scrapple. Since farmers can only afford to get away once or twice a week (to sell at Germantown and at Reading Terminal in Philadelphia, for example), the more commercial markets tend to augment the local goods with gourmet stalls selling everything from deerskin to candy and souvenirs. And the low-ceilinged, air-conditioned spaces you'll find there lack the flavor of, say, **Central Market** in Lancaster (see "Lancaster," above), with its swirling fans and 1860 tiles and hitching posts, or Friday at **Green Dragon Market** (see "Ephrata," above), North State Street in Ephrata.

A notable contemporary market is the **Bird-in-Hand Farmers Market** at Route 340 and Maple Avenue (☎ 717/393-9674). It's open 8:30am to 5:30pm on Friday and Saturday year-round, as well as Wednesday and Thursday during the summer. They have homemade ice cream and are linked to Good 'n' Plenty Restaurant nearby. I also like **Meadowbrook Farmers Market** on Route 23 in Leola (☎ 717/656-2226), open Friday 8am to 7pm and Saturday 8am to 5pm, with 180 stands. **Root's Country Market and Auction,** just south of Manheim on Route 72, is a very complete market on Tuesday.

Among the dozens of roadside stands you'll see, try the homemade root beer, breads, and pies at **Countryside Stand,** on Stumptown Road. Take a right turn from Route 772 heading west out of Intercourse and follow Stumptown for one-half mile. **Fisher's Produce,** on Route 741 between Strasburg and Gap, sells baked goods along with fresh corn and melons in the summer.

OUTLET CENTERS

With over 120 stores, **Rockvale Square Outlets,** Route 30 East, is Lancaster's largest outlet mall. Jonathan Logan, Harvé Bernard, Evan-Picone, Nautica, Izod, Jockey, London Fog, and Bass Shoes are represented, with Oneida, Lenox, Dansk, and Pfaltzgraff for housewares. I prefer the newer **Tanger Outlet Center at Millstream,** 311 Outlet Drive, Route 30 East, for shops like Donna Karan, Ann Taylor, Reebok, J. Crew, Guess?, London Fog, and Brooks Brothers. It's slightly closer to Lancaster and more compact. The project also includes a 125-seat bakery and deli run by Miller's, of Miller's Smorgasbord fame. My children love the selection of leggings (and movies) at So Fun, Kids! Both complexes are open Monday to Saturday 9:30am to 9pm, and Sunday noon to 6pm.

Manufacturers Outlet Mall, at the junction of Exit 22 off the Pennsylvania Turnpike and Route 23 in Morgantown, has more than 50 stores, including Levi Strauss, Munsingweat, and Van Heusen, in an entirely enclosed mall with a food court. A Holiday Inn with indoor recreation for guests rounds out the premises. It's open Monday to Saturday 10am to 9pm and Sunday 11am to 5pm.

I don't have the space or the adjectives to fully describe the new "Outlet Capital of the World" in **Reading,** built out of former textile mills along the Schuylkill. Some 6 million shoppers are drawn here annually to 260 separate centers. It's 30 minutes from Lancaster or 75 from Philadelphia, via I-76 to I-176 north to Route 422. The two largest destinations are **Vanity Fair Factory Outlet Complex,** just west of the city in Wyomissing, and **Reading Outlet Center,** a multistory rehab in the heart of the city.

6 Where to Stay

From campsites and bedrooms in working Amish farms, to exquisite inns and luxury conference resorts, there's a wide variety of places to stay in Lancaster County. The higher the price level, the more advance notice is recommended; this also goes for some farms that only have two or three rooms.

HOTELS & RESORTS

✪ **Best Western Eden Resort Inn and Conference Center.** 222 Eden Rd., Rtes. 30 and 272, Lancaster, PA 17601. ☎ **800/528-1234** or 717/569-6444. Fax 717/569-4208. E-mail: eden@edenresort.com. 275 units. A/C TV TEL. $119 double; $185 suite. Up to two children under age 18 free in parents' room. 10% AAA/AARP discount. AE, CB, DC, DISC, MC, V. Free parking.

The amenities of this hotel are incongruous with the region; that is, they provide comforts you'd almost forgotten about, including plush, if bland, rooms (request poolside), coffeemakers, and a tropically landscaped atrium and pool. Some Club Suites include kitchenettes. The resort has two restaurants: Arthur's overlooks the atrium courtyard; Garfield's is in a more relaxed family setting. Facilities include two movie theaters, indoor and outdoor pools, tennis and basketball courts, shuffleboard, health club, and Jacuzzi.

✪ **The Inns at Doneckers.** 322 N. State St. (near junction of Rtes. 322 and 222), Ephrata, PA 17522. ☎ **717/738-9502.** Fax 717/738-9554. www.doneckers.com. 40 units in 4 houses. A/C TEL. $69–$105 double; $210 suite. Rates include full buffet breakfast. Rollaway bed $12; crib charge $10. AE, CB, DC, DISC, MC, V. Free parking.

Bill Donecker started building his customer service empire on Ephrata's north side in the early 1960s, beginning with a complex of stores featuring gifts, accessories, fashions, and collectibles. He's since added the fine Restaurant at Doneckers serving all meals (see "Where to Dine," below), the Artworks loft spaces for contemporary artists to work in and market their crafts, the Farmer's Market (see above), and four inns, spicing the mixture with frequent events and festivals. Of the four, the 1777 House, built by a clock-maker member of Ephrata Cloister, is the most stately and distinguished; I also like the Gerhart House for its small size and removal from main streets. All rooms have hand stenciling, local antiques and objects, and each site has a parlor with TV and library. The staff is outstanding; five rooms have Jacuzzis.

Willow Valley Family Resort. 2416 Willow St. Pike (3 miles south of Lancaster on Rte. 222), Lancaster, PA 17602. ☎ **800/444-1714** or 717/464-2711. www.willowvalley.com. E-mail: info@willowval.com. 352 units. A/C TV TEL. $125 double; add $17 per person for all-you-can-eat dinner and breakfast smorgasbord. Children under 6 free in parents' room; $5 for children above 6. Special packages available. AE, DC, MC, V. Free parking.

This Mennonite-owned resort (no drinking or smoking is permitted on premises) started out as a farm stand in 1943 and now combines modern comforts like a 9-hole golf course, lighted tennis courts, and indoor and outdoor pools with local touches such as a bakery specializing in apple dumplings and fresh-baked pies (shoofly, among others). A skylit atrium is home to two smorgasbords and a restaurant. Free bus tours of the Amish country are offered Monday to Saturday.

INNS

✪ **General Sutter Inn.** 14 E. Main St. (junction of Rtes. 501 and 772), Lititz, PA 17543. ☎ **717/626-2115.** Fax 717/626-0992. 16 units. A/C TV TEL. $78–$105 double; $105–$140 suite. Additional guests $3. AE, DISC, MC, V. Free parking.

The General Sutter Inn has operated continuously since 1764 at this charming intersection complete with fountain and overlooking verandas and marble-topped tables. While wings have been added and the lobby and restaurant renovated, most of the rooms occupy the original building and are decorated in solid Victorian style with folk art touches. There is a coffee shop for breakfast, lunch, and a notable Sunday brunch; the dining room offers a solid continental gourmet menu.

BED & BREAKFASTS

✪ **Alden House.** 62 E. Main St. (Rte. 772), Lititz, PA 17543. ☎ **800/584-0753** or 717/627-3363. 5 units. A/C TV TEL. $85–120 double and suite. MC, V. Free parking.

This 1850 brick Victorian house is at the center of the town's historic district. It was recently completely renovated, with private baths installed in all rooms. Two suites can be accessed either through the house or an outdoor spiral staircase to the second-floor porch—and they may soon renovate the carriage house for more quarters. The morning brings a full breakfast with waffles or cinnamon-chip pancakes served in the dining room or overlooking the charming gardens outside. Be warned: The two cats have the run of the house.

Churchtown Inn Bed and Breakfast. Main St. (Rte. 23), Churchtown, PA 17555. ☎ **800/637-4446** or 717/445-7794. Fax 717/445-0962. 8 units. A/C. $75–$135 double. Two-night weekend minimum. DISC, MC, V. Free parking. Children under 12 not accepted.

This completely restored 1735 stone inn has evening cocktail hours in the Victorian parlor, and the opulent breakfast is served in a glassed-in porch overlooking the garden. Guest rooms all have private bathrooms. You can arrange for dinner with nearby Mennonite or Amish families. Innkeeper Stuart Smith believes in camaraderie and good fellowship between guests. The Cornwall iron forge nearby, still functioning as a working historic site, supplied Revolutionary War troops with cannonballs and musket shot.

Historic Smithtown Inn. 900 W. Main St., Ephrata, PA 17522. ☎ **717/733-6094.** www.smithtoninn.com. 8 units. A/C TEL. $75–$125 double; $145–$175 suite. Rates include full breakfast. Children welcome: under 12, $20 additional; over 12, $35 additional. Two-night minimum on weekends and holidays. MC, V. Free parking.

This inn, near Ephrata Cloister, is a pre–Revolutionary War stagecoach stop whose owner, Dorothy Graybill, has restored each room, with canopy feather beds and collector-quality quilts, working fireplaces, sitting areas, and leather upholstered chairs. Triple-pane windows for quiet, magazines, and fresh flowers are typical thoughtful touches; the grounds have lovely gardens and a gazebo. There is a restaurant on the premises. Smoking is not permitted.

✪ **Strasburg Village Inn.** 1 W. Main St. (Rte. 896), Strasburg, PA 17579. ☎ **800/ 541-1055** or 717/687-0900. www.strasburg.com. 11 units. A/C TV TEL. $80–$140 double. AARP discount. Children $10 extra. AE, DISC, MC, V. Free parking.

You couldn't be more central than at this vaguely 18th-century inn set on 58 acres. Rooms are colonial-themed, with poster beds. There's a nice reading room upstairs, and a second-floor porch. A full breakfast is served in the adjacent ice-cream parlor. There is a restaurant on the premises as well as an outdoor pool.

MOTELS

✪ **Best Western Revere Inn and Suites.** Rte. 30, Paradise, PA 17562. ☎ **800/ 429-7383** or 717/687-7683. Fax 717/687-6141. www.revereinn.com 95 units. A/C TV TEL. $69–$99 double. Rates include continental breakfast. Children under 12 free in parents' room. AE, MC, V. Free parking.

Eight miles east of Lancaster, the original motor inn is built off a historic 1740 post house now used as a restaurant and lounge. A 1999 new main building houses 65 oversize rooms and suites. Recently installed room amenities include coffeemakers, hair dryers, and refrigerators, as well as fireplaces and Jacuzzis in suites. It's close to the outlet malls and has both indoor and outdoor pools.

Bird-in-Hand Family Inn & Restaurant. Rte. 340, Bird-in-Hand, PA 17505. ☎ **800/ 537-2535.** Fax 717/768-1117. www.bird-in-hand.com. 125 units. A/C TV TEL. $52–$91 double. Packages available. Children under 16 free in parents' room. AE, CB, DC, DISC, MC, V. Free parking.

This motel's location puts you directly into the heart of Amish country. It has a three-diamond AAA rating, and 70% of the guests are repeat customers or came through word of mouth. I prefer the back building, with rooms off an indoor hallway, to the front building's motel setup. The simple utilitarian rooms were recently renovated, with 25 new rooms and a pool and mini-golf added in 2000. The hotel restaurant serves all meals buffet style and is a popular stop for tours. Grandma Smucker's Bakery offers wet-bottom shoofly pie and apple dumplings. Facilities include indoor and outdoor pools, two lighted tennis courts, game room, playground, and free 2-hour bus tour of country roads.

Harvest Drive Family Motel & Restaurant. Box 498, Intercourse, PA 17534. ☎ **800/ 233-0176** or 717/768-7186. 50 units. A/C TV TEL. $75–$85 double. Two-night minimum on holiday weekends. $5 for children over 14 in parents' room. AE, MC, V. Free parking. Take Clearview Rd. south off Rte. 340 just west of Intercourse, then bear right to 3370 Harvest Dr.

Good farmland was converted to create this family owned motel, but it's surrounded by corn and alfalfa fields on a quiet back road next to the family farm. The motel building has rooms with one to three double beds and pleasant but utilitarian decor. The simple restaurant features Dutch home cooking all day, and there's a gift shop in the barn.

Mill Stream Country Inn. Rte. 896 (between Rtes. 30 and 340), Smoketown, PA 17576. ☎ **800/444-1714** or 717/299-0931. 52 units. A/C TV TEL. $79–$89 double. Two-night minimum on weekends. Children under 6 free in parents' room; additional $5 for ages 6–11. Package including breakfast adds $3 per person. AE, MC, V. Free parking.

Of the dozens of motor lodges in the vicinity, this more modest sister of Willow Valley Family Resort in Lancaster (see above) is one of the most popular, with three floors of simple rooms. The rear rooms are away from the road and overlook a stream. It's owned by Mennonites, and most rooms are nonsmoking. The restaurant serves breakfast and lunch (no alcohol).

Your Place Country Inn and Restaurant. 2133 Lincoln Hwy. East (Rte. 30), Lancaster, PA 17602. ☎ **717/393-3413.** Fax 717/393-2889. E-mail: YPCI@800padutch.com. 125 units. A/C TV TEL. $64–$139 double. Packages available. Children under 12 free in parents' room. AE, MC, V. Free parking.

Thomas Dommel's Your Place is very convenient to Lancaster, just east of the Route 30 bypass. More to the point, its back building overlooks beautiful Amish farmland, the decor is unusually charming, and the amenities—such as elevators for all second-floor guests and a large heated pool, open 9am to 9pm—are impeccably maintained. Most furnishings are handmade locally, from Amish quilts to branch wreaths, and all rooms have porches or balconies with wooden rocking chairs. The complex includes two buildings, each with several complimentary breakfast stations, an adjoining restaurant (you can get discount coupons for any meal there), and an extensive gift shop.

FARM VACATION BED & BREAKFASTS

What better way to get the flavor of Amish life than by staying with a farm family? The **Pennsylvania Dutch Country Convention & Visitors Bureau** (☎ **800/PA-DUTCH**) has a complete listing of about 40 working farms that take guests. Reservations are recommended since most offer only three to five rooms; expect simple lodgings, hall bathrooms, and filling, family-style breakfasts, all at less than motel rates. Dinners with the family are sometimes offered at an additional charge. You'll be able to chat with the women in the family (the men start and end their days with the sun) and get suggestions on local routes, walks, and crafts producers. One tip: Stay away from dairy and poultry farms if you have a sensitive nose!

Belmont View Bed & Breakfast. 5204 Newport Rd. (Rte. 772, 0.8 miles north of Rte. 30 west of Gap), Gap, PA 17527. ☎ **717/442-5269.** 2 units. A/C. $65–$75 double. Additional person 12 and up $9.

Although there are only two rooms, this is an unusually pretty place, with spectacular views of a 117-acre dairy farm and a 200-year-old ambience. Both rooms have antique beds and modern bathrooms, refrigerator, and microwave, and there's a common living room. No smoking or alcoholic beverages are allowed.

Green Acres Farm. 1382 Pinkerton Rd., Mount Joy, PA 17552. ☎ **717/653-4028.** Fax 717/653-2840. www.castyournet.com/GreenAcres. 7 units. A/C. $75 double. Additional child $5. Summer reservations are recommended. MC, V. Pinkerton Rd. is south of Rte. 772 just west of Mt. Joy's town center. You'll wind past Groff's Farm Restaurant and a creek before you get to the farm.

Wayne and Yvonne Miller can sleep 29 people in this 150-year-old farmhouse, with private bathrooms in all rooms. It's a corn and soybean farm but also offers hay wagon rides, farm pets, a playhouse, and swings and trampoline for kids. All rooms have one double or queen-sized bed plus bunk beds. There's no smoking, but you're allowed to bring your own alcohol.

Rayba Acres Farm. 183 Black Horse Rd., Paradise, PA 17562. ☎ **717/687-6729.** www.800padutch.com/rayba. E-mail: Rayba@aol.com. 9 units, 6 with private bathroom. A/C TEL. $45–$65 double. MC, V. From Paradise center, south from Rte. 30 onto Black Horse, follow 2 miles.

Ray and Reba Ranck offer clean, quiet rooms on a working fifth-generation dairy farm. (You're welcome to try milking.) Rooms are in a modernized 1863 farmhouse with a private entrance, or with private bathroom and TV in two motel-like units. A common room has a microwave and refrigerator. There's complimentary coffee in your room, but no smoking. Outside features a pretty pergola and gardens.

7 Where to Dine

While Ben Franklin would probably be staggered at the size of a modern Pennsylvania Dutch meal or smorgasbord, he'd recognize everything in it—you'll still find the same baked goods, meat and poultry, and fruits and vegetables that have been offered here since colonial times. The Amish way of life calls for substantial, wholesome, long-cooking dishes, rich in butter and cream. Don't look for crunchy vegetables—if they're not creamed, they're marinated or thoroughly boiled. The baked goods are renowned, and even the main courses tend to the sweet. Shoofly pie, a concoction of molasses and sweet dough (hence its attraction to flies), is probably the most famous. Decor tends to take a back seat to quantity and cost.

Included here are the most representative family style and smorgasbord dining spots, as well as restaurants that update local ingredients and traditions. Family style means that you'll be part of a group of 10 or 12, ushered to long tables and brought heaping platters of food, course after course. At a smorgasbord, you construct your own plate at central food stations, with unlimited refills. Prices are fixed per person at both.

And when looking for a meal, don't neglect the signs along the road, or "Community Event" listings in the Thursday "Weekend" section of the *Lancaster New Era*, for church or firehouse pancake breakfasts, corn roasts, or barbecue or game suppers. These generally charge a minimal amount for all the food you can eat and all the iced tea or soda you can drink; and they're great chances to meet the locals. You can also catch annual festivals, such as the rhubarb fair in Intercourse and the Sertoma Club's enormous chicken barbecues at Long's Park in Lancaster, both in May. The Dutch Food and Folk Fair is held in Bird-in-Hand each June.

FAMILY STYLE/SMORGASBORD

Good 'N' Plenty Restaurant. Rte. 896 between Rtes. 30 and 340, Smoketown. ☎ **717/ 394-7111.** Reservations not accepted. Adults $15.50, children $7.50 for ages 4–12, free for children under 4; tax included. MC, V. Mon–Sat 11:30am–8pm. PENNSYLVANIA DUTCH.

They've added the 500-seat Dutch Room to the original 110-seat farmhouse here. The location is very convenient, tables seat 10 to 12. Expect waits at peak dining hours. You can purchase baked goods and other gift items.

Miller's Smorgasbord. Rte. 30 at Ronks Rd., 5 miles east of Lancaster. ☎ **800/669-3568** or 717/687-6621. Reservations accepted. Dinner $18.75 adults, $5.95 for children 3–8, $8.95 for children 9–12; breakfast $8.95 adults, $4.95 for children 3–12; tax included. AE, DISC, MC, V. Open in summer Sun–Fri 8am–8pm, Sat 8am–9pm; weekend breakfast Nov–April. SMORGASBORD.

In 1929, Anna Miller prepared chicken and waffles for truckers while Enos Miller repaired their vehicles. For millions since then, Miller's has been the definitive Pennsylvania Dutch smorgasbord. Homemade chicken corn soup, slow-roasted carved beef, turkey, and ham, chicken pot pies, and a rich apple pie are just the tip of the iceberg. The breakfast smorgasbord offers made-to-order eggs and omelettes, along with local sausage and pastries. The health-conscious diner will find plenty of choices here too.

Plain & Fancy Farm & Dining Room. Rte. 340, 7 miles east of Lancaster, Bird-in-Hand, PA. ☎ **717/768-4400.** Reservations recommended. Adults $15.95, $5.95 for children 4–11; tax included. AE, DISC, MC, V. Mon–Sat 11:30am–8pm, Sun noon–7pm in summer. PENNSYLVANIA DUTCH.

This 40-year-old family style restaurant started out as a barn, as you can see by the posts that still support the front dining room. A back addition gives it a capacity of 260. The newly renovated complex now includes a village of craft shops and a bakery. Smoking is not permitted.

Shady Maple. Rte. 23, East Earl, PA (1 mile east of Blue Ball, at intersection with Rte. 897). ☎ **800/238-7365** or 717/354-8222. Reservations not accepted. Dinner $10.50–$15; breakfast $6–$7. Children 4–10 half-price; 10% discount for seniors. AE, DC, DISC, MC, V. Mon–Sat 5am–8pm. SMORGASBORD.

This is somewhat north of most of the attractions, but it does an enormous business, with waits of up to 30 minutes on Saturday for one of the 600 seats. Tourist buses have their own entrance and seating. The Pennsylvania Dutch buffet is a mind-boggling 140-feet long, with 46 salads, 14 vegetables, 8 meats, 8 breads, 27 desserts, and a make-your-own-sundae station. Breakfast includes everything you've ever imagined eating at that hour. There's a touristy gift shop and a fast food version (why bother?) downstairs. The cheapest days are Monday, Wednesday, and Friday; the dinner price of $11.49 includes tax, tip, and all nonalcoholic beverages. Smoking is not permitted.

MORE DINING CHOICES

Groff's Farm Restaurant. 650 Pinkerton Rd., Mount Joy, PA. ☎ **717/653-2048.** Reservations recommended. Family style all-inclusive meals $16–$26 or a la carte. CB, DC, DISC, MC, V. Dinner seatings Tues–Sat 4–8:30pm. AMERICAN/PENNSYLVANIA DUTCH.

At Groff's, the Pennsylvania Dutch cuisine's emphasis on fresh ingredients and rib-sticking heartiness is tempered by a lighter, contemporary touch. Betty Groff, who still personally greets every guest, was born Mennonite, and she and her husband Abe began cooking reinterpreted meals as a hobby for friends. Famed food writer James Beard came, tasted, and raved about the results, and the next 20 years saw an expansion of the facilities and the menu. The 1756 farmhouse overlooks meadows and ponds (and, as of 1998, an 18-hole Lynx-style golf course). The appetizer plate still features a famous cracker pudding, celery relish, and a sweet such as chocolate cake. Many a la carte dishes have been added recently, but most first-timers will prefer the family style entree of beef or chicken Stoltzfus, served creamed over little buttered pastry diamonds. Drinks are extremely reasonable, with an emphasis on local porters and lagers.

The Restaurant at Doneckers. 333 N. State St., Ephrata. ☎ **717/738-9501.** Reservations recommended. Main courses $17–$27. AE, CB, DC, DISC, MC, V. Mon–Sat 11am–10pm. CONTINENTAL.

This restaurant has one of the closest approaches to an urban cuisine in the area, mixing classic French dishes such as chateaubriand and veal Oscar with American techniques of infused oils, lighter ingredients, and healthier cooking. If you're in the mood for creamy sauces, though, they'll be more than happy to indulge you. Sorbet is served to cleanse the palate, and breads and desserts are baked on the premises daily. For lighter fare, there's a bistro-style menu offered from 4 to 10pm. The wine list is extensive.

Stoudt's Black Angus Restaurant and Brew Pub. Rte. 272, 1 mile north of Exit 21 from I-76, Adamstown, PA. ☎ **717/484-4385.** Reservations recommended. Main courses $14–$35; brew pub $6.50–$9.50. AE, CB, DC, MC, V. Mon–Thurs 4:30–11pm, Fri–Sat noon–11pm, Sun 11:30am–9pm. STEAKHOUSE/BREW PUB.

Stoudt's Golden Lager, Pilsner, and other German-style varieties are brewed here and make a perfect conclusion to the famed Sunday antiques market next door. The family has added a steakhouse specializing in aged prime beef, a clam and oyster bar, and an agreeable pub with Pennsylvania Dutch ham and chicken dishes alongside burgers, wursts, soups, and salads. The restaurant has a 1928 Packard in the lobby, and the pub offers country dancing Friday and Saturday. The complex also includes a medieval German-style village of shops and homes.

Appendix:
Philadelphia in Depth

At the beginning of the 21st century, Philadelphia is prepared to attract visitors with a new convention center, a major sports arena, improved theaters for the performing arts, a gleaming inner Center City core filled with new skyscrapers, and a revitalized cultural and street life.

The opening of the $522-million Pennsylvania Convention Center in 1993, only minutes from both historic and business districts, has been a tremendous boon for the city and its visitors. The Train Shed, Grand Hall, permanent art exhibition, and Ballroom are all breath-taking, and it's a miracle that the historic Reading Terminal facade and its street-level Market have been preserved.

The South Philadelphia sports complex of Veterans Stadium, the Spectrum, and Comcast–Spectacor's First Union Center combines all four professional teams—the Phillies in baseball, the Eagles in football, the Flyers in hockey, the 76ers in basketball—along with mass-market events, from rock shows to evangelical services and one-of-a-kind events. There's a bid to construct a new baseball stadium just east of the Convention Center, although the price tag and necessity of government subsidy to make it work may doom the concept.

No one can ignore that Philadelphia has finally entered the age of the superskyscraper, starting with the graceful One Liberty Place, an energetic and gracious 945-foot spire, and the 150,000-square-foot ground-level Shops at Liberty Place. A dozen more have joined it in the past decade.

The arts are finally attracting major projects and investment, particularly along South Broad Street, where the city is trying hard to establish a safe, convenient core zone for the performing arts. This "Avenue of the Arts," which has been called a "strung-out Lincoln Center," includes the Wilma Theater, the Pennsylvania Ballet's new home, the Arts Bank Theater at South Street, and the American Musical Theater Festival home a block away. The Philadelphia Orchestra and others will occupy a new $245 million Regional Performing Arts Center with a 2,500-seat concert hall opening at Spruce Street in the fall of 2002, leaving the Academy of Music free to book traveling orchestras and the like. The Rafael Vinoly design also incorporates a 650-seat recital theater to be the home for the Chamber Music Society, Concerto Soloists, and Philadanco, in a dramatic glass enclosure.

The city has developed a lively nightlife scene, with something for all tastes. The Delaware River waterfront's transformed piers and warehouses, and the Old City area, are major centers for clubs and bars and other entertainment.

1 History 101: The Philadelphia Story

Dateline

- **1644** William Penn born.
- **1682** The 300-ton *Welcome*, with William Penn aboard, lands at New Castle (Delaware). Penn rows up to the tongue of land between the Delaware and Schuylkill rivers and names the area Philadelphia.
- **1723** Sixteen-year-old Benjamin Franklin arrives by boat from Boston.
- **1748** First Philadelphia Assembly, an annual ball that in the 1990s still represents "making it" in social circles.
- **1752** Franklin performs his kite-flying experiment, proving that lightning is a form of electricity, in an open field that's now the location of St. Stephen's Episcopal Church at 10th and Ludlow streets.
- **1755** Franklin and others open America's first hospital at 8th and Spruce streets.
- **1765** Mass protests on news of English Parliament's passage of the Stamp Act, with boycotts of imports and office "strikes."
- **1774** First Continental Congress held in the State House (now Independence Hall).
- **1776** Declaration of Independence debated and adopted on July 2.
- **1777** General Howe, moving up from Maryland, takes Germantown on October 4 and occupies Philadelphia soon after; members of the Continental Congress flee, with the Liberty Bell, to Lancaster.

continues

Although Philadelphia may conjure up thoughts of William Penn and the Revolutionary period in the minds of most Americans, it was in fact a tiny group of Swedish settlers that first established a foothold here in the 1640s. Where does William Penn fit in? Well, his father had been an admiral and a courtier under Charles II of England. The king was in debt to Admiral Penn, and the younger Penn asked to collect the debt through a land grant on the west bank of the Delaware River, a grant that would eventually be named Pennsylvania, or "Penn's forest." Penn's Quaker religion, his anti-Anglicanism, and his contempt for authority had landed him in prison, and the chance for him to set up a Quaker utopia in the New World was too good to pass up. Since Swedish farmers owned most of the lower Delaware frontage, he settled upriver, where the Schuylkill met the Delaware, and named the settlement Philadelphia—City of Brotherly Love.

COLONIAL PHILADELPHIA When Philadelphia celebrated its 300th anniversary, in 1982, Penn's original city plan still adequately described the Center City, down to the public parks and the site for City Hall. Penn, who had learned the dangers of narrow streets and semi-detached wooden buildings from London's terrible 1666 fire, laid out the city along broad avenues and city blocks arranged in a grid. As he intended to treat Native Americans and fellow settlers equally, he planned no city walls or neighborhood borders. Front Street, naturally, faced the Delaware, as it still does, and parallel streets were numbered up to 24th Street and the Schuylkill. Streets running east to west were named after trees and plants (Sassafras became Race Street, for the horse-and-buggy contests run along it). To attract prospective investors, Penn promised bonus land grants in the "Liberties" (outlying countryside) to anyone who bought a city lot; he took one of the largest for himself, now Pennsbury Manor (26 miles north of town). The Colonies were in the business of attracting settlers in those days, and Penn found that he had to wear a variety of hats—those of financier, politician, religious leader, salesman, and manufacturer.

Homes and public buildings filled in the map, but slowly—that's why all the colonial row houses of Society Hill and Elfreth's Alley (continuously inhabited since the 1690s) are so near the Delaware docks. Thomas Jefferson, when he wrote the Declaration of Independence in 1776 almost a century later, could still say of his boardinghouse on 7th and Market that it was away from the city's noise and dirt!

Even later, the city spread west to Broad Street, around 1800. Philadelphia grew along the river and not west as Penn had planned. Southwark, to the south, and the Northern Liberties, to the north, housed the less affluent, including many sailors. These were Philadelphia's first slums—unpaved, without public services, filled with taverns set up in unofficial alleys, and populated by those without enough property or money to satisfy voting requirements.

Although Philadelphia was founded after Boston and New York, manufacturing, financial services, excellent docking facilities, and fine Pennsylvania farm produce soon propelled it into the first city of the colonies, and the largest English-speaking city in the British Empire after London. Despite its urban problems, colonial Philadelphia was a thriving city in virtually every way—boasting public hospitals and streetlights, cultural institutions and newspapers, stately Georgian architecture, imported tea and cloth, and, above all, commerce. The "triangle trade" shipping route between England, the Caribbean, and Philadelphia yielded estimated profits of 700% on each leg.

One man who will always be linked with Philadelphia is the multitalented, insatiably curious Benjamin Franklin. Inventor, printer, statesman, scientist, and diplomat, Franklin was an all-around genius. It sometimes seems that his hand appears in every aspect of the city worth exploring! Colonial homes were protected by his fire-insurance company; the post office at 3rd and Market streets became his grandson's printing shop; and the Free Library of Philadelphia, the University of Philadelphia, Pennsylvania Hospital at 8th and Spruce streets, and the American Philosophical Society all came into being thanks to Franklin's inspiration.

FROM REVOLUTION TO CIVIL WAR
Like most important Philadelphians, Franklin considered himself a loyal British subject until

- **1778** British troops abandon Philadelphia in June to advance on New York City.
- **1780** Pennsylvania becomes the first state to abolish slavery, calling for general emancipation by 1827.
- **1787** Constitutional Convention meets in the State House.
- **1790–1800** Philadelphia is the capital of the United States.
- **1805** First permanent bridge spans the Schuylkill, connecting the city to Pennsylvania's rich farmlands.
- **1812–15** English blockade of international trade shuts down Philadelphia shipping, though its Navy Yard outfits most of the U.S. Navy.
- **1820s** Transformation of the seaport city into America's first major industrial city.
- **1832** Railroad to Germantown built.
- **1854** Consolidation Act expands Philadelphia tremendously, creating a city of 154 square miles.
- **1860** First baseball game played in Philadelphia.
- **1860–90** Rise of the saloon (6,000 by 1887) as a focus of German and Irish immigrant society.
- **1861** Civil War begins. The city elite, wealthy through Southern trade, oppose the war, despite strong popular antislavery sentiment.
- **1862** Philadelphia is an armed camp with tremendous demand for locomotives, uniforms, and supplies manufactured here.
- **1863** Battle of Gettysburg in July saves city from Confederate attack but brings loss of thousands of local troops.

continues

- **1865** Antiblack riots culminate in an ordinance forbidding blacks to ride in the horsecars; Jim Crow laws persist until the 1870s. Lincoln's body lies in state in Independence Hall on its way to burial in Illinois.
- **1866–72** Chestnut Street bridge spurs the quick development of West Philadelphia; University of Pennsylvania moves there in 1872.
- **1874** Groundbreaking on July 4 for both City Hall and the Centennial Exhibition in Fairmount Park.
- **1876** First public demonstration of the telephone and other wonders of the age at the Centennial Exhibition.
- **1878** First use of electric lighting for houses and offices; first Bell telephone exchange at 400 Chestnut St.
- **1884** Mayor King appoints the city's first African American police officer.
- **1890** Drexel University founded at 32nd and Chestnut streets.
- **1892** First trolley car, on Catharine and Bainbridge streets.
- **1893** Reading Terminal built for Reading Railroad.
- **1899** First motorcar arrives in Philadelphia, brought from France by a local merchant.
- **1900** More people own houses in Philadelphia than in any other city in the world; a middle-class house with seven rooms rents for $15 per month. City's population is over 1.25 million.
- **1901** First Mummer's Parade marches up Broad Street on New Year's Day.
- **1910** First airplane flight from New York City to Philadelphia.

continues

well into the 1770s, though he and the other colonists were increasingly subject to what they considered capricious English policy. Colonists here weren't as radical as those in New England, but tremendous political debate erupted after Lexington and Concord and the meeting of the First and Second Continental Congresses. Moderates—wealthy citizens with friends and relatives in England—held out as long as they could. But with the April 1776 decision in Independence Hall to consider drafting a declaration of independence, revolutionary fervor gained a momentum that would become unstoppable.

"These are the times that try men's souls," wrote Thomas Paine—and they certainly were for Philadelphians, who had much to lose in a war with Britain. Thomas Jefferson and John Adams talked over the situation with George Washington, Robert Morris, and other delegates at City Tavern by night and at Carpenter's Hall and Independence Hall by day. On July 2, their declaration was passed by the general Congress; on July 8, it was read to a crowd of 8,000, which tumultuously approved.

Your visit to Independence National Historical Park will fill you in on the Revolution's effect on the City of Brotherly Love. Of the major colonial cities, Philadelphia had the fewest defenses. The war came to the city itself because British troops occupied patriot homes during the harsh winter of 1777 to 1778. Woodford, a country mansion in what is now Fairmount Park, was hosting Tory balls while Washington's troops drilled and shivered at Valley Forge. Washington's attempt to crack the British line at Germantown ended in a confused retreat. The city later greatly benefited from the British departure and the Peace of Paris (1783), which ended the war.

Problems with the new federal government brought a Constitutional Convention to Philadelphia in 1787. This body crafted the Constitution that the United States still follows. In the years between the ratification of the Constitution and the Civil War, the city prospered. For 10 of these years, 1790 to 1800, the U.S. government operated here while the District of Columbia was still marshland. George Washington lived in an executive mansion where the Liberty Bell is now; the Supreme Court met in Old City Hall; Congress met in Congress Hall;

and everybody met at City Tavern for balls and festivals.

After the capital moved to Washington, Philadelphia retained the federal charter to mint money, build ships, and produce weapons. The transportation revolution that made America's growth possible was fueled by the city's shipyards, ironworks, and locomotive works. Philadelphia vied with Baltimore and New York City for transport routes to agricultural production inland. New York eventually won out as a shipper, thanks to its natural harbor and the Erie Canal. Philadelphia, however, was the hands-down winner in becoming America's premier manufacturing city, and it ranked even with New York in finance. During the Civil War, Philadelphia's manufacturers weren't above supplying both Yankees and Confederates with guns and rail equipment. Fortunately for Philadelphians, the Southern offensive met with bloody defeat at Gettysburg before reaching the city. With the end of the Civil War in 1865, port activity rebounded, as Southern cotton was spun and shipped from city textile looms.

Philadelphia became the natural site for the first world's fair held on American soil: the Centennial Exposition. It's hard to imagine the excitement that filled Fairmount Park, with 200 pavilions and displays. There's a scale model in Memorial Hall, one of the few surviving structures in the park; it gives a good idea of how seriously the United States took this show of power and prestige. University City in West Philadelphia saw the establishment of campuses for Drexel University and the University of Pennsylvania, and public transport lines connected all the neighborhoods of the city.

INTO THE 21ST CENTURY Philadelphia's history has been checkered in the 20th century, and the city enters the 21st century with mixed fortunes. A new convention center, major sports arena, improved theaters for the performing arts, and selective Center City reclamation balance out many of the problems that plague urban centers throughout America—homelessness, drugs, crime, and inadequate resources for public services. Philadelphia's biggest challenge over the next few years is to create jobs through tourism in the urban core and to increase visitors from the current 5 million a year to 10 or even 15 million. This concept translates into investments that improve the city's attractiveness and quality of life for visitors.

- **1913** Women's suffrage marches.
- **1917–18** Philadelphia is a beehive of activity in World War I, with the world's largest ship-construction plant.
- **1922–26** Delaware River Bridge connects Philadelphia and New Jersey; ferry trade persists until the 1950s.
- **1926** Jack Dempsey–Gene Tunney prizefight, movie "talkies," and electric refrigerator all featured at the Sesquicentennial Exposition.
- **1928** Philadelphia Museum of Art opens.
- **1940** Stokowski and the Philadelphia Orchestra record the soundtrack to Walt Disney's *Fantasia.*
- **1944** Due to World War II labor shortages, African American workers make substantial gains, despite union opposition.
- **1946** First computer, ENIAC, developed at University of Pennsylvania for the U.S. Army.
- **1950** Restoration and renovation of Society Hill begins.
- **1950s** Pop singing stars like Fabian, Frankie Avalon, and Chubby Checker emerge from Philadelphia neighborhoods.
- **1951** National Park Service establishes Independence National Historical Park.
- **1954** Philadelphia International Airport (domestic flights since 1940) dedicated.
- **1960** Dr. John Gibbons invents heart-lung machine at Jefferson Medical Center.
- **1964** Society Hill Towers, symbolic of old and new in the neighborhood, constructed to design of I. M. Pei.

continues

- **1964–1967** Eruption of racial disturbances, said to have been aggravated by Police Commissioner Frank Rizzo, who would serve as mayor from 1972 to 1980.
- **1974** Chestnut Street urban mall project built; seen as a failure by 1980 and reversed by the late 1990s.
- **1976** Liberty Bell moved from Congress Hall to the new Independence Mall; America's bicentennial celebrated.
- **1982** Philadelphia's 300th anniversary celebration. Tall ships line Penn's Landing.
- **1984–92** Administration of Wilson Goode, Philadelphia's first African American mayor, tainted by the 1985 MOVE bombing of a city block in West Philadelphia in the name of law and order.
- **1987** Bicentennial of U.S. Constitution celebrated at Independence Hall.
- **1993** Pennsylvania Convention Center opened with celebration and speech by President Bill Clinton.
- **1994** Reading Terminal Train Shed at Convention Center reopens; City Hall reemerges from scaffolding.
- **1997** National Park Service announces plan to remake Independence Mall and build National Constitution Center.
- **2000** Republican National Convention held.

If you go to the top of City Hall and look around, you'll see a panorama of factories, the old Navy Yard, warehouses, and docks—virtually all shuttered or turned to other uses. You'll also see block after block of row houses built a century ago by new immigrants, whose more successful descendants have left for greener pastures. In terms of urban homeowners—an area in which Philadelphia led the world for decades—there have been good reasons for successful citizens to leave for more pleasant suburban areas, although the urban-renewal projects at Society Hill, the boom period of expansion along the northeast and Parkway, and the establishment of Independence National Historical Park have combated the migration somewhat. Although port and petroleum-refining operations bolstered its position as an industrial center until the 1980s, manufacturing in general has moved out of the city and the region. Half of the city's workforce was once employed in manufacturing—a figure that has shrunk to 9% today. As industry has moved out, the city has tried to develop its service businesses.

The opening of the $522 million Pennsylvania Convention Center in 1993, only minutes from both historic and business districts, has been a tremendous boon for the city. The hundreds of conventions, millions of visitors, and billions of dollars projected in revenues from the center over the next decade are crucial, after some lean years, to keeping afloat the restaurants, hotels, sights, and entertainment we recommend. And there's appreciably more nightlife and sidewalk safety.

Pennsylvania Convention Center dollars also tie into great infrastructure improvements, with lots of repaving, new lighting, and curb cuts along lower Market Street, Columbus Boulevard and the waterfront, and the Italian Market.

A dark blue "Direction Philadelphia" signage program that's clear and coherent can guide you on and off a reconstructed expressway system, now connecting I-95 and I-76 (along the two rivers), with plenty of easy entrances and exits. The burgeoning airport, now a USAirways hub, is undergoing a $1 billion capital improvement, with new terminals, a new hotel connected to Terminal B, a state-of-the-art shopping mall, and new runways. The nation's second busiest Amtrak stop, 30th Street Station, has completed a $100 million restoration, with a new bakery, charcuterie, and rejuvenated services like bookstores. Hot areas in town have radiated out from the city core. The Delaware River waterfront's piers and warehouses have been transformed into frenetic pleasure domes: bars, clubs, sports palaces, and beach resorts. On the other side, the once blue-collar terraced streets of Manayunk along the Schuylkill

> *Of all goodly villages, the very goodliest, probably, in the world; the very*
> *largest, and flattest, and smoothest. . . . The absence of the note of the perpet-*
> *ual perpendicular, the New York, the Chicago note, . . . seemed to symbolize*
> *exactly the principle of indefinite level extension and to offer, refreshingly, a*
> *challenge . . . to absolute centrifugal motion.*
> —Henry James, *The American Scene* (1905)

River host fashion—from high to funky—cuisine, and shopping, along with a new farmer's market.

Corporate headquarters punctuate the northwest quadrant of Center City, and conventions throng Market Street east of City Hall. Major corporate headquarters in Philadelphia now include SmithKline Beecham (pharmaceuticals); Aramark (food and hospitality); Advanta (financial services); and CIGNA (insurance). With all those universities to train entrepreneurs and scientists, plenty of Internet and biogenetic firms are sprouting like Kennett Square mushrooms, with local financing.

But tourism and hospitality are even more critical for revenue replacement, with coordination of public and private efforts in Center City under recent mayors Ed Rendell and John Street. The city, now done with the various historic bicentennials, looks toward the 21st century with a keen sense that visitors are the key to a vibrant urban core.

Major projects being implemented or on the drawing board include:

- **Improvement of Independence Mall.** To make the Liberty Bell's current home and the stretch of city cleared north of it less of an eyesore, the city and the National Park Service are carrying a $130 million renovation plan. The Bell will be moved into a larger new pavilion near the corner of 6th and Chestnut streets, along with an interpretive center and a new National Constitution Center, all with beautiful walkways and landscaping. The park has also started making itself sexier, with initiatives like a revamped City Tavern and the new "Lights of Liberty" sound-and-light show.

- **Development of the waterfront at Penn's Landing.** The persistent dream is coming close to reality, with a 300,000-square foot complex including an IMAX theater, multiscreen cinema, more commercial and cultural attractions, and a 350-room Hyatt hotel.

- **Increased hotel capacity in Center City.** 5,000 hotel beds have been added in the last 5 years, most within walking distance of the Convention Center and historic district. The new 600-room Loews Hotel in the classic PSFS skyscraper; more Marriott rooms near and attached to the Convention Center; and the stunning Ritz Carlton rehab of an old bank are all noteworthy. Rittenhouse Square is witnessing a rehab Sheraton, an expanded Warwick Hotel, and a new Sofitel.

- **Landscaping and gardens around the Art Museum and the Schuylkill.** The gardens are now being revitalized by the Pennsylvania Horticultural Society, and the 19th-century Waterworks will be modernized and refashioned into a restaurant with one of the city's most spectacular views.

- **Redevelopment of West Philadelphia.** Energetic management at the University of Pennsylvania has brought major retail, cinemas, a wonderful Inn at Penn, and mixed use around the campus.

A Portrait of the Philadelphians

The first European settlers in Philadelphia, arriving in the 1640s, were from Sweden. (You can see models of the two ships that brought them over in Gloria Dei Church.) Unusual tolerance, epitomized by the Quakers, helped lead to two separate strains of immigration during the first centuries of the city's history. One was made up of large European families drawn to the new world by the promise of cheap farmland—English, Scottish, Sephardic Jews, and Germans (*Deutsch* in German—hence the term *Pennsylvania Dutch*). The other group included thousands of London-based craftsmen, servants, and sailors, including London-based French Huguenots. German immigrants specialized in linen and wool weaving and ironwork; French Huguenots in fine silver; and all immigrants farmed and built ships.

In general the quality of life was high, despite a disastrous 1793 yellow fever epidemic. Franklin's legacy flourished. The resources of the Library Company became available to the public, and both men and women received "modern" educations—that is, more emphasis on accounting and less on classics. The 1834 Free School Act established a democratic public school system. Private academies, such as Germantown Friends School and Friends Select, are still going strong today. Culture flourished—the Walnut Street Theater, founded in 1809, is the oldest American theater still in constant use, and the Musical Fund Hall at 808 Locust St. (now apartments) hosted operas, symphony orchestras, and chamber ensembles. The 1805 Pennsylvania Academy of Fine Arts, now at Broad and Cherry streets, taught such painters as Washington Allston and the younger Peales. Charles Willson Peale, the eccentric patriarch, set up the first American museum in the Long Hall of Independence Hall; its exhibits included a portrait gallery and the first lifelike arrangements of full-size stuffed animals.

The 19th century saw the arrival of English commoners fleeing the industrialization of their countryside in the 1820s; Irish escaping from the 1840s potato famine; and waves of Germans and central Europeans seeking peace and stability during the 1870s. From the 1880s to the 1920s, Russians and Jews from eastern Europe, Italians, and free blacks from the American South all migrated in record numbers to the city. In recent years, Asian and Hispanic immigrants have filled in the gap left by the suburban exodus of earlier groups, creating a more multicultural Philadelphia than ever before.

2 Recommended Books & Films

BOOKS

HISTORY It is impossible to read about the transition from the Colonies to the United States and the first 50 years of independence without learning about Philadelphia. Christopher and James Collier, two brothers—one a writer on jazz, the other a history professor—have an intensely novelistic and readable summary of the 1787 Constitutional Convention with *Decision in Philadelphia* (Ballantine, reissued 1987). Carl Bridenbaugh's *Rebels and*

Gentlemen (Oxford University Press, 1965) is a good summary of events leading up to independence. Catherine Drinker Bowen's *Miracle at Philadelphia* (Atlantic–Little, Brown, 1960) is a vivid retelling of the 1787 Constitutional Convention. A Bancroft Prize–winner is Thomas Doeflinger's *A Vigorous Spirit of Enterprise: Merchants and Economic Development in Revolutionary Philadelphia* (University of North Carolina Press, 1986).

E. Digby Baltzell's *Puritan Boston and Quaker Philadelphia* (Free Press, 1960) is a thoughtful and amusing comparison between these two preeminent colonial cities, explaining why their histories turned out so differently—in particular, why the emphasis placed on keeping a civil society dampened outstanding individual achievements in Philadelphia. Baltzell's first classic effort here was *Philadelphia Gentlemen: The Making of a National Upper Class* (Free Press, 1958).

The transformation from ideal seaport to ideal manufacturing city is covered in *Civil War Issues in Philadelphia 1956–1965* by William Dusinberre (University of Pennsylvania Press, 1965). *Magee's Illustrated Guide of Philadelphia and the Centennial Exhibition* (1876) is a treat of civic pride, with wonderful lithographs throughout.

W.E.B. Du Bois's *The Philadelphia Negro* (University of Pennsylvania Press, 1899) is a classic analysis of racism and its social effects in the North since the Civil War. Jean Seder has edited *Voices of Another Time: 3 Memories* (Institute for the Study of Human Issues, 1985), three oral histories of Afro-American women who were born in the South but who spent their lives in Philadelphia, complete with recipes, cures, and proverbs.

Edwin Wolf II's *Philadelphia: Portrait of an American City* (Stackpole Books, 1975) is one of the more engaging histories, with beautiful and appropriate illustrations. The building of the Benjamin Franklin Parkway, a swath like the Champs Elysees in the midst of a colonial grid, is covered in David Bruce Brownlee's *Building the City Beautiful* (Philadelphia Museum of Art catalog, 1989).

From the moment the superb mayor, Ed Rendell, took office, he allowed Buzz Bissinger complete behind-the-scenes access to his thoughts and meetings. The essential recent history of the city is being played out as sketched by this experience, as recorded in Bissinger's *A Prayer for the City: The True Story of a Mayor and Five Heroes in a Race Against Time* (Random House, 1998).

THE ARTS   There is a surfeit of material on Philadelphia's architecture; try *Philadelphia's Architecture* (MIT Press, 1984), which goes into environmental issues as well, or the more coffee-table *An Architectural Guidebook to Philadelphia* (Gibbs Smith, 1999) by Frances Morrone and James Iska. Roslyn Brenner's *Philadelphia's Outdoor Art: A Walking Tour* (Camino Books, 1987) has a makeshift text but contains good photography.

Old Philadelphia in Early Photographs, 1839–1914 (Dover, 1976) by Robert F. Looney is a superb photographic history. Robert Llewellyn has also assembled a sensitive book of more recent photographs in *Philadelphia* (Thomasson-Grant, 1986).

Philadelphia is the fount of the classical art tradition as translated to America, and the Philadelphia Academy of Fine Art has published various catalogs detailing this for sculpture, painting, and textiles.

FICTION   Try Pete Dexter's *God's Pocket* (Warner Books, 1990) for a gritty contemporary look at the city by a former newspaper reporter turned big-league novelist and scriptwriter. Lisa Scottoline's various fast-read thrillers from Harper involving snappy women lawyers are set in Philadelphia but not really evocative of it. Donald Zochert's *Murder in the Hellfire Club* (Holt, Rinehart & Winston, 1978) is an amusing historical mystery, with Colonists framed in London of the 1770s and Ben Franklin on hand to solve the case.

TRAVEL   If you find old guidebooks fascinating, consult *Magee's Illustrated Guide* for the 1987 city (see "History," above) or the *Federal Writer's Project Guide to Philadelphia* (1937; Scholar Press reprint 1978). The playwright Christopher Morley was witty and perceptive and a selection from his *Travels in Philadelphia* has been published as *Christopher Morley's Philadelphia* (Fordham University Press, 1990).

BIOGRAPHY   John Lukacs's *Philadelphia: Patricians & Philistines 1900–1950* (Farrar, Straus & Giroux, 1981) is a charming, slightly offbeat collection of profiles of seven colorful figures who flourished during this period and have faded into obscurity since. It opens and concludes with wonderful ruminations on what made Philadelphia so different—its geniality and datedness.

One of those chronicled by Lukacs, Albert C. Barnes of the legendary Barnes Foundation and its French Impressionist masterworks, is further examined in Howard Greenfield's *The Devil and Dr. Barnes: A Portrait of an American Art Collector* (Viking, 1987).

The Kelly family—John, Jack, and Grace—receives a hagiographic and slightly dated treatment in John McCallum's *That Kelly Family* (A.S. Barnes, 1957). Another "immigrant made good" story, although more measured, is the biography of former Mayor Frank Rizzo, Joseph Daughen's *The Cop Who Would Be King* (Little, Brown, 1977).

FOR KIDS   See the box "A Little Book Learnin'" in chapter 2 for a description of books kids might enjoy reading before the trip. Katherine Milhous's *Through These Arches: The Story of Independence Hall* (Lippincott, 1965) tells the history of the famous site. In *The Treasure Code* by Milton Dank (Delacorte, 1985), six junior-high students search for a dragonring, a valuable treasure buried somewhere in the city; included are lots of clues and comments. Elizabeth Gray Vining's *The Taken Girl* (Viking, 1972) is the story of an orphan girl who becomes involved in the antislavery movement. Susan Lee's *The Fall of the Quaker City* (Children's Press, 1975), is about a Quaker family's decision to support the American Revolution. John Loeper's *The House on Spruce Street* (Athenaeum, 1984) concentrates on Philadelphia history during the restoring of a grand old Society Hill house. For younger readers there's Elvajeen Hall's *Today in Old Philadelphia* (Children's Press, 1975), and Robert Lawson's classic is *Ben and Me* (Little, Brown, 1998 ed.).

FILMS

The classic *Philadelphia Story* (1940), adapted from a play by Philip Barry, involves a headstrong Philadelphia socialite who learns to find love with her first husband, on the eve of her wedding to a very proper second husband. The film stars Katherine Hepburn, Cary Grant, and Jimmy Stewart (who won a Best Actor Oscar). Films of the 1970s and 1980s include Sylvester Stallone's *Rocky* (1976), in which the young Kensington (*not* South Philadelphia) boxer searching for a future jogs through the Italian Market and up the Art Museum steps; you can do the same and meet the bronze commemorative statue, in one of those art-meets-life moments. In *Blow Out* (1983), John Travolta as a sound technician hears mysterious noises when a presidential candidate's car runs off a Wissahickon Creek bridge. In *Witness* (1985), Harrison Ford plays a detective forced to go undercover in Amish country.

The city has seen a spate of films made here in the 1990s, attracted by the wide-open spaces and friendly culture. Notably, Tom Hanks and Denzel Washington star in Jonathan Demme's 1993 tearjerker and Oscar winner (Hanks for acting, Bruce Springsteen for best song) *Philadelphia,* in which a young lawyer with AIDS battles discrimination, from City Hall to Famous Deli. City Hall and Eastern State Penitentiary are reimagined in *Twelve Monkeys* (1995), a grim post-apocalyptic thriller with Bruce Willis. The young director M. Night Shyamalan of *The Sixth Sense* (1999), set in Philadelphia, lives and frequently works in the city.

Index

See also Accommodations and Restaurant indexes, below.

GENERAL INDEX

A World of Options, 16

Academy of Music, 150, 172–173

Academy of Natural Sciences, 114–116

Access-Able Travel Source, 16

ACT UP/Philadelphia, 17

Advance Purchase Excursion (APEX) fares, 25

Afro-American Historical and Cultural Museum, 116

Airlines
  contact numbers, 19, 25
  fares, 19–21, 25
  Visit USA discounts, 26

Airport
  accommodations near, 60–61
  getting downtown from, 30–31
  layout, 30

American Association of Retired Persons (AARP), 18

American Automobile Association (AAA), 27

American cuisine, 64

American Express, 38

American Music Theater Festival, 12

American Swedish Historical Museum, 15, 116

Amish lifestyle, 206–208

Amtrak
  accommodations for disabled travelers, 17
  information for foreign visitors, 26
  service to Philadelphia, 21–22

Annenberg Center, 173

Antiques shopping, 155–156, 215

Aquariums, 121–122

Arch Street Meeting House, 109

Architectural landmarks, 106–108, 139

Art galleries, 2, 156–157

Art museums, 3, 15, 103–105, 118–119, 152

Associated Services for the Blind, 17

Association of Bed and Breakfasts in Philadelphia, Valley Forge, and Brandywine, 43

Athenaeum of Philadelphia, 113

ATMs, 10

Atwater Kent Museum, 116

Audubon Wildlife Sanctuary (Audubon), 196

Auto clubs, 27

Baby-sitters, 38

Balch Institute, 116

Barnes Foundation Gallery, 2

Bars, 181–183

Baseball, 132

Basketball, 132

Bed-and-breakfasts, 5, 43, 218, 220

Belmont Mansion, 124

Ben and Me, 18

Ben FrankLine, 36

Benjamin Franklin Bridge, 106–107

Benjamin Franklin Parkway, 122, 147–152

Betsy Ross House, 14, 111

Biking, 129, 132, 191–192

Bishop White House, 140

Black History Month, 12

Blackwell Center for Women, 17

Bloomsday, 14

Boat House Row, 4, 122

Boating, 129, 132

Boating tours, 128

Book and the Cook Festival, The, 12

Books about Philadelphia, 18, 231–232

Bookstores, 157–158

Bourse, 137–138

Bowling, 184

Brandywine Valley, 198–203

Brazilian cuisine, 64

Broad Street, 31

Bucks County, 187–194

Buggy rides (Amish country), 213
Bus tours, 127–128
Bus travel
    getting around town, 36
    information for foreign visitors, 26
    to Philadelphia, 22
Business hours, 27, 38
Business services, 39

Cabs, 38
Calendar of events, 11–15
Canadian citizens, 23
Candlelight strolls, 128
Car rental companies
    accommodations for disabled travelers, 17
    at airport, 31
    choices, 37
    information for foreign visitors, 26
    insurance offered, 37
Car travel
    auto clubs, 27
    getting around town, 37–38
    getting to Philadelphia, 21
    information for foreign visitors, 26
    safety, 25
Carpenters' Hall, 111, 136
Cathedral Basilica of Sts. Peter and Paul, 151
Cedar Grove, 124
Cemeteries, 108–109, 111
Center City
    accommodations, 48–56
    layout, 31–32
    music clubs, 177
    restaurants, 74–84
Chadds Ford, 199–200
Cheesesteaks, 2, 91–92
Chestnut Hill, 32

Children
    accommodations for, 18, 57–58
    Amish country attractions, 213–214
    books for, 232
    entertainment for, 127
    museums for, 118, 126–127
Chinatown, 32, 89–90
    restaurants, 89
Chinese cuisine, 64
Chinese New Year celebration, 12
Christ Church, 108, 109–110
Christmas celebrations, 15
Churches, 109–111, 140–142, 146
Cinema, 185
Cirrus network, 10
City Hall, 107
    location, 32
    parking near, 38
    routes to, 21
    touring, 148
City layout, 31–32
City Tavern, 142–143
Classical music, 13–14, 169–171
Coffee, 72, 75, 83, 90
Coffee bars, 93
Columbus Day Parade, 14
Comcast U.S. Indoor Tennis Championships, 12
Comedy clubs, 181
Commuter rail, 22, 36
Concerts, 169–172
Congress Hall, 137
Consolidators, 20
Constitutional Convention, 100–101
Consulates, 27
Contemporary cuisine, 64
Continental cuisine, 64

Council on International Educational Exchange, 19
Council Travel, 21
Country inns (New Hope area), 192–193
Country music, 180
Covered bridges (Lancaster County), 211
Crafts, 158–159, 214–215
Credit cards
    information for foreign travelers, 24
    insurance through, 16
    reporting lost or stolen, 11
Crime, 40
Currency information, 24, 27
Curtis Institute, 170
Customs requirements, 24, 26

Dad Vail Regatta, 13
Dance. See performing arts
Dance clubs, 180–181
Declaration House, 112
Declaration of Independence, 100, 226
Delaware waterfront, 3, 174–176
Devon Horse Show, 13
Dining. See Restaurant Index
Disabled travelers, 16–17
Doylestown, 193–194
Drinking laws, 27, 39
Driving safety, 25
Du Ponts, 202

E-Savers programs, 20
Eclectic cuisine, 64
Edgar Allen Poe National Historic Site, 114

General Index

Elderhostel, 18
Electricity, 27
Elfreth's Alley, 112
Elfreth's Alley Days, 13
Embassies, 27
Emergencies, 27, 39
English cuisine, 64
Entry requirements for foreign citizens, 23–24
Ephrata, 212
Episcopal Diocese of Philadelphia, 140
Expedia Web site, 20

Fairmount Park
  Christmas tours, 15
  festival, 14
  location, 32
  outdoor activities, 130–131
  spring tour, 13
  touring, 2, 122–124
Fall of the Quaker City, The, 18
Families
  accommodations for, 18
  Amish country attractions, 213–214
  entertainment for, 127
  Please Touch Museum, 118
  restaurants for, 84
"Family-Friendly Philadelphia", 57
"Fare Tracker" (Expedia), 20
Farm vacation bed-and-breakfasts, 220
Farmer's markets, 216. See also markets
Fashion, 161–163
Fax machines, 29
Federal style, 139
Festivals, 12–14
Films, recommended, 232–233
Fire-insurance markers, 138, 140
Fireman's Hall Museum, 144

First Bank of the United States, 134–136
First Union Pro Cycling Championships, 13
Fisher Fine Arts Library, 107
Fishing, 129
Flag Day celebrations, 14
Flifo Global Web site, 20
Food courts, 94
Football, 132
Foreign travelers
  fast facts for, 27–29
  getting to U.S., 25–26
  preparations needed, 23–25
  transportation in U.S., 26
Franklin, Benjamin, 225–226
Franklin Court, 102
Franklin Institute Science Museum, 12, 105–106
Franklin Mills, 154
Free Library of Philadelphia, 113–114, 152
Free Quaker Meeting-house, 147
French cuisine, 64
Front Street, 31, 143
Fusion cuisine, 64

Gallery at Market East, 154
Gardens (Brandywine Valley), 200–201
Gasoline prices, 28
Gay and lesbian travelers, 17, 183–184
Geography of city, 1–2
Georgian style, 139
Germantown, 32
Germantown Christmas tours, 15
Giovanni's Room, 17
Gloria Dei Church, 110
Golden Age Passports, 18

Golf, 129–130
Greek cuisine, 64
Greyhound Bus Lines
  accommodations for disabled travelers, 17
  information for foreign visitors, 26
  service to Philadelphia, 22
Greyhound/Trailways, 17
Guesthouses, 43

Hagley Museum (Wilmington, DE), 202
Head House Square, 13, 141–142
Health clubs, 130
Health insurance, 24
Hershey, 214
Highway access to Philadelphia, 21
Hiking, 130, 191–192
Historic Ship Zone, 126
History of Philadelphia, 224–228, 230
Hoagies, 2
Holidays
  information for foreign visitors, 28
  special events, 12–15
Horse racing, 132–133
Horseback riding, 130
Horse-drawn carriage rides, 128
Hospitals, 39
Hostels, 62
Hotels. See also Accommodations Index
  accommodations for families, 18
  best bets, 4–6
  Brandywine Valley, 202–203
  Bucks County, 193
  Center City, 48–56
  City Line and northeast, 61–62
  family-friendly, 57–58

growth, 42
historic area, 46–48
in Amish country, 217
near airport, 60–61
University City, 58–59
Valley Forge area, 196
weekend packages, 42
House on Spruce Street, The, 18

Ice hockey, 133
Ice skating, 130–131
Independence Hall tours, 99–101, 137
Independence Mall, 99, 146
Independence National Historical Park tours, 98–103, 134
Independence Seaport Museum, 117
Independence Square, 2, 101, 137
Indian cuisine, 64
Insurance, 15–16, 24
Intercourse, 211–212
international cuisine, 64
International Theater Festival for Children, 13
International Visitors Center, 23
Irish cuisine, 64
Israel Independence Day celebration, 13
Italian cuisine, 64–65
Italian Market, 94, 164

Jam on the River, 13
Japanese cuisine, 65
Japanese House and Gardens, 124
Jazz and blues, 13, 14, 179

Kids. *See* children; families

King of Prussia Court and Plaza, 155
Kosciuszko National Memorial, 141

Labyrinth, 17
Lancaster, 210–211
Landis Valley museum, 214
Latin American cuisine, 65
Laurel Hill Cemetery, 108–109
Legal aid information, 28
Lemon Hill, 124
Lesbian Hotline, 17
Liberty Bell, 1, 101–102, 137
Liberty Belle II, 128
libraries and literary sites, 113–114, 152
Library for the Blind and Physically Handicapped, 17
Library Hall, 137
Lights at Night, 2
Lights of Liberty, 102–103, 185
Lititz, 212
Logan Circle, 122, 151
Longwood Gardens (Brandywine Valley), 200–201
Lord & Taylor, 148, 159
Lucia Fest, 15
Luggage, insuring, 16

Mail services, 28, 40
Man Full of Trouble Tavern, 142
Manayunk
music clubs, 178
popularity, 32
restaurants, 90–91
shopping, 160
Mann Music Center, 170
mansion tours, 3
Mantua Maker's House, 112

Manufacturing decline, 228
Market Place East, 155
markets, 83, 93–94, 210, 216
Masonic Temple, 112
Mayor's Commission on People with Disabilities, 17
Medical requirements, 24
Mediterranean cuisine, 65
Mellon Jazz Festival, 14
Mennonite Information Center, 209
Mennonites, 206–207
Metrokids, 19
Mexican cuisine, 65
Microsoft Expedia Web site, 20
Mid-City loop, 36
Mikveh Israel Cemetery, 109
Millennium Coffee, 17
Mobility International USA, 16
Mother Bethel African Methodist Episcopal Church, 110
Mount Pleasant, 124
Movie theaters, 185
Mozart on the Square, 13
Mummer's Parade, 11
Museums
Academy of Natural Sciences, 114–116
Afro-American Historical and Cultural Museum, 116
American Swedish Historical Museum, 15, 116
Atwater Kent, 116
Balch Institute, 116
Barnes Foundation, 103–104
Brandywine River (Chadd's Ford), 200

General Index

Museums *(cont.)*
Franklin Court, 102
Franklin Institute
Science Museum,
12, 105–106
Hagley Museum
(Wilmington, DE),
202
Independence Sea-
port Museum, 117
Landis Valley, 214
National Museum of
American Jewish
History, 117,
146–147
Pennsylvania
Academy of Fine
Arts, 105, 148
Philadelphia
Museum of Art, 3,
15, 104–105
Physick House,
117–118
Please Touch
Museum, 118
Rodin, 118–119,
152
Rosenbach Museum
and Library, 114
single-interest, 115
tours, 103–106
University of Penn-
sylvania, 119–120
Winterthur (Brandy-
wine Valley), 201
Music
classical, 13–14,
169–171
clubs, 3, 174–181
folk and country, 14,
180
jazz and blues, 13,
14, 179
opera, 169

**National Museum of
American Jewish
History, 117,
146–147**
Neighborhoods, 32–33
New Hall, 136

**New Hope area,
190–193**
**New Jersey State
Aquarium, 121–122**
New Jersey Transit, 22
**newspapers and
magazines, 39–40**
Nightlife
bars, 181–183
music clubs,
174–181
**Norwegian Seaman's
Church, 144**
Nutcracker **Ballet, 15**

**"Official Visitors
Guide", 10**
Old City, 32–33
music clubs,
176–177
walking tours,
143–147
Old City Hall, 137
**Old First Reformed
Church, 146**
**Old Pine Presbyterian
Church, 141**
**Old St. George's
Methodist Church,
146**
**Old St. Joseph's
Church, 110**
**Old St. Mary's
Church, 140**
**Old Swedes' Church,
110**
Open house tours, 3
Opera, 169
**Outdoor activities,
128–131, 191–192**

Package tours, 10, 95
Parades
Columbus Day, 14
Mummer's Parade,
11
St. Patrick's Day, 12
Thanksgiving Day,
15
**Parking information,
38**

Parks
Brandywine Battle-
field (Chadds
Ford), 200
Fairmount Park, 2,
32, 122–124
Independence
National Historical
Park, 98–103
Penn's Landing,
124–126
Ridley Creek (Bucks
County), 197
Valley Forge,
195–196
Washington Crossing
State Park (Bucks
County), 188
Passports, 23
**PATCO commuter rail,
36**
Pemberton House, 136
**Penn, William,
224–225**
Penn Center, 151
Penn Station, 31
**Penn's Landing, 3, 124,
126**
**Penn's Landing Trolley,
36**
**Pennsbury Manor
(Morrisville), 190**
**Pennsylvania Academy
of Fine Arts, 105**
**Pennsylvania Ballet,
172**
**Pennsylvania
Convention Center,
107–108, 228**
**Pennsylvania Dutch
Convention & Visi-
tors Bureau, 208**
**Pennsylvania Dutch
Festival, 14**
**Pennsylvania Hospital,
113**
**Performing arts,
169–174, 223–224.**
See also **music**
**"Personal Fare
Watcher"
(Travelocity), 20**

Peter Pan/Trailways, 22

Pharmacies, 40

Philadelphia Antiques Show, 12

Philadelphia Citypass, 95

Philadelphia Contributionship, 140

Philadelphia Convention and Visitors Bureau, 10, 31–32

Philadelphia Distance Run, 14

Philadelphia Exchange, 108, 142

Philadelphia Flower Show, 3, 12

Philadelphia Folk Festival, 14

Philadelphia Fringe Festival, 14

Philadelphia Gay News, 17

Philadelphia history, 224–228, 230

Philadelphia International Airport, 25, 30, 60–61, 154

Philadelphia Lesbian and Gay Task Force Hotline, 17

Philadelphia Marathon, 15

Philadelphia Museum of Art, 3, 15, 104–105

Philadelphia Open House, 13

Philadelphia Orchestra, 14, 170–171

Philadelphia Zoological Gardens, 120–121

Philosophical Hall, 137

PHLASH Bus, 36

Physick House, 117–118

Playgrounds, 127

Please Touch Museum, 118

PLUS system, 10

Poe National Historic Site, 114

Postal services, 28, 40

Powel House, 113

Pretzels, 92, 146

Prices, 10

Professional sports, 131–133

Public transportation
  accommodations for families, 18
  air travel to Philadelphia, 19–20, 30
  buses to Philadelphia, 22
  for disabled travelers, 17
  for getting around town, 33, 37
  for seniors, 18
  information for foreign travelers, 26
  trains to Philadelphia, 21–22, 31

Queen Village, 33

Quilts, 214–215

Radio stations, 40

Rapid transit, 36

Reading Terminal Market, 4, 83

Regattas, 4

Rest rooms, 29, 40

Restaurants. *See also* Restaurant Index
  best bets, 6–9
  Brandywine Valley, 203
  Bucks County, 193
  by cuisine, 64–65
  Center City, 74–84
  Chinatown, 89–90
  coffee bars, 93
  family-friendly, 84
  in Amish country, 221–222
  in historic area, 65–74
  late night, 185–186
  local favorites, 91–94

Manayunk, 90–91
South Philadelphia, 84–86
University City, 86–89

Ridley Creek State Park, 197

Rittenhouse Square, 33
  Easter celebration, 13
  Fine Arts Annual, 13
  Flower Market, 13
  Mozart on the Square, 13
  restaurants, 4
  touring, 150

RiverLink, 128

Rock clubs, 178–179

Rodin Museum, 118–119, 152

Rollerblading, 129

Rosenbach Museum and Library, 114

Safety, 25, 40

Sales taxes, 28

Schuylkill River regattas, 4

Seafood restaurants, 65

Second Bank of the United States, 136

Second Continental Congress, 100

Second Street, 31

Senior Travelers, 18

"Seniors on the Go", 18

SEPTA commuter trains, 22

SEPTA DayPass, 18

SEPTA Special Services transit guide, 17

Sesame Place (Langhorne), 188–190

Sheraton Rittenhouse Square, 55

Shippen Way Inn, 49

Shopping
  antiques, 155–156, 215
  art, 156–157
  crafts, 158–159

General Index

Shopping *(cont.)*
  fashion, 161–163
  first Fridays, 2
  gifts and souvenirs,
    164
  in Lancaster County,
    214–216
  outlet malls and
    shopping centers,
    153–155, 216
Shops at Liberty Place,
  155, 216
Society Hill, 33,
  138–143
South Broad Street,
  148–150
South Philadelphia
  atmosphere, 4, 33
  music clubs, 180
  restaurants, 84–86
South Street neighbor-
  hood, 33, 177
Spectator sports,
  12–13, 15, 131–133,
  223
Spirit of Philadelphia,
  128
Sporting goods, 167
Sports
  participation, 14–15,
    129–131, 184
  spectator, 12–13, 15,
    131–133, 223
St. Augustine's Roman
  Catholic Church, 146
St. Joseph's Church,
  140
St. Patrick's Day
  Parade, 12
St. Paul's Episcopal
  Church, 142
St. Peter's Episcopal
  Church, 110–111
State stores, 167
Steakhouses, 65
Strasburg, 212–213
Strawberry Mansion,
  124
Street layout, 31–32
Subways, 36

Sunoco Welcome
  America!, 14
Super Sunday, 14
Sweetbriar, 124
Swimming, 131
Sydenham Street, 4

Taken Girl, The, 18
Taxes, 28, 40
Taxis, 38
Telephone, 29, 38
Television stations, 40
Ten Eleven Clinton, 49
Tennis, 131, 133
Thai cuisine, 65
Thanksgiving Day
  Parade, 15
Theater, 171–173
Through These Arches:
  The Story of Indepen-
  dence Hall, 18
Ticket information,
  168–169
Time zones, 29, 41
Tipping, 29
Today in Old
  Philadelphia, 18
Todd House, 139–140
Toilets, 29, 40
Tourist information,
  10
Tours. *See also* **walking**
  tours
  Amish country, 209
  Fairmount Park
    Christmas tours,
    15
  guided, 127–128
  Independence
    National Historical
    Park, 98–103, 134
  museums, 103–106
  options, 2
  Philadelphia Open
    House, 13
  suggested itineraries,
    98
  trollies, 36
Track and field, 133

Train travel
  from airport, 30
  getting around town,
    36
  information for
    foreign visitors, 26
  to Philadelphia,
    21–22, 31
"Travel Agent"
  (Expedia), 20
Travel Information
  Service, 16
Travel insurance,
  15–16
Traveler's checks, 11,
  24
Travelers Aid Society,
  27
Travelocity Web site,
  20
Trip.Com Web site, 20
Trollies, 36, 127

U.S. Mint, 119
Universities, 19
University City, 33,
  86–89
University of
  Pennsylvania, 120
University of
  Pennsylvania
  Museum, 119–120
Urban renewal, 99,
  228–230
USA Railpass, 26

Valley Forge, 195–198
Vegetarian cuisine, 65
Vietnamese cuisine, 65
Virginia Slims
  Women's Tennis
  Championships, 15
Visas, 23–24
Visit USA, 26
Vsitor information, 10,
  31
Visitor information
  (Amish country),
  208–209

General Index

Walking tours, 128
  midtown and the Parkway, 147–152
  Old City, 143–147
  Society Hill and historic highlights, 134–143
Walnut Street, 4
Walnut Street Theatre, 171–172
Washington Crossing State Park, 188
Washington Square, 138
Washington's Birthday celebration, 12
waterfront, 3
Waterworks, 122
Weather, 11
Web sites
  events, 168
  for travel arrangements, 20
  Independence Hall Association, 100
  restaurant reviews, 63
  visitor information, 10
Weekend packages, 42
Welcome Park, 143
Western Union, 25
Wheelchair access, 16–17
Wheelchair Getaways, 17
Wheelers East, 17
William Way Community Center, 17
Wilma Theater, 171
Winterthur (Brandywine Valley), 201
Women's Switchboard, 17
Woodford, 124

Zoos, 120–121

ACCOMMODATIONS
Adam's Mark Philadelphia, 61–62
Alexander Inn, 56
Bank Street Hostel, 62
Best Western Independence Park Inn, 47
Chamounix Hostel Mansion, 62
Clarion Suites Convention Center, 56
Comfort Inn at Penn's Landing, 47–48
Crowne Plaza Philadelphia Center City, 57–58
Doubletree Hotel Philadelphia, 52
Embassy Suites Center City, 5, 52–53
Four Seasons Hotel, 2, 4, 5, 6, 7, 48–49
Gables, 59
Hawthorn Suites, 5, 56
Holiday Inn—Independence Mall, 46
Hotel Sofitel, 53
Inn at Penn, 4, 58
International House, 59
KormanSuites Hotel, 53–54
Latham Hotel, 54
Loews Philadelphia Hotel, 54
Omni Hotel at Independence Park, 5, 46
Penn Tower Hotel, 58–59
Penn's View Hotel, 4, 6, 48
Philadelphia Airport Hilton, 61
Philadelphia Airport Marriott, 60
Philadelphia Marriott, 4, 55
Philadelphia Park Hyatt at the Bellevue, 4, 5, 49–50, 150, 153–154
Philadelphia Renaissance Hotel Airport, 61
Rittenhouse Hotel, 5, 50–51
Ritz-Carlton Hotel, 5–6, 51
Rodeway Inn, 58
Sheraton Philadelphia Airport, 60
Sheraton Society Hill, 46
Shippen Way Inn, 5
Ten Eleven Clinton, 5
Thomas Bond House, 48
University City Guest Houses, 59
Westin Philadelphia, 51–52
Wyndham Franklin Plaza, 5, 55–56

RESTAURANTS
Azalea, 69
Bassett's Ice Cream, 9
Beau Monde, 73
Bellevue Hotel, 94
Bertucci's, 82
Bleu, 9
Bookbinder's, 76
Bourse Food Court, 94
Brasil's, 73
Brasserie Perrier, 76
Buddakan, 8, 68
Café Spice, 73
Capital, 89
Cassatt Lounge, 8
Chart House, 6, 68
Ciboulette, 76–77
Circa, 6, 80
City Tavern, 8, 69
Cutters, 80

Devon Seafood Grill, 9
Dickens Inn, 8, 70, 142
DiNardo's Famous Crabs, 70
Dock Street Brasserie, 82
Dock Street Brew Pub–Terminal, 8, 82
Down Home Diner, 8
Downey's Pub, 70–71
Food Court at Liberty Place, 7
Fork, 7, 71
Founders, 50, 74
Fountain, 5–7, 49, 74–75
Friday Saturday Sunday, 77
Gallery Food Court, 94
Garden, The, 6, 77–78
Golden Pond, 89
Harmony Vegetarian, 89
Hikaru, 90–91
Imperial Inn, 89
Jack's Firehouse, 7, 78
Jim's Steaks, 91–92
Joe's Peking Duck House, 89–90
Johnny Rockets, 73
Judy's Cafe, 71
Kansas City Prime, 90

La Famiglia, 6, 68
La Terrasse, 86
Le Bar Lyonnais, 76
Le Bec-Fin, 6–8, 75–76
Le Bus Main Street, 91
Lee's Hoagies, 92
Liberty Place Food Court, 94
Marathon on the Square, 82–83
Marra's, 8, 85
Meiji-en, 71
Metropolitan Bakery, 8
Morton's of Chicago, 7, 78
New Deck Tavern, 88
New Delhi, 88
Old Original Book-binder's, 65
Painted Parrot Cafe, 6, 8, 72
Palladium, 86–87
Paris Bar and Grille, 6, 51
Pasion!, 7, 78–79
Pat's King of the Steaks, 92
Philadelphia Fish & Company, 72
Pizzeria Uno, 92
Ralph's Italian Restaurant, 85
Ray's Coffee Shop, 90

Restaurant School, 88
Rex Pizza, 84
Ristorante Panorama, 6, 72
Rouge, 9
Ruth's Chris Steak House, 7, 80–81
Saloon, The, 7, 85
Sansom Street Oyster House, 81
Sawan's Mediterranean Bistro, 84
Shiao Lan Kung, 9, 90
Society Hill Hotel, 74
Sonoma, 8, 91
Striped Bass, 7, 79
Strolli's, 86
Susanna Foo, 7, 81–82
Swann Lounge, 2, 49
Tacconelli's, 93
Tangerine, 69
Thai Palace, 74
Toto's, 8, 79–80
Triangle Tavern, 86
Victor Cafe, 85
Walt's King of the Crabs, 74
White Dog Cafe, 8, 87
Wichita Steak + Brews, 72–73
Zanzibar Blue, 82
Zesty's, 91
Zocalo, 88–89

FROMMER'S® COMPLETE TRAVEL GUIDES

Alaska
Amsterdam
Arizona
Atlanta
Australia
Austria
Bahamas
Barcelona, Madrid &
  Seville
Beijing
Belgium, Holland &
  Luxembourg
Bermuda
Boston
British Columbia & the
  Canadian Rockies
Budapest & the Best of
  Hungary
California
Canada
Cancún, Cozumel &
  the Yucatán
Cape Cod, Nantucket &
  Martha's Vineyard
Caribbean
Caribbean Cruises & Ports
  of Call
Caribbean Ports of Call
Carolinas & Georgia
Chicago
China
Colorado
Costa Rica
Denmark
Denver, Boulder & Colorado
  Springs
England
Europe

European Cruises & Ports
  of Call
Florida
France
Germany
Greece
Greek Islands
Hawaii
Hong Kong
Honolulu, Waikiki & Oahu
Ireland
Israel
Italy
Jamaica
Japan
Las Vegas
London
Los Angeles
Maryland & Delaware
Maui
Mexico
Montana & Wyoming
Montréal & Québec City
Munich & the Bavarian
  Alps
Nashville & Memphis
Nepal
New England
New Mexico
New Orleans
New York City
New Zealand
Nova Scotia, New Brunswick
  & Prince Edward Island
Oregon
Paris
Philadelphia & the
  Amish Country

Portugal
Prague & the Best of the
  Czech Republic
Provence & the Riviera
Puerto Rico
Rome
San Antonio & Austin
San Diego
San Francisco
Santa Fe, Taos & Albuquerque
Scandinavia
Scotland
Seattle & Portland
Shanghai
Singapore & Malaysia
South Africa
Southeast Asia
South Florida
South Pacific
Spain
Sweden
Switzerland
Thailand
Tokyo
Toronto
Tuscany & Umbria
USA
Utah
Vancouver & Victoria
Vermont, New Hampshire
  & Maine
Vienna & the Danube Valley
Virgin Islands
Virginia
Walt Disney World &
  Orlando
Washington, D.C.
Washington State

FROMMER'S® DOLLAR-A-DAY GUIDES

Australia from $50 a Day
California from $60 a Day
Caribbean from $70 a Day
England from $70 a Day
Europe from $70 a Day

Florida from $70 a Day
Hawaii from $70 a Day
Ireland from $60 a Day
Italy from $70 a Day
London from $85 a Day

New York from $80 a Day
Paris from $80 a Day
San Francisco from $60 a Day
Washington, D.C.,
  from $70 a Day

FROMMER'S® PORTABLE GUIDES

Acapulco, Ixtapa &
  Zihuatanejo
Alaska Cruises & Ports of Call
Bahamas
Baja & Los Cabos
Berlin
California Wine Country
Charleston & Savannah
Chicago
Dublin

Hawaii: The Big Island
Las Vegas
London
Los Angeles
Maine Coast
Maui
Miami
New Orleans
New York City
Paris

Puerto Vallarta, Manzanillo
  & Guadalajara
San Diego
San Francisco
Sydney
Tampa & St. Petersburg
Venice
Washington, D.C.

FROMMER'S® NATIONAL PARK GUIDES

Family Vacations in the
  National Parks
Grand Canyon

National Parks of the
  American West
Rocky Mountain

Yellowstone & Grand Teton
Yosemite & Sequoia/
  Kings Canyon
Zion & Bryce Canyon

FROMMER'S® MEMORABLE WALKS

Chicago
London

New York
Paris

San Francisco
Washington, D.C.

FROMMER'S® GREAT OUTDOOR GUIDES

New England
Northern California

Southern California & Baja
Southern New England

Washington & Oregon

FROMMER'S® BORN TO SHOP GUIDES

Born to Shop: France
Born to Shop: Italy

Born to Shop: London
Born to Shop: New York

Born to Shop: Paris

FROMMER'S® IRREVERENT GUIDES

Amsterdam
Boston
Chicago
Las Vegas

London
Los Angeles
Manhattan
New Orleans

Paris
San Francisco
Seattle & Portland
Vancouver

Walt Disney World
Washington, D.C.

FROMMER'S® BEST-LOVED DRIVING TOURS

America
Britain
California

Florida
France
Germany

Ireland
Italy
New England

Scotland
Spain
Western Europe

THE UNOFFICIAL GUIDES®

Bed & Breakfasts in
  California
Bed & Breakfasts in
  New England
Bed & Breakfasts in
  the Northwest
Bed & Breakfasts in
  Southeast
Beyond Disney
Branson, Missouri

California with Kids
Chicago
Cruises
Disneyland
Florida with Kids
Golf Vacations in the
  Eastern U.S.
The Great Smoky &
  Blue Ridge
  Mountains

Inside Disney
Hawaii
Las Vegas
London
Miami & the Keys
Mini Las Vegas
Mini-Mickey
New Orleans
New York City
Paris

San Francisco
Skiing in the West
Southeast with Kids
Walt Disney World
Walt Disney World
  for Grown-ups
Walt Disney World
  for Kids
Washington, D.C.

SPECIAL-INTEREST TITLES

Frommer's Britain's Best Bed & Breakfasts and
  Country Inns
Frommer's Britain's Best Bike Rides
The Civil War Trust's Official Guide
  to the Civil War Discovery Trail
Frommer's Caribbean Hideaways
Frommer's Adventure Guide to Central America
Frommer's Adventure Guide to South America
Frommer's Adventure Guide to Southeast Asia
Frommer's Food Lover's Companion to France
Frommer's Gay & Lesbian Europe
Frommer's Exploring America by RV
Hanging Out in Europe

Israel Past & Present
Mad Monks' Guide to California
Mad Monks' Guide to New York City
Frommer's The Moon
Frommer's New York City with Kids
The New York Times' Unforgettable
  Weekends
Places Rated Almanac
Retirement Places Rated
Frommer's Road Atlas Britain
Frommer's Road Atlas Europe
Frommer's Washington, D.C., with Kids
Frommer's What the Airlines Never Tell You